Antoinette Clark Wire *is*
Professor of New Testament at
San Francisco Theological
Seminary and the Graduate
Theological Union.

The Corinthian Women Prophets

The Corinthian Women Prophets

A Reconstruction through Paul's Rhetoric

Antoinette Clark Wire

Fortress Press • Minneapolis

THE CORINTHIAN WOMEN PROPHETS
A Reconstruction through Paul's Rhetoric

Material in this book is reprinted by permission of the publishers and the Loeb Classical Library—

From *Dionysius of Halicarnassus,* Volume II, translated by Earnest Cary, Cambridge, Mass.: Harvard University Press, 1939.

From *Pausanias: Description of Greece,* Volume I, translated by W. H. S. Jones, Cambridge, Mass.: Harvard University Press, 1918.

From *Pausanias: Description of Greece,* Volume IV, translated by W. H. S. Jones and H. A. Ormerod, Cambridge, Mass.: Harvard University Press, 1918.

Acknowledgements are continued on page 294, which constitutes a continuation of the copyright page.

Library of Congress Cataloging-in-Publication Data

Wire, Antoinette Clark.
  The Corinthian women prophets : a reconstruction through Paul's rhetoric / Antoinette Clark Wire.
     p. cm.
  Includes bibliographical references.
  Includes index.
  ISBN: 0-8006-2434-3 (alk. paper)
     1. Women, Christian—Greece—Corinth—History. 2. Women in the Bible. 3. Prophets in the New Testament. 4. Bible. N.T. Corinthians, 1st—Criticism, interpretation, etc. I. Title.
BS2655.W5W57 1990
227'.2067—dc20   90-35519
                                                                       CIP

Manufactured in the U.S.A.   AF 1-2434

94   93   92   91   90   1   2   3   4   5   6   7   8   9   10

Contents

| Preface

WRITING ABOUT PREVIOUS WRITING should be short and to the point, turning us quickly back to the original text to see if the point is useful for understanding it. I plead indulgence in this case on two counts. First, my purpose extends through and beyond understanding Paul to understanding a group he is addressing, which is a more elusive task. Second, this group has been seldom considered in its own right, and the letter's addressees considered with such prejudice, that the undertaking itself seemed quixotic at the start, and no part of it could be convincing unless a full review made possible a new perspective. Becoming acquainted with the women prophets in Corinth has been for me a lesson against my own antithetical mode of thinking, a challenge to learn from people different from myself, and a pleasure to discover in them aspects of ourselves as women of faith two millennia later. In the process Paul has become a familiar and never dull traveling companion.

I have tried to keep this study as clear and accessible as possible. Rather than arguing with other exegetes on each page, I have written appendices outlining the history of recent Western research on issues central to this study. Occasionally an excursus within a chapter takes up specialized questions necessary to the analysis of Paul's argument or arising from it. The volume ends with a collection of many people's translations of texts on women who speak for the divine in the Early Roman Empire. I cite these excerpts seldom in interpreting 1 Corinthians because parallel passages can prove nothing about each other until each complete text has been read in light of its own rhetoric and historical implications. I want to draw attention to that task.

Because many readers interested in the Christian women prophets of first-century Corinth do not read Greek, I have translated the New Testament texts. This is feasible because Paul's arguments appeal to the structures of Hellenistic culture and human experience more than to the structure of the particular language he uses. The occasional exception, such as a play on words, can be explained as such.

Gender language has been the most difficult to deal with. Greek also subsumes women into masculine language when addressing mixed groups, but today's English-speaking readers no longer hear masculine language as inclusive. Where Paul unmistakably addresses both men and women, I have tried to communicate this in English, sometimes being forced from singular to plural to avoid tongue twisters, or using the archaic "brethren" to keep the ambiguity of his usually inclusive meaning. Otherwise I have translated his gender language as literally as possible. I considered using the feminine throughout, with the stipulation of a generic meaning, if only to reveal the futility of such stipulations. But because I am trying to determine the implications of Paul's argument for the women within his address, the use of a generic feminine could be heard as special pleading.

Everything I have seen has come out of interaction with others. My students and colleagues at San Francisco Theological Seminary and the Graduate Theological Union have been especially important. I want to thank the Asilomar workshop and Mary Criscione for reading and Mary for indexing, Francis Chapelle and Douglas Jenkins at the keyboard, John Hollar, Marshall Johnson, and Renee Fall at Fortress Press, Hugh, Annette, and Joseph Wire at home, and, from the beginning, Hal and Antoinette Clark. My hope is that through this study the Corinthian women prophets can become the challenge to others that they have been to me.

1 | Introduction

Aim

THE PURPOSE OF THIS STUDY is to reconstruct as accurate a picture as possible of the women prophets in the church of first-century Corinth. I am interested in their behavior, daily and occasional, their position in society and the church, and their values and theology. Broad studies are available on women in the Greco-Roman world[1] and women in the ancient church,[2] recently even on women in the Pauline churches[3] But these wide-angle views are more suggestive than conclusive because the specific texts they depend on have not been analyzed with reconstructing the women's lives in mind. The next step is to read and reread the key texts until they yield all they have to say about the women.[4] As one stage of this process I take up Paul's first extant letter to the Corinthians, focusing attention on the women who prophesy. Second Corinthians, Acts, and 1 Clement speak of the same community in the same half century. But it is 1 Corinthians that refers repeatedly to the women, addresses them at times, and works to persuade the community and its women. As such it offers the best opportunity for reconstruction.

Method

Due to the nature of this source document, the historical and sociological methods commonly used to reconstruct a social group are not immediately useful. Gerd Theissen has proposed that reconstruction can proceed both from direct social statements in a text and from the social implications of norms, events, and symbols within the text.[5] But even the most explicitly social statements in 1 Corinthians, such as Paul's "not many of you were wise by standards of the flesh, not many powerful, not many prominent" (1:26), cannot be taken as objective evidence about people's status because it is part of Paul's defense as he begins an argument. The question is whether we can know anything about the Corinthian community beyond the writer's viewpoint. Groups such as the women prophets who come in for Paul's criticism would seem most likely to elude our grasp.

This impasse diverted me into the study of rhetoric, the art of persuasion. If Paul's intent is to persuade rather than to describe the Corinthians, can Paul's rhetoric lead to the people he is trying to persuade? Paul's rhetoric is not a new area of study.[6] Rhetoric was one of the pillars of classical advanced education. On a popular level, Paul's hometown of Tarsus was known for its lively public debates.[7] And the rabbinical system Paul was apparently educated in taught a wisdom generated and preserved in oral sayings and dialogues. Paul's own letters, oral both in their writing and reading (1 Cor. 16:21; Gal. 6:11; 1 Thess. 5:27), seem to have functioned as speeches *in absentia*. Rhetorical analysis could be applied in studying these letters to try to reconstruct how Paul understood his own speech. Such a study would begin with the Greek and Jewish canons of rhetoric Paul may have studied, and the question of Paul's education and self-conscious application of rhetorical methods would stand in the foreground.

But my aim is narrower. Just as a child can speak her native tongue correctly without schooling, so a man can sell a horse or a conviction very persuasively without reflecting upon how he does it. In Paul's case the data we have is this persuasion itself. Even his reflections on his own speaking and how it is received are an integral part of his effort to persuade. So the question whether Paul composed with conscious rhetorical technique or analyzed in retrospect the way he had spoken can be set aside. His argument can be the focus of this study and the proper and sufficient access point to his audience.

I look to the modern revival of classical rhetoric for my primary analytical tools in this task, the movement called in Chaim Perelman and L. Olbrechts-Tyteca's comprehensive description "The New Rhetoric."[8] The major distinctions made in the ancient discipline are retained. For example, the writer's self-presentation (ethos) is expected to dominate the introductory part of a speech, the rational argument (logos) — often including a narration of the case — is anticipated in the body of the discourse, and direct appeals to the audience (pathos) are looked for in conclusions.[9] The names given to specific arguments are often translations of their Greek or Latin titles. But the study of rhetoric has changed significantly; its scope is both broader and more clearly delimited than before, and there is a concomitant change in the precision of its work.

Today, rhetorical analysis takes as its province all persuasive discourse, recognizing that its major contribution is not in generating or dissecting proper speeches but in illuminating how words function to persuade. Once we focus on function it is clear that all argument — some say all speech — is shaped for an effect and works to persuade. This means that the ambiguous position of Paul's letters as written discourse orally given and received is no longer a methodological problem, since the words function to persuade in any case. And by its functional definition modern rhetoric has been able to delimit its field of inquiry. It does not deal with certain strictly declarative or performative speech acts such as lists, chants, and curses, nor with what the philosopher calls self-evident or incontrovertible truth. Rejecting modern philosophy's obsession with self-evident logic and conclusive proof since René Descartes, Perelman and Olbrechts-Tyteca choose to study the broad world between what is arbitrary and what is necessary, where most of human life is lived. Here some things are better than others in some ways, and it falls to rhetoric to study how people deliberate in this world. Rhetoric observes how people who have any freedom use it to persuade each other, "to induce or to increase the mind's adherence to the theses presented for its assent."[10] This world of reasoning, standing in contrast to self-evident truth, may seem like shifting sand upon which to build a historical reconstruction. But the fact that Paul is arguing his case indicates that he operates in this world. The best procedure is to use the technology of rhetorical analysis that is appropriate to this sandy soil of argument.

The precision of the new rhetoric comes from its axiom that all argument serves the function of persuasion. In no detail can a persuader afford to ignore those who are to be persuaded. Because everything spoken must be shaped for them, the measure of the audience as the speaker knows it can be read in the arguments that are chosen. It has taken the computer generation to discover the precision with which one person speaks to another in human communication, drawing on elaborate "programs" that both share. These programs tell far more about an audience than the occasional descriptive comment. A rhetorical analysis of 1 Corinthians can give us accurate information about the Corinthian women prophets as Paul knew them by reading Paul's letter as an attempt to persuade in a particular argumentative situation in which they play some role. Granted they are often hidden within a generic address, only occasionally spoken about, and still less often spoken to; but their repeated appearance shows that they are not without a role within the rhetorical situation. This rhetorical or argumentative situation includes both the goals of the speaker and the counter-arguments that are anticipated as the speaking progresses. Perelman and Olbrechts-Tyteca define it as "the influence of the earlier stages of the discussion on the argumentative possibilities open to the speaker."[11] Access is gained to it through the text, not by other readings about first-century Corinth, and it offers much more specific knowledge of the person who is writing and of those who are intended to receive a text than other sources.

Here rhetoricians are suggesting that an argumentative text does not give only one side of an argument—unless the speaker is completely incompetent—because to argue is to gauge your audience as accurately as you can at every point, to use their language, to work from where they are in order to move them toward where you want them to be. So what we have is not just one individual's viewpoint but a window into a volatile situation, volatile yet not amorphous because certain points of agreement are clear in premises taken and authorities cited; certain points of conflict vanish by one argument while others congeal into Gordian knots.

In classical rhetoric the three types of discourse were distinguished by the audience's role in each case: *forensic speech* before those who judge right from wrong concerning past actions, *deliberative speech* before those who weigh good and bad proposals for future action, and *epideictic speech* before those who celebrate or censure present values. But these three settings of court, assembly, and cult seldom appear in pure form; and struggling to classify more diverse texts into one of these categories may not be fruitful.[12]

Modern rhetoric has given up the prescriptive side of classical rhetoric with its canon of the single-function speech, but this has intensified its sensitivity to the key role of the rhetorical situation in which the speaker and audience are related as that which shapes the argument at each point. Granted, this is the audience as seen by the speaker, and any evidence of blind spots in the speaker's vision must be watched for. But the more intent the speaker is to persuade, the less he or she can afford to misjudge the audience. An accurate reading of the audience is integral to the self-interest of any persuader, all the more so when part of the audience stands in opposition. This suggests that those in clear disagreement with Paul should be the ones most accessible through his rhetoric.

But even so, is it possible to call a reconstruction based largely on rhetorical analysis a historical reconstruction? Rhetoricians evade this question by limiting themselves to reconstructing the rhetorical situation and disclaiming any interest in history. Recently, literary critics have created an entire hierarchy of figures—from the real author to implied author to narrator to narratee to implied reader to real reader—in order to insulate fiction's fragile world from the heavy hand of history.[13] But Paul's letter is as close to history as writing can get—a proxy for his presence in a specific historical context. Historians cannot ignore this fact. Where others see history as a monolithic reality set in a determined past outside the literary creation, historians know history is a piecing together of fragile textual and material remains.

Modern historians study texts with the same tools as do the literary and rhetorical critics in order to determine the interests of writers and intended audiences. They find this data as crucial for historical reconstruction as whatever the text says about particular events or social institutions. It is plain what a significant historical source 1 Corinthians is when read along with Jerome Murphy-O'Connor's recent collection of texts about ancient Corinth.[14] This letter does not simply describe the place as the geographers do. It attests a struggle in a particular community as it occurs and from within, the author himself being implicated in the conflict and at work persuading other parties by appeal to common assumptions and attacks on certain conduct. Of course, this data cannot be generalized to apply to all Corinthians or to all early Christians—the social implications depend on wider local evidence and on careful use of social models from comparative contexts—but the historian willing to settle for the reconstruction of a particular conflict in a particular year can only see this source as a bonanza. When each ancient text is read with attention to its rhetorical situation the result can be a more intricate and accurate kind of history drawn from the mutual informing of the rhetorical situations of all extant texts. Literary scholars may call this "intertextuality" and deny any interest in reconstructing what was going on at the time. The literary critic's peelings make the historian's banquet!

To reconstruct a group that is part of a larger group to whom an author writes is a project in social history. The social questions asked of the text must tailor themselves to the data available through rhetorical analysis. As this method of reconstructing social history is developed it may come to have tools of its own, but in the meantime I adapt social models from various quarters. For example, in his argument Paul gives multiple indications of how the Corinthians perceive their social status. Therefore I analyze their status at the time of the letter writing using a multifactor approach that charts status for each variable independently (see excursus to chapter 3). These results can be compared to indications of the social status they had before entering the community as it is found in Paul's argument and in data from other sources on Greek women of the time. On this basis the change in their social status can be compared to social status changes of others in this community and society. Theissen's proposed analytic methods of social reconstruction are useful, particularly the focus on conflict as it exposes structures of communal life and the caution that in conflict situations norms, events, and symbols may indicate a situation opposite to what they say.[15] Victor Turner's studies and Bruce Lincoln's work on initiation rituals suggest some ways to read the different experiences of baptism in the Corinthian church.[16] Mary Douglas in her study of trance states in the Nuer and Dinka societies makes observations that have implications for Christian prophecy.[17] Her "group-grid" structure can be used in social reconstruction of an argumentative situation (see chapter 9).[18] For example, Paul's efforts to persuade the Corinthian church to strengthen its group boundaries could indicate relatively weak existing group boundaries. Bruce Malina's work on the use of challenge and riposte in the Mediterranean world makes some of Paul's rhetoric clearer.[19] Comparative models of group life, drawn from the ancient Roman East, are particularly important as, for example, Wayne Meeks and Elisabeth Schüssler Fiorenza apply them.[20] No one study can pursue all these approaches; it is their integration that will eventually make an effective social reconstruction of early Christianity.

Finally, a feminist must defend herself against charges of special pleading in the use of rhetorical analysis. Since almost all extant texts from the ancient world were written by men from their viewpoints, women have a special interest in finding ways of reconstructing the viewpoints of those who were not writing or whose writings were not preserved. The rhetorical method, which reconstructs the audience's conduct and views in its understanding of a writer's argument, deals with women's views where they had a significant role in an audience. The work that women do on this front is parallel to the work of other groups today who seek out their own history and thereby extend the knowledge of the past. When priests kept the records, the records listed the priests. When history was written in the courts of kings, history was about kings. When the educated men of the cities began to write, they wrote their own political and economic history. The new, broader social history reflects today's authors.

In this context, women's research proposes to bring to light the other half of the human race. This is not in any new sense a work of the imagination, since women were as active as men in all the societies of the past and have left their mark. But the methods a new group develops to reconstruct its history are part of the act of taking power. I say this not to take them out of the arena of criticism, but to underline the need to meet this criticism with solid argument if power is to be gained by persuasion rather than by force. Women who have in the past lacked the personal power of the pen and the institutional power to preserve their own writings will reconstruct their past by reading given texts and artifacts in new ways, particularly by recovering embedded oral traditions, interpreting scattered pieces of data about women, and identifying and mining texts that women provoked men to write. In the latter case we will be making a double contribution. The aim will be an accurate and full picture of the women in that rhetorical situation. The by-product will be a clearer picture of the author's act of writing in the rhetorical situation that gives us our only access to these women.

Procedure

Two different approaches are useful to better understand a particular text as argument. On the one hand, specific arguments can be identified and traced as they appear and reappear throughout the document. The arguments that prove to be most characteristic of the text, especially when seen to be distinctive among parallel texts of the time and other writings of this author, can reveal what the writer considered most persuasive to the intended readers. I begin with this analysis in chapter 2 because it provides an overview of the key arguments and certain indications of the situation for which the letter was written, meanwhile accustoming us to hear the text as persuasion rather than as dogma, historical record, or imaginative literature. The simplicity artificially created by separating a recurring argument from the mass of argumentation in a text also helps to distinguish and name types of arguments. I call the result of this kind of analysis the textual rhetoric of 1 Corinthians because it is argumentation characteristic of this particular text.[21] A comprehensive textual rhetoric of 1 Corinthians is not possible within the scope of this study, but the thread of certain arguments can be traced through the fabric and their colors seen as they recur, provoking certain theses about the Corinthian women prophets.

A second approach to the same arguments is to work on one unit of the text at a time as in chapters 3–9. Here all arguments in the context are important as they are interwoven in one effort to persuade, yielding much fuller implications about the people being addressed or mentioned. This can be called the letter's structural rhetoric because unit by unit the structure of the combined arguments becomes visible until the structure of the whole is apparent. The integration of warp and woof—gauge, color, texture, and weight together—give the text its whole impact and allow whatever reconstruction of the situation is possible.

To catalogue Paul's textual rhetoric in 1 Corinthians I follow Perelman and Olbrechts-Tyteca's distinction of four kinds of argument.[22] Their classification rejects the traditional view that all arguments are either inductive or deductive, and particularly the modern prejudice in favor of incontrovertible arguments deduced from self-evident axioms or built up inductively from empirical evidence. They consider the latter of minor importance among the multiple grounds for adherence to one view rather than another. In place of what some call deduction they speak of two kinds of argument, quasi-logical arguments and arguments based on the structure of reality. By quasi-logical they mean having the logic of common sense: wholes are made up of parts, contradictions exclude each other, things the same or similar are to be treated as such. Arguments from sacrifice and justice derive from such assumptions. The second, more general kind of deduction they call argument from the structure of reality. These arguments appeal to relations of cause and effect and relations people have to their acts, the latter including arguments from authority, custom, and other more symbolic kinds of coexistence.

Arguments of a third class that seek to establish the structure of reality do not deduce from common sense or from assumptions about how reality is structured but work to establish this structure. Here the argument moves from the particular to the general: examples seek to prove a rule; illustration is satisfied to highlight a rule; models or anti-models stand for more than themselves; analogy and metaphor speak through particular images. The fourth and final type of argument Perelman and Olbrechts-Tyteca call the dissociation of concepts. Here assumed structures of reality are broken apart to provoke new understanding, as when reality is dissociated from appearance, the concrete from the abstract, or the divine from the human.

When analyzing Paul's textual rhetoric in these categories (chapter 2) and Paul's structural rhetoric in each unit of the letter (chapter 3–9), I ask my primary question about the Corinthian women prophets at every point.

Normally, when the text is in motion, an author's argument is not interrupted to ask for the implications of what is said for problems that may not be the primary focus of the writer's attention. This means that the way the author argues at each stage is seldom factored to decipher what is indicated about the groups or issues more marginally referred to. Because this loss cannot be made up by sweeping conclusions at the end, I will pursue the question at each step. This interruption can be tolerated if particular attention is given to the author's point in each argument and care is taken to make the distinction between what is focusing the pupil of the writer's eye at the moment and what is in the wider field of vision.

I use the analogy of vision to explain what is meant by "factoring" for the role of these women within the argumentative situation. An argument is like a stare that focuses on one point but incorporates a wide background, all in relation to the focal point. The interpreter's eye can therefore choose a different focus and consider what this arrangement indicates about a peripheral element. For example, this is done in the best theological reading of Paul's letters where the interpreter focuses on a reference to God used in the background of an argument. Another useful analogy drawn from hearing is suggested by the title of Michael Polanyi's book, *The Tacit Dimension*. He proposes that knowledge is largely unvoiced background to the little that we think we know.[23] I suggest that hearing the background silence is possible if its relation to our conscious knowledge is never abandoned as the key to our access.

My word, "factoring," comes from an analogy to the algebraic equation that answers its own questions but can be reorganized to define the peripheral "x." This is possible because the relation between all the elements is given within the original equation. The danger of this analogy is that it might be thought to claim something like empirical or, in the case of argument, historical validity for what is factored, whereas the validity is restricted to the relations between the elements in the rhetorical equation. The integrity of a rewritten equation depends upon its faithfulness to the initial statement's data, not upon correspondence to the world at large; so too, any implication for women drawn from Paul's arguments has its integrity within his argument as a whole. Whatever correspondence Paul's arguments have to the reality of the Corinthian women is a different question depending strictly on the level of Paul's openness to the situation, his skill in argument, and the firmness of his intent to persuade real people in Corinth.

To state my assumptions should be useful in evaluating the adequacy with which this "factoring" is done. First, Paul is writing this letter to persuade the Corinthians. Everything he says and the way he says it must be understood according to its function in this aim. Second, whatever Paul says about human beings, Corinthians, believers in Christ, women, and prophets is a possible resource for understanding the women prophets in

Corinth's church. But nothing he writes can be considered reliable unless it serves his purpose of persuasion. In other words, everything spoken as description or analysis is first of all an address to the intended readers. Third, on whatever points Paul's persuasion is insistent and intense, showing he is not merely confirming their agreement but struggling for their assent, one can assume some different and opposite point of view in Corinth from the one Paul is stating.

Fourth, the women prophets in Corinth's church have a place in the group Paul is addressing, some role in the rhetorical situation. If this role were known from the start, the significance of Paul's arguments for a reconstruction of these women could be determined. Because this is not initially known, it must be discovered in conjunction with its use in reconstructing whatever we can know about them. This role could be presented as a hypothesis and tested for its adequacy in helping lay out a comprehensive understanding of Paul's argument. But because research in this area is still at a beginning stage I am neither able to do this nor would it be convincing to hear something so new presented as *fait accompli*. To avoid some reality and the appearance of manipulation of the text, I work simultaneously to determine what place these women have in the developing event of persuasion that is 1 Corinthians and whatever light this sheds on themselves, testing both by their adequacy in helping to provide an account of Paul's argument.

It needs to be stated that the Corinthian women prophets are only one part of Paul's audience; other parts could also be reconstructed in this way. A parallel study of some group of men in the Corinthian church would be particularly helpful for comparative purposes. This is discussed briefly at the end of chapter 3 in the excursus on the Social Status of the Corinthian Women Prophets and of Paul.

Argument and Authority

The appropriateness of rhetorical analysis to scriptural texts is not self-evident. Rhetoric can be seen as embellishment or even distortion of the truth, not to be credited to biblical authors. Even when rhetoric is taken as the language of persuasion, there is hesitancy in describing the New Testament defense of the gospel as rhetoric. We may say, "To the unbeliever it may be persuasion, but to us it is truth." It is necessary to respect this position and the problem that lies behind it if room is to be made for rhetorical study of these texts, whose analysis is carried out largely within believing communities. Granted, rhetoric is not concerned with demonstrating absolute truth, scientific or dogmatic, but with argument concerning what is probable, aiming to increase adherence to theses presented for approval. In so far as biblical authority is taken in the popular sense as the absolute authority of the biblical writer's point of view, there is no experience of Paul's letter as rhetoric. Respect for biblical authority presupposes that Paul is right and excludes the possibility of weighing his arguments in the balance. Because an argument Paul makes cannot be rejected as unconvincing, it also cannot convince. In this way the authority we attribute to Paul prevents him from persuading us.

This dogmatic reading of Paul's letters is present as much in the academy as in the pulpit. Particularly in the Lutheran and Reformed traditions where Paul's theology is absolutized because it was persuasive to the Reformers, every study begins and ends with the assumption that Paul's view is normative. In spite of the great advances in Pauline research in the historical-critical study of 1 Corinthians, extending from Friedrich Christian Baur to Johannes Weiss to Hans Conzelmann,[24] Paul's opponents are still seen as no more than the contrasting background to his own exemplary humility. At the same time, all these people recognize that Paul was not understood in his own time as the standard of valid Christian faith and that, in all cases, his major opponents are also believers in Christ. Yet our interpreters remain bound by their heritage in Protestant Orthodoxy to cast these opponents negatively in order to affirm Paul. It is as if every opinion the interpreters hold is Pauline and every opinion of Paul's their own.

This has put Paul in the straitjacket of each generation's self-understanding; those who begin from the foregone conclusion that Paul's viewpoint is authoritative read Paul in the way that justifies him by their own standards. Paul's contemporary, Philo, may seem arbitrary or sexist in his allegorical exegesis; Josephus may be seen as an opportunist vis-à-vis his Roman patrons—all without disparaging the great gifts of each writer. But Paul is required to be pristine, our Protestant alter ego. This not only does great disservice to the memory of Paul. It has taken Paul's letters out of the public domain where argument is in order and where Paul's strong arguments could have social impact. Those reacting against this domestication of Paul tend to avenge themselves by seeing Paul as the devil incarnate or by ignoring his arguments altogether.[25]

Understanding Paul's letters as argument may be possible in the church only when there is a shift in its view of the Bible's authority. Two appropriate standards for determining a text's authority are the way it claims authority and the authority it actively exercises with the receptive reader. Paul claims a hearing on the basis of insistent arguments from God's calling, from revelation, from hard work, and from modeling Christ. The letters do not claim to be authoritative in their own right or this argument would be redundant. For Paul, such intrinsic authority belongs to God alone. Paul's letters' authority depends on free assent to Paul's arguments because they are convincing.

The same point applies to the authority that the text exercises with the thoughtful reader. Again, any independent determination of a text's authority works against hearing the arguments in the text because it sets up an alternative authority to the conviction won by the arguments given. This explanation is not a sleight of hand to cancel out the authority of the text. It is a necessary defense of authority that operates through persuasion as found in the form and functioning of Paul's letters.

If we take on the role of the reader that Paul sets up and locate the Bible's authority not in given dogmas or individual authors but in the event where the persuasive word meets conviction, this event may occur where we do not expect. The book of James may win an argument against Paul; the Corinthian women prophets may convince us at a point where Paul does not; voices from outside the canon may speak with authority. None of these would surprise Paul or he would not put such effort into persuading. Paul's reader is programmed to be involved in a debate that believers are carrying on about the issues he discusses, not to be a non-believer seeking enlightenment nor a new believer receiving training (if these passive stereotypes have ever appeared in the flesh). Paul expects controversy—provokes it in fact—and he is confident that the best argument will win. The way he writes challenges the reader not to memorize verses but to fearlessly weigh what he says against other views. It is a competitive market: "Do you not know that all the runners in the stadium run, but only one takes the prize? So run that you seize it!" (1 Cor. 9:24). If a runner only becomes as good as his or her competition requires, that says something about both Paul and his opposition in Corinth.

A view of biblical authority emerges that has more the form of witness and debate than of a party line. This is appropriate to the biblical canon whose witness is already a lively debate, one that can reach its full stereophonic sound only when the silenced voices within and around it are recovered. This also says something about human community, about the freedom we can allow each other to have, though we do not have agreement on the most crucial issues. It assumes that none of us is God and yet that the authority to hear God and to speak for God can come to us in the human task of effective persuasion.

2 | The Rhetoric Characteristic of 1 Corinthians with Implications for the Corinthian Women Prophets

THE ARGUMENTS PAUL USES repeatedly in 1 Corinthians qualify as textual rhetoric, as argumentative features characteristic of this particular text. In order to keep the catalogue of Paul's rhetoric in 1 Corinthians within manageable length, the only arguments listed are those that have particular significance for a reconstruction of the Corinthian women prophets. Certain rhetorical features that are not in themselves arguments — the rhetorical question, the statement of objections, the various tropes or alterations in word meaning — are mentioned only when they consistently appear within one of these arguments. Perelman and Olbrechts-Tyteca's division of arguments described previously provides a framework that fits Paul's writing. Arguments that deduce particular claims from an assumed structure of reality are distinguished from arguments that seek to establish the structure of reality from particulars, with the latter including all arguments from example, model, analogy, and metaphor. Two other kinds of arguments are also identified, on one extreme the most strictly deductive arguments of a quasi-logical or commonsense nature, such as arguments from identity and contradiction, and arguments that move beyond positive construction of reality into negative construction on the other. The identification of this last argument by dissociation of concepts is the contribution of Perelman and Olbrechts-Tyteca, one very useful in understanding Paul.

The catalogue below, even though partial, indicates by its broad distribution of arguments that Paul's persuasion is complex. His strong use of arguments from the structure of reality shows how much he appeals to given authorities in matters related to the women. Even the argument by dissociation of concepts draws on basic cultural oppositions that stand almost beyond question. To clarify this least self-explanatory category of argument, I begin with Paul's arguments by dissociation.

Arguments by Dissociation of Concepts

Argument Dissociating Principle from Practice

6:12a All things are authorized me, but not all things are useful.

6:12b All things are authorized me, but I will not fall under the authority of anything.

6:13a Food is for the stomach and the stomach for food. But God will do away with both stomach and food.

7:1b-2 It is good for a man not to touch a woman. But because of sexual immorality, let each man have his own wife, and each woman her own husband.

8:1b, 7a For we all have knowledge. . . . But knowledge is not in all.

10:23a All things are authorized, but not all things are useful.

10:23b All things are authorized, but not all things are constructive.

Paul's argument of agreement in principle and qualification in practice only appears in the long central section of 1 Corinthians on sexual immorality and idolatry, but its spread throughout chapters 6–10 qualifies it as part of Paul's textual rhetoric. The first half of each of these arguments may be a direct quotation of slogans used by the Corinthians (note RSV quotation marks) that Paul responds to in the second half. Or it may be that Paul is commenting on key statements from his earlier preaching in Corinth, although the absence of the slogans in his other letters makes this less probable. In any case, the persuasiveness of Paul's argument depends on Paul so well reflecting the hearers' present views in his agreement with them on principle that they will be open to his qualification in practice. If Paul were stressing the opening statement of agreement, this would be an argument from the structure of reality. But his point is that their authority claims, which he concedes in principle, are not functional for themselves or others.

In fact, Paul's agreement masks the extent of his qualification. What is offered as a simple qualification of the principle turns out to be a reversal in terms of advised conduct. Not only are sexual immorality and eating in temples out of bounds, but so are celibacy and acting on one's knowledge where others whose lives are affected do not share the same commitment. Paul could counter that the basic freedom still remains, since it is by an exercise of authority or knowledge that people are asked to limit themselves. Yet the result is limitation. And it is not clear that Paul will respect those who do not think it right to restrict this expression.

Note the impersonal form of the opening statements claiming authority: "it is good . . . ," "it is authorized . . . ," "food is for. . . ." If these are Corinthian slogans, they may be imitating a judicial "it is forbidden," the series of permissions functioning as a kind of parody of legal prohibitions, perhaps formulated by those who teach. On the other hand, the claim, "we all have knowledge," with its first-person plural form, suggests another possible origin for the slogans. All of them are brief, self-legitimating assertions that could have arisen as prophetic legitimation oracles justifying certain conduct or claims.

Both the impersonal and first-person forms leave us in the dark about the sex of those who speak. The one statement that refers to male initiative, "It is good for a man not to touch a woman," is met by Paul with the response that each man should have his own wife and each woman her own husband. Since Paul indicates that women are as active as men in making choices in this case, it does not seem reasonable to read a less-inclusive meaning into Paul's understanding of the other claims to authority. This suggests that there are women prophets in Corinth claiming that they have authority to do all things, that they all have knowledge, that they may eat what they like, that they have authority not to be touched by a man. These principles may have been practiced in Corinth and provoked Paul's dissociation of principle from practice.

Argument Dissociating Thought from Reality

3:18 If any among you in this age think they are wise, let them become fools that they may become wise.[1]

8:2-3 If any think they know something, they do not yet know as they need to know. But if any love God, they are known by him.

10:12 So let any who think they stand watch out not to fall.

11:16 If any think they want to make an issue of this, we ourselves have no such custom [as women prophesying with uncovered heads], nor do the churches of God.

14:37-38 If any think they are prophets or spiritual, let them recognize that the things I write you [about silence in the church] are a command of the Lord.[2] Whoever does not recognize this is not recognized.

This provoking of confident boasts, suddenly to deflate them as mere thought and not reality, is found only twice elsewhere in Paul's letters (Gal. 6:3; Phil. 3:4).[3] In 1 Corinthians the argument spans the entire letter, appearing in five separate contexts.

The final two uses of this argument come at the end of Paul's instructions about women in worship. His challenges are in the masculine plural, the form used to address men and women together. He anticipates that some people will want to make an issue of the requirement that women cover their heads when praying and prophesying. The words I translate "want to make an issue of this," sometimes read "to be contentious," and literally meaning "to be victory-loving," show that Paul is expecting opponents. Women who prophesy are obvious candidates.

Immediately after insisting that those who speak in tongues without interpreters, those who prophesy simultaneously, and those who are women be silent in the church, Paul challenges any who think they are prophets or spiritual to recognize what he says or not be recognized. Women prophets, among others, must be intended. In this argument and the one described above the same technique is applied to cut off debate, namely a challenge to those who claim to be confident to see that their confidence is based on what they think but not on reality—unless they concede his point and restrict themselves. The double use of this argument in contexts where Paul's instructions concern women suggests that women are not only intended among others but could be the focus of his attention. If so, the women within this address consider themselves "prophets" or "spiritual," are willing to contest Paul, and they expect to win.

The question is whether the first three uses of this argument in the letter, also addressed to "any among you," may be preparing for the final challenges where women who prophesy are explicitly mentioned. In so, the net is intentionally thrown wide. Those who think they are wise are challenged to become fools, those who think they have knowledge are challenged to love, those who think they are firmly founded are challenged not to fall. Although Paul concedes they gain their confidence in Christ (1:4-7, 30; 4:10; 8:6), it is rhetorically interpreted as self-assertion in contrast to humble modesty. The basic argument remains the same each time it is used and indicates, not separate and unrelated problems in the church, but one problem: a wisdom, freedom, and fluency in the church—perhaps particularly among its prophesying women—that threatens Paul's gospel and leadership.

Argument Dissociating Private from Public

7:2, 8-9, 36 Due to sexual immorality, let each man have his own wife and each woman her own husband. . . . And I say to the single and widows . . . , if they cannot exercise self-control, let them marry. . . . And if anyone thinks he is acting improperly toward his virgin . . . let them marry.

10:25 Eat [privately] whatever is bought in the market without any considerations of conscience because the world is the Lord's and all that is in it.

11:5a But every woman who prays and prophesies [in church] with uncovered head shames her head.

11:21-22a, 34a Each one goes ahead in eating his or her own meal with this one hungry and that one drunk. Have you no houses for eating and drinking? . . . If anyone is hungry, let him or her eat at home so that you do not gather to be judged.

14:18-19a, 28 I thank God that I speak in tongues more than you all. But in church I would rather say five words with my mind in order to instruct others. . . . If there is no interpreter, let [the speakers in tongues] be silent in church and speak rather to themselves and to God.

14:34-35 Let the women be silent in the churches. . . . And if they want to learn, let them inquire of their husbands at home, for it is shameful for a woman to speak in church.

16:2 On the first day of each week let each of you put something aside at home and save up whatever you can so that collecting will not be necessary when I come.

At several points Paul proposes that the Corinthians do at home activities that he considers disrupting or difficult when they gather. His argument dissociates the private from the public sphere of life and locates the church in the public sphere. Home is the place to satisfy hunger and thirst, not church. Even idol food bought in the market can be eaten at home without question. The money for the poor in Jerusalem is to be saved up at home. There are also kinds of speech that do not belong in church. Speaking in tongues is not to be permitted in church when there is no one on hand to interpret. This speaking should be done in private, "to self and to God," as Paul claims he does "more than you all." Finally, "If the women want to learn, let them inquire of their husbands at home."

In order to keep the church undefiled, Paul seems to be making the home into a buffer zone for the people's energy, a place conceded to their lively interest in such things as food, sex, unveiled prayer, money, inquiry, and ecstasy. All these matters, including money, are volatile, liable to stir up feeling and differences of opinion, and Paul may be trying to cool off the communal situation by sending these activities back to each home. This would not mean defiling the homes to Paul since he understands the pollution to be located less in the act than in the threat of individual confidence to the community at large.

Certain implications of this argument suggest further testing for women prophets. Paul's argument assumes that the Corinthians know the distinction of public and private but do not practice it in his sense. They may classify the church as a home, certain women's homes having become home to others. Paul's advocacy of marriage to prevent immorality only makes sense if many have chosen to live without marriage. Women, as the more socially restricted sex, would have particular advantage in taking on the less sex-specific roles within a community that included many single people. Paul's directive would threaten this. Paul's interest in sending the community meal home would also have particular impact on the women who were responsible in Greece for family food preparation. That he thinks money should be saved at home indicates that money once gathered is prone to be spent, possibly by women for food or drink.

Paul's regulations of worship conduct and speech as public behavior are particularly telling for the women, beginning as they do with his demand for their head covering and ending by silencing their voices in the community. They do not cover their heads when praying and prophesying, probably are active in speaking in tongues with or without interpretation, and are not asking their own men questions at home. Paul's dissociation of private from public spheres suggests that the yeast Paul wants cleaned out of the church could be female. Or, to change the image, he may be trying to send back home a Pandora's box of women's spiritual and physical energy that has given the church the richness and disruptiveness of a home.

Argument Dissociating Self-Benefit from Community Benefit

1:10; 3:3 Brethren, I beg you through the name of Jesus Christ our Lord that you all agree and that there not be schisms among you, but that you be restored in the same mind and the same knowledge For while there is jealousy and strife among you, are you not fleshly and living in a human way?

8:9-11 Watch out lest your authority itself become a stumbling block to the weak. For if someone should see you who have knowledge seated in an idol's temple, will that one with a weak conscience not be encouraged to eat food offered to idols? So by your knowledge the one who is weak is lost, the brother for whom Christ died.

9:22 To the weak I have become weak so I might win the weak. I have become all things to all people so that in all ways I might save some.

10:24, 28-29a, 32-33 Let no one seek what is for himself or herself but what is for the other. . . . But if someone should say to you, "This food has been offered to idols," do not eat it due to the one who pointed it out and to conscience. And I mean not your own conscience but the other person's. . . . Cause no offense to Jews or to Greeks or to God's church, as I myself please all people in all things, not seeking my own benefit but that of the many so they might be saved.

11:21-22 Each one goes ahead in eating his or her own meal with this one hungry and that one drunk. Have you no houses for eating and drinking? Or do you despise God's church and shame those who have nothing?

12:7, 24b-25 To each is given the manifestation of the spirit for the common benefit. . . . But God has so arranged the body, giving greater honor to the lesser part so that there might be no schism in the body but that the parts might have the same care for each other.

13:5b [Love] does not seek its own benefit.

14:3-4, 12 Those who prophesy speak to people to build up and encourage and strengthen. Those who speak in tongues build themselves up, but those who prophesy build up the church. . . . So you yourselves, since you are zealots of the spirit, seek the upbuilding of the church in order to excel.

The argument dissociating self-benefit from community benefit is developed most explicitly in the two parts of 1 Corinthians "concerning idol food" (8:1–11:1) and "concerning spiritual gifts" (12:1–14:40). In each case it appears that Paul has picked up an exclamation of their God-given strength from the Corinthians' letter. They know that idols are nothing and demonstrate it in public eating of idol food. They exercise spiritual gifts and show that they are spiritual people. Paul affirms both their knowledge and gifts, but he wants to subordinate them to the common good. If by their knowledge a fellow believer reverts to idol worship, or by their gifts another person is discouraged or confused, then the church is not built up, the community is not served, and God's purpose for giving the knowledge and spirit is not realized. Instead each one is serving him or herself, which Paul's dissociation takes as the opposite of serving the common good.

Paul makes the same distinction more indirectly in two other sections of the letter. He has heard of conflict within the church concerning leadership and the Lord's meal (1:10–4:21; 11:17-34), and he charges them with mutual jealousy and preference for their own meals with the implication that this is not for the common good.

Paul does not dissociate self and community in other matters such as sexual offenses, marriage decisions, head covering, and resurrection. This is worth noting because Paul's argument from the common good in 1 Corinthians has sometimes been overdrawn, as if it were not one argument among others but an objective description of the situation. Then he appears to be addressing a clique of egomaniacs flaunting their powers against a cowering majority.

Paul's dissociation of self-benefit and community-benefit would be no use to him if the people he addresses were not committed to the community. They probably see their freedom from food restrictions as a sign of their common new identity—as Paul does in other contexts (Gal. 2:11-21; 3:27-28; 5:1-3)—and their simultaneous prophecy and tongues as God's empowering of the community. Here they conceive the common good differently than Paul. He sees the common good served in Corinth by people restricting their self-expression of God's Spirit to prevent offenses. They apparently see the common good served by freely celebrating their own empowerment and drawing others into this orbit. If so, they would not dissociate the community benefit from their own benefit.

It is remarkable that Paul nowhere uses the argument from the common good explicitly to defend or restrict women. The sexual offenses are never seen to be against women, nor to be committed by women against the good of others. Women's head covering is not said to benefit the church nor their bare heads to harm the church. Even the silencing of women, which appears within the argument preferring prophecy to tongues for the common good, is defended on other grounds. The closest thing to it, Paul's challenge to the women, "Did God's word originate from you? Or did it reach you alone?" (14:36) is more likely an argument against the Corinthians' originality, when compared to his original preaching in Corinth and beyond Corinth, rather than a call for those who prophesy to hear each other in the community. It may not have been credible to argue directly that the restricting or silencing of women was a benefit to the community.

Argument Dissociating Shame from Honor

1:27-29 God chose the world's foolish things to shame those who are wise. God chose the world's weak things to shame those that are strong. God chose the world's common and despised things, even things that are nothing, to make nothing those that are something, so that no human being might boast before God.

4:10, 14 We are fools for Christ's sake but you are intelligent in Christ, we are weak but you strong, you are honored but we disgraced . . . I write these things not to shame you, but to warn you as beloved children.

11:3-7 But I want you to know that of every man the head is Christ, and the head of woman is man, and the head of Christ is God. Any man who prays or prophesies with his head covered shames his head. Any woman who prays and prophesies with her head uncovered shames her head, for it is one and the same as being shaven. For if a woman is not covered, let her even cut her hair. But if it is shameful for a woman to cut her hair or shave herself, then let her be covered. For the man should not cover his head since he is the image and glory of God. But the woman is the glory of the man.

11:13-15 Judge for yourselves. Is it proper for a woman to pray to God uncovered? Or does nature itself not teach you that if a man has long hair, it is a disgrace to him. But if a woman has long hair, it is an honor to her. For long hair was given her as a covering.

11:21-22 Each one goes ahead in eating his or her own meal with this one hungry and that one drunk. Have you no houses for eating and drinking? Or do you despise God's church and shame those who have nothing?

12:23a And the parts of the body we consider more disgraceful we clothe with extra honor.

14:34-35 Let the women be silent in the churches since it is not fitting for them to speak, but let them be subordinate as the law itself says. And if they want to learn anything, let them inquire of their husbands at home, for it is shameful for a woman to speak in church.

15:42-43a Even the resurrection of the dead is like this. It is sown perishable; it is raised imperishable. It is sown in disgrace; it is raised in honor.

In other letters Paul speaks of shame when denouncing shameful sins (Rom. 1:26; 6:21; 2 Cor. 4:2; Phil. 3:19), or he speaks in the first person about not being ashamed of his work or the gospel (Rom. 1:16; 5:5; 2 Cor. 7:14; 9:4; 10:8; 11:21; Phil. 1:20). In 1 Corinthians he dissociates shame from honor to warn that it is possible to forfeit the dignity befitting a certain human station.

Sometimes the contrast is explicit and the word "disgrace" (*atimia*) is used — Paul is disgraced while they are honored; the disgraceful body parts are clothed with honor; long hair disgraces the man and honors the woman; the body disgraced in death is raised in honor. Otherwise Paul uses the word "shameful" (*aischros*) or the transitive verb "to shame someone" (*kataischunein, entrepein*) and the focus shifts from the contrast with honor to the act that brings shame on a person. God actively chooses those not wise, powerful, or privileged to shame the wise, powerful, and privileged by not respecting the honor befitting their station (1:26-29).

Yet there is no sign that Paul sees this as a reversal of stations, because later he comes close to shaming the Corinthians for claiming just such honor for themselves (4:10-14). Although Paul does not conceive that those who are weak could become strong, he thinks that they should not be shamed by having their weakness exposed. So the poor should not be shamed into begging by others eating in front of them who would do better to eat at home if they are hungry, leaving the community to eat together what all eat (11:21-22, 33-34).

Likewise women should not shame themselves by being shaven, by praying or prophesying with head uncovered, or by speaking in the church

(11:5-6; 14:34). This seems to reflect received views of how a woman should not expose her weakness and bring herself into shame: "Judge for yourselves, is it proper for a woman to pray to God uncovered?" (11:13) But even in the Mediterranean context this argument may have had little force, because Paul goes on to bolster it with various amplifications of the same argument: a woman's praying uncovered is no better than cutting or shaving her hair; praying covered is as natural as the long hair that naturally covers her. Intimations of homosexuality in men with long hair and perhaps men with covered heads also seem to be brought in as an indirect sanction against women who put off the head covering. Why women's head shaving—or male homosexuality—is shameful is not investigated, there being more persuasive force from the untested assumption that femininity is a weakness not to be exposed.

Paul thinks it possible to shame another by association: "every woman who prays and prophesies uncovered shames her head" (11:5), since "the head of woman is the man" (11:3). Paul even fears the women will shame the angels as well and "should have authority on the head because of the angels" (11:10). This reversed meaning of the words "have authority" suggests that Paul is reinterpreting these women's claim to have the right to prophesy uncovered: "to have authority on the head because of the angels" as they honor the angels by speaking in angels' tongues (11:10; 13:1).

Argument Dissociating Human from Divine, Flesh from Spirit

2:12-15; 3:1a, 3b Yet we have not received the spirit of the world but the spirit that is from God so we might know the things given us by God. And we do not speak in words taught by human wisdom but taught by the spirit, determining spiritual things among the spiritual. But the ordinary person does not receive the things of God's spirit, for they are foolish to the person who is not able to know them, since they are spiritually discerned. The spiritual person, on the other hand, discerns all things but is not discerned by anyone. . . . I myself, brethren, cannot speak to you as spiritual people but as fleshly. . . . As long as there is still envy and strife among you, are you not fleshly and living in a human way?

6:15-17 Do you not know that your bodies are members of Christ? Will I then take members of Christ and make them members of a prostitute? Impossible! Or do you not know that the one who joins himself with a prostitute is one body with her? For it says, "the two will be one flesh." But the one joined to the Lord is one spirit with him.

7:32b-34 The unmarried man is worried about the Lord's affairs, how to please the Lord. But the man who has married is worried about the world's affairs, how to please his wife, and he is divided. The unmarried woman and also the virgin is worried about the Lord's affairs so that she may be consecrated in body and spirit. The woman who has married is worried about the world's affairs, how to please her husband.

10:21-22 You cannot drink the cup of the Lord and the cup of daemons. You cannot partake in the table of the Lord and the table of daemons. Or are we to provoke the Lord to jealousy? Are we stronger than he?

11:7 For the man should not cover his head since he is the image and glory of God. But the woman is the glory of the man.

11:20-21 When you come together it is not the Lord's meal that you eat. For each one goes ahead to eat his or her own meal with this one hungry and that one drunk.

15:50 But I say this, brethren: flesh and blood cannot inherit the kingdom of God, nor can the perishable inherit the imperishable.

Paul's rhetoric in 1 Corinthians again and again stresses the dissociation of divine and human, spirit and flesh. Using accumulation in argument and the shock tactics of the rhetorical question, antithesis and negation, he contrasts two kinds of conduct in Corinth. Whatever is not of the spirit is of the flesh and is antithetical to it. Envy and strife are human so they are not spiritual, one's own meal cannot be the Lord's meal, the man's glory cannot be God's glory, the perishable cannot be imperishable. In these arguments Christ is not a mediating figure but represents the divine side of the disjunction. To participate in Christ excludes participating in anything human or fleshly or semidivine (as the Greeks saw daemons to be). Paul does not give arguments to support this dissociation but assumes it and appeals to it by attacking certain Corinthian conduct.

This suggests that he could be appealing to a dissociation they already are making when claiming to be spiritual. Yet their understanding of spirit and flesh, Christ and world, has led to conduct different than Paul's view supports. In the leadership struggle and in the practice of the Lord's meal, they are able to tolerate more variety of opinion and practice than Paul. They do not expect the Lord's spirit to produce resolution of the leadership struggle or an ordered meal in contrast to strife, disorder, and arbitrary spiritual experience in the world. Rather, the spirit seems to be known for generating multiple authorities in contrast to a world of stated authority.

In sexual practice, some Corinthians abandon marriage while others form irregular alliances and no one adjudicates. In prayer and prophecy they exhibit the spirit without distinguishing gifts or determining proper dress. Paul meets this by requiring marriage where necessary to block the greater threat to men of the prostitute's flesh, and by requiring the woman to cover her head because she is the glory of the male over against God's glory reflected in Christ, man's head. At these points Paul's male perspective dissociates human from divine by taking woman as the fleshly or dangerous side of man that must be spurned or tamed before God. But there is no sign that the Corinthians see women as less spiritual or take the wealth of the spirit among them as competing with God's glory. On the contrary, they may claim in their prayer and prophecy to mediate between God and humanity so that through the spirit the perishable does inherit imperishability and the primal dissociation is breached.

Quasi-Logical Arguments

Argument from Definition

1:18 For the word of the cross is foolishness to those who are perishing, but to us who are being saved it is the power of God.

11:3 But I want you to know that of every man the head is Christ, and the head of woman is man, and the head of Christ is God.

13:4-8a Love waits patiently; love shows kindness; it does not envy, love does not boast; it does not exalt itself, does not act shamefully, does not seek its own advantage, does not provoke, does not count up evil, does not rejoice in injustice but joins those rejoicing in the truth. It bears all things, believes all things, hopes all things, endures all things. Love never fails.

14:33 For God is not the God of disruption but the God of peace as in all the churches of the saints.

Definition as an argument depends less on correspondence with empirical reality than on its own claim that something logically or universally has a certain character. So Paul does not set out to justify his definitions with evidence. But defining seldom happens where meanings are not contested, and competing definitions are at least implied. Paul's definitions argue for themselves indirectly by incorporating as much common sense and folk wisdom as can be combined with his point, and the definitions cited previously also confirm themselves by defining the term in more than one way.

Paul's definition of "the word of the cross" takes from the apocalyptic worldview the image of one group perishing and another being saved to show that the cross can be both the world's foolishness and God's power. The triple definition of "head" leans on common views of Christ being both Lord of the believer and son of God, sandwiching between them the phrase on woman. The parallel statements about men and women that follow depend on the definition and seem to confirm it. "Love" is defined by a long series of verbs that tell what it does, in contrast to statements telling what knowledge, tongues, and prophecy do. Finally, even "God" is defined antithetically so that God's standard association with peace turns out to require the absence of the disruption that Paul wants to silence.

There is no direct evidence showing that the Corinthian women or men used definitions that Paul is reworking or that they reworked his definitions, although some of this is almost unavoidable in verbal confrontations. Paul's definitions do indicate that those he is trying to persuade do not share his views. They do not consider the cross as God's foolish wisdom and God's weak power. Yet he assumes they possess a basic knowledge that Christ was crucified and some cultural understanding that crucifixion means execution and shame. To them the weakness and foolishness of the cross more likely represent the obvious weakness and foolishness of human life, the life out of which God raises Christ and those who are in Christ. Paul's definition of "head" indicates that they do not see Christ as one who links woman through man to God in a chain of dependency or subordination. The opposite view must, in some way, take Christ as an effective mediator of divine presence and as an agent of human participation in this mediating. The self-humbling that Paul extols in his definition of love would not have been their mode as much as the self-expressing possible in tongues, knowledge, and prophecy with which he contrasts it. If God is praised among them as the God of peace, it would have been in a different sense than the peace kept by restrictions to prevent disruption.

Definition is a powerful rhetorical tool because it gives universal warrant to affirmative claims. The way it accomplishes this provides not a precise pinpointing but a general indication of the views that are being denied.

Argument from Justice

3:5-8 (continued in 9-15; 4:1-6, 15) What then is Apollos? What is Paul? Servants through whom you believed, as the Lord gave to each. I planted, Apollos watered, but God caused growth. He who plants and he who waters are equal and each will receive his own reward according to his own labor.

7:2-4 (continued in 10-11, 12-14, 16, 28, 32-34) But due to sexual immorality, let each man have his own wife and each woman her own husband. Let the man give what he owes to his wife, likewise also the wife to the husband. The wife does not have authority over her own body but the husband does. Likewise also the husband does not have authority over his own body but the wife does.

9:5-6 Do we not have the authority to have our sister-wives travel with us, as do the rest of the apostles and the Lord's brothers and Cephas? Or do Barnabas and I alone lack the authority not to work for a living?

11:4-5a, 11-12 Any man who prays or prophesies with his head covered shames his head. And any woman who prays and prophesies with her head uncovered shames her head. . . . But the woman is not apart from the man nor the man apart from the woman in the Lord. For just as the woman is [created] from the man, so the man is [born] through the woman, and all things are from God.

It is logical that identical treatment be given in identical cases and equivalent treatment in equivalent cases. Rhetoric calls this the rule of justice. Paul combats divisiveness in Corinth by comparing himself and Apollos to coworkers who are both due respect. Since cases are never exactly equal, Paul manages to draw out of the argument from justice the conclusion that he has a greater claim on them. He argues for his right to have church support from the rights given the other apostles—though he later refuses to use this right and claims an advantage from this refusal (9:1-18). From these two arguments we learn that the Corinthian women and others in Corinth do not see their itinerant leaders as equivalent. They apparently value some leaders more than others and may show this financially.

In the other two passages the equivalence is between men and women. Paul invokes the argument from justice ten times in his discussion of marriage. What is expected of the men is also expected of the women and vice versa. This could show Paul's respect for the Corinthian women in a culture where there is no equivalence in marriage. But this does not explain the repetition and amplification of parallel clauses so far beyond what would be necessary to make the point. The handy word, "each other," used only once in the chapter, could have made the same point more quickly. Paul may be dramatizing equivalence in order to gain support from those whom it would most benefit—the women. But why an appeal to them? It may be that the women are less ready than the men to return to the marriage commitments that Paul now widely advocates in the wake of sexual offenses in the church.

The fact that the rule of justice may be used to give two groups "equally" what one group wants or takes for granted and the other group does not want can be seen in the argument on head covering. The different points of view of the two parties are clearer because the equivalence is only rhetorical. Each party is said to shame his or her head when praying and prophesying. But a foregoing definition and several following explanations use the form of equivalent speech to argue its exact opposite, namely that the different head covering is a sign of one group being subordinate to the other.

Argument from Divine Reciprocity or Retribution

3:16-17 (cf. 6:18-20) Don't you know that you people are God's temple and God's spirit lives in you? Anyone who corrupts God's temple, God will bring down to corruption. For God's temple is holy, and you are that temple.

5:1, 4b-5, 13b It is even heard that there is sexual immorality among you, and such immorality as is not even practiced among the Gentiles, so that someone has his father's wife. . . . When you are gathered with my spirit in the power of our Lord Jesus, such a man as this is to be delivered to Satan for the destruction of the flesh in order that his spirit might be saved in the day of the Lord. . . . "Cast the evil one out from among you!"

10:7-10, 14 (continued 10:19-22) Do not be idolaters as some of them were, as it is written, "The people sat down to eat and drink and stood up to play." And let us not be sexually immoral as some of them were and twenty-three thousand fell in one day. Nor let us test the Lord as some of them tested the Lord and perished by the snakes. Nor conspire as some of them conspired and were destroyed by the Destroyer. . . . Therefore, my loved ones, flee idolatry!"

11:20, 27-30 So when you come together it is not the Lord's meal that you eat. . . . Therefore whoever eats the loaf or drinks the cup of the Lord unworthily is guilty of the body and blood of the Lord. But let the people all test themselves and in this way eat from the loaf and drink from the cup. For those who eat and drink without discerning the body seal their own sentence with eating and drinking. This is the reason many among you are weak and sick and several die.

Divine reciprocity or retribution for human acts appears in 1 Corinthians in two ways. On the one hand, the "divine passive" is used to state that God reciprocates and surpasses all human knowledge of God: "If any think that they know something, they do not yet know as they need to know. But if any love God, they are known by him" (8:2-3). "Now I know in part, but then I shall know even as I have been known" (13:12b). "Whoever does not recognize this is not recognized" (14:38). In the last of these Paul uses God's withholding of recognition as a threat against any prophets who do not recognize as valid his silencing of uninterpreted tongues, simultaneous prophecy, and all women's speech in the church.

The full citations above show a second kind of argument from divine reciprocity or retribution in which a sentence of death is announced for violating God. After Paul indicates that some leader in Corinth, perhaps

Apollos, has been building with materials that will burn at God's judgment though he will be saved "as through fire" (3:12-15), he concludes by saying that whoever corrupts God's temple, which they are, will go down to corruption in the grave. Later Paul uses the same image of the body as the spirit's temple to warn the Corinthians against associating with prostitutes (6:18-20). Here he does not explicitly threaten them with death, but this could be implied in his first pollution warning, "Flee immorality!"

In the case of the man living with his father's wife, Paul almost moves out of the realm of argument by announcing the sentence of destruction as a self fulfilling curse.[4] But a careful reading reveals that Paul understands that the judgment he has passed depends on their communal execution of it. The sentence he gives is part of his effort to persuade them and remains an argument in the form of a proleptic curse.

Paul's second pollution warning, "Flee idolatry!" shows that he opposes their eating idol food, not so much because it offends others, but because it violates God (10:1-22). The Israelites in the desert are taken as the type or model of idolatry, and for their conspiring they are said to have been destroyed by the Destroyer. The problem Paul sees for the Corinthians at the daemons' tables is that they worship nonexistent daemons in place of God and provoke God's jealous retribution. The same critique is applied to their common meals which, in Paul's judgment, are not the Lord's meal. Because "some are hungry and some drunk" they do not "discern the body" in the loaf, making them guilty of Christ's death so that "many are weak and sick and several die" (11:21-30). These deaths come from a sacral violation of God's exclusive claim on them as a body, which is identified as the Lord's body in the meal.

In these arguments from retribution, the primary group addressed is not the Corinthian women, but they are included because Paul attacks the community at large for being "bloated" by claiming that "we all know" and that "all things are authorized" (4:8; 5:2, 6; 8:1; 6:12; 10:23). Apparently they do not see God on the defense, vindicating the divine glory by capital punishment, but on the offense, giving people gifts whose exercise glorifies both themselves and God.

Twice Paul draws on the threat of divine retribution when trying to control the Corinthian women's speech. He requires head covering for women because he sees them reflecting the glory of men, thus competing with God's glory in worship (11:5-10). Does Paul avoid threatening destruction because women are too weak and the threat of shame should be sufficient or because women in this community are too strong? Paul's words after silencing the women, "Whoever does not recognize this is not recognized" (14:38), do not explicitly call down death, but they function much like his earlier words handing over the man "for the destruction of the flesh" (5:5).

Arguments Based on the Structure of Reality

Argument from What Is Written

Quotations stating part of an argument

14:21 In the law it is written, "In strange tongues and with foreign lips I will speak to this people and so they will not hear me, says the Lord." Therefore tongues are a sign not to believers but to unbelievers.

5:13 You are supposed to judge the insiders, are you not? But God judges the outsiders. "Cast the evil one out from among you."

See also 1:30-31; 2:9; 15:54; and without formulary introductions 10:20; 14:25; 15:32, 33.

Quotations confirming an argument already stated

9:4, 8b-10a Do we not have the right to food and drink? . . . Or does the law not also say these things? For in the law of Moses it is written, "Do not muzzle the threshing ox." Is it the ox that God is concerned about? Does he not rather speak completely on our account?

10:7b, 11 Do not become idolaters like some of them were. As it is written, "The people sat down to eat and drink and rose up to play." . . . But these things happened to them typologically and were written down as a warning for us upon whom the end of the ages has come.

See also 1:19; 3:19, 20; 6:16; 10:26; and without formulary introductions 2:16; 15:25-27.

Allusions to particular written traditions

5:7b For our passover has been sacrificed, Christ.

10:5-6 But God was not pleased with most of them, for they were strewn out in the wilderness. But these things have become prototypes for us, in order that we not become people who crave evil as those people craved.

11:7-9 For a man ought not to cover his head, being the image and glory of God, but the woman is the glory of man. For man is not from woman, but woman from man. And man was not created on woman's account, but woman on man's account.

See also 10:21, 22; 11:25; 13:5; 15:45, 47; possibly 11:3, 10.

Appeals to the written tradition or the law in general

4:6 But I have applied these things to myself and Apollos on your account, brethren, so you might learn by our example the principle of not going beyond what is written and so no one of you become bloated in favor of one against the other.

14:34 Let the women be silent in the churches, for it is not fitting for them to speak, but let them be subordinate as the law itself says.

See also 7:19.

Quotations are less frequent in 1 Corinthians than in the letters where Paul works out the new believer's relation to Israel, but he nonetheless often appeals to written authority. Once he cites an unknown text (2:9) and once the poet Menander (15:33). But his basic authorities are the Jewish law and writings that he quotes on matters from the community's moral, financial, and worship practices to the most general truths and signs of the time. Paul not only applies these texts to Corinth but claims they were written down precisely to warn and encourage God's people in the present final days (9:10; 10:11).

The accent is on warning. Paul primarily uses the Scripture as a rein on the Corinthians, including the women. He thinks that they have abandoned the principle of not going beyond what is written when they become bloated in favor of one leader over another (4:6). Comparing them to the Israelites in the desert, they are tempted by the sheer weight of gifts to overestimate their strength and become lost in the wilderness. He warns: "It is written, 'I will wipe out the wisdom of the wise'" (1:19), and "Cast the evil one out from among you" (5:13). Even the positive words written about God's gifts tend to come down on the Corinthians in a restricting way: God has revealed "what eye has not seen," but they are too human to receive it (2:10; 3:1-4); "The world is the Lord's and its fullness," but do not eat the food on account of someone else's conscience (10:26-29a); "Our passover is sacrificed, Christ," but this means that their yeasty faith must be cleaned out of the church. If the Corinthians themselves quote what is written, it is more probable they do so to affirm what is taking place among them.

Twice Paul appeals to what is written to define roles in the community by telling what women should and should not do (11:3-10; 14:34). The women are to cover their heads when praying or prophesying. As in his warning from what happened to the Israelites in the desert (10:5-10), Paul emphasizes his point by drawing on several topically related stories (Gen. 1:27; 2:18, 22-23; possibly 3:16 and 6:2). The women have not covered themselves in worship and have made something of this that he opposes. The fact that he alludes to these texts without quoting them shows that he thinks they are known in Corinth and also suggests the possibility that the Corinthian women are using them to speak about God's image and glory in a different way, as a direct quotation of the key text might encourage:

"So God created the human being in his own image, in the image of God he created him, male and female he created them" (Gen. 1:27).

The second time Paul regulates women's conduct he says they are not to speak in the churches but should be subordinate "as even the law itself says" (14:34). Lacking a written text requiring women's silence as traditional in the synagogue, this short, categorical statement may be the best leverage he can get from the law. If there is an exegetical tradition justifying women's prophecy in Corinth, Paul does not want to take it on directly. What he does say shows that women's speech in the Corinthian church is of such significance that his final rule concerning prophecy should be devoted to excising it with the quick, wide brush of the law.

Argument from God's Calling

1:1-2, 9 Paul, called by God's will to be an apostle of Christ Jesus, to God's church which is in Corinth, to those sanctified in Christ Jesus, called to be saints together with all those in every place who call on the name of our Lord Jesus Christ, theirs as well as ours. . . . God is faithful, through whom you were called into the partnership of his son Jesus Christ.

1:22-24, 26-27a, 29 Whereas the Jews ask for signs and the Greeks seek for wisdom, we ourselves preach Christ crucified, to the Jews an offense, to the Gentiles foolishness, but to those who are called, both Jews and Greeks, Christ the power of God and the wisdom of God. . . . For look at your calling, brethren. There were not many wise by human standards, not many powerful, not many privileged. But God chose the world's foolish things to shame those who are wise . . . so that no human being might boast before God.

7:15-18ab, 20-21, 24 But if the non-believer leaves the believer, let him or her leave. The brother or sister is not bound in this case. But God has called you in peace. For what do you know, wife, but that you might save your husband? Or what do you know, husband, but that you might save your wife? Only let each person live as the Lord has portioned out to each one, as God has called each one. It is this that I command in all the churches. Was anyone called already circumcised? Let him not reverse it. . . . Let each remain in the calling in which that one was called. Were you called a slave? Do not let it bother you. . . . Brethren, let each one remain with God in the state that he or she was when called.

In the salutation and opening prayer of thanks Paul sets up the rhetorical situation in terms of God's call. He is called to be apostle to them and they are called to be saints, people set apart, consecrated, and holy. This much is typical of Paul's letters. But in this letter he goes on to stress the communal nature of this call. It extends to all those in every place who call on Christ's name—Christ is "theirs as well as ours" (1:2)—and it is a calling into the "partnership" of Christ (1:9). This could indicate that the Corinthians affirm their own distinctiveness among churches when they speak of God's call. Paul's accent on the wider partnership of Christ serves to remind them of the broad base of his own authority and set the stage for his discipline of them in terms of what other churches do.[5]

Paul's second point is that God's call reverses all peoples' desires and values but not their concrete social status. The Jews who want signs and the Greeks who want wisdom both find, when they are called, that the crucified Christ is God's power and wisdom. Paul says that not many of the Corinthians were wise, powerful, or privileged and concludes that God chose the foolish to shame the wise and silence their boasts before God. He does not say that the one-time foolish do this by becoming wise. Rather they shame the wise by sharing in God's own foolishness that is wiser than human beings.

This argument indicates two things about the Corinthians. They were largely uneducated and without economic power and social standing when they were called. Otherwise Paul's argument on this basis would not be credible. But at the same time it tells us that they did not stay in this state. Otherwise Paul's argument defending the foolishness of the gospel would be unnecessary. Everything they are they have become since their calling— rich, filled, and ruling; wise, powerful, and honored (4:8, 10; 1:5-7). They may see themselves called out of lowness, not into it. But Paul, who began his life in privilege, made a choice: "I chose to know nothing among you but Jesus Christ and him crucified. And I was among you in weakness and fear and trembling" (2:2). Here he argues from God's calling that those who had no choice belong in the low station they had when called.

Similarly in chapter 7, Paul charges the "brother or sister" married to a nonbeliever: "Only let each live as the Lord has portioned out to each one, as God has called each one" (7:15-17). This might be taken to mean a general commitment to God, not the need to stay in a social position, were it not for the social examples of circumcision and slavery that follow and reassert the general rule on remaining as called. In the middle of this discussion Paul can only mean that marriage, like circumcision and slavery, should not be a matter of Christian freedom but is given by one's situation when called. The contrary position of the Corinthians must reflect, among other factors, that most of them lacked Paul's social standing when called. The same rule would have much less impact on him as a circumcised, single, free male—even where he can choose not to use certain rights— than on the non-Jewish, married, slave woman.

Argument from Universal Church Practice

4:16-17 I beg you then, be imitators of me. For this very reason I sent Timothy to you who is my loved and faithful child in the Lord. He will remind you of my ways in Christ Jesus as I teach them everywhere in each church.

7:17 Only let each one live as the Lord has portioned out, each one as God has called. And so I have directed in all the churches.

11:16 If any think they want to make an issue of this, we ourselves have no such custom [as women praying and prophesying with uncovered heads] nor have the churches of God.

14:32-34, 36 Even the spirits of the prophets are subordinate to the prophets, for God is not the God of disruption but the God of peace, as in all the churches of the saints. Let the women be silent in the churches since it is not fitting for them to speak, but let them be subordinate as the law itself says. . . . Or did God's word originate from you? Has it reached as far as you only?

At least four times in 1 Corinthians, and only in this one of his letters, does Paul cite the conduct of the churches at large as normative for one church. After defending his preaching of the cross for four chapters against what he calls the worldly wisdom of some in Corinth, Paul warns them as a father and points to Timothy as a model. Through him they can imitate Paul's ways that he claims to teach "everywhere in each church" (4:17). Paul is appealing to the whole church in an effort to sanction his way of life, which he has described as the burlesque act and scum of the world in contrast to the Corinthians' own rich and regal posture (4:6-13). This first use of the argument from church practice indicates the distinctiveness of the Corinthian church and their confidence in their position.

The argument is used a second time to get the Corinthians to curtail their withdrawals from marriage partners. In a situation where some abstain within marriage and others have left each other or left nonbelievers (7:1-16), he says, "Let everyone live the life that the Lord has portioned out to them, in which God has called them. This is my arrangement in all the churches" (7:17). This rule is then grounded in church practice concerning circumcision and slavery, and each example allows him to repeat the rule again. Far from being a digression from Paul's theme, this section is carefully constructed to coin a rule that gives the sanction of "all the churches" to the married staying married in Corinth, a rule greatly impacting women in a society where marriage for women was almost universal and quite restrictive.

The final two uses of the argument from church practice are directly related to restrictions on women, suggesting the possibility that it is particularly the Corinthian women's conduct that stands out from other churches. Paul ends his string of arguments for women's head covering with words that anticipate opposition, "If any think they will make an issue of this, we have no such custom, nor do the churches of God" (11:16). For the third time the authority of what other churches do is identified with Paul's own ways, arrangements, or customs, indicating that what sound like claims about the church everywhere are more likely arguments based on other churches he has founded.

The fourth use of the argument from church practice appears just before Paul's silencing of the women: "Even the spirits of the prophets are subordinate to the prophets, for God is not a God of disruption but of peace, as in all the churches of the saints" (14:32-33). Whether it is the subordination of all the prophets' spirits or God's nature as a God of peace that Paul claims is found in all the churches, this argument from universal church practice claims confirmation from many cities that peace in God's church reigns everywhere else but in Corinth. It justifies the silencing of the women that follows abruptly, this without requiring Paul to claim that everywhere women are forbidden to speak, which he could hardly have made credible.

The contrast between Paul's and the Corinthians' relation to other churches is evident in his final questions directed to the women in Corinth, "Or did God's word originate from you? Has it reached as far as you only?" The masculine plural form of the final word, "only," shows that Paul cannot mean the women are claiming to be the font of wisdom against the men in Corinth. The context suggests an inclusive masculine in which the women addressed represent all those in Corinth who claim through prophecy to be an independent source and destination of God's word. In contrast, Paul sees the word being carried by people like himself from Palestine to and beyond Corinth, making the Corinthians essentially receivers who should accept and practice the faith in the way he has taught it elsewhere.

Argument from the Lord's Command

7:10-11 To the married I order, not I but the Lord, that a woman not separate from her husband—but if she should separate, let her remain unmarried or be reconciled to her husband—and that a man not divorce his wife.

9:13-15a Don't you know that those who perform the temple rites eat food from the temple, those who serve at the altar partake at the altar? So also the Lord ordered those who proclaim the gospel to get their living from the gospel. But I myself make use of none of these things.

14:27, 29, 34, 37-38 If any speak in tongues, let two or at most three speak, and one after another, and let one interpret. . . . And let two or three prophets speak and let others discern what they say. . . . Let the women be silent in the churches since it is not fitting for them to speak, but let them be subordinate as the law itself says. . . . If any think they are prophets or spiritual people, let them recognize that the things I write you are a command of the Lord. Whoever does not recognize this is not recognized.

Paul gives the final weight to an order by citing a command of the Lord three times in 1 Corinthians, and not elsewhere in his letters.[6] On his own authority he has begun to exclude divorce when he substitutes the Lord's command that wife not separate from husband nor husband leave wife. The argument that the church must feed its leaders has already been made by analogy, Scripture, and tradition when Paul secures it with the Lord's order that those who proclaim the gospel are to get their living from it. In both of these cases the command is very specific and synoptic parallels confirm that these were known as instructions handed down from Jesus.[7]

The third instance is Paul's final argument for church order after he has given specific grounds for silencing those who speak in tongues without interpreters, those who prophesy simultaneously, and women who speak in church. He concludes by challenging all who consider themselves prophets or spiritual people to recognize what he has said as the Lord's command. This challenge to the spiritual suggests that Paul is not referring to some unattested saying of Jesus but to a command he has received spiritually (cf. 2:6; 2 Cor.12:8-9; 13:3; Gal. 1:16). The authority Paul attributes to this command seems to be greater than the authority of the first two words of the Lord that are immediately followed by exceptions. Here the next words are, "Whoever does not recognize this is not recognized."

These arguments from the Lord's command apply to the whole church but particularly to the women. The command against divorce is applied to women first and an additional line is spoken about them alone: "But if she should be separated, let her stay unmarried or be reconciled with her husband." Whereas the synoptic prohibitions against remarriage define it as adultery (Mark 10:11-12; Matt. 5:32; Luke 16:18), Paul's conditional clause and positive advice show he wants to draw women back toward their husbands. But to do this the concession of staying single seems to be necessary, a kind of second line of defense where the tide of women leaving marriage cannot be held back by the Lord's word alone.

The command of the Lord to feed those who carry the gospel falls more on the women who do the feeding. Paul does not interpret the order as his obligation to depend on their hospitality (cf. 9:14; Luke 10:4-8; Matt. 10:9-11), but as their obligation to support him. This means that his refusal to take what is his due can be interpreted as an unpaid obligation on the Corinthians' part and a "ground for boasting" on his own part (9:15).

Immediately after silencing women in the church Paul appeals to the Lord's command to regulate the prophets. His inclusive masculine address shows he is speaking not only to women but to all who claim to be spiritual including those speaking in tongues without interpreters and those prophesying simultaneously or at length. But because his restrictions on speakers in tongues and on prophets require only some adjustments in their conduct, it is the women's categorical silencing that best explains the heavy sanctions of the Lord's command and the final "Whoever does not recognize this is not recognized." Intent on persuading them, Paul chooses their prophetic mode of challenging with the divine word. In this spiritual showdown he demands that they demonstrate their spiritual insight by recognizing the prophetic command of the Lord that they no longer speak in the community as prophets. They have only two options. They can capitulate in silence. Or they can take up Paul's rhetorical challenge to all who think themselves prophets or spiritual to test his spiritual judgment of what is and what is not the Lord's command.

Arguments Establishing the Structure of Reality

Argument from the Model of Paul and of Christ

4:15-17b Though you have many caretakers in Christ, you do not have many fathers, for it was I who gave you birth in Christ Jesus through the gospel. So I plead with you, become imitators of me. For this very reason I sent to you Timothy, my loved and faithful child in the Lord, who will remind you of my ways in Christ Jesus.

7:6-7 I say this [about the need for sexual partners] as a concession, not as a command. I would rather have all people be as I myself am. Yet each one has his or her own gift from God, some in this way and some in that.

8:9, 13 Watch lest your very authority become a stumbling-block to the weak. . . . For if food offends my brother, I will never again eat meat so my brother will not be caused to stumble.

9:23-24 I do all things for the gospel's sake in order to become a participant in it. Don't you know that all the runners in the stadium run, but only one takes the prize? So run that you seize it!

10:32 — 11:1 Be no offense either to Jews or to Greeks or to the church of God, just as I please everyone in all things, not seeking my own advantage but that of many, so they might be saved. Become imitators of me as I myself am of Christ.

13:9-11 For we know partially and we prophesy partially. But when the perfect comes, what is partial will be done away with. When I was a child, I thought like a child, I reasoned like a child. When I became a man, I did away with childish things.

14:18-20 I thank God that I speak in tongues more than all of you. But in the church I would rather speak five words with my mind than a thousand words in tongues. Brethren, do not be children in thought. Rather be children in evil but be mature in thought.

In 1 Corinthians Paul presents himself as a model for one purpose, to encourage the maturity of voluntary sacrifice. He either cannot or will not require them to give up the conduct in question, but he draws them in that direction by holding up his own voluntary sacrifice as a model. In the passages quoted he models for them hardship and shame, celibacy, not eating meat, not using apostolic rights and freedom, not seeking one's own advantage, not settling for the partial knowledge of prophecy, and not speaking to the church in tongues. His arguments suggest that those he addresses are wise, confident, sexually active, meat-eating, nondisciplined, and self-seeking prophets and speakers in tongues. This may be more caricature than solid fact, but Paul's argument can only work if they are gifted in speech and expressive in life style.

In various ways Paul appeals to the structure of reality in order to establish himself as an example for the Corinthians—he was their father in Christ, all must serve the community benefit, hard work wins the reward, and maturity is better than childishness. But as a model for them Paul goes beyond these arguments to establish himself as a new structure of reality from which generalizations can be drawn. Through him, he says, they can imitate Christ, the ultimate particular model (11:1). The effectiveness of this argument depends on the hearers and Paul sharing a common understanding of Christ by which he can support the voluntary giving-up that he is advocating. Paul is apparently thinking of Christ's death as a sacrifice— —"Christ our passover is sacrificed"; "You were bought at a high price"; "The brother for whom Christ died"; "This is my body for you" (5:7; 6:20; 8:11; 11:24). Elsewhere Paul applies this early Christian view more schematically as a model for believers, describing Christ's downward path from equality with God to the cross and God's corresponding act raising him to enthronement as Lord over all creation (Phil. 2:1-11).

There are signs that the Corinthians do not share Paul's interpretation of Jesus' death and rising and do not imitate the life he has modeled after it. His strong accent on the crucified Christ as God's chosen foolishness (1:17—2:8) seems to oppose some view in Corinth of Christ as God's exalted wisdom and glory. And Paul's final argument that reserves resurrection as a future hope for the dead, only then including survivors, may be countering a Corinthian affirmation of Christ as the present and expanding life of those who believe. If the Corinthians take Christ's death as their point of entry into identification with him and model their lives on his resurrection as their new and powerful upward path, they would not be persuaded by Paul's model of Christ's voluntary down way—unless Paul were able to generate in them a new experience of Christ according to this model.

Argument by Analogy to Christ's Subordination to God

3:21-23 So let no one boast in human beings. For all things are yours, whether Paul or Apollos or Cephas or world or life or death or present or future, all things are yours and you are Christ's and Christ is God's.

11:3 But I want you to know that of every man the head is Christ, and the head of woman is man, and the head of Christ is God.

15:23-28 But each in its own order: Christ, the first fruit, then those who are Christ's at his coming, then the end when he hands the kingdom over to God and father after he has destroyed every rule and authority and power, for he must rule until "he puts all enemies under his feet." The last enemy destroyed is death. For "he subordinated all things under his feet." But when it says that "all things" are subordinated, it is clear that it excludes the one who subordinates all things to him. Yet when all things are subordinated to him, then the son will subordinate even himself to the one who subordinated all things to him, in order that God may be all in all.

Paul speaks explicitly of a subordination of Christ to God only in 1 Corinthians.[8] Three times in this letter Paul takes up a pair of terms in human experience and subordinates one term to the other as lower to higher, the higher term to Christ, and Christ to God. In each context the point being debated is not the relation of Christ and God but the order of the original two terms. This indicates that Christ is being subordinated to God as an argument to confirm a distinctive ordering of two other terms, possibly a reversal of their order in the minds of the hearers. The analogy here does not appeal to a better-known human relation but to a divine relation, constructing human reality less by a suggestive parallel case than by an authoritative divine case.

In the first instance Paul responds to the Corinthians' "I'm Paul's!" "I'm Apollos'!" "I'm Cephas'!" with his own argument and conclusion, "All these are yours, whether Paul or Apollos or Cephas . . . , but you are Christ's and Christ is God's" (1:12; 3:21-23). He reverses their possessive language by saying that they possess their leaders. He also substitutes Christ as their possessor and confirms this subordination to Christ by Christ's subordination to God. Apparently the Corinthians do not understand their relation to Christ through baptism as one of being owned — at least not in a way that conflicts with their allegiance to persons who baptized them. Corinthian prophets may see their baptizers as mediators of the Christ who now speaks prophecies through them.

Near the end of 1 Corinthians Paul again speaks of Christ's subordination to God in a complex argument against certain Corinthians. He argues that, in spite of Christ's resurrection, they remain subject to death until death is at last made subject to Christ at his triumph, and then ultimately

Christ will be made subject to God. Paul's final doxological statement of God's single sovereignty becomes a sanction for this chain of subordinations. This suggests that the Corinthians, whom Paul wants to persuade, do not accept Paul's ordering of the first two terms by which their lives are still seen to be under the power of death. In contrast, they see death having already given way to the life that became theirs through Christ, a dynamic probably expressed differently than in any sequence of subordinations.

Midway in Paul's letter a third argument from Christ's subordination to God is presented as a triple definition of "head": Christ is man's head, man is woman's head, and God is Christ's head. By placing woman's subordination to man between the two theological subordinations, Paul tries to defend it from the opposition he anticipates (11:16). If the pattern seen in the two earlier arguments holds in this instance, and Paul is reversing the Corinthians' order of two terms, his subordination of woman to man counters some Corinthian experience of male dependence on women. The cultic context of this argument suggests the possibility of some special role of women in worship, perhaps in the mediation of God in prayer and prophecy, the two roles Paul named as requiring head covering (11:5a). If women's authority is based on their prophetic role, any subordination of others to them would have been functional rather than prescribed by law or legitimated by subordination of Christ to God.

Paul's appeal to divine subordination in each instance shows that the people he wants to persuade already consider Christ as their key link to God. The fact that they do not understand Christ as a middle term between levels of subordination to God raises the question of how Christ is understood. The first argument suggests the model of mediating Christ rather than being owned by Christ, the second, dynamic life rather than assured waiting, the third, women's spoken expression of Christ rather than their subordination. The common element is Christ as God's transforming presence being extended in and through them. Paul expects them to oppose exchanging this active role for one defined by subordination and exchanging this Christ who is the mediating spirit of God for a Christ who is the cosmic model of submission.

3 | Women Rich in God's Wisdom: 1 Corinthians 1–4

LIKE PEOPLE IN A SOCIETY, arguments in a text do not exist in isolation. They work together in complex networks of argumentation and one layer builds on another. In the following chapters each unit of the letter is made the focus of attention in order to see Paul's structural rhetoric and understand the people it is shaped to persuade.

From Paul's first word—his name—followed by his greetings and prayers for the Corinthians, to the last lines of the fourth chapter where he calls himself their only father in Christ, Paul is presenting himself to them. There are considerable differences between these two self-presentations. The opening presentation is cordial and modest as Paul praises God for gifts given to them and claims little for himself. The closing presentation is stern. Paul demands that they imitate him and prepares to launch attacks on their immorality and idolatry. Between the two Paul must think he has established the authority he needs to bring off the changes he is about to demand in Corinth. Because the primary intent of this passage is not descriptive, we cannot begin by asking if Paul meant to include women prophets in this or that description of the Corinthians. Only when we weigh each argument as it functions in Paul's self-presentation can we gain, as a by-product, some picture of the church he is addressing and of its women prophets.

The opening four chapters of this letter pose two problems. In the first place it is not clear why Paul takes so long to clarify his relationship with them. Almost a fourth of the letter goes into this introduction, considerably more than one would expect where two correspondents have the good relationship that Paul's cordial opening implies. Is this a sign that the fissures in the church are deeper than he makes explicit, or that his own base has eroded more than he says? His extended discussions of the church's relation to its leaders should answer this. Second, it is not clear why he bursts into an attack on worldly wisdom and then defends his own different wisdom in the middle of this discussion of Corinth's leaders. Any such extended digression in an argument, even if unplanned, has major rhetorical functions. The kind of data it provides about the Corinthians is both restricted and enlarged from what a quick reading suggests, restricted in that he is not doing a descriptive comparison of their views and his own, but enlarged in that the indirect way he tries to persuade them — as well as what he says — is geared precisely to them.

Paul's sex-specific statements in these chapters are few, but there are multiple implications for the women prophets in the way he addresses the leadership struggle and in his digression on wisdom.

Paul as One Among Their Leaders

Paul the Witness to God's Gifts and the Corinthians' Speech and Knowledge: 1:1-9

Before mentioning the divisions in the Corinthian church Paul takes a certain stance toward them in his greeting and prayer. He stresses their calling into a partnership of Christ that is not limited to Corinth (1:2, 9), perhaps wanting to edge them toward more awareness of the wider church and of God's ultimate judgment by which to gauge themselves. But above all he affirms God's grace that has made them "rich in Christ in all speech and knowledge" so that they are "lacking in no spiritual gift" but "anticipating the revelation of our Lord Jesus Christ" (1:5-7). Paul presents himself as a praising witness to God's work in them and in response he expects them to open up to him.

There is no reason to doubt his sweeping characterization of this community's verbal, mental, and spiritual wealth — any exaggeration on his part would threaten to turn his praise of God into irony. It must have been an extraordinary community. To contrast this picture with the pictures Paul paints when thanking God for other churches, these Corinthians are outstanding not in faith (Rom. 1:8), nor in mutual comfort through suffering (2 Cor. 1:3-7), nor in love and endurance (1 Thess. 1:2-3), nor in partnership in the work of the gospel (Phil. 1:3-6), but in speech and knowledge, spiritual gifts and revelation (1 Cor. 1:4-7). Whether they expressed their powers in terms of God's gift and Christ's indwelling as Paul does here is not known, but because he is seeking their positive response, the way Paul praises God for what has happened in Christ cannot be foreign to them.

There is no sign that any part of the church is being excluded from Paul's description, least of all its prophets. It is safe to say that the women prophets are rich in speech and knowledge, lack no spiritual gift, and are strong enough, not only to inspire Paul's praise to God, but to make Paul articulate their praiseworthiness before he goes on to qualify it. Yet the length of Paul's argument is not taken up in this praise but in its extended qualification that begins immediately, "But I warn you, brethren" (1:10), and does not end until the last words of the fourth chapter, "What do you want? Should I come to you with a rod, or in love with the spirit of gentleness?" (4:21)

Paul the Champion of Unity and
the Corinthians' Contention about Leaders:
1:10-13; 3:21-23

Paul first takes conflict as his theme, quoting from Chloe's people the Corinthians' first-person singular claims, "I am Paul's!" "I am Apollos'!" "I am Cephas'!" Initially he charges them with tearing up Christ and finding their salvation and baptism in others. Later he calls them not spiritual at all but fleshly, like animals, because they are jealous and fighting (3:1-3). This picture from the jungle may be caricature. Yet when a group is young, fast-growing, and "lacks no spiritual gift," it attracts and generates many leaders and can tolerate considerable diversity. Paul's quick quotations from their conflict show that they remain within shouting distance and are building up their positive claims in interaction with each other.

The originators of this shouting cannot be Paul's group who would have been the whole church from the time Paul founded it until notified to the contrary by the shouts of others. Yet Paul quotes his group first, and he begins to berate them immediately, "Was Paul crucified for you? Were you baptized into Paul's name?" Like the mother who breaks up a children's fight by admonishing her own child, Paul's criticism must begin at home if it is eventually to be heard elsewhere. This caution shows that Paul's base for direct action is quite narrow and many Corinthians cannot be presumed to support him. In fact, none of the Corinthians quote their leaders but use the leaders' names in their own assertive, first-person claims.

Paul refers to "those belonging to Chloe," a group identified by a woman's name, as the oral source of his information. She must be known to the church as one who has her own emissaries to Paul, perhaps a widow with slaves on out-of-town business, or a woman whose husband or father is not a believer or does not join her in sending Paul some men or women from her house-church. More important, we learn that this woman takes the lead in spreading what might be called an alarmist view of the divisions in Corinth, a view at cross-purposes with the bold confidence of those whose written claims Paul responds to later in the letter.[1] Most significant is the fact that Paul chooses, against his usual practice (5:1; 11:18; 15:12, 35), to cite his source. Her name must add in some way to the credibility of his description, not to the credibility of the facts they already know, but to the credibility of his attitude. Her name says that someone of significance shares his response to their divisions. She may model the kind of alarm about divisions in Corinth that Paul thinks could prepare others— perhaps especially women—to seek a solution from him.

Paul calls the Corinthians "brothers" (1:10-11) when rebuking his own faction and again when citing Chloe's people. Four other times in the letter's first four chapters he uses this address, in each case returning to this fraternity as the relationship within which he wants to address another aspect of the Corinthian situation (1:26; 2:1; 3:1; 4:6). It is unlikely that Paul intends to exclude Chloe from this address (1:11) any more than he does Euodia and Syntyche when he calls the Philippians "brothers" (Phil. 4:1-2) or than he does the women among "all God's beloved in Rome" (Rom. 1:7, 13). The Greek word for sister is the same root with feminine endings. For these reasons I will translate "brethren." Yet this broad, familial address, adapted from a similar usage among Jews (Rom. 9:3; Acts 7:23; 13:26; 22:5), carries over from its masculine plural form a tendency to see all members of the community in light of its men. For example, when the Thessalonians are called as brethren not to live immorally but each to take a wife for himself and not to transgress against his brother in this matter (1 Thess. 4:1-6), the women have faded out of Paul's address. In Corinth both men and women who hear Paul's letter might be computing the relative cost of Paul's much-pledged fraternity to themselves, the women with added awareness that the unity of brethren is not always to their advantage.

The nature of the supposed anarchy in Corinth is first described in their claims to belong to separate leaders. The series ends with the cry, "I am Christ's!" exposing the absurdity of this shouting match. The questions that follow, "Is Christ divided? Was Paul crucified for you?" continue the retort, suggesting that it is not one group in Corinth nor the reporters sent by Chloe who say "I am Christ's!" but Paul himself. By the end of the third chapter Paul's position is clear. Against their partisanship he claims ownership for Christ alone, who is owned by God: "All are yours, whether Paul or Apollos or Cephas or the world or life or death or the present or the future—all are yours, but you are Christ's and Christ is God's." Cephas reappears only here in these chapters and may be functioning as the standard apostle in Paul's argument, as he does later in the letter (9:5; 15:5), rather than being a significant figure in the Corinthian debate. The names of Paul and Apollos always appear first; elsewhere in this argument they appear alone (3:4, 5, 6; 4:6).

If the real struggle in Corinth is polarized around the names of Paul and Apollos, with Cephas introduced to defuse the conflict and Christ to stop it, Paul has reason to use a singular form when he speaks of "another" who is building on the foundation he has laid, and when he warns about someone threatening to defile God's temple, which they are (3:10, 17). Paul's complaint at the end of the section, that they do not expect him to return to Corinth, can be compared with their having apparently written for Apollos to come (4:18; 16:12). Even the wisdom argument built into this section shows Paul fighting on only one front. And experience teaches that generalized tensions turn into social conflicts precisely by polarization.

The best evidence that there is a single struggle between the followers of Paul and the followers of Apollos in Corinth is Paul's response to the challenge. Before he can insist on "my ways in Christ Jesus as I teach them everywhere in each church" (4:17), he first spreads the blame among multiple factions and dissociates himself from his own faction's claims, downplaying any competition between himself and Apollos. This suggests that the Apollos group is too strong for Paul to attack directly, to marginalize, or to neutralize. Apparently a major new experience of faith has swept over the church, expanding its confidence and size, and Paul is unable to regain authority by building solely on the remnant faithful to him.

Paul's positive strategy is to present himself as the champion of unity. He ridicules their claim to be Paul's or Apollos' by making the single statement that they all belong to Christ who belongs to God. In this way he lifts himself above the conflict and associates himself with the higher authority of Christ and God, and finally claims their obedience as their father in Christ. This shows that the intended readers share a common commitment to Christ to which Paul can appeal. Yet they do not understand Christ in a way that excludes allegiance to separate leaders because of an exclusive possession by Christ who is possessed by God. Positive indications of their experience of Christ and of God are not found in this section. But Paul's rhetoric of unmediated subordination to a single divine hierarchy suggests that they, in contrast to him, may experience Christ as God's power or wisdom fully mediated and present in human beings.

Paul the Servant Worker and the Corinthian Rejection of Instrumental Leadership: 3:5-17

Paul presents himself and Apollos as workers: "What then is Apollos? And what is Paul? Servants through whom you came to believe as the Lord gave [tasks] to each. I planted, Apollos watered, but God caused the growth" (3:5-6). The point of this farming analogy and of the following one from building is to undermine any tendency of the Corinthians to choose between leaders, since all workers have distinct roles that are strictly functional and complementary. Paul neither criticizes Apollos directly nor singles out his followers but attacks all who take sides, himself remaining above the conflict, or rather—claiming the advantage of modesty—below it as a worker.

Yet he manages to turn the second analogy from building to his advantage. Although the planter may be no more essential than the irrigator in a Mediterranean climate, a "wise master builder" who lays the single valid foundation—Jesus Christ—is more basic than another worker who builds on this foundation. Paul notes that if inferior building materials are used, fire will destroy what is built and that worker will survive only "as through fire." Anyone who corrupts God's temple, which they are, will personally go down to corruption by God's retribution. Apparently the Corinthians whom Paul wants to persuade do not see their leaders as hired workers doing specific tasks for God. Opposite to this instrumental view is one that takes the leader as integral to what is being done. A strong group of Corinthians may take Apollos and themselves as mediators of the presence of Christ in the community. Then the issue would not be whether the leader carries out an assignment and receives a reward but whether that person's words realize God's presence, in which case a reward is redundant.

Paul the Dishonored Apostle and the Corinthians Filled, Rich, and Ruling: 3:21—4:13

At first Paul focuses judiciously on Apollos and himself as independent stewards of God's mysteries, teaching the Corinthians the principle of not exceeding what is written, of not being bloated against one another when all that they have is from God. The bottom line in this is God's gift, God's written word, God's judgment, God's possession of them, in each case presented as the limit to human claims. But the tone changes when Paul moves from teaching the Corinthians their limits into mocking their strength. His parody of them as filled, rich, and ruling becomes the foil for a contrasting pathetic presentation of himself as dying and despised, hungry, homeless, and beaten, "the garbage peelings of the world" (4:8-13).

Where is Apollos in this? When Paul says to the Corinthians, "without us you have begun to rule," and Apollos was not with him but with them during that time, he hints at Apollos' complicity in their triumph. And when Paul says, "God has shown us apostles up as last of all," he leaves the reader to try on Apollos this harsh apostolic garment and find that it does not fit. In this way Paul has discredited Apollos without the attack that could mobilize his supporters. Instead he shames the Corinthians for faring so well while he suffers, like children who feast while their parents starve, and he exploits this in his final paragraph. But here Paul takes reality as they see it — their own fulfillment and his bungling — and reverses the valuation, ridiculing their achievements and exalting his hard life as proof of his apostleship from God, in order to leave them without the groundwork to champion Apollos against him.

Paul's self-presentation gives us additional clues about the Corinthians. When Paul initially confirms their possession of everything, and when he claims his own freedom from all human judgment, he may be reaching to meet their demand for total freedom from human restrictions in a newly structured world — only to subordinate both to God. In contrast, they do not see that their new life has opened up in order to be subordinated to a total divine possession or judgment. The articular phrase, in which he challenges them to learn "the not-exceeding-what-is-written" (4:6), indicates a principle on which he and they disagree. It is not that they disobey some statute but that they lack the basic acceptance of limitation or subordination. He disparages them as "bloated" and "boasting," and claims they do not remember that all they have comes from God (4:6-7).

Paul could be misinterpreting their insubordination to him as a lack of subordination to God. On the other hand, they may not conceive their relation to God in terms of subordination to an owner, dependence on gifts, or responsibility before a judge in line with a written code. Instead they may know God in Christ as they are lifted up to rejoice/exult/boast. Paul's mocking words reflect what was apparently their positive claim: Already we are filled! Already we are rich! Already we have begun to rule! These words, though not without spiritual implications, mean having plenty to eat, having possessions, and having authority with other people—as they do in the kingdom tradition proclaimed in the synoptic beatitudes and woes.[2] Whereas Paul's life in Christ has taken him from a full plate, warm home, and prestigious work into hunger, homelessness, and working with his hands, their life in Christ has taken them from obscurity, restriction, and want into what they experience as authority, fullness, and wealth (see Excursus on Social Status at the end of this chapter).

It is understandable that Paul's theology reflects his experience and that he should interpret God in terms of a demand to jeopardize all human security for Christ's sake. It is also possible that Corinthian theology reflects their experience of a completely full life in Christ evolving from nothing. Paul finds freedom from judgment of his unlikely ministry only in God's single and ultimate judgment; he tries to argue the same for them—everything belongs to them only because they belong to Christ. But judgment may not be the issue for them. If their one-time oppression was not to the world's values but to its structures, then the different nature of their new freedom in Christ is not to accept restrictions and shame because God assigns, adjudicates, and vindicates, but to accept honor and life because God is present among them.

When Paul moves from berating their claims to rule and begins to contrast their life in Christ with his own, it is possible that he is accepting the difference between them: "We are fools on Christ's account but you are wise in Christ, we are weak but you strong, you are honored but we shamed" (4:10; cf. 1:26; 2:1-5; 2 Cor. 13:3-4). But as he intensifies the pathetic picture of himself, his irony becomes unmistakable. Paul is unwilling to let their sudden wisdom and power stand as a shock to the world and a preview of what is to come. He insists that their wisdom is dependent on the dishonored apostolate and on their learning his ways. In contrast, they take their new life as a full, independent, and self-confirming presence of the divine Spirit in them.

Paul Their Only Father and the Corinthians Come of Age: 4:14-21

By the end of four chapters Paul has made his way from pleading with them to agree as brethren, to warning them as their only father in Christ to return to his ways before he arrives with a rod. Paul gets the final leverage for making this demand by denying himself the rhetorical fruit of his tale of apostolic dishonor—the chance to shame them for not supporting him. He turns this self-denial to his advantage; it proves his great love for his children; it even proves that he alone is their father and all the other leaders are simply slave attendants or hired tutors. The historical grounds for this paternity, that he has given them birth in Christ through the gospel, appears after Paul has made the claim, probably because it is convincing only for the community as a whole. Individually many or even most of its participants will be new converts who first heard of Paul from others and do not expect him to come back. Paul uses the image of apprenticeship when calling them to imitate him, their father, or in his absence to learn his ways from his faithful child Timothy before he comes to test what power stands behind their speech.

The implications concerning the Corinthians are mixed. Paul would not speak so confidently if he did not think that by this point in his argument his readers were ready to accept his authority and take on his ways. This must be given considerable weight. But Paul also recognizes that his role as threatening father is a direct affront to their independence and as such is a major rhetorical risk. If it does not make them capitulate, it will have the opposite effect. Paul sets it up that way; he will come either with the rod or in love with a meek spirit, depending on their reaction.

Although Paul intends that his threat will work, the text points in the other direction. The father image fully subordinates the widely favored Apollos to Paul as a tutoring slave to a masterful father. The apprentice image with its rote learning of a given family trade could not be farther from their experience of being divinely filled. The appeal to the churches at large as a standard for Corinth discredits their unique gifts. And finally Paul's direct reference to those who are "bloated" and think he will never come shows they are ready to rule in God's kingdom without him.

Does Paul gear his fatherly persuasion in any way that suggests its reception by the Corinthian women? He calls the Corinthians "children," not "sons." At most this is a general recognition of females in the church at large, not a conscious inclusiveness in Corinth, since Paul never speaks of those dependent on him as "sons" (1 Thess. 2:7, 11; Gal. 4:19; 2 Cor. 6:13; Phil. 10). But this passage does include several distinctly male images. It is sons who are assigned slaves as tutors to take them to school and back and see they do their lessons.[3] This not only disparages any leaders who followed Paul in Corinth, but it pictures the Corinthians as male and young. And Timothy, their positive image of how to be Paul's "beloved and faithful" child, who is not called "tutor" as might have been appropriate, is also male when he arrives in the flesh. Paul's advice to all the Corinthians is thus more difficult for some to learn from than for others.

Perhaps these two images could be laid to the restricted nature of Paul's male social experience and the availability of subordinates he could control, but the third and dominant male image, his own fatherhood, is carefully chosen. Elsewhere Paul can describe himself as a mother who is in labor giving birth to the Galatians and as a wet nurse who comforts her Thessalonian children (Gal. 4:19; 1 Thess. 2:7). Here he is a father because his focus is on control; control by showing he could shame them for shaming him, control unlike that of their tutors, control through his favorite child, and finally the control of one who threatens punishment with the rod. The women prophets' gender gives them no immunity from Paul's authority claim now that his guise of neutrality and impartiality is put off, but neither does it make their compliance more likely.

Paul Not Speaking Wisdom in Corinth: The Wisdom Digression, 1:18—2:16, and Its Framework 1:14-17; 3:1-4, 18-19

The Wisdom Digression as Self-Defense and the Women Among Those Charging Paul

I have put off until now discussing Paul's argument on wisdom because it deviates from the major theme of these chapters, the Corinthian divisions. Rhetorically it is a digression. A digression, by a change in theme or tone, relieves pressure on the audience about the matter at stake in such a way that serves the main argument indirectly and returns to it from a stronger position. The challenge is to determine how this digression helps Paul reassert his presence and authority in the Corinthian struggle and what, if anything, this can tell us concerning the women prophets.

When dealing with the conflict in Corinth, Paul has preferred the persona of the peacemaker and denied himself any direct self-defense, perhaps in order not to stir up the flames of the debate. But in the digression on God's wisdom Paul defends himself and shows that he has been charged with not speaking wisdom in Corinth. He concedes this charge by dissociating himself from all worldly wisdom through negation, antithesis, irony, and paradox. At the same time he contradicts their charge by demonstrating that he can speak God's wisdom, appealing here to assumed structures of reality, first by definition, proofs, maxims, and experience, and second by divine revelation. Finally he makes a countercharge by moving beyond both dissociation and association to build a new model of wisdom or structure of reality, drawn inductively from his account of the acts of God.

These three kinds of argument provide clues for reconstructing the kind of wisdom the Corinthians demand of Paul and consider authoritative among themselves. This should have implications for Corinth's women prophets since Paul is addressing the whole community. Yet, because Paul is defending himself against a charge that he has not spoken wisdom in Corinth, his attention may be focused on those making the charge, very likely those who identify themselves with Apollos rather than Paul. It is necessary to consider the women prophets' relation to this group demanding wisdom from Paul.

There are definite links between Paul's digression on wisdom (1:18 – 2:16) and his later argument on spiritual gifts (12:1 – 14:40). These suggest that the women and men who have prophetic gifts are the same ones who demand wisdom from their leaders. In both contexts Paul is speaking about "spiritual things" or "things granted" that are known through the spirit (2:12, 13) or fueled by the one spirit (12:1-11). Although when he accents the diversity of gifts he can call one gift prophecy, another wisdom, and another knowledge (12:8-10), when he is contrasting all gifts with the love that lasts, he speaks of tongues, prophecy, and knowledge all passing away (13:1, 2, 8), just as he speaks in the letter opening of their word and knowledge as one phenomenon (1:4-7). Similarly, in the wisdom digression he virtually identifies wisdom, the things prepared for those who love God, the depths of God, the things of God's spirit, and the mind of Christ (2:6-16). Paul rejects any consistent nomenclature or demarcation of gifts that support a sharp distinction between some who seek wisdom and others who prophesy.

And his basic argument in both contexts is consistent. Though his language changes, he confirms again and again the gifts given them and then puts their Corinthian manifestation in question. He charges them with immaturity three times. In his digression on wisdom Paul reserves esoteric wisdom for the "perfect" or "mature," whereas the Corinthians with all their fighting receive only milk, not meat (2:6; 3:1-3). In his praise of love he tells them that when what is "perfect" or "mature" arrives, then prophecy, tongues, and knowledge will pass away (13:8-11). And he critiques public speaking in tongues, "Brethren, don't be children in your thinking . . . but be mature!" (14:18-20)

These important ties between Paul's opening argument on wisdom and his later argument on tongues, knowledge, and prophecy are best explained if Paul is fighting on one front throughout. Topics change as he responds to their reports or their letter; forms of speech change as he completes his self-presentation and speaks more directly, but the letter does not indicate a change of address midstream. Paul continues to attack the same verbal fluency and bold action. Therefore it is probable that the women and men known for prophecy, tongues, and knowledge in chapters 11 through 14 are not different people from those who demand a leader speaking wisdom in the opening chapters.

If the women prophets among other Corinthians have demanded that Paul provide a defense of his gospel because he has not spoken wisdom in

Corinth, Paul's argument in the wisdom digression should help to reconstruct these women's behavior and thought. First I consider his arguments from the structure of reality—a definition with supporting evidence and an esoteric wisdom claim, each appealing to values of his hearers and of the women prophets among them. Then I consider how Paul moves by negation, antithesis, and paradox into a full dissociation from his hearers. Finally I show how Paul works to establish a new model of reality that the Corinthian women prophets would not share.

Paul's Appeal to the Structure of Reality Using Definition (1:17–2:5) and Esoteric Claim (2:6-16) and the Corinthian Women Prophets' Corresponding Wisdom

Paul's wisdom digression begins with his definition of the word of the cross: to the lost it is foolishness, but to those being saved it is God's power. The antithesis in this will be taken up later for its dissociative function, but definition appeals first to the structure of reality for its credibility, or, more precisely, to the logic that says a thing is identical to itself. The thing being defined is neither a single object—a wooden cross—nor the past event of Jesus' crucifixion, but the recurring event of the word of the cross. This speech-event is identified by its content, the cross, and defined by its two kinds of hearers, the lost and those being saved. The rejection of some hearers is then supported from Scripture, appealed to as the written structure of reality (1:19), and shown to be fulfilled in four rhetorical questions and a summary explanation (1:20-21). Paul rephrases the positive side of the definition—the Christ crucified he preaches is "Christ God's power and God's wisdom" (1:22-24)—and draws everything together in a maxim, the proverbial statement of a fundamental principle—"God's foolishness is wiser than human beings" (1:25). Finally the definition is demonstrated empirically, first from the Corinthians' experience as hearers of the speech-event (2:26-31) and second from Paul's experience as its speaker (2:1-5), with each justified in terms of the divine purpose accomplished. In all Paul sustains his definition of the word of the cross and fills it with the rich content and heavy authority of Scripture, fulfilled history, universal axiom, and personal experience.

Paul's appeal to these structures of reality when addressing the Corinthians provides the basic foundation on which to begin building an understanding of wisdom as acclaimed by the women prophets in Corinth. Apparently Paul is constrained by his audience to step back, define the issue, cite authorities, and give evidence. Paul's argument here suggests that the Corinthians speak not only in invocation and confession but discursively, reflecting on words and meanings, proposing to each other distinctions that clarify usage and can be supported by mutual experience. Maxims, definitions, and short quotations may become slogans to summarize their stand and opportunities to demonstrate common commitment. An important incentive for such thinking and speaking would be the polemical situation in Corinth where new converts with a different experience of Christ would have to defend it, whether as Scripture fulfillment, as general truth, or as an account of what has happened to themselves in Christ.

At least Apollos must have been known for such articulation of the faith, since it is in the wake of his visit and in his name that the Corinthians have questioned Paul's wisdom. The description of Apollos in Acts 18:24-25 shows that his reputation as a man eloquent in scriptural interpretation survived until Luke's time. Luke also notes that it is Priscilla and Aquila in Ephesus who take Apollos aside to explain to him God's way more accurately before he first comes to Corinth (Acts 18:26-28). According to Luke, Priscilla had been a woman in the Corinthian church for some time before this, a relation Paul confirms by transmitting her greetings to the church at the end of 1 Corinthians (Acts 18:1-3, 18; 1 Cor. 16:19). Luke's witness to her teaching Apollos has no dramatic or theological function in Acts that would suggest his own invention,[4] so it is best taken as an earlier story—one of the few points where another document may contribute to the study of Christian women in Corinth at the time of Paul's writing of 1 Corinthians.

The evidence from Acts suggests that Apollos was indebted to one woman and man who knew Corinth well for his understanding of the meaning of baptism into Christ. Before this instruction Luke speaks of Apollos as "knowing only the baptism of John" (Acts 18:25), by which Luke means a baptism that lacks the transforming power of the spirit (Acts 19:1-7; cf. 8:14-17). As Paul's coworkers, Priscilla and Aquila probably shared the early baptismal tradition, "You who were baptized into Christ have put on Christ . . . there is no male and female," with its programmatic rejection of sexual and other social discrimination.[5] When Paul dissociates himself from baptizing (1 Cor. 1:13-17), he may be reacting to some understanding of this new identity by Priscilla and Aquila or by Apollos. If this was the history, Apollos was not the single shining light of a new Corinthian movement. It may have antedated him in Corinth, outlasted him there, and may even have flown his banner because he had been able to learn its ways and foster its power.

Priscilla's teaching role, though attested several decades later than Paul's letters, is a significant parallel to Chloe's role of informant to Paul, and Phoebe's role of deacon and defender of the church in Corinth's eastern port of Cenchreae (Rom. 16:1-2)—individual pictures of the variety of leadership functions carried out by believing women in and near Corinth. Whether these three women prophesied is unknown and depends on many factors yet to be weighed, including to what extent different gifts were seen to be mutually exclusive. But the women of Corinth's church, including their prophets, cannot be identified as a hysterical fringe. They

expect wisdom from those who speak among them; in at least one case they
are said to tutor an outsider in this wisdom; and some of them form a faction
independent from Paul in Apollos' name. Paul shapes his argument to
appeal to the wise even when he knows that Apollos is not in Corinth
(16:12).

Paul's definition of the word of the cross as God's foolish wisdom
culminates in identifying Christ as God's wisdom, his ultimate appeal to the
structure of reality (1:24, 30). One interpreter explains that the Corinthians see Christ as one among many guides to God's wisdom, with some
saying, "I am Christ's," while others claim Paul or Apollos or Cephas as
their guides,[6] and Paul responds that Christ alone is God's wisdom (1:12-13;
3:21-23). This reading, which assumes that Paul is dealing with a random
factionalism of many groups in Corinth, cannot account for the fact that
only Paul and Apollos are mentioned elsewhere in the argument (3:4, 5, 6;
4:6), nor for Paul's ability to shock them with the reply, "Is Christ divided?"
(1:13) But if Paul is meeting a struggle between his own followers and
those of Apollos by a mocking "I am Christ's!" and a rebuking "Is Christ
divided?" he is appealing to a shared faith in Christ. What, then, has he
accomplished when he concludes that Christ is "the wisdom of God"?

Paul's new contribution may be in the way he has argued to dissociate
the crucified Christ from all worldly wisdom (see next section). But this
would be meaningless unless he had simultaneously confirmed by appeal
to commonly assumed structures of reality that Christ is indeed God's
wisdom. His distinctive achievement is this identification of the "Christ
crucified we proclaim" as "Christ God's power and God's wisdom" (1:23-24).
The repetition of the word "Christ" here, not required for clarity in the
Greek sentence, along with the reversal of Paul's usual word order so that
the genitive precedes the noun it modifies—literally, "Christ, of God the
power and of God the wisdom"—suggests that Paul may be co-opting a
Corinthian phrase to make this affirmation. Whether their coinage or his,
this affirmation becomes Paul's claim that the crucified Christ is Christ the
divine wisdom whom the Corinthians know and will not want to deny.

Paul moves from speaking of Christ to identifying the Corinthians in
the same way, dissociated from all possible wisdom and power, and yet, "By
God's act it is you who are in Christ Jesus, who has become wisdom for us
from God" (1:26-31). Finally Paul's own proclaiming of Christ in Corinth,
after being radically dissociated from all wisdom, is identified as God's
power (2:1-5). If this third case seems to stop short of the claim that his own
speech is God's wisdom, it may be because at this point Paul is answering
the charge that he has not spoken wisdom in Corinth by conceding that,
for good reason, he has not. In any case Paul's practice of ending each argument with a positive appeal to the structure of divine reality does not prove
that these final statements are his point of disagreement with the Corinthians or that the Corinthians deny God's wisdom in Christ. If they denied

it, Paul would have been forced to develop arguments to prove Christ was God's wisdom, whereas in the letter there is no persuasion to that effect. Instead he gives them their own affirmation of Christ as God's wisdom, but by a coup of rhetorical dissociation it now confirms the peculiar crucified Christ whom he preaches.

The Corinthians' understanding of Christ as God's wisdom appears only in the brief affirmations of these capstone statements of Paul. The accompanying language Paul uses to identify Christ as God's power and as their righteousness, holiness, and freedom could be Paul's own argument rather than their description of how they experience Christ as God's wisdom. But the noun "wisdom" and the adjective "wise"—which appear in these four chapters twenty-six times and only seven times in all of Paul's other letters—are very likely his effort to use Corinthian terminology. This is further supported by his challenge, "if any think themselves wise . . ." and by his peculiar choice of the word "wisdom" to put their confidence in question, calling it "human wisdom," "verbal wisdom," and "wisdom of this world" (3:18; 1:17; 2:4-6, 13). Apparently the Corinthians understand that God in Christ has become present to them as wisdom. This wisdom may be demonstrated through the kind of speech Paul engages in to get their attention. There is no sign that Christ is identified as God but, by Paul's witness, Christ "has become wisdom to you from God"—representing, realizing, or mediating God among them and through them, especially as they hear and speak.

There is a certain analogy here to the understanding of God's wisdom that appears in two sayings attributed to Jesus in Matthew and Luke's common sayings source (Q): "The wisdom of God said, 'I will send them prophets and messengers, some of whom they will kill and persecute, so that the blood of all the prophets from the world's foundation might be reclaimed from this generation'" (Luke 11:49-50); "John the baptizer came not eating bread nor drinking wine and you say, 'He is possessed!' The Human One came eating and drinking and you say, 'Look, a glutton and a drunkard, a friend of tax-collectors and sinners!' Yet wisdom is vindicated by all her children" (Luke 7:33-35). The analogy is that God's wisdom appears in prophets and messengers, in "her children," and this mediation is vindicated in spite of or even through their rejection.

This depiction of God's wisdom speaking through representatives is widespread in Hellenistic Judaism (Wis. 7:13, 27; 9:10-12) and could have influenced the Corinthians independently of Jesus' sayings. In any case Paul probably did not introduce this wisdom tradition to Corinth, both because it is not prominent in his other letters and because it is a problem to him in this letter. The hypothesis closest to hand concerning the origin of Corinthian Christian wisdom—granted that we lack proof—would trace it back through Apollos to the arrival of the baptism of John and the proclamation of Jesus into the context of Hellenistic-Jewish wisdom in

Alexandria (Acts 18:24 — 19:7). Such a double parentage of the Corinthians' wisdom in the sayings of John and Jesus on the one hand and Hellenistic Jewish wisdom on the other could mean that the Corinthian church knew of the traditional feminine personification of God's wisdom in Judaism, which appears in Jesus seeing himself and John among "all her children." If so, our lack of evidence for this would come from Paul's choosing not to adopt this aspect of the Corinthian view of Christ as God's wisdom when reformulating his faith in Christ crucified as wisdom in the context of this struggle. A Corinthian characterization of Christ as God's wisdom as she reaches out to give wisdom to all who respond could be seen by Paul as not securely bound to the humiliation of the cross, not adequately identifying the male Christ and the female wisdom of God, or particularly prone to inspire women as her voice. This hypothesis of origins aside, there are strong indications that the Corinthians affirm Christ as God's wisdom present in their own hearing and speaking and expected in their leaders.

Paul's own positive wisdom claim that follows (2:6-16) fills out considerably our picture of Corinthian wisdom. He continues to appeal to the structure of reality by citing experience, quotations, and maxims. But now every argument serves his claim to speak the wisdom beyond all human knowledge, available only by revelation through God's spirit. He seems to have conceded to their demand to speak wisdom and be about to speak wisdom before them. Only when the wisdom claim is complete does he identify them, not with the mature among whom he does speak wisdom, but with those who are mere souls or flesh and cannot be fed spiritual meat. This surprise ending shows that he shaped his wisdom claim to draw them in, to offer them the wisdom they want in the way they want it. Therefore this positive claim by Paul to speak wisdom must reflect their own wisdom. Any simultaneous use of the material didactically to correct their views would hamper his double aim to show them that he can speak wisdom as they recognize it and in closing, to shame them for being unable in his judgment to receive it.

Paul's wisdom claim (2:6-16) appeals to the structure of reality in three ways, at each point reflecting Corinthian claims. First, he says that he can speak *God's* wisdom. This is both the wisdom belonging to God and the wisdom concerning God. That it belongs to God is seen in the fact that "God has ordained it before the ages for our glory" and "has prepared these things for those who love him" (2:7, 9). That it concerns God is seen in its being called "the deep things of God," "the things of God which no one knows except God's spirit," "spiritual things," "the mind of Christ," or even "all things." It is no less than the interior mind of God, prepared before the ages for their glory, which the Corinthians claim to know.

Second, it is a *speaking* of this wisdom that Paul claims. The focus is on oral expression. Although Paul also mentions receiving, knowing, having, and interpreting this wisdom, he accentuates at the beginning, middle, and after the end of his wisdom claim that he speaks this wisdom. Paul is able to draw the Corinthians effectively into this speaking claim because they demand such speech of their leaders and are themselves speakers.

Third, the speakers are *plural* and speak among themselves: "We speak wisdom among the mature"; "We speak God's wisdom in a mystery"; "We interpret spiritual things by spiritual means"; "We have Christ's mind." This contrasts with Paul's first-person address immediately before and after the wisdom claim. He can only be referring to himself throughout, but in the wisdom claim he adopts a traditional communal way of speaking. In Corinth the claim must be communal not individual. Paul's prepositional phrase, "We speak wisdom among the perfect," shows that the speech happens within the community. Apparently, it works less as an instrument to inform people who do not know wisdom than as a good in itself to express God's glory and to inspire and knit together all who speak.

Paul's argument here appeals to a structure of reality in Corinth called wisdom, which is identified with Christ, which reveals itself communally and orally, and has God as its origin and content.

Paul's Argument by Dissociation Using Negation, Antithesis, Irony, and Paradox and the Corinthian Women Prophets' Affirmation

Everything Paul has established by arguing from the structure of reality proves essential to keep his wisdom digression from being submerged under massive dissociations. Negation alone seems to take back everything that is given, with thirty-four negative particles appearing in thirty verses between 1:14 and 3:4. These negations fall into five kinds of sentences. People are said not to know or receive God's wisdom or Spirit (1:21; 2:8, 9, 11b, 14). Conversely, Paul's preaching and their faith are not in words of wisdom (1:17; 2:4, 5, 6, 13). God chooses those who are "nothings" and Paul decides to know nothing but the cross (1:26-28; 2:2). These strange choices are made so people cannot boast in their own wisdom (1:17, 29; 2:5). And finally, negative rhetorical questions—"Is it not the case that . . . ?"—force positive recognition of human foolishness (1:20b; 3:3, 4) and positive rhetorical questions without any negative particle—"Where is someone wise?"—force negative answers about human wisdom (1:20a; 2:11, 16). The cumulative impact is shattering, leaving a great abyss between human reality and divine reality, both of which are present within human experience but directly contradicting each other.

Antithesis accentuates this further. Corrective antithesis occurs constantly, both in short "not this but that" phrases (2:4, 5, 12, 13) and in recurring adversative clauses or sentences built on the same pattern. Apparently the expected view must be denied in order to state the surprising positive reality. Only when negation has excluded any identification of Paul's message with human wisdom can it be called God's power, wisdom, or spirit.

Other means of dissociation include comparison, irony, and a kind of quotation that undermines tradition. The proof that God is known only by God's own spirit comes by comparing God to a human being who also is known only by his or her own spirit. In turn this comparison reveals the irony that human and divine spirits are incomparable—impermeable to each other—and God's spirit alone has access to God. Quotations are used repeatedly to undermine standard assumptions about divine accessibility: "Who has known the mind of the Lord?" Once the negative answer is understood, this is followed in corrective antithesis by "but we have the mind of Christ."

This claim, that what cannot be known is known, shows negation and antithesis become paradox, Paul's ultimate dissociative device. The implications of all Paul's arguments by dissociation for Paul's Corinthian opponents can best be seen where the various devices come to a head in paradox. It is not yet paradoxical to say in antithetical parallelism that the word of the cross is absurd to the lost and wise to the saved, since two points of view can account for the contradiction. But Paul goes on to say that the scandal the Jew finds and the absurdity the Greek finds become God's power and wisdom to both Jew and Greek once they are called. This paradox is finally condensed into the unthinkable "foolishness of God" and "weakness of God." To insure against any danger that the tension might be relaxed by some diminishing of God as the measure of all wisdom and power Paul adds—"is wiser/stronger than human beings." In this comparison the understatement gives the maxim a final ironic twist.

The Corinthian women prophets and their colleagues cannot be read directly from Paul's caricature of either wisdom-seeking Greeks or power-seeking Jews, although his focus on wisdom suggests he is addressing the Greeks and assuring them that Jews seeking power are no better. In any case, their ears are shaping his mouth throughout. His claim to reflect the structure of reality in definitions, Scripture quotes, and maxims must appeal to their interest in a comprehensive understanding. Paul also assumes they know of the cross and cannot deny its weakness and foolishness. They must admit that they were weak and foolish when called, and that Paul came to Corinth without power or wisdom. But these three points of foolishness—in Christ, themselves, and Paul—would not have been taken in Corinth as the locus of God's wisdom in such a way as to justify the paradoxical characterization of God's wisdom as foolish. The three points could only have been seen as the "before" of a great "before and after," as a contrasting foil to set off God's powerful act of resurrection and new life. The cross of Jesus and the believers' original harsh lives are not glorified or romanticized in Corinth but become a measuring stick for the remarkable change that has taken place.

Paul's weakness, on the other hand, has continued, and this is the problem in Corinth. He responds to their objections with the paradox of the cross as wisdom in foolishness and power in weakness to justify his lack of transparent wisdom and power. His way of proclaiming the cross becomes his accusation against the Corinthians who insist that wisdom and power have been accomplished in Christ, in themselves, and can be expected in Paul as well. Whereas Paul's argument by dissociation represents his active dissociation of himself and of Christ from the Corinthians' demands for wisdom and power, we can expect that the Corinthians are not given to dissociative arguments but to direct demonstrations of wisdom.

After Paul has shown from the paradox of God's foolishness in the cross why he has refused to speak wisdom (1:18−2:5), he goes on to argue from their immaturity that they could never have received wisdom, had he spoken it to them (3:1-4). This requires him to make an intervening claim that he is able to speak wisdom (2:6-16). In this claim the paradox of wisdom in foolishness is not carried through. Wisdom is not called foolish (2:6, 7), and the person who thinks God's spirit is foolish is not called wise (2:14). But a different kind of dissociation typical of wisdom claims takes its place. The essence of a wisdom claim is that something hidden is revealed to the speaker, something that even the elite of the world do not know is about to be spoken. Early in this passage and again at its end two quotations proving universal human ignorance of God are juxtaposed to a contrary claim to know God's depths and have Christ's mind (2:9-10, 16). Between these two the paradox of the known unknown reality is explained in four corrective antitheses (2:11, 12, 13, 14-15). In each case the negative side of the antithesis leads off and clears the boards of all preconceptions, making room for a positive claim: no one knows what is in a person except that person's spirit, so no one knows God except God's spirit; we have not received the world's spirit, but we have received God's spirit; we do not speak in taught words of human wisdom, but we interpret spiritual things by spiritual means; and, finally, the natural person does not receive God's spirit and cannot know it, but the spiritual person tests all things and can be tested by none. By this sequence the innocent argument from human self-knowledge to prove that only God's spirit can know God leads into a deepening antithesis between the human and the divine. This becomes paradox because human beings who are limited to self-knowledge have by revelation a divine spirit within them that searches God's depths, knows God's gifts, and interprets spiritual things, to the extent that a human person can be called a "spiritual one" who discerns all things and is discerned by none.

Paul immediately refuses to speak this wisdom to the Corinthians because they are immature (3:1-4), thus giving the primary clue concerning their relation to his wisdom claim. His rebuke is often misread in one of two ways. Traditionally it signifies the Corinthians' spiritual bankruptcy in contrast to Paul's just-demonstrated wisdom. More recently it is read as an exposé that Paul's entire wisdom claim has been a parody of their empty boasts against each other, revealing that neither he nor they have wisdom except in the paradox of the cross. Each reading has a point. The old interpretation is correct in that Paul has made a serious claim to wisdom; it is not a trick. His appeal to revelation by the spirit and to Scripture cannot be sheer parody. On the other hand, the second misreading of the claim as parody recognizes that Paul does not set the standards for wisdom in Corinth and can only prove that he can speak wisdom by adopting in full the Corinthians' wisdom claim. He takes from them not only their argument from the structure of reality just described—that divine wisdom appears, that it is spoken, that the speaking is communal—but also their dissociation, that this divine wisdom revealed by God's spirit is eternally hidden from human beings. The paradox of knowing the unknown God is already theirs, and Paul's advantage from this argument is not in claiming something they lack but in being recognized for what they have and demand from him. His comparative advantage over them can only follow the wisdom claim when he refuses them what he has to offer, contending that their spiritual wealth has overextended itself and become nothing but fleshly strife against each other.

Whether Paul's esoteric claim can provide a comprehensive view of the positive content of Corinthian wisdom depends on whether he is mirroring their wisdom speech or only their preliminary claims to be able to speak wisdom. His final statement that he could not before, and cannot now, speak wisdom to them due to their fighting (3:1-4) shows that he has only claimed the ability they have, but has not executed the wisdom speech. In this case the first misreading of Paul's digression as wisdom, in contrast to the Corinthians' empty and competitive claims to speak wisdom, must be abandoned. The second hypothesis is no stronger. Paul's claim to speak wisdom without doing so cannot be a parody of similar Corinthian claims that were not carried out. This is because Paul's final retort that they are not fit to receive his wisdom depends for its impact on their expecting his wisdom claim to be carried out. They would expect him to speak wisdom at this point only if that is the normal pattern in Corinth.

This points to a third interpretation of the passage: the Corinthians already speak the kind of wisdom that Paul only claims he could speak—and therefore expect him to do so until the end. If so, it is Paul, not the Corinthians, whose claim to speak wisdom turns out to be strictly a demonstration in a competitive situation, a promise without delivery. In his effort to dissociate himself from the contending Corinthians, Paul does not put himself above contention but catches himself in his own net. The Corinthians, on the other hand, speak to their own satisfaction the wisdom of

God that shapes his claim—oral, communal, hidden, and yet revealed, unknown and yet known—the wisdom that Paul aborts before term. Unfortunately, because we are dependent on this Pauline exemplar here, we see only the fetus of wisdom and do not see how wisdom is born in Corinth nor the form of its active life.

Paul's Argument Constructing Reality According to the Model of Choosing Loss and the Corinthian Women Prophets' Model of Accepting Gain

Paul does construct his own positive statement in the wisdom digression. While arguing from the structure of reality and arguing by dissociation from reality, he also develops an argument building a new structure of reality. Deduction and deconstruction lead to a new construction. A model takes shape that was not there before, indicating something not present in the Corinthian wisdom, and suggesting, by contrast, something about the model of wisdom in Corinth.

To construct his new model of reality Paul draws on the worldview and language of Jewish history-writing as it comes to him through apocalyptic and wisdom traditions of his time. Human life is characterized by its place in a divine-human drama that stretches from creation to consummation, beginning and ending in God's glory and human benefit, but in the present time suffering a mutiny of human glory against God that threatens to destroy humanity. Paul's particular rendition of this drama introduces the new model. The initiative is God's, prefigured in the prophetic word, "I will destroy the wisdom of the wise and I will thwart the comprehension of the comprehending" (1:19). A series of questions indicate that the fulfillment has come: "Where is there a wise person? . . . Has God not made foolish the wisdom of the world?" (1:20) Then the new divine act is described: "For since in God's wisdom the world did not know God through wisdom, God was pleased to save those who believe through the announcement's foolishness" (1:21). When Paul goes on to say, "We preach Christ crucified . . . , Christ God's power and God's wisdom" (1:23-24), it is clear that this act of God's choosing foolishness over wisdom has shaped the model for Paul's preaching.

The same model recurs in Paul's view of the Corinthians' calling and in how he describes his own work among them. They were "not many wise," but "God chose the world's foolish things to shame the wise" (1:26-27). He acclaims the remarkable wit of God to choose such a people, shaming those who expected to be chosen and cutting off any human boast before God. Paul's arrival in Corinth without eloquence, in fear and trembling, is explained as the same kind of wise decision: "for I determined to know nothing among you but Jesus Christ and him crucified . . . in order that your faith might not be in human wisdom but in God's power" (2:2-5).

"God pleased," "God chose," and "I determined," all refer to free choices of loss over gain in order that people might know the God who chooses foolishness and alone is wise.

The assumed context of this argument is a cosmic conflict for glory between the One who made all reality, to whom all glory belongs, and the human creatures who seek their own glory through achieving knowledge of God. By choosing to be known in the foolish word of the cross, God becomes accessible to human beings open to this foolishness. Therefore they cannot boast their own wisdom but only this preeminent foolish wisdom of God. This is not an argument from the structure of reality but from a contingent event; it is not an argument by dissociation but an argument traced to a positive act. A divine, contingent act of choosing the lesser becomes the new model for true wisdom — or, more precisely, a new model is presented in the language of a narrative about God. The human location of that model is the word of the cross, Paul's preaching of Christ crucified. When this is seen as Paul's answer to the charge that he did not speak wisdom in Corinth, it is his defense in the form of a narrative giving the facts in the case. God chose loss in the word of the cross; therefore Paul chooses loss. He virtually responds to his accusers, "I wouldn't speak wisdom if I could!"

But then he goes on to claim wisdom. This claim in the wisdom digression (2:6-16) does not explicitly sustain the new model. The initial and concluding focus is not on a divine act of choosing the lesser but on a human claim to speak God's wisdom. Yet in terms of his self-defense Paul has not reversed himself. He has said the same thing in reversed language. Once God's act of taking loss has redefined the nature of wisdom, then the narrative of what God has done can be told as a revelation of wisdom, both to Paul's defense and, from his viewpoint, to the Corinthians' exposure. So his response becomes, "I do speak wisdom, but you aren't up to it!"

Because this wisdom claim is formed to impress the Corinthians and draw them in by mirroring their claims, it provides a beginning point for understanding their different model of God's activity. Its primary verbs do not affirm God's actions but human ones — "We speak wisdom," "We speak God's wisdom," "We have received God's spirit," "The spiritual person discerns all things," "We have Christ's mind" (2:6, 7, 12, 15, 16). At no point is knowing and speaking interpreted as a choice of loss or as any kind of self-limitation. It is in the form and content of an unabashed human boast in God's wisdom. Yet "boast" here is not braggadocio, self-glory, or the desire to exclude anyone else. The verbs speak in a communal first-person plural, and the only dichotomy is between those who speak God's wisdom together in a mystery and the ignorant rulers of the world who reject God's wisdom (2:12-14). The entire genre is positive, confident, even jubilant. Paul's wisdom claim mirrors a human celebration of common gain.

The narrative line does refer to divine action in subordinate and explanatory clauses: this is the wisdom "which God ordained for our glory"; these are things "which God prepared for those who love him"; this happens because "God has made a revelation to us through the spirit" (2:7, 9, 10). Remarkably there seems to be no anxiety in Corinth about upstaging God by receiving the divine spirit that alone knows God. What God is so bold as to give is received not as a danger but as a blessing to be exercised and celebrated. And, correspondingly, the act of revelation is depicted as God's achieving an eternal purpose and gaining a long-sought expression of spirit. In Corinth God's act models gain not loss.

It has been suggested that the Corinthians understand their experience less in terms of an apocalyptic divine action in the end time than in terms of a distinctive initial creation. Paul's mention of three kinds of human beings — the fleshly, those with souls, and the spiritual (2:14 – 3:4) — could indicate an anthropological assumption of three kinds of created beings — animals, mere living people, and those with God's spirit.[7] Yet in Paul's wisdom claim, which is our closest evidence for the Corinthians' understanding of wisdom, the spirit is not depicted as a privilege of some from birth but as a recent gift in revelation. It is better not to separate the Corinthians from the apocalyptic milieu more radically than Paul does, but instead to delineate how a wisdom-oriented apocalyptic scenario may have been conceived in Corinth.[8] Although the Corinthians reject Paul's view that God chooses to save through foolishness, they may share his traditional affirmations about creation and consummation. In the initial event "before the ages" God ordains, prepares, or hides away a secret wisdom intended eventually to glorify those who love God. In the present consummation God reveals the Lord of Glory, exposing the ignorance of the world rulers who have crucified him, and giving the spirit that knows God's secret wisdom "to us." There is a progression from original glory to present glory without any radical break in God's intention by an act of choosing foolishness.

In contrast, Paul's argument shows scriptural intimations and empirical evidence of a reversal of expectations when God chooses foolish people through the foolish preaching of the cross. Paul hedges against attributing an ignorance to God that requires a correction in midstream; it is "in God's wisdom" that "the world did not know God through wisdom" so that "God pleased to save those who believe through the announcement's foolishness" (1:21). The primordial event of preparing and hiding wisdom that Paul describes may be seen by him as a planning of this divine anomaly. The issue at stake between Paul and the Corinthians is how God's purposes are fulfilled in the present — for Paul by shaming the wise and limiting all glory to God, for the Corinthians by giving the spirit so that "we have the mind of Christ" as ordained from the beginning "for our glory." That Paul can adopt their wisdom claim in order to subordinate it to his own word of the cross does not diminish the essential difference between the two. Paul claims that all glory is restricted to God, and returns to God; the Corinthians claim that God's glory is being realized among them.

This is particularly clear in how Paul appeals to the Corinthians' own experience to support his model. He does not say that they chose to be foolish or weak. He argues that it is God who chose them, foolish and weak, and this choice signifies that God took a loss, not the Corinthians. Paul sees their calling as God's way of rejecting the values of the world and shaming those who excel in what the world values. God prefers the Corinthians because they are foolish, weak, and common. Without choosing loss they, being already foolish, are chosen by God "in order that they might shame the wise." Because Paul gives no hint that the wise are likely to understand God's foolishness in the present, this shaming of the wise is probably anticipated at God's judgment. Paul sees the present change limited to two phenomena, a transvaluation of values with consequent loss of social standing among those like Paul who choose with God to take a loss (2:2), and a representation of God's values in those like the Corinthians who are chosen to remain foolish (1:26-30). Since the social situation remains dominated by the values of the world's wise and the strong, the social standing of those already foolish and weak does not change. If this is an accurate reflection of Paul's view in this text, the present salvation he affirms is above all a transvaluation of values; only secondarily, where that requires it, does it become a change in social circumstances (see Excursus on Social Status at the end of the chapter).

Paul's wisdom claim mirrors the Corinthians' different view. They see themselves doubly blessed, having been given the long-hidden wisdom through proclamation and then having received God's own Spirit, which alone can understand these "things of God" (2:6-12). The wisdom of God is seen flowing freely to reach even those least expected to understand. The Corinthians do not receive this wisdom and power as a confirmation that God has chosen foolishness but as the ultimate demonstration that all can receive the surpassing value of God's wisdom so long beyond reach. The Corinthians now know themselves to be wise, as can be seen in Paul's retort, "If any among you think they are wise in this age, let them become foolish that they may be wise" (3:18). The same point is made in what might be called Paul's lament, "We are fools for Christ's sake but you are wise in Christ, we are weak but you strong, you are honored but we shamed" (4:10).

What Paul sees as a reversal of values intended by God's choice of people who are not wise, powerful, or honored, has been experienced by them as a reversal of their social situation. They have become wise, powerful, and honored. Paul thinks they are subverting God's transvaluation of all values for their own social advantage. They think Paul is subverting God's transformation of social reality to legitimate his own losses. When

Paul says God chose the foolish to shame the wise so that none can boast before God, he sees their calling demonstrating, above all, God's exclusive right to glory and, secondarily, the subordination of the world's wise to the glory of God. To Paul, the Corinthians are simply God's instruments to shame the wise who have not chosen God's model of foolishness and to vindicate those like himself who have. When the Corinthians say that God chose the foolish to make them wise and glorify God, they see that their calling demonstrates God's glory—not simply its preservation but its extension—through the dramatically changed social reality of the once foolish of the world. Those already wise are left no distinctive role.

Excursus on the Social Status of the Corinthian Women Prophets and of Paul

Recent research on social structures in Roman Corinth (Appendix 7) points to a society with multiple, rather diverse bases of social power. Rome gave grants of land in colonies such as Corinth to freed slaves to get them out of Rome and grants to retiring veterans to prevent them from returning to Rome and leaving its borders exposed. These lesser Roman citizens probably had to compete for dignity with prime Greek families who returned to Corinth after it had been destroyed and rebuilt as Rome's colony. They also had to compete for wealth with foreign merchants and traders and compete for power with the governor's slaves managing the province. Survival required that people on every social level broker their possessions and connections to gain the patrons, peers, or dependents necessary in times of need. No one factor of citizenship, wealth, family, or office could tell the whole story of one's status in this complex world made increasingly volatile throughout the first century by arbitrary exercise of imperial power. For this reason it is appropriate to apply to a Corinthian population a multifactor analysis of social status adapted from certain American sociologists.[9]

In 1 Corinthians Paul refers more than once to six factors in the social status of his intended readers. Three factors are named in describing their status when called to believe and in stating their status at the time he writes: wisdom, power, and family name or honor (1:26; 4:10). Though Paul qualifies his description of their former state—"not many wise"—and may exaggerate for pathetic contrast with himself concerning the present—"we are fools on Christ's account but you have insight in Christ," the credibility of his argument in each case requires that the readers recognize themselves in his description.

Three other factors of ethnic group, condition of servitude, and gender are indicated when Paul names the social divisions of Jew and Greek, slave and free, and male and female. He appeals to these when arguing that men and women should maintain the specific relations they had at the time they were called into the community, just as Jew and Greek and slave and free have done (7:17-24). When calling for unity of all believers in Christ whether Jew or Greek, slave or free, he does not specify male and female, but this pair was present in the tradition Paul uses (12:13; Gal. 3:28; see chapter 6). Strictly speaking, ethnic group, caste (servitude), and gender factors do not admit application on a sliding scale because each names a basic relation in Paul's social world between privileged and deprived groups that an individual escapes only if reversal into the opposite class is possible. Yet in these areas status is conferred by one's associations as well as by one's own identity; and there are intermediate categories of proselyte, freed person, and celibate, indicating a possible range of status. Additional factors such as wealth or office might also be pursued, but a six-factor gauge should be broad enough to reveal the basic inconsistencies and changes in social status within this community. It is recognized that status is a perceived rather than objective reality, and self-perceived status will be favored where known.

The Social Status of the Corinthian Women Prophets

I first ask the status of the Corinthian women prophets when they enter the community. It has been shown that the women prophets are among those who demand wisdom from Paul and therefore are among those of whom he says "Look at your calling, brethren, not many wise according to the flesh, not many powerful, not many of prominent families" (1:26). Their "calling" may incorporate for Paul the meaning that God called them to this station, but any such argument depends on their first recognizing themselves in this description of their social situation, if not in the present at least in the past. That the three qualities of wisdom, power, and rank apply to social station and not to character traits is clear in the accompanying phrase, "by human standards" (literally, "according to the flesh"), and is confirmed by the focus on shaming others that follows immediately (1:27-28), by the later appearance of this triad to describe Paul's social debasement (4:10), and by Paul's subsequent use of "calling" to mean a social condition (7:14-24).

It is unlikely that the women prophets fall among the "not many" who arrive with some power and status in Corinth's church. A society where women are not found in schools, courts, or councils cannot produce many learned or politically powerful women for religious recruitment. As to family rank, Paul's letters mention occasional women with homes large enough for church gatherings or with some kind of resources to help others (16:19; Rom. 16:2, 5), but the data Paul gives suggests that they are more likely artisans or traders than people from prominent families. Even toward the end of the century when upper-class Gentile women are said to be attracted into Jewish and Christian worship, they could not have been a large percentage.[10]

Ethnic identity gave Jews privileges Greeks did not have in a city once Greek, destroyed by Rome for insubordination and left nearly-abandoned for a century before being rebuilt as a Roman colony with a Roman government. Whereas Rome granted Hellenistic Jews, on the basis of a long-standing if rocky alliance, the rights to assemble, have their own courts and councils, and send money to Jerusalem,[11] Greeks lost their citizenship in Corinth and many Greek religious practices no longer functioned.[12] Attacks upon Jews in various cities seem to have risen more from local resentment of Jewish privileges than from any consistent Roman disfavor.[13] Although the tide changes by the time the Jews of Palestine revolt against Rome about fifteen years after this letter, some Jews continued to live well in cities of the Roman East throughout the century.[14]

The ethnic status of the Corinthian women who were to become Christian prophets could be Jew or Greek. Although a number of Paul's early associates in Corinth were apparently Jews (1:14-16; 16:15; Acts 18:2, 8, 13), Paul's arguments in 1 Corinthians show his audience is now largely Gentile. He deals with the wisdom that Greeks seek rather than the power Jews want; he does not discuss the law; he appeals less often to Scripture; and he prefers the more honorable term "Greeks" to the word "Gentiles," except when speaking of their earlier idolatry or immorality (1:24; 12:2; cf. 5:1; 10:20). There may be Romans in the church or Jews and Greeks with Roman citizenship, but Paul's address gives no clear evidence of this. It is safe to assume that most of Paul's audience are Greek and lack positive ethnic identity and support. If they die without family or a voluntary association such as the church, their burial will be in question.

Paul assumes that Corinth's church includes both slave and free in roughly the proportion that entered the community (7:21-24) without saying what that was. Demographers refuse to make estimates of the number of slaves in the urban Roman East, but they do say that the percentage of slave to free does not change greatly in this period and suggest a common figure of about three slaves to a slaveholding family, indicating that slightly over one-third of the urban population may be slave.[15] Corinth as a Roman colony, provincial capital, and commercial center would probably exceed in slaves the average city in the percentage of slaves, and the Corinthian church where not many are powerful would exceed in slaves the average association there. It may be that slaves in well-placed households would have less need than the free poor to seek the security of a voluntary association. But Paul's caveat that they use the chance to become free if they have it suggests that slaves in this society look toward their freedom, whether through death of an owner, as a reward for special acts of devotion, or by increasing their own social and economic connections so that they can eventually buy their freedom—the latter being one reason to join an open group. The existence of this intermediate group of freed people complicates the statistics further. We have to settle for the general determination of a mixed-caste community, approximately half slave and half free. This is the first factor discussed for which it is possible that as many as half the Corinthian women prophets when converted have a positive social status—freedom.

The final factor of the women prophets' status when entering the community, their gender, is by definition female. The disadvantage of this status can be seen in basic statistics. Literary sources show that girls married at twelve to fourteen, men not before twenty. Burials suggest the life expectancy of females was roughly seven years shorter than of males, probably due to widespread death in childbirth.[16] The exposure of infants by the father's decision, the primary method of birth control, fell largely upon girl babies because of the dowry system and the economic advantage of sons. Some of these girls were found and raised as slaves. Many others died, and that is one factor in the severe depopulation problem in Greece during this period.[17] The low proportion of women in the population increased pressures on them to marry early and, if widowed, to remarry quickly. It can be assumed that virtually all adult women who were to become prophets in the Corinthian church were married when entering the community, bearing children regularly, and keeping the hearth either for their husbands' or their masters' households.

In brief, the social status of the Corinthian women prophets at the time that they are called seems to be mixed on one indicator (free/slave) and low in every other indicator: wisdom, power, rank, ethnic support, and gender.

Their status at the time that Paul is writing can be determined more quickly. Concerning their wisdom, power, and honor, Paul says, "We are fools on Christ's account, but you have insight in Christ, we are weak but you are strong, you honored but we shamed" (4:10). Granted that he speaks ironically, he can only hope to shame them with this contrast if this is widely perceived to be their present situation. And what brought these changes about? Concerning wisdom, Paul dissociates himself from baptizing in Corinth and simultaneously from "worldly wisdom," suggesting that in Corinth baptism has become an occasion for wisdom instruction (1:5-7; 13–18). Their prophecy and tongues may allow for further cultivation of "the depths of God" and "the mind of Christ" (2:10, 16; 12:8-11; 14:22-26). Such wisdom would also give them significant power in a community where prophecy seems to have shaped future goals, warned about dangers, and kept given commitments in view. Paul ranks prophets second only to apostles (12:28). The women prophets' rank, in the sense of being "from prominent families," can hardly change with time, but it could be interpreted in terms of a new household, a new inheritance, even a new *cursus honorum* within the community. To the Corinthian housewife at the hearth, or slave at the churn, it would appear that the whole city were now coming to the door to see and hear, whether at her home or that of other women.

In the Greco-Roman world, ethnic identity is less racial than social — one can become a Jew or a Roman overnight with its major privileges. In Christ the women prophets are putting on a single identity with other believers, realized in each act of eating and speaking together. This binds them into the history and destiny of God's people Israel (6:2-3; 10:1-11). Though not calling themselves Jews or ceasing to be Greeks, those not a people become a people and care for each other accordingly. The Corinthian woman prophet who was a slave when called is probably still a slave as Paul writes or he would hardly bring in the example of slavery to confirm the rule for remaining married as when called (7:21-24). But a slave's status would be different in a community where slave and free are "baptized in one spirit into one body" (12:13) and where Paul can argue for stable slave/free roles only by conceding that an opportunity to gain one's freedom must not be wasted (7:22). In gender there would seem to be no escape from bearing the disadvantaged social status. However, the boundary appears to be somewhat porous in that women in the community from every age group and marriage status are choosing to withdraw from sexual relations and enter a less sexually defined state. This seems to be linked with another move of women into the public roles of prayer and prophecy, since women prophets otherwise attested in the Hellenistic churches are expected to be chaste, and Paul links sexual abstinence and prayer (Luke 2:36; Acts 21:9; Rev. 2:20-22; 1 Cor. 7:5).

In all, it appears that the Corinthian woman prophet has experienced a surge of status in wisdom, power, and honor and has reshaped her ethnic identity, caste, and gender in ways that give her more scope. Free women and even the occasional woman from a prominent family are not exceptions to this rule. Rather, their status inconsistency disappears as their freedom or dignity is matched with the wisdom and power attributed to independent women prophets in a committed community. The dominant event is the great change upward in the social status of all the women prophets, especially as it affects relations to others whose status has been constant or declining.[18]

The Social Status of Christian Men in Corinth and of Paul

There will be men in the Corinthian church who also experience rising status in certain factors since entering the community—most slaves, those lacking any education, men in ethnic groups without any self-rule. But all men have the social advantages across each factor that accrue to the dominant gender, and the few who are wise, powerful, and honored when called are virtually all male.

More precise determination is possible about the people Paul names in 1 Corinthians. None of them appears to be among those Paul is trying to persuade to limit the use of their authority, to follow the practices of his other churches, or to respect his coworkers, that is, among those whose rising status is problematic to Paul. Instead he introduces them as reliable sources (Chloe 1:11), as his converts (Crispus, Gaius, Stephanas 1:14-16), his coworkers (Apollos, Cephas, Prisca, Aquila, and Stephanas 3:5-6; 16:3-5, 15-16, 19), his helpers (Stephanas, Fortunatus, Achaicus 16:17-18), and his representative (Timothy 4:17). If the evidence from Luke's Acts of the Apostles is also taken into account, many of these people can be shown to have come from the synagogue in complete households, have Latin names, have travel opportunities and/or live in homes large enough to host Paul or the new community (1:16; Acts 18:8; 19:29).[19] The women among them—Prisca who came from Rome with a trade and now hosts a church, Chloe who has slaves or emissaries—may have gained status in the community without taking heavy losses (Acts 18:2-3; 1 Cor. 1:11; 16:19). But the status of the men has fallen. According to Luke, Crispus forfeits a position as synagogue head; Stephanas and Timothy do not get the respect Paul thinks they deserve in the church; and all the men are seen associating with Gentiles, slaves, and women (Acts 18:8; 1 Cor. 16:10-11, 15-18). The people saying, "I belong to Apollos," have reduced these "first fruit of Achaia" to a faction echoing, "I belong to Paul," not without further loss of status (1 Cor. 1:14-16; 16:15).

Our best documentation of status loss for a male believer is that of Paul. A sketch of his status in each indicator before and after he is called illustrates how status changes may be experienced by others who are like him in certain respects. Before Paul is called to believe in Christ, he is wise, powerful, and a person with rank. His wisdom is attributed by Luke to his teacher Gamaliel, by Paul to his having applied himself to "the traditions of the fathers" with zeal beyond all his peers (Acts 22:3; Gal. 1:14). Both demonstrate his power primarily in the authority he is given to persecute the church (Gal. 1:13; Phil. 3:6; Acts 8:1-3; 9:1-2). As to rank, Luke speaks of Roman citizenship; Paul boasts he is "Hebrew of Hebrews, as to the law a Pharisee" (Acts 16:37-38; 22:25-29; 23:27; Phil. 3:5; 2 Cor. 11:22). Together they suggest he comes from a Hellenistic Jewish family with the wealth to foster a son's education and with political influence used in Rome's favor to win citizenship. Paul is also favored in the other three status indicators—Jew, free, and male. The significance of these factors is basic to what he is able to accomplish before he is called. The lack of any would have been prohibitive.[20] In wisdom, power, rank, ethnic security, caste, and sex, Saul—to use Luke's name for him at this stage—has status.

Paul's calling to preach Christ to the Gentiles has a direct impact on his social status, cutting off his promising career among the Pharisees without providing him the kind of wisdom that can be a solid power-base in the Greek world. Paul concedes that he has not spoken wisdom in Corinth, arguing both that God prefers the foolishness of the cross and that the Corinthians are too immature to be addressed with wisdom. Instead he claims to represent the crucified Christ as the measure of God's paradoxical wisdom. But he knows this kind of argument does not cancel out their judgment of him by all normal standards, and he uses that to get their sympathy: "We are fools on Christ's account but you have insight in Christ, we are weak but you are strong, you honored but we shamed" (4:10). To be without wisdom in the Corinthian church means to be without power—they do not expect him back (4:18)—which also means his honor in this adopted community of identification is bankrupt. In response he claims the right to their financial support in order to say he has given it up voluntarily, trying to recover what honor he can with words (9:1-18).

In ethnic identity, caste, and gender there is a certain stability; Paul remains in society at large a Jew, free, and male. There is no way that his status can fall even to equal the level to which the Gentile slave woman's status has risen in the Corinthian church. Yet the privileges of his Jewish status have been severely compromised, his rights as a free person have been limited by the Christian slave's freedom in Christ, and his position as a male is now being lived out in the same world with the Corinthian women prophets. Paul unquestionably sees himself having lost status.

Social Status and Theological Claims

There is a close parallel between Paul's view of his status loss and his view of what God is doing in Christ. He says that God did not become known through wisdom and therefore chose to save those who would trust in the foolish announcement of Christ crucified (1:20). This puts in terms of wisdom what he says elsewhere in terms of honor (Phil. 2:5-11), that Christ did not grasp equality with God but emptied himself to take on the form of the human being, the slave, and the criminal. For Paul these two statements, the original wisdom of God in the one case and the original preexistence of Christ in the other, provide the precondition for the voluntary downward plunge of the divine. The final identification of the crucified Christ as God's wisdom and the final exaltation of Christ to God's right hand are told in each context to vindicate the divine path of chosen loss. The relation of this theology to Paul's losses in social status needs to be determined. Can any more be said than that the relation is reciprocal and intensifying, the content of such a message bringing on Paul's loss of status, and Paul's loss of status in turn making him interpret Christ in this way?

To Paul, both the content of his gospel and his own measurable status are abstractions from the single, concrete event of the "word of the cross." This speech-act of announcing the gospel is the core reality, simultaneously the insane weakness of the cross in the proclaimer's life and God's wisdom and power for all who believe. Three times in 1 Corinthians 1–4 Paul distinguishes this kind of speaking from the way other Christians are teaching Christ in Corinth, each time providing a new justification for it. First, he insists that it was Christ who sent him to tell the good news without verbal wisdom rather than to baptize people with whatever initiations in wisdom that involves (1:17). Second, he claims that he decided to know nothing in Corinth but Christ crucified rather than to declaim God's mystery with an overflow of wisdom (2:1-2). And finally, he lays it on their doorstep. Their fighting disqualifies them for solid spiritual food and forces him to address them with the basics of the cross (3:1-3).

Far from simplifying why there is a correlation between Paul's own status loss and his proclaiming Christ's downward way, Paul adds this third causative factor beyond Christ and himself, namely the Corinthians' zeal and strife or, the sociologist might say, their upward mobility. Even it can be seen as sufficient cause of the way of chosen loss.

These arguments do not prove anything about historical or logical causality. Nor has Paul any interest in going behind this Christ crucified as a shameful speech/hearing event to a past historical event of the cross or to a general concept of God's nature in order to establish the validity of his gospel. Paul focuses history on this one present event that in its content, in his expression and in their reception, is God's saving foolishness. His own loss of status before the Corinthians is the visible exemplar of this wisdom/wit/way of God. Paul's highly unified and complex affirmation of triple causality can be taken as a caution against oversimplification in any direction—against assuming with the idealists that a Christology of self-emptying pitted Paul against Corinth, or with psycho-social determinists that Paul's status loss is simply projected onto Christ and the church, or with audience rhetoric that the hearer determines the shape of all argument. Message, speaker, and hearers are all taken as effective determinants in this much overdetermined argument against another way to present Christ in Corinth.

The status gain of the Corinthian women prophets across multiple factors also seems to mirror their view of God's wisdom in Christ. This is directly stated each time Paul attributes their high self-image to their experience in Christ: "In everything you are rich in him in all reason and knowledge" (1:5); "You yourselves are in Christ Jesus who became wisdom from God for us" (1:30); "You have insight in Christ" (4:10). These are statements, not arguments with justifications, showing that the Corinthians do not need to be persuaded to take Christ as the location of their present experience of rising status. In Christ they have found a new identity, not of self-abasement and shame but of self-expression and honor.

Paul states the Corinthians' theological rationale for this when he bids to outplay them in their strong suit of speaking wisdom (2:6-16). He echoes their conviction that only God's spirit knows God so that the world's rulers do not recognize God's hidden wisdom in Christ and they crucify Jesus. But shame and honor are reversed when God raises Christ as Lord of Glory, breaking the perfect internal security system by giving away the self-understanding divine spirit that knows "the depths of God" (2:7-10). On this basis they claim that their wisdom is nothing less than this self-knowing mind of Christ occurring in them (2:16), their power is Christ's rising from death to life in their rising, and their rank is that of the Lord of Glory ordained before the ages for their glory (2:7). There is no hint of fear that they might overstep human limits and violate God in this, apparently because God is known as the initiator of this complete self-revealing in Christ.

The concrete settings in life where the Corinthians' status is being realized are indicated when Paul three times rejects some speaking in Corinth that competes with his own. Paul says that Christ did not send him to baptize (1:17). This suggests some process of baptismal instruction and confession, perhaps fostered by Apollos, where Corinthian women prophets can demonstrate in their speech their entry into the mind of Christ and initiate others in putting on God's image that is not Jew and Gentile, slave and free, male and female. Paul also points to the mission setting when he protests that he did not come to Corinth to declaim Christ's mysteries with overflowing wisdom (2:1-2). Their status rises from effective outreach in synagogues, streets, and the open homes where they meet. In later letters Paul refers to the church of Phoebe in Cenchreae and to "all the saints in the whole of Achaia" (Rom. 16:1-2; 2 Cor. 1:1), pointing to successful local missions beyond Corinth. How such work is done is only suggested in Paul's pejorative "declaiming Christ's mysteries in an overflow of word and wisdom" (2:2). The word "overflow" does not specify narrative or discourse but is some demonstration of Christ's risen presence, perhaps as he speaks through many voices to expose deceit and call forth new life (14:23-25).

Paul's final disclaimer—that he is unable to speak to them as "spirituals" due to their zeal and strife (3:1-3)—indicates a final setting in which the wise speak, "among the perfect" or "mature" (2:6). This internal setting of community life may be the primary location of the Corinthians' wisdom in Christ, because here Paul is at last pressed to match their wisdom with a wisdom claim of his own. His focus on their zealous advocacy and strife indicates that Christ is not known within this community in a formal or routinized way but in speech that is not univocal and leads to conflict in a process of testing which voices speak for Christ.

In contrast to Paul's paradoxical word of Christ crucified as God's wisdom, the Corinthians exhibit the exaltation of the crucified One in outreach, baptism, and communal life. This cannot be dissociated from their rising social status, which is seen as Christ's wisdom and power, giving them honor, group solidarity, and respect as women and/or slaves.

The Social Context

Although it can only be done in a cursory way, the comparison of the social status changes of Paul and the Corinthian women prophets, and the theologies related to each, must be set in the social context of the cities of the first-century Roman East.[21]

Paul's rhetoric reflects his position as an educated Hellenistic Jew. His experience of voluntary status loss, his exhortation to take on this loss, and even his theology of status loss are not unique but appear in different ways in a number of documents from the period such as the Wisdom of Solomon, *IV Maccabees*, the Gospel of Mark, and Philo's *Life of Moses*. The social context reflected is that of the educated, free, Jewish male reared to take for granted his rising prospects in the urban Roman East. But the religious tradition that gives him his rich identity and significant political freedom also puts moral and legal restrictions on his advancement within the Roman Empire. To remain an influential Jew he must learn to accept these restrictions as a voluntary self-limitation.[22] These losses are intensified by the collapse of Rome's alliance with the Herodian dynasty during the first century ce. All of this takes place in the same context as Greek-speaking city gentry see their independence disintegrate under Roman rule and the Roman senatorial class finds itself a front for the emperor's personal power. Many of these educated men seek dignity in Stoic talk of self-denial.

In the century before Paul, Hellenistic-Jewish wisdom circles produced the Wisdom of Solomon, purporting to be Solomon's challenge to the world's powerful to join him in admitting weakness and pleading for God's Wisdom. She was promised to accompany them as a personal presence through the world's taunts and into immortality, as she also accompanied Joseph into Egypt:

> She did not abandon a just man when he was sold but saved him from sin. She went down with him into the pit and did not leave him when he was chained until she had brought him scepters of kingship and authority over those who oppressed him. She exposed the lies of those who had accused him and gave him eternal glory. (Wisdom 10:13-14)

Philo is speaking to highly cultivated Jews in Alexandria of Paul's time when he exalts Moses as the model of virtue, using the specific schema of voluntary loss divinely rewarded:

> When he gave up the lordship of Egypt, which he held as son to the daughter of the then reigning king, because the sight of the iniquities committed in the land and his own nobility of soul and magnanimity of spirit and inborn hatred of evil led him to renounce completely his expected inheritance from the kinfolk of his adoption, He Who presides over and takes charge of all things thought good to requite him with the kingship of a nation more populous and mightier. . . . For he was named god and king of the whole nation, and entered, we are told, into the darkness where God was, that is, into the unseen, invisible, incorporeal and archetypal essence of existing things. Thus he beheld what is hidden from the sight of mortal nature, and in himself and his life displayed for all to see. . . . a model for those who are willing to copy it. Happy are they who imprint, or strive to imprint, that image in their souls.[23]

Paul's Christ belongs among these heroic figures who bear loss faithfully until they receive a royal kingdom, figures formulated out of the experience of a class of people who had to accept loss of status in order to remain faithful to God:

> Take the attitude among yourselves which is also in Christ Jesus who, though he was in the form of God, did not count equality with God as his rightful spoil, but emptied himself, having taken the form of a slave and the likeness of human beings. Found in human form, he humbled himself and became obedient to the point of death, even death on a cross. Therefore God has exalted him and has given him the name which is above every name, that at the name of Jesus every knee should bow, in heaven and on earth and under the earth, and every tongue confess that Jesus Christ is Lord, to the glory of God, the Father. (Phil. 2:5-11)

The Corinthian women prophets occupy a different position in the social context of the urban Roman East. Whether or not a woman has some measure of status inconsistency—she may be free or have good connections in family or ethnic group—she is nonetheless gaining in status in the church because the community attributes wisdom and power to its prophets in a society where women are not educated or politically active. She belongs in the category of persons who are experiencing rising prospects in the Hellenistic city after the empire is established. The *pax Romana* was oppressive to the peasant and rural slave producing the surplus capital on which it flourished, and ambiguous to old wealth whose lands could be confiscated by imperial power; however, it provided space between for more aggressive artisans, traders, soldiers, freed people, well-placed slaves, and women to meet the rising demand for goods and services—including religious services.[24] The relative stabilization of taxes and transportation across the empire allowed people without much to lose to take risks and see improvements in their status.

The best evidence of this, outside military records and dedicatory inscriptions by freedmen, are literary satires, laments, and exhortations in which people of rank or education decry the rising hordes.[25] Seneca describes the upstart freedmen, Juvenal satirizes provincial boors and Roman women. Christian texts, such as James and the Gospel of Thomas, disparage merchants and traders. Finally, the well-documented flash flood of religious traditions from the East, including Isis devotion and the Christian gospel, with their incorporation of past suffering into an essentially affirmative and—in contrast to local political cults—voluntary faith, is evidence of the spiritual creativity of this population.

This analysis of the changing status of the Corinthian women prophets and Paul, with their different Christian theologies, has several implications for the study of religion. First, the integral relation of social experience and theological confession shows that neither should be studied in isolation from the other. Any confession assumed to have universal validity in a religious tradition is probably not yet fully understood. A Christology such as Paul's may challenge people like himself profoundly and yet have no effect, or unintended effects, on people of different social experience. Second, religious texts that argue against another position have not been fully researched until everything possible has been done to reconstruct the confession and social stance of the people against which they are written. Third, where conflicts within a religious tradition are understood in light of the different social experience of each party, it may be possible to move toward genuine mediation of the conflicts through discovery of what can be commonly believed. Otherwise there tends to be increasing polarization of the kind seen in Corinth. Fourth, confessions of God in different religious traditions may have important social and theological parallels, even where common language and historical links are absent. Such similar beliefs will not be identical, but locating them could encourage mutual understanding and prevent misdrawn contrasts, such as between a Christian theology of the cross and Jewish boasting in the law.

4 | Women Consecrated in Body and Spirit: 1 Corinthians 5–7

NEXT PAUL TAKES UP ISSUES rising from sexual conduct in the Corinthian church. He first responds to what he has heard (5:1 – 6:20) and then to their letter to him (7:1-40). Though Paul's self-presentation gives way at this point to addressing their situation and trying to affect specific aspects of their behavior, his speech is no more descriptive of them than it was previously. Just as a "NO FISHING" sign can signal where there is good fishing, Paul's reactions against certain behavior may reveal that it is in vogue. On the other hand, what he seems to concede may not be what they want at all; at one point his strong advocacy shows their opposition to some action and at another his effort builds commonality by agreeing with them. The challenge is to explore the possible meanings of each part of the argument and then find the pieces that fit together as a whole. How the entire text wants to persuade can reveal the rhetorical situation between the author and the intended readers—including the Corinthian women prophets.

Upon first reading two elements of the rhetorical situation present themselves. First Corinthians 5 and 6 show that sexual behavior, which Paul considers radically offensive, is going on. A man has his father's wife, some go to prostitutes, there are court cases that may be provoked by sexual conduct. First Corinthians 7, on the other hand, shows Paul's ambiguous response to a pattern of withdrawing from long-term sexual relationships in the Corinthian church. Some people have remained formally married, others have left believing spouses, still others have left non-believing spouses. This suggests that married people who come to believe do not automatically, perhaps do not normally, continue in previous sexual relationships. We learn that single people are unlikely to marry from Paul's telling those living alone that they may marry if they cannot abstain, widows that they are free to marry if they wish, and virgins that they and their partners are not sinning if they marry.

To piece together Paul's full argument and ferret out the specific roles of women in this situation, I will change the focus three times. First the broad lens: Paul's polemic against immorality in chapters 5 and 6 does not seem to be integrally connected to his judicious considerations on marriage in chapter 7. How are these linked in one unified strategy of Paul, and what does that link suggest about the women? Second, focusing on Paul's peculiar rhetoric in chapter 7 where he seems to weigh marriage over against the single life, what does this approach tell concerning the women? And finally, how does each particular unit of the argument in chapter 7 add data about the women, and specifically about women prophets? I end with proposals concerning women's sexual behavior, roles, self-understanding, and theology in the Corinthian church.

The Unifying Link in Paul's Argument: Marriage Due to Immorality

The link between the immorality Paul describes in 1 Corinthians 5 and 6, and his concern about marriage in 1 Corinthians 7, could not be more explicit. Between the two statements he says, "Concerning what you wrote, 'It is good for a man not to touch a woman,' but due to immorality let each man have his own wife and each woman her own husband" (7:1-2). In response to their letter he concedes that life without sexual relations is the ideal, but calls for marriage in practice. The reason is that marriage solves the problem of immorality. At this key point, where he first speaks directly to their letter — "Concerning what you wrote" — the success of his argument depends on their being ready to understand immorality as a present threat and a severe danger. Without the premise that the existing state of immorality is intolerable, it would not make sense to argue that marriage is necessary in order to prevent it. So the prelude to Paul's many-faceted defense of marriage as a valid Christian option — in spite of singleness being better on principle — is his tirade against immorality in chapters 5 and 6.

It is not yet clear how Paul conceives that people leaving marriages have contributed to immorality — whether they became single in order to seek other sexual partners, whether their commitments to single devotion did not last, or whether one person's commitment left his or her spouse or fiancé to seek partners elsewhere. Knowing the gender of those Paul is persuading to reconsider marriage in chapter 7 and the gender of those Paul presents as immoral in chapters 5 and 6 could contribute to answering this question. The issue is whether the people who are practicing what Paul calls immorality and the people living without sexual relations are gender-specific groups or whether both groups are made up of equal numbers of women and men.

Paul's argument against immorality in chapters 5 and 6 follows a warning against overconfidence already mentioned in 4:14-21 and makes two direct charges: someone has his father's wife and someone has taken another believer to court. In neither case does he bring charges against a woman. When the man is charged with having his father's wife, the woman is not charged with having her husband's son. A number of explanations can be proposed for Paul not accusing the woman, the most obvious being that a public charge against the man would also implicate her. But Paul's verdict of expulsion spoken in the singular, not the plural (5:3-5, 13b), cannot include her. It could be that she is not a believer, or cannot be held responsible because she is not free, or is too young, or is known not to have chosen what happened. Yet she may be a responsible believer. The fact remains that Paul's leading individual example of immorality in the community is male. And the verdict that Paul has decided on — though it remains up to the gathered community to actualize — is the most extreme possible. The man's violation of his father is taken as a violation of God effectively excluding him from God's people and delivering him over to God's enemy "for the destruction of flesh." Violation of God is echoed in the last line of the chapter, "Cast the evil one out from among yourselves!" — the Deuteronomic refrain attached to the death sentence for idolatry and for other extreme offenses against God (Deut. 13:5; 17:7; 19:19; 22:21, 24). Paul's view that this happens for the man's own good, that "his spirit might be saved on the Lord's day" (5:5), does not diminish the weight of the sentence or even assure us that Paul does not expect the man to die immediately.

In the second case, where one believer takes another to a public court, Paul speaks of "brother" going to court against "brother." This language does not necessarily exclude women's involvement because Paul can use brother-to-brother language to stress the tie that binds community members and not their gender (8:11-13; Rom. 14:10-21). Yet it is likely that he is not specifically thinking of women since he can speak of "brother and sister" (7:15). The stronger indication that Paul means men comes from reading the text in light of what we know about institutions at that time. In the early empire women in Greece and Rome go to court indirectly through the representation of their fathers, husbands, or guardians — the related male being understood to be the legally wronged party.[1] Of course women may be interested parties to the case. But Paul's accusing someone who takes another to court is probably not a charge against a woman.

At the end of the chapter when Paul alludes to a third kind of offense in the community, the patronizing of prostitutes (6:15-17), the offender can only be male. Even if the female word used for the "prostitute" were understood not to exclude male prostitution in Paul's vendetta (cf. 6:9), the male prostitute in Greece was also patronized exclusively by men. Because Paul charges no particular man, we can question if the pattern was so general as to make that unnecessary, or if he has no direct evidence. At least he has heard that men do go to prostitutes and believes it to be true, because the credibility of his argument depends on some recognition of actual incidents by the reader.

Paul does not charge women with these three offenses, but what he does say in each case gives some data about women in Corinth. In the first place a woman, either in the church or on its periphery, is living with her husband's son. Moral judgment set aside, this woman's original marriage, probably to a man with children near her age, was not exceptional in Hellenistic Greece. Most women married men considerably older than themselves. Plato had recommended that men first marry between ages thirty and thirty-five and women sixteen and twenty. Xenophon said thirty and fourteen respectively.[2] These may be ideal figures, weighted to allow long periods of military service for men in earlier times, but a five-to-ten year differential seems to be standard throughout the ancient period, and longer than that for second marriages. At the same time, childbirth deaths and widespread exposure of female infants meant lower life expectancy for Greek women—thirty-four for women and forty for men based on skeletal remains.[3] The shortage of marriageable women meant that free men sometimes married their own slaves or freedwomen, which gave these women the added disability of servile status or background in marriage, but the relation could be better for her married than unmarried. Women in the Christian community were not immune from the radical systemic disadvantages of women in that society as a whole—inferiority by age and possible slave heritage in marriage, dependency on men in all civil and judicial matters, and special vulnerability to death at birth and again at giving birth.

The court case would have particular implications for women if the "matters of daily life" being adjudicated are sexual. Three things suggest this. First, Paul makes the charge without any transition just after he has called for the Deuteronomic sentence against the man living with his father's wife (5:13). Second, Paul says it is better to be defrauded than to defraud; he uses the same verb later when referring to spouses denying each other sexual intercourse (6:7-8; 7:5). Perhaps one man is claiming damages from another for defrauding him of sexual access to his wife or fiancé, or for defrauding his daughter or sister of her marriage rights, or for something more explicitly financial such as denying the return of the dowry in a separation. This claim is pressed so hard that Paul considers a reverse injustice to take place. Has the public court decision vindicated someone whom Paul thinks is already overconfident or immoral? Third, Paul maintains the focus on sexual offenses. Four of the first five groups Paul lists as unrighteous are sexual offenders. And when Paul adopts the Corinthian slogan, "All things are authorized me," he warns them not to lose authority over themselves or give their bodies over to immorality. These three points suggest, but do not prove, that a sexual matter is at stake. If it is, women as well as men are experiencing significant changes in their sexual relationships, changes that in at least one case—and Paul anticipates others—have led to disputes within the church. Though women do not normally go to court, their actions may have played a part in generating the dispute and they may be crucial in settling such disputes out of court.

By challenging the practice of going to prostitutes Paul indicates the existence of a double standard that commonly applied in Corinthian marriages. The husband might have many sexual partners with impunity, but the wife did not. Eastern Mediterranean marriage agreements of this period sometimes make the point that the woman's dowry must be returned upon separation or that the man may not keep a second legitimate household, but the sexual freedom of husband and wife are never comparable.[4] This is only general data. But it cautions against the common assumption that Corinthian women and men in the church share the same view of marriage or interpret their Christian freedom in the same way when it comes to sexuality. The fact that Paul does not censure the prostitutes themselves suggests that they are not to his knowledge participants in the community. Yet most cross-class urban groups would include some prostitutes. Paul does say that many Christians practiced immorality before their freedom was purchased by Christ (6:9-11), and among these could be prostitutes living single or married lives in the community.

These implications for women can be drawn from Paul's charges against men, but the data is general and indirect. The fact that Paul does not charge any women with sexual offenses may be significant but remains an argument from silence. The possibility of a more positive and specific view of Corinthian women in these two chapters depends on a third factor, the role of the women in the group Paul is addressing throughout. Paul's charges against offenders are embedded in a sustained challenge to all his readers to put an end to immoral conduct. The blame does not fall on the individuals who have strayed, but on the community that has not reacted appropriately: "It is even reported that there is immorality among you, such immorality that . . . a man has his father's wife. And you yourselves are elated! Ought you not rather to mourn?" (5:1-2) And in connection with the court case, "Is there no one wise among you who can adjudicate in a brother's case?" (6:5) And finally in the matter of prostitution, "Flee immorality!" (6:18) All these pleas, directed in the second-person plural to the community, are to women as well as to men. Paul expects the change that will put an end to men's offensive conduct to originate from the church at large.

How Paul argues for this change shows the kind of people he is trying to persuade. His tone is one of shocked disbelief, as if he expected something different from them. He says repeatedly, "Don't you know . . . ?" and each time he recalls them to some tradition as the basis for a change in their present self-understanding and consequent action.

In the case of the man living with his father's wife, Paul charges the community with being "bloated" and then compares them to yeast at passover: "Don't you know that a little leaven pollutes the whole lump? Clean out the old leaven in order to be a new lump, just as you are, unleavened. For Christ, our passover, is sacrificed. . . . Cast out the evil from among you!" (5:6-7, 13) The traditional threat of yeast pollution at Passover is used to legitimate an interpretation of the believer and of Christ that requires separation from those who pollute. Paul's argument shows that they do know the seriousness of Passover housecleaning—the women from experience if they have been close to the synagogue—and they do accept Christ's death as a key event for Christian self-definition. But he would not be working to persuade them if they understood the yeast and Christ's death in the way that Paul does.

A different use of the yeast image appears in Jesus' antitraditional story about God's kingdom: a woman hides yeast away in fifty pounds of flour until the whole is leavened. According to this story the threat would not be the pollution of Christ by forbidden yeast, but the isolation of the yeasty believers so that Christ's new life in them comes to nothing. Of course the contrast between this image and Paul's does not assure that it represents the Corinthians' view. But it is obvious that the Corinthians are unafraid of polluting Christ's death feast. His death, and also the meal in his honor, may be seen as the generating point for new life, a life that has no reason to be defensive, being by nature on the offense and offensive. Yet at the same time, Paul must have some basis for thinking they can be shocked into a reversed view and conduct.

Concerning the second case of those going to court, Paul's "don't you know" takes another form: "Don't you know that we will judge angels? . . . Don't you know that the unrighteous will not inherit God's kingdom?" (6:3, 9). This shows that they know of their God-given inheritance and authority—perhaps in an expressive sense that discourages evaluation of each other, or as a judgment on the outside world that rejects what they express. But they see no threat from within the community, no need to represent God's judgment over against each other. Paul thinks they can be made to feel this threat.

Finally, in the light of those who go to prostitutes he says, "Don't you know that the one who is joined to the prostitute is one body with her, since it says, 'the two will be one flesh,' whereas the one joined to the Lord is one spirit with him?" (6:16-17) This sentence appears in a series of rhetorical questions, antitheses, and shocked denials, showing horror that a body God has prepared to raise with Christ be united with a prostitute. The model of union with Christ, which they apparently share, has become Paul's basis for an antimodel of union with the prostitute by dissociating the divine incorruptible and the human corruptible. In summary, at the end of his argument Paul uses a plural "your" with the singular "body" to show that he is addressing the whole church: "Don't you know that your body is the temple of the holy spirit which is in you? . . . Glorify God in your body!" (6:19-20) This makes clear that Paul's threatening antimodel, the man united with the prostitute, is not intended to curb certain wayward men as much as to shock the church at large to take action so that Christ's body, in which they all participate, will not be violated.

But why does Paul think he can persuade them if they don't mourn over the man who has his father's wife, don't judge each other, and don't see their common body violated by prostitution? He dramatizes these events as if some people will be susceptible to his shock tactics. These could be people who have worshiped in the synagogue and have sufficient qualms about being associated with offenses "not even found among the Gentiles" that they might be persuaded to expel the yeast of wickedness from their midst (5:1, 8). Or it could be separatist or perfectionist Christians who followed Paul's earlier letter by withdrawing from the world's evil, knowing that those not redeemed and set apart could not inherit the kingdom (5:9-11; 6:9-11). But would such people have supported the man with his father's wife?

Paul choosing to highlight sexual sins committed by men suggests another possibility. Women in the community would be particularly vulnerable to the offense of such acts. Even those ready to support the young woman and man against his father would have a sense of the limits of men's sexual freedom in Christ. Paul's words would be most congenial to women who have used their freedom to live separately from men, although the next chapter shows that he has no intention of ruling out sexual union for those in union with Christ. But his use of the Genesis quotation, "the two will become one flesh," to build the stark antithesis of two kinds of union appeals to those whose union with Christ replaces sexual union.

To these people Paul concedes "it is well for a man not to touch a woman," and continues, "but due to immorality let each man have his own wife and each woman her own husband" (7:1-2). (This could be translated "due to prostitution," yet its hinge location suggests that it refers back to Paul's entire exposé of immorality.) The immorality he exposes is male. The solution he calls for is marriage, and here, for the first time in the letter, he refers to women as an explicit group. Paul is not telling the offending men to marry. This cannot happen without the cooperation of others and the others cannot be male. Women are necessary in Paul's plan to put an end to immorality in the community.

It is possible that the role of women in marrying these men to stop immorality could be an afterthought on Paul's part. But the three indicators developed earlier point toward a concerted strategy of persuading women. First, throughout the argument against immorality it is not the offending men Paul has addressed but the community, including its women, which must make structural changes in its life. Second, the way Paul has appealed to the community with images of yeast pollution and violation of the union with Christ suggests that he may be addressing those who have set aside sexual relations for the gospel. Third, men who renounce sexual relations are the least important for Paul to persuade, since their choices already ward off immorality. It is the women rejecting sexual contact who must be persuaded if he is to succeed in stemming immorality by Christian marriage or remarriage of those men not willing to forgo sexual relations. Apparently Paul sets out to persuade women to give up what they have gained through sexual abstinence in order that the community and Christ himself may be saved from immorality.

Judicious Rhetoric for a Difficult Task

Once we see that Paul's warnings about immorality are not separate from his instruction on marriage but are dramatized to shock the people into restoring, wherever necessary, the traditional marriage bonds that preserve morality, the issue becomes why Paul's words on marriage do not continue in the same tone. A few lines before Paul asked in horrified disbelief, "Will you then take the parts of Christ's body and make them parts of a prostitute?" (6:15) In this chapter he appears to be seated calmly behind the dais adjudicating successive cases with strict impartiality (7:1-40). Every word is chosen to present what he says as the most measured, modest, balanced, and impartial solution to the Corinthians' problems. He gives his advice to each group in turn—the married, the single, the divorced, the virgins, and the widows. His words are modest in that at each point he states frankly whether he speaks on divine authority— the Lord's command, God's call (7:10, 17)—or from his own best judgment in God's spirit (7:6, 12, 25, 40). Where his own desires for them break through, he says openly, "I wish that . . ." and then goes on to admit that they may lack the gift for sexual abstinence or may be more swayed by practical arguments (7:7, 32-34).

Even more stress is put on balance. Paul repeatedly weighs what are for him life's two options: life without sexual relations and sexual commitment of a husband and wife. "It is good not to touch . . ." but due to sexual immorality each should marry. "It is good" if the single remain as I am, "but if they cannot control themselves, let them marry." "It is good" to be a virgin, "but . . . if the virgin marries, she does not sin" (7:1-2, 8, 26-28). In these sentences the phrase "it is good" has a comparative value and could be read "Better . . ." or even "It would be ideal. . . ." This last rendition shows most clearly how principle and practice are being dissociated. That singleness has value is already being qualified as not fully practical or appropriate. Yet when the weight falls toward the option of marriage, this can be balanced by Paul's own preference for singleness or by the urgency of the time and the need for full devotion to the Lord.

Finally, and with the most repetition among all these rhetorical devices, there is the rhetoric of equality or justice. Paul goes far beyond what is required in Greek to make the point that men and women have the same responsibilities toward each other. Ten times an instruction is rephrased twice, once for the male in relation to the female, and once for the female in relation to the male. Sometimes one precedes, sometimes the other. There is no question that Paul is rhetorically accentuating the equal and reciprocal nature of sexual responsibilities. The lack of a common noun for "spouse" in Greek does not require Paul to delineate each responsibility twice in full. Paul goes far beyond the needs of clarity to stress in diction, tone, and repetition his own impartiality and reasonableness.

What accounts for the sudden metamorphosis of Paul the agitator into Paul the thoughtful judge? One explanation is suggested by the first words of the chapter, "But concerning what you wrote. . . ." Paul may be responding differently to a letter he has received than he has responded in the earlier chapters to things he got wind of orally. He may speak soberly to written questions about marriage, virgins, idol food, spiritual people, the collection, and Apollos — to note all the issues Paul identifies as writing topics by prefixing the word "concerning" (7:1, 25; 8:1; 12:1; 16:1, 12)[5] — whereas in response to alarmist reports of factions, incest, immorality, and drunkenness in the community his own rhetoric follows suit (1:10 — 6:20; 11:1-34).[6]

But there is little evidence of Paul answering written questions. Instead, a number of Paul's responses to the written topics open with a confident assertion that he qualifies immediately. This suggests that he has received a string of statements rather than questions, very straightforward or even provocative statements. He deals with them where he can by affirming the principle stated but then denying its practice. For example,

> Concerning idol food; we know "we all have knowledge." Knowledge bloats but love builds. If any [of you] think they know something, they do not yet know as they need to know. But if any love God, they are known by him (8:1-3).

Chapter 7 begins with a similar construction,

> Concerning what you wrote, "It is good for a man not to touch a woman," but due to immorality let each man have his own wife and each woman her own husband (7:1-2).

This suggests that Paul is not answering questions but questioning answers. If so, the judicious language, careful distinctions between groups, and rhetoric of equality in this chapter cannot be laid to his relaxed frame of mind as he takes up their thoughtful questions. On the contrary, his careful rhetoric may reflect wariness in approaching strong and fixed positions at odds with his own. What more crucial place to maintain a judicious air than when beginning to address the statements of confident people whose position one wants to modify?

This rhetoric has implications for the Corinthian women. Paul's measured, case-by-case address to each group, always noting the women, not only indicates that there are women of every sexual status in the church, but it shows that some women in each group are living without sexual relations against the social custom—widows of various ages, young women already of the age for marriage, women separated from non-believers (perhaps upon becoming Christians), women who have left believing husbands, and even women who still live in the same house with their husbands. This must be a movement of considerable proportions, involving some kind of general calling. But Paul wants them to consider the differences between themselves and to weigh the practical consequences of their decisions.

Paul's modesty in distinguishing between areas in which he speaks with divine authority and those in which he only thinks he knows what is right could be taken at face value as evidence to show that Paul is feeling his way when he moves beyond the tradition. But why does he call attention to his insecurity? He may sense that this will disarm opponents in matters where opposition is strong. His diffidence could be expressed to encourage discussion of the possibility that perhaps Christians need not leave pagan spouses, need not remain virgins, need not stay widows, even in a community where that is expected. As a closer look at the texts will show, it is in these categories that women are distinctively mentioned as choosing to be single. So Paul's demurs could be geared toward them.

The rhetoric by which Paul carefully balances what is "good" in theory and what is advised in practice has been shown to have a special impact on women when it appears in the first lines of the chapter. They are the only ones who, by sacrificing what Paul concedes to them is "good," can prevent the kind of pollution of the community that Paul has dramatized in the two previous chapters. It is unlikely that Paul has shocked the immoral, but he can hope to have shocked their actual or potential spouses and thereby to have accomplished his purpose. Rhetorically speaking, he concedes the ideal they have chosen in return for the practice he has chosen, applying this with the "it is good . . . but" formula, first to those who have been sexually abstaining in marriage (7:1-7), then to the single and widows (7:8-9), and finally to the virgins and their male counterparts (7:26, 38). Although he does not say explicitly to the separated that singleness would be better in principle, he does find ways, even against the word of the Lord, to allow divorce to a woman if she does not remarry and to those deserted by unbelievers. It is not only his own preference for singleness that makes him give it so much room. The Corinthians whose conduct he wants to change seem themselves to be single by choice and have to be conceded their choice in principle in order to consider yielding it in practice.

Finally, Paul's rhetoric of equality, his laying all sexual responsibilities reciprocally on men toward women and women toward men, appeals more to women and, in this case, demands more from women. It is not difficult to see that women more than men would be attracted to an argument from reciprocal rights in a society where their rights are minimal. To say that Paul uses this as an argument that appeals to them does not prejudice the case about whether or not Paul accepts such sexual equality as a consistent standard for his own conduct. Here it draws women toward his position. And it is not just a change of subject matter that causes this change in speech. Paul has been talking about sexuality without reciprocal language in the preceding chapters, as he can also talk about marriage (1 Thess. 4:4). But here he apparently wants to influence women's choices and shapes his argument accordingly.

And how is it that the same argument demands more of the women? This is true only if the life style laid down for the men and the women is an advantage to most men — or an advantage in most ways to men — and a disadvantage to most women. There would be exceptions in cases where women of low status marry men of high status. But in that culture the relative social position of men and women within marriage makes it probable that a viable alternative to marriage would be more attractive to women, hence its loss a greater sacrifice. It remains to be shown from other parts of the letter whether this community functions in a way that singleness is more necessary for women than for men to fulfill key community roles. In this chapter granting marriage to eliminate immorality, Paul's rhetoric of equality requires him to avoid admitting that he is asking more of one sex than the other. But considerable data suggests otherwise, as the individual sections of the chapter reveal.

Women Apart from Husbands, the Virgins, and the Widows

Paul's program of marriage to prevent immorality is first applied to those who withhold sexual relations within marriage. He tells the man that he has sexual duties to his wife, and argues from equality that the woman owes her husband the same.

It is possible that there is a positive Corinthian slogan behind Paul's negation, "The woman does not have authority over her own body, but the husband has it" (7:4). If Paul were not intent on contradicting such a claim one would expect him to state the matter positively, "The husband has authority over the wife's body," or not repeat what he has just said — "Let the man give to his wife what he owes her, and likewise the wife to her husband." The verb "to have authority" is the key word in another Corinthian saying that Paul quotes four times, "All things are authorized to me" (6:12; cf. 10:23). Although Paul denies husbands authority over their own bodies as well, any slogan in Corinth claiming authority over one's own body must have come from women because it would be redundant in that society for a man to claim such authority over himself. If married women were with-holding sexual relations under the slogan, "The woman has authority over her own body," it is obvious why Paul begins here before he fights immorality with marriage, since marriage of this kind would not solve the problem.

Why Corinthian women prophets in particular might have claimed authority over their own bodies is also suggested by Paul. He associates sexual abstinence with prayer (7:5). Women who prophesied in Corinth were known for prayer as well (11:5), and may have practiced sexual abstinence to predispose them for communion with God. In Greek cults women were often chosen for the roles most intimate to the god or goddess and then expected to abstain from sexual relations, at least for a time. Children and the elderly were also given such service because they were presumed to live without sexual relations.[7] Significantly, all the women identified as prophets in the New Testament are described in terms of their sexual lives — Anna at the temple, eighty-four years old and a widow since the seventh year of her marriage (Luke 2:36-38); the four daughters of Philip who are virgins (Acts 21:9); and Jezebel against whom the polemic is made that she "calls herself a prophet and teaches and leads my servants astray to act immorally and eat idol food" (Rev. 2:20). This charge of immorality may be a reference to leaving a marriage or to drawing other women away from sexual relations. The same association of prophecy with virginity or widowhood is found throughout the Roman East, with exceptions of married visionaries in some Jewish texts (see Selected Texts, pp. 240–45, 260, 267).

In contrast the sexual status of men prophets is seldom discussed, even where extended narratives survive, such as those about John the Baptist and Jesus in the New Testament. It is conceivable that the contrast between Jesus and John in ascetic practices concerning food, drink, and clothing also applied sexually, but if so, only the barest hints survive in the images of the bridegroom and his non-marrying friend, of Jesus' friendship with sinners, and John's desert isolation (Luke 7:24-35; Matt. 11:7-19; Mark 1:6; 2:15, 22 par; John 3:29). In any case, sexual abstinence seems to be considered more essential for female participation in prophecy than for male.

Paul affirms the value of sexual abstinence for prayer, but insists that the married practice it for a limited time by mutual agreement, "so that Satan might not test you because of your lack of self-control" (1 Cor. 7:5). The "you" here is plural, but the call to mutual agreement and temporary practice suggests Paul is addressing the cases in which one partner has chosen to abstain beyond the measure acceptable to the other, either unilaterally, permanently, or both. Paul does not deal with this differential explicitly, for example by calling on the stronger not to use their right to abstain out of deference to the weaker. Instead he uses the rhetoric of equality and closes this section by calling his position a concession, not a command. What he concedes is the return to sexual relations after times of prayer, or more broadly the practice of sex within marriage, since he goes on to say that he would prefer all people to be like himself but knows that some have this gift and some do not.

By conceding sexual relations in marriage to these who lack the gift of abstinence, Paul commands sexual relations for their partners. Yet he rejects the rhetoric of command that he uses in other contexts. Instead, he seeks the compliance of those who would like to be chaste by reminding them that his heart is on their side, that he wishes more people shared this gift, that he would never command anyone against what is admissibly the "good." His delicacy does not disguise the fact that some people are being maneuvered back into sexual relations within their marriages. Why does Paul act against his own chosen life style, sensibilities, and ideals? He has argued that some people's lack of self-control pollutes the community's celebration of Christ's sacrifice, defiles the body consecrated to Christ, and desecrates the temple of God's Spirit. In order not to leave the community vulnerable to Satan, those wanting a life set apart for prayer are to settle for short periods if the partner agrees to it.

The instruction to unmarried people and widows that follows is similar. Remaining single is "good," but if their feelings are not in control they should marry. Paul's contrast of the ideal and the practical does not so much support the sensibilities of those who remain single as reassure those who want to remain single but find themselves conceding to a partner who "is being consumed with fire." Paul does not say here if the passion is the man's or the woman's, but, at the end of the chapter, when he returns to discussing widows without reference to their male counterparts he does not mention that they might lack self-control.

The passage on divorce has been repeatedly interpreted because of its possible ties with gospel traditions of Jesus' sayings and because divorce is a current issue. Three points stand out within Paul's statement. First, he forbids divorce himself and then steps back to substitute for his own authority ("not I") the greater sanction of the Lord's word. Second, he speaks of the woman "separating" and the man "divorcing," but several lines later a woman "divorces" and a man "separates" (7:13, 15), so sex-linked legal distinctions are not demonstrable here. Third, he qualifies the prohibition to the woman with the words, "but if she even so should separate, let her remain unmarried or be reconciled to her husband."

Why is this remarkable exception to the Lord's command spoken to women only? The use of this Greek word for "if" with the subjunctive verb does not refer to past events but to the present and future, so it cannot be explained as Paul's advice to an already separated woman.[8] Apparently he thinks that some women will leave their husbands even after being instructed by the Lord's word. The lack of a similar aside to the men does not mean that they are free to marry twice—how can they be if they are not free to divorce?—but it suggests that the men are not the problem to

Paul on this front, the women are, and so a general prohibition suffices. It could be that they are included to apply the argument from justice, rather than because men are divorcing their wives.

But the women are a problem to Paul, hence the precaution after he forbids divorce that the women who leave their husbands are to remain single or be reconciled to their husbands. This is witness to the strength of the movement of women away from marriage, also perhaps to the integrity of it that Paul seems to respect. And it shows that remaining single is possible for once-married women in Corinth—in their parents' homes? in other believing homes? together? with or without children? At the same time Paul directs them toward the option of reconciliation to their husbands. The difficulty with this option is probably not the danger of physical abuse or the recurrence of something that forced them to leave. Paul would have been better off dealing with the husbands to solve such problems. Here he is addressing believing couples; only later does he turn to "others" who are married to people outside the community. But if women are leaving marriage for some positive reasons based in the community, then this instruction that the woman herself be reconciled would be necessary, as would be the concession that some remain single.

Next Paul speaks in his own name, not the Lord's, to "the rest," which turns out to mean the man married to a nonbelieving woman and the woman married to a nonbelieving man. He repeats the rhetoric of equality four times in four sentences, alternating which couple he speaks of first. He calls on the believers to continue living with their nonbelieving spouses who will be made holy through them in the same way their children are made holy. In the third of these sentences is it apparent why Paul has not included marriage to nonbelievers under the Lord's word against divorce. He has been preparing the groundwork to make another exception: if the nonbeliever leaves the believer, "the brother or sister is not enslaved in such cases" (7:15). But Paul keeps this exception tightly within the context of his appeal to stay married, arguing that God has called them in peace so that each one might save his or her spouse.

Concerning the women, Paul is explicit that some have left nonbelieving husbands (7:13). The intensity of his argument from justice suggests that he is focused on the women. He specifically mentions the "sister" not being enslaved. The one place he does not manage full equivalence he uses a masculine article to refer to the spouse: "If the unbeliever leaves, let him leave" (7:15). Women married to nonbelievers would have sought assurance that their children were holy because Greek children shared their father's political and religious identity; hence reference to that issue suggests an address to women. Even the graphic verb Paul chooses to say that believers are not "enslaved" to spouses who have left them suggests that he is freeing abandoned women, not giving men license to seek out new partners (7:15; cf. verbs in 7:27, 39). First-century Jewish and

Christian texts confirm that these communities attracted many wives of prominent unbelievers[9] and must have been open also to poorer women entering without their husbands. In all, there are good indications that Paul is dealing in Corinth more with women than with men who have left non-believing spouses. Since Paul concedes freedom to the abandoned, it is evident that those he wants to persuade to stay with spouses have taken the initiative to leave.

At this point Paul establishes a general principle from God's call to keep the peace: each one should remain as they were when called. He presents this in a way that minimizes any apparent demand that has been made on them, and at the same time applies the sanctions of God's gifts and call and his own church practice: "Only as the Lord has portioned out to each, as God has called each, so let everyone live. It is this that I insist on in all the churches" (7:17).

He confirms this rule by examples from two areas of church life — circumcision and slavery — where he assumes that people normally continue to live as they were living when called into the community. After each example he repeats the rule of remaining in one's original state to accentuate its broad application — in this chapter he must mean in sexual relations. Evidently the practice of continuing to live as before entering the community was not taken for granted in sexual conduct, and specific changes in sexual life style may even have been expected. In the matter of circumcision, Paul elsewhere says only that circumcision is of no significance for faith (Gal. 5:6; 6:15; Rom. 2:25-26; 1 Cor. 7:19), but here he coins from this a positive rule about remaining how one was when called (1 Cor. 7:20). As a second example he is able to integrate the churches' practice concerning slavery, though only with some difficulty by conceding an exception where freedom becomes possible for the slave.[10] He keeps the exception strictly parenthetical and emerges with a rule restricting definite change in male/female relations because there has been no parallel change in the other two major forms of social privilege overcome by baptism into Christ: "There is neither Jew or Greek, slave nor free, not male and female, for you are all one in Christ Jesus" (Gal. 3:28).

The rhetoric of equality is clear throughout — it is "each one" who is to remain as called. This is thin cover for the great difference between Paul's situation when called — as a free Jewish single male — and that of the slave Gentile married woman (see Excursus on Social Status, chapter 3). In the example of the slave, Paul becomes aware of the absurdity of arguing from equality and remonstrates that the slave is a freedman of the Lord just as the free person is a slave bought by Christ who must not be enslaved to anyone else. These metaphors of redemption by Christ and enslavement to Christ shore up the rhetoric of equality at this tenuous point. This is done not to prevent freeing of slaves — which is conceded parenthetically and is not in any case the occasion for this argument — but to stop and then reverse a movement away from marriage by those, especially women, who seek independence from sexual partners. He secures the argument by adding to his rhetoric of equality a pastoral address and the legitimating divine presence, "Each one in the state he or she was called, brethren, in that state let each remain with God" (7:24).

With this foundation Paul goes on to the case of the virgins. One would expect a quick answer according to the rule, encouraging them to remain as they were when called but allowing marriage if immorality threatens, in the same way he spoke to the "unmarried and widows" (7:8-9). Instead he takes longer to say this than he has taken to speak about any other group (7:25-38). The heading "concerning the virgins" shows that Paul is probably addressing a topic from the Corinthian letter, but he can speak to their topics briefly elsewhere (16:1-4, 12). There must be something in the Corinthian claim concerning virgins that Paul has difficulty approaching directly. This should become evident in the way he argues.

First Paul disclaims any authority for his words beyond his own trust-worthiness due to the Lord's mercy. Then he says confidently, "I consider that it is good to be this way due to the present crisis, since 'it is good for a man to be like this'" (7:26). The second clause of this sentence, which often is not translated independently, is shown by the articular infinitive to be referring back to something already mentioned or well known,[11] probably to the Corinthians' claim that "it is good for a man not to touch a woman" (7:1). This Greek word for "man" can have a generic meaning, but in the context of not touching a woman it obviously means a man. By alluding to this saying, Paul shifts the focus from the virgin to the man involved. In short questions and answers he advises the man neither to seek a sexual commitment nor try to escape one already made. Paul does not repeat the same words to the woman but continues to the man, "But if you marry, you do not sin, and if the virgin marries, she does not sin" (7:28). In this way Paul manages to incorporate the rhetoric of equality, although the woman is only talked about, not addressed.

Paul continues speaking to the man of the urgency in the last days so that "even those who have wives live as though they had none" (7:29). He warns of the anxiety married men and women have that keeps them from full devotion to the Lord. The parallel phrasing in this last argument suggests that now he may be seeking to persuade both men and women. But this is not sustained. He reassures them he wants only propriety of them and explains: "If anyone thinks he is acting improperly toward his virgin, if he is over-wrought (or: if she is of full age)[12] and so it needs to happen, let him do what he wants. He does not sin. Let them marry. But if anyone stands firm in his resolve, not being under pressure, but has control over his own desire[13] and makes his own decision to keep her virginal, he does well" (7:36-37).

Multiple attempts have been made to understand what the relation is between the man and the virgin that explains why Paul leaves everything up to the man's decision in this way (see Appendix 9). In the early centuries of the church it was understood that the man called on to choose here was the girl's father who would cause her to marry if she seemed overwrought. But a man being torn between "impropriety" and "having control over his own desire/will," does not sound like a father. Others have proposed that both male and female are virgin, bound to each other in a strictly spiritual marriage, with Paul's focus on the man whose resolve is weakening. Yet in all but the opening phrase, "concerning the virgins" — where the genitive plural does not indicate gender (7:35) — it is unmistakable that Paul is using "virgin" to refer to a marriageable woman in the normal way (7:28, 36-38),[14] and there is no reason for the meaning of the word to be different in the first line. There could be an engagement implied, either in Paul's question, "Are you bound to a woman?" or in the man's resolve "to keep her as his own virgin" (7:27, 37). Or this being "bound" could refer to a spiritual marriage, and Paul could be challenging the man to "keep her inviolate."

Whatever the exact bond between the virgin and the man involved, Paul's choice to direct himself to the man rather than the woman or to both should not be rationalized by transforming the man into an anguished father or a male virgin. In advising abstinence but conceding marriage with sexual relations, Paul begins, "If you do marry you do not sin, and if a virgin marries she does not sin," and ends, "He who causes his own virgin to marry does well, and he who causes her not to marry does better" (7:28, 38). This unusual causative form of the verb, "to cause to marry," is more often used in Greek of fathers concerning their daughters. But here it fits the male suitor because it is not his right to marry that is contested so much as his right to cause this virgin to marry. The danger of sin is not mentioned in marrying widows or the "unmarried" generally. Apparently the women called "virgins" in Corinth are seen as consecrated and able to be desecrated by being caused to marry. The fact that they are a topic of the Corinthian letter suggests special regard for their faithfulness, witness, or wisdom. It is not said what keeps the man from going elsewhere to marry. Perhaps it is his own choice, a binding engagement, or Paul's preference for marriages within the community (7:39). In any case, Paul ends by saying that the man is better to choose abstinence but good to choose marriage.

Why Paul approaches the man rather than the woman or both man and woman is indicated in the rhetoric Paul uses to persuade the man. In the first place, Paul applies to the man his rule that each person continue to live the way he or she was living when first called to believe — the rule he has just used to direct the married back toward their marriages — in order to challenge the single man to remain single. The advantage of remaining single is argued with force. Paul cites the present crises in which all must live as if they had no wives, the need not to be torn between serving a wife and serving the Lord, even the chance for a man to prove he has authority over his own desire. That the woman's viewpoint is considered only in the second of these three arguments indicates that those who are not yet persuaded are male. And Paul's argument to them cannot be a specious one, since it has Paul's example on its side.

But Paul is not so committed to single devotion to the Lord that he expects the men to continue to live their sexual lives within the limitations set by other people's decisions for chastity. Due to the dangers of impropriety—a word that conjures up the descriptions and warnings in preceding chapters—if the man does not find himself able to choose continence, then "if you do marry, you do not sin"; "he does not sin, let them marry"; "the one who causes his virgin to marry does well" (7:28, 36, 38). These concessions both before and after Paul's arguments for continence show that his vigorous and various effort to persuade the men not to marry the virgins is imbedded in a wider argument to overcome immorality by regularizing sexual partnerships in the Corinthian church.

The second function of Paul's rhetoric in this passage is to demonstrate to the virgins and their many supporters in the church that he wants what they want, that their ideals are his, and therefore that his concession to reality—if the men are not convinced—can become theirs as well. His intense fraternal persuasion directed to the men (7:29, 32, 35) will be overheard by the women who want nothing more in the church than the single devotion that Paul advocates. It is in such rhetoric, congenial to the virgin, that Paul leaves the marriage decision up to the man. This disguises the fact that the rhetoric of equality does not reappear at the critical point to give the woman a corresponding challenge to decide whether she has control of her desire. At the end Paul has replaced the balance of male and female with the balance of two options facing the man (7:36-38). Only at the end of the chapter does the woman receive corresponding options. If her husband dies, she may marry whom she wants or stay single. But to reach this option requires a marriage and a death. The poignant reality is the virgin bound sexually against her decision to the man for his lifetime if he lacks "authority over his own desire" (7:37).

The length and complexity of Paul's argument about virgins and the fact that he concedes sexual relations as merely "good" alongside of abstinence as "best," show the strength of the virgins in Corinth. Community support for them is also evident in Paul's assumption that some think it a sin for the virgins to marry. This may explain why he does not directly address the virgins with instructions on how to prevent immorality but speaks instead to their partners. Paul's rhetoric "concerning the virgins" reflects the same confidence in Corinth about them as he later reflects when speaking "concerning the spiritual." In the one full argument from equality in this passage, where pleasing the spouse is said to conflict with full devotion to the Lord, Paul describes the purpose of the women's commitment in a distinct phrase: "The unmarried woman and the virgin are worried about the Lord's concerns, that they might be consecrated (or holy) both in body and in spirit" (7:34). Note that other unmarried and no-longer-married women (cf. 7:11) are included with the virgins, that the "consecration" is both physical and spiritual, and that it is not thought to be possible in conjunction with marriage either by Paul or the Corinthians.

It is this consecration that Paul is trying to persuade many women to give up. When speaking about the virgins, his argument is to agree whole-heartedly that the commitment they have chosen is also the best thing for men and to try to persuade men of this fact, but, if the men are not per-suaded, to require marriage from the virgins to ward off the specter of immorality in the community. Although Paul is convinced that the gospel is best served by those who are completely devoted to the Lord, immorality is such an overriding danger that most people are to marry.

The reasons for Paul's fear of immorality do not become fully clear until he also attacks idolatry in a parallel way in the next section of the letter. The references that Paul is making to people being "tested by Satan because of self-indulgence" or being "delivered over to Satan for destruc-tion of the flesh" (7:4; 5:5) cannot demonstrate a substantive cosmic dualism in which human immorality serves Satan's reign. Paul also uses the language of yeast pollution, catalogues vices that exclude "entry to the kingdom," and speaks of physical union with the prostitute excluding spiri-tual union with the Lord. The only explanation developed theologically for the danger of immorality argues that a body destined for resurrection with the Lord is no longer neutral ground subject to human authority but becomes the spirit's temple, which may not be violated. This would seem to require sexual abstinence of all believers. Instead Paul locates immo-rality in "your (plural) body," meaning the community as a whole, and calls for marriage to prevent immorality in this body, conceding parenthetically the ideal of abstinence (7:1-2). Because Paul does not ask the strong to help the weak but uses the rhetoric of equality, he disguises the gross inequality in his treatment of the woman who has chosen abstinence and the man who lacks "authority over his own desire" (7:37). The intervening sentences— "You are not your own. You were bought at a high price. So glorify God in your body" (6:20)—bring all the sanctions of Christ's sacrifice to bear upon them. Paul argues that it is not the new commitments that some have made to live out their confession, but the compromises that he wants made to prevent male immorality, which will "glorify God in your body." This suggests a different understanding of God's glory in Corinth.

Women Consecrated in Body and Spirit

The Sexual and Social Behavior of the Consecrated Women

The women's sexual behavior has its background in the situation of women in that time and place. The incident of the man who "has his father's wife" reflects a world where women are married at puberty and often die in childbirth, leaving the man to marry another woman possibly close in age to his surviving children. Though women have a dowry, if it is not returned upon divorce it is the father who sues the husband to get it back. The need to provide this dowry for daughters encourages female infanticide as the primary method of birth control, practiced so widely that Hellenistic records show most families without daughters and very few families who rear more than one daughter.[15] This could not be more debilitating for women because they have to risk their lives to bear children, because female children are most often exposed, because the husband makes the decision, and because this kind of birth control results in a shortage of women and pressure on all surviving women to marry young and, if widowed, to remarry quickly. Some abandoned girls are raised to be slaves or prostitutes, but the slave has no legal rights and the prostitute has less protection than the slave. Although Corinth as a Roman colony and provincial capital during a prosperous century offered more than usual room for a gifted woman to maneuver sexually as well as commercially, there were also no limits to misfortune when it hit. So most women were married young, bore many children, and had little scope for a life beyond the hearth except where poverty taught them to sell some home-learned skill.

In this context we see significant numbers of people in the small Christian community of Corinth leaving long-term sexual relationships or refusing marriage. The group includes male and female, young and old, married, no longer married, and never married. Their apparent motivations will be considered later; here we concentrate on what they do, first focusing on sexual behavior.

At no point does Paul charge a woman with what he calls immorality. This suggests that as far as Paul knows the women who have left partners are living without sexual relations in contrast to some of the men. Yet there are pressures on these women to return to sexual life. Paul recommends that the married woman remain in the sexual relationship she had when called, that the divorced woman return to her husband, and that the virgin marry if her suitor or fiancé cannot control his desires. This pressure is witness that women have voluntarily chosen the single life and are not readily conceding marriage.

The life-support arrangements of these women—where they live and what they do—are suggested only indirectly in the various domestic situations Paul describes. Slave women, as well as free women who continue to live in the home of their husbands, probably retain traditional domestic responsibilities, as do—perhaps on a lesser scale—virgins living with parents, widows living with children, and divorced women staying with relatives or other believers. Paul's reference to children shows that many women have children and must care for them. A key consequence of sexual abstinence for younger women would be the end to further childbearing.

Conversion might also mean a separation from one's children when leaving the man whose children they legally are — except if he cannot afford to care for them.

In Paul's only direct reference to domestic responsibilities, he contrasts the woman who must worry about her husband's concerns with the woman who is devoted to the Lord. Paul's argument is shaped by the rhetoric of equality and may reflect his single life more accurately than that of a once-married woman who may have family members to care for. But it would be an ineffective argument if it were not generally true for women also. The subordinate role of women in Corinthian marriages would tend to make the contrast of married and unmarried life greater for women than for men.

The Corinthians' reference to the virgins in their letter to Paul shows their particular interest in this group. Because Paul responds "concerning the virgins" (7:25) as he does to some of their other topics, affirming what they say in principle and qualifying it in practice, they probably have made some strong affirmations of the virgins. It is possible that other members of Christian households carry the domestic or economic work so that those who are "consecrated" are free for "the Lord's concerns." The virgins with strong community support are probably teenagers and unlikely to mount a movement alone. In fact Paul refers to the consecrated women as those "not married" as well as "virgins" (7:34),[16] indicating a cross-generational group that would provide mutual support among consecrated women. Food and lodging could even be available to some of these people in the same way they are to itinerant leaders (9:4-5). Community financial support is assumed for Christian single women by the time that 1 Timothy 5:1-16 is written, and not all of the women in that setting are "true widows," suggesting that there are virgins and divorced women in the group.

At the same time it appears that the consecrated women provide some kinds of support for others in the community. When Paul tries to raise fears that the community may be polluted by the man living with his father's wife, he says to the church, "And you yourselves are bloated . . . your boast is not good" (5:2, 6). If this extended argument is directed especially to chaste women to motivate them into accepting marriage in order to prevent immorality, they have not isolated themselves into a closed group but support others who exercise the new freedom in different and seemingly contrary ways to their own. Such support presupposes ties based on grounds other than sexual abstinence, perhaps on links among young women or common opposition to family patriarchs and those who force others into traditional patterns.

The more specific community roles of these women can be determined to some extent. Paul concedes that sexual abstinence may assist in prayer (7:5) and recognizes that women pray in the community (11:5). It is clear that spoken public prayer is meant when Paul criticizes prayer in tongues because others can hardly say "amen" to what they cannot understand (14:16). Prophecy, the gift most strongly associated with the divine spirit by Paul, is also attributed to the women (11:5). Again this is definitely a public act that may convert a visitor (14:25). In general, the first-century Christian women recognized as prophets were known for their chastity (Luke 2:36-38; Acts 21:9; Rev. 2:20). Yet it is important that those "consecrated both in body and spirit" were not a formally instituted group in the church. Had they been, Paul's reform efforts would have been directed to reshape the church's vows and practices rather than to persuade individuals concerning their personal decisions. These were believers whose sexual decisions intensified both their own and other people's expectations that they would bear particular fruits of the spirit in the community, in prayer, and in prophecy, but possibly also in miracle working, healing, teaching, helping, or administering.

We may tend to picture a decision for asceticism as a withdrawal from the social scene, but here the women were moving out of relative seclusion into wider and more direct participation in public life. Of course they do not do this without discipline, nor without tradition. Their decision has roots in Hellenistic women's religious practice including some Hellenistic Jewish sects. The Therapeutes's monastic and scholarly life as described by Philo allows women to study and compose biblical interpretations and songs and to share in extended and ecstatic group worship.[17] The temporary continence expected of participants in many Greco-Roman religious rituals was for the sake of public participation, not for seclusion.[18]

It is Paul who understands authority in terms of a man having "authority over his own desire" (7:37; cf. 9:12, 18), that is, authority sufficient for self-understanding and self-denial. In contrast, the women of Corinth appear to have claimed what they lacked, authority over their own bodies (7:4). They therefore do not undergo internal struggle and self-abnegation but social struggle and self-determination within a newly structured social unit. When Paul tries to persuade the Corinthian women to return to sexual relations wherever their partners require, he knows enough to appeal not only to ideology but also to the community's social and religious needs. If he is successful in restoring earlier sexual behavior, this can put in jeopardy the structures of life through which these women have extended their social roles.

The Self-Understanding and Theology of the Consecrated Women

As in sexual behavior, so in self-understanding, the Corinthian women prophets are not focused on avoidance of evil but on participation in a divinely sent good. This might seem to be disproven by the slogan that a man is not to touch a woman—a prohibition. Such a low valuation of sexuality in Hellenistic culture is traced by H. Strathmann to oriental folk traditions, which are present in Greece as early as the Dionysian cult and call for sexual abstinence to avoid pollution from the death-world.[19] This may underlie the widespread expectation that a woman prophet will be chaste, but it does not explain the strong positive self-understanding of the women prophets in Corinth's church.

Paul's repeated argument dissociating principle from practice shows their positive self-understanding. Their principles, which he accepts, speak for themselves. Even the slogan, "it is good for a man not to touch a woman," is phrased in a way that is restrictive for the male but not necessarily for the female (7:1). "All things are authorized me," is a direct and unlimited claim of authority (6:12). These two slogans may have been combined in a third, "The woman has authority over her own body" (7:4). Paul's concession in theory and qualification in practice of these slogans is evidence of the opposition the Corinthians met from him, but their slogans in themselves are anything but restrictive.

The way that Paul argues here also demonstrates that here there was no doctrinaire "libertine party" whose excesses threw others into self-denying asceticism. The same people claim authority and knowledge and reject the man's touching the woman. It is Paul who highlights the danger of immorality in their radical commitments, which they apparently do not experience. Whatever immorality he hears about he blames on their lack of self-judgment, then warns them to "flee immorality," and tries to shock them with images of the union with the prostitute that supplants union with Christ. Far from reflecting polarization in the church, Paul is fostering polarization in order to make them see what he considers to be the consequences of their confidence and their sexual independence in the church.

The quality of their positive self-understanding is clarified when Paul moves from shocking his readers to appealing to their own values in his instructions on marriage. We learn that they expect to be dealt with according to their diversity with equal respect for every age and station. They appreciate a leader who speaks modestly as the spirit gives insight, not from dogmatic claims. Their values are clear in Paul's personal preference for single-minded commitment to the Lord and his respect for the virgin's wise choice. His rhetoric of equality appeals to their interests. The fact that he applies this rhetoric to purposes that are not theirs does not prevent the arguments from being an excellent mirror of them.

Finally, the women prophets' self-understanding is reflected in the way Paul describes the choices they have made. He prepares women to concede marriage where a man requires it in practice by validating unequivocally in theory their decision and its motivation: "the unmarried woman and the virgin are absorbed with the Lord's concerns in order that they might be consecrated both in body and in spirit" (7:34). This phrase reflects their self-understanding as he sees it. The "both . . . and" particles[20]

stress their commitment "even in body as well as in spirit," in contrast to
that of the married women. Consecration in body must refer to their
virginity, which leads to a new life-orientation and distribution of energy
through the work of the spirit. Paul later contrasts speaking mysteries in
the spirit through prayers or psalms with speaking rationally in the mind
(14:2-4), and such ecstatic powers would certainly be among the gifts
expected of those "consecrated . . . in spirit." The adjective "consecrated"
or "holy," a word not used to characterize the single men in the previous
sentence, may suggest some heightened sense of the meaning of chastity
for women. This is also suggested by it being considered a sin to cause one
of the virgins to marry (7:28, 36). These women may be seen as special
channels for the divine due to their simplicity and their isolation from male
influence and control. Plutarch indicates this as the reason for choosing a
young virgin as the Pythian prophet at the Delphic oracle:

> Having been brought up in the home of poor peasants, she brings nothing as
> the result of technical skill or of any other expertness or faculty, as she goes
> down into the shrine. On the contrary, just as Xenophon believes that a bride
> should have seen as little and heard as little as possible before she proceeds
> to her husband's house, so this girl, inexperienced and uninformed about prac-
> tically everything, a pure, virgin soul, becomes the associate of the god
>
> Plutarch, *The Oracles at Delphi*, 405CD

This innocence, far from signifying stupidity, is taken as the natural
setting for divine insight and true wisdom. It is not based on characteristics
unique to certain individuals but on those common to all and only later lost
by people who use reason to gain control. Similarly the community uses the
term "consecrated ones" — also translated "holy ones" or "saints" — to apply
to all believers. Whether the Corinthian women understand themselves in
the cultural image of innocent wisdom or strictly as those sanctified
through baptism into Christ, they apparently see their virginity as an inten-
sification of their consecration to Christ. Set apart from any possible conflict of interest between a man's plans and God's will, they do not have a
stake in the human competition to supplant God's glory. Physically and
spiritually free, they can re-present God's own glory in the community.

Some aspects of the theology of the consecrated women can be reconstructed from Paul's persuasion. Both he and they draw a sharp distinction
between devotion to things of the world and devotion to the Lord, and both
express this in a totally committed life. But Paul thinks immorality within
the community is so great that it threatens Christ with pollution and,
although single devotion is preferable, marriage may be the only effective
antidote to such immorality. He sees Satan present among them, tempting
those whose self-control wavers and punishing the whole church with the
physical consequences of their acts. In contrast they are confident, even
exultant. Yet there is no indication that they think they have built up a

physical barrier against sin. Where sexual abstinence is thought to have such a purpose, stress is put on avoiding contact with others in matters of food and clothing in order to ward off pollution. But these factors are absent. The alternative to such a mechanistic basis of confidence is a dynamistic one. They apparently see Christ working in and through the community with such a generating spirit and liberating force that Satan appears deposed and fleeing, if Satan is conjured at all. They will not take time sitting in judgment over vestiges of pollution when Christ is risen and lives out this transformation in widening circles of people. In Christ all have authority and none are subject to each other but only to the spirit who speaks in prophecy and is praised in prayer.

In these chapters Paul refers to God as the God of the future, the present, and the past. In the future those in Christ will be God's agents to judge the world and angels (6:2-3). The Corinthians may accept this as a sign of God's glory in them but not as an act of discrimination, since all their standards are positive rather than negative. The world's sin can only be seen as the fear and ignorance that prevents it from receiving its own transformation.

Paul also speaks of God present in the community making its common body a temple through the varying gifts to each (6:19; 7:7). But the Corinthian women will not accept the way that Paul sacrifices the authority of God's spirit present in them to the authority of purity standards legitimated by God the future judge.

And Paul affirms the God of the past who assigns each to live in the station in which he or she was first called and to remain there with God (7:15, 17, 20, 24). When exposed, this is a theological appeal to a God who has made arrangements in the past that benefit the speaker at the expense of others. Such a calling is not out of death into life nor darkness into light but a calling to stay in a situation where one already is in order not to put burdens of change on others. It is here that Paul first introduces the God of peace, who appears again near the letter's end in struggle with the God of disruption to confirm the silencing of certain prophetic voices (7:15; 14:33).

The women who have moved away from traditional sexual relationships to devote themselves to the Lord must also have some experience of a God of the past. Paul appeals to this: "But you were washed, you were consecrated, you were justified . . ." (6:11). Paul uses this as reason for them to guard against sin, whereas they take it as a demonstration of their present authority (6:12). In the same way Paul argues from the presence of God's spirit in them to their need to reform their conduct. But for them this "holy spirit in you which you have from God" and in which "you glorify God" is the primary experience of the present God, an end in itself not to be made the basis for fear and restriction (6:19-20). Apparently God does not call the women of Corinth to remain as they were when called but transforms their social lives through new sexual choices and responsibilities. Without doubt this is the God of disruption, not the God of peace and order. On this basis they reject every attempt to bring forward a God of past structures or future judgment to compromise the living God to whom they are consecrated in body and spirit.

5 | Women Having Authority as Participants of Christ: 1 Corinthians 8–11

Paul: Eating and Idolatry

THIS SECTION, TITLED "Concerning what has been sacrificed to idols . . . ," appears on first reading to deal with an arcane cultic practice of sacrificed meat and with certain dress and eating customs in the Corinthian church. A caution is needed in order that we do not dismiss this argument. Here the immorality already discussed is linked with idolatry, which clarifies an integral connection between the two in Paul's theology. On this basis, and in conjunction with an argument from the common good, Paul adjudicates the key questions of who participates in social and communal life and how their authority as participants is to be exercised.

The primary issues are the following: Does participation in the Lord's meal, by which this community is identified, exclude or include participation at other tables—that is, does Christ demand an exclusive commitment, or does the believer sit at one table with all people? And is the authority that rises from participation in Christ to be restricted by each person so as not to offend others and God, or is it to be exercised openly and fully as a witness of the one God to all people? Put in terms of idolatry, do the conflicts among people reflect aspects of their social and religious identity so basic and essential to the common good that to violate these identities violates God? Or does the ultimate and single claim of God override all boundaries and require conduct cutting across every division in order to demonstrate that idolatry is no longer a threat? Such questions about how the one God is to be worshiped in a divided world indicate the field in which Paul's argument takes place.

Once Paul introduces their letter topic, "Concerning what has been sacrificed to idols" (8:1),[1] and concedes in this matter, "we all have knowledge . . . that there is no God but one" (8:1, 4), he begins to dissociate himself—and he hopes them—from the consequences they draw from this view. He dissociates mere thought from reality: "If any think they know something, they do not know as they need to know" (8:2). He dissociates mere knowledge from love: knowledge "bloats" but love "builds up," and the one who loves God is known by God. And he dissociates mere principle from what is true in practice: though "we all have knowledge" yet "knowledge is not in all" in that some still take eating sacrificed meat as worship (8:1-7). These arguments, trying to dissociate them from a thorough-going monotheism by preferring what is loving and practical, lead Paul into further appeals to the common good. These end in two concluding arguments—the first from the threat of causing the death of the one for whom Christ died, the second from Paul's model of not eating meat to spare his brother (8:11-13).

Paul puts it in one sentence, "Watch that your very authority not become a stumbling block to the weak" (8:9). In the next chapters he provides two examples of the use of authority, one positive and one negative. Its proper use is illustrated by his own life in matters of financial support and law-keeping, a long argument from himself as their model (9:1-27). Note the lengths to which he goes—arguments from apostolic practice, from common life, from what is written, from justice, from their debt to him, from the cult, even from the Lord's command—all to prove that he has the right to be supported by the church. It is only on this basis that he can exemplify one who does not use his authority. He also claims freedom not to keep the law, but does not always use it, adjusting his conduct toward whatever helps him persuade people. So Paul defends himself as a model of serving the common good, adding credibility by admitting he is not sacrificing himself but seeking God's reward—or rather he is adopting intensive athletic training so that their coach will not end up disqualified.

The improper use of authority is exemplified by Israel in the desert (10:1-13). Israel's full spiritual resources, mirroring those of the Corinthians, are depicted in five parallel clauses: all Israel were under the cloud, all passed through the sea, all were thus baptized into Moses, all ate the spiritual food, and all drank the spiritual drink from the rock that prefigured Christ. Yet most of them were scattered in the wilderness because they misused this authority. By citing five different stories of what Israel did in the desert and the mortal retribution of God (Num. 11:1-35; Exod 32:1-35; Num. 25:1-18; 21:4-9; 14:1-45)—stories Paul says were written down expressly for the Corinthians—he threatens them with the same consequences if they also desire what is bad, worship idols, are sexually immoral, test God, or conspire to rebel. A final warning dissociates their thoughts about themselves from reality: "Let whoever thinks they stand—watch out not to fall!" And he promises God will provide some escape from this testing.

In these two examples of himself and Israel Paul has dramatized his argument that those given divine authority, whether apostolic rights or spiritual nourishment, are expected to limit themselves and not to exploit their authority. Paul's focus has shifted to show that the need for self-limiting is less the external necessity of the weak than an internal necessity of those who have authority. This is applied to the Corinthians in Paul's final challenge concerning sacrificed food (10:14 – 11:1). It is a warning of cultic pollution directed to his loved ones – "Flee idol worship!" – and supported by an argument from the exclusive nature of cultic commitments, which he commends to their consideration as "discerning people." Sharing the cup and loaf makes people participants of Christ, one body. Eating Israel's sacrifices makes people participants of the altar. Eating sacrificed food makes people participants of daemons, a word used in Greek for semidivine beings. Paul's caveat, "What am I saying then . . . that an idol is anything?" shows that Paul is not introducing a new kind of living spirit in these daemons. Rather the issue is, as he quotes, "The things they offer in sacrifice, 'they offer to daemons and not to God.'" What is given elsewhere is taken from God. Twice Paul says, "You are not able . . . ," attributing the problem not to God but to their inability to be two things at once, participants of Christ and of another. The identity of the believer depends on an exclusive participation. Yet rhetorical questions name the danger as idolatry, "Or 'are we to provoke the Lord to jealousy?' Are we stronger than he?"

In his summary Paul once again takes up the Corinthian theme, "All things are authorized," but, he adds, "not all are constructive." He encourages total freedom of conscience in the market and the banquet hall with thanks to God, yet limits their eating whenever needed for another's sake. The final message is not to use one's authority but to imitate Paul as he imitates Christ. This argument from self-limitation for the common good gets the last word here as it does in the letter (16:13-14). It is the kind of persuasion that is clear and practical and makes a simple framework for community ethics.

But this does not cancel out what Paul has said about the ultimate sanction of death in the desert for provoking God to jealousy. At the heart of Paul's argument the ultimate danger is not the other person's weakness but one's own strength. The Corinthians "on whom the end of the ages has come" (10:11) live in an ideal time of God's total spiritual provision, as when God's gifts made Israel so strong that the people made and worshiped idols and conspired to rebel against God. Paul is expressing the classic religious taboo against overstepping the limits of human mortality. The Greeks tell of the healing god Asclepius being struck dead by a lightning bolt from Zeus when he presumes to raise the dead. In Paul's own tradition it is Eve's desire to "be like a god, knowing good and evil" that results in her and Adam being cast out of the garden, lest they "eat from the tree of life and become immortal" (Gen. 3:5, 22; cf. 2 Cor. 11:3). People who try to be like God receive retribution for their hubris.

Paul applies this to eating sacrificed food and concludes that the different tables are mutually exclusive. It is not daemons that make the Lord jealous but the people who worship at many tables, thinking they can create and destroy gods. It is these people who bring on their own destruction. If Paul's last word is the warmer appeal to the community benefit and the welfare of the weak, his bottom line is the threat of death that falls upon the strong for violating God. Paul explains the basis for his appeal to community benefit, namely that Christ has died for the weak whom they offend. The basis for his appeal to divine retribution seems to be that those strengthened by God do not stay weak but become strong and threaten to make God jealous. Idols and daemons turn out to be nothing. The divine jealousy and retribution apparently directed against these figures is really directed against human beings who "go ahead with eating their own meals." In this way Paul reduces the entire pantheon of divine rivals to the strong human being.

The charge of idolatrous eating is carried by Paul into the heart of the community's life, to the Lord's meal. The intervening instruction on head covering in worship is best considered afterwards, in light of this framework. Paul states that he cannot praise them concerning their eating, though he concedes that the factions he has heard about have some positive function in testing who is right (11:18, 22c). This censures those who celebrate their common life, expecting him to follow suit, and supports those shocked enough to report their dissent to him. His charge of idolatry is that someone other than the Lord is being worshiped in this meal. "When you gather together it is not the Lord's meal that you eat because each goes ahead to eat his or her own meal and one is hungry while another is drunk" (11:20-21). By sharply dissociating "his or her own meal" as a self-benefit from the common benefit, Paul is particularly persuasive that such a human interest must be dissociated from the divine; the meal cannot simultaneously be theirs and the Lord's. He also dissociates private from public — have you no houses for eating and drinking? — and shame from honor — will you shame those who have nothing?

As his final basis for critique he appeals to the Christian tradition about Jesus' last meal, featuring himself as its transmitter, "I myself received from the Lord. . . ." The tradition as Paul gives it stresses remembering Jesus' death until he comes, not celebrating Jesus' resurrected life in the community. From the link of the bread and wine to Jesus' body and blood Paul concludes that their unworthy eating will make them guilty of the body and blood of the Lord. He even attributes recent sicknesses and deaths in the congregation to people's "eating judgment on themselves" by not "discerning the body."

That Paul resorts to a threat of death as divine retribution seems overdrawn. We want to read this as hyperbole, a shock tactic intended to bring them around to "discerning themselves," to waiting for each other at the meal, to taking care of their hunger at home before they gather, in short, to doing all that he advises in his brotherly closing. But this means his strong language about meeting for the worse, about it not being the

Lord's meal, about guilt, sickness, and death would have to be discounted. In spite of the fact that Paul chooses to conclude with the appeal to the common good, the appeal to divine retribution acts as the argument's turning point that makes Paul ready to bring it to a close.[2] At the same time, the charge of idolatry with its consequences consistently draws on the argument from community benefit: it is not the Lord's meal because they all go ahead with their own meals; they eat unworthily and die for "not discerning the body," but "if we discern ourselves we will not be judged" (11:20-21, 29, 31). Paul's chapters on idolatry are incomplete until he has traced it down to the community meal and identified the offense against others in the community as the offense against God, which is idolatry and punishable by death. The authority in Christ, which comes from knowing that God is one, cannot be exercised for the common good at large but is restricted to this one table for the benefit of those participants who are not sure that God is one.

The Corinthian Women Prophets: Eating and Idolatry

Behavior

To begin with the most concrete questions of how women are related to eating in the Corinthian church, Paul says that as apostle he can expect the church to feed and house not only himself but "a sister as wife" (9:5). By the word "sister" Paul means a female fellow-believer (7:15). The second word in conjunction with it cannot mean simply "woman" because that would be redundant after "sister," and therefore must mean "wife," or some other female relative who travels with an apostle. Though Paul makes this claim in order to set the example of not using his rights, it shows that the wives of the Lord's brothers and Cephas were known to travel with them. Whether this practice arose from Jewish mission customs in Hellenistic cities or was initiated by Christian missionary couples (16:19; Rom. 16:3-5, 7), possibly as an adaption of Jesus' practice of traveling with both men and women (Mark 15:40-41; Matt. 27:55-56; Luke 8:2-3), here it is an issue of the right of an apostle to food and lodging for both himself and his wife. The fact that these women are expected to be "sisters" indicates that they may have participated in various leadership roles in the communities visited and received hospitality for their work and not just as their husband's right—but Paul does not refer to this.

For the Corinthian women prophets who apparently are not married, nor—at least in their local capacities—itinerant, the impact of the itinerant wives would be at least twofold. In the first place, as Corinthian women the prophets might be made physically responsible for the work involved in caring for these couples, though this may not be as difficult a position as

Paul puts them into by not permitting them to discharge the debt that he claims they owe him. Second, because Paul sees the rights of support to belong to itinerant male apostles and by extension to their wives regardless of the wives' contribution, this puts in question the relative rights of single women, of local residents, and of those whose authority is based on spiritual gifts—three characteristics of the Corinthian women prophets. From Paul's argument it is clear that the Jerusalem leaders' mission practices are putting pressure on male apostles such as Paul who choose sexual and financial independence. How much more would the rights given their wives impact independent local women prophets.

The Corinthians whom Paul joins in affirming the principle that "we all know" (8:1) act from this principle in some way that Paul wants to restrict. He objects to eating any meat that is said to be "sacrificed to idols," whether in a private setting after it has been identified or in a temple (10:21, 28-29). In contrast this shows that the Corinthians are choosing to make a public witness, even in cultic settings, that the sacrificed meat will not harm them, that "the stomach is for food and food for the stomach" because there is no God but one (6:13; 8:6).

The question must be raised whether women eat in public often enough to take part in those demonstrations or whether they lack access to the banquets where such offensive witness might be given. There are differences of opinion about the propriety of women appearing at public banquets during the Roman period. Well-to-do Jewish families, who would not serve such sacrificed meat in any case, kept the women in the family secluded in the inner part of the house.[3] Greco-Roman literature reflects in a stylized form the conventions of its educated classes when it depicts the banquet as a male preserve appropriate only for women who are flute players, courtesans, and prostitutes.[4] But there is evidence that women in the Hellenistic and Roman imperial periods took an increasing part in public social life, especially in Rome, its provincial capitals, and colonies such as Corinth. When moralists decry how the Roman matron abandons spinning and hearth for the games, courts, and luxury shops,[5] it shows that such behavior is widely known if not universally accepted. And at the other, and much broader, end of the social scale, cultic banquets and food distributions including meat were provided for the population at large on the emperor's accession or at the festivals of a city's deities.[6] In general, the participation of women in cultic celebrations and meals seemed to be taken for granted,[7] except in a few cults such as the Mithras mysteries reserved for soldiers. In veneration of female deities or in Dionysian rites women could make up the majority of the worshipers, or in local cases all the worshipers.[8] It could not have been difficult for Corinth's women to find opportunities to demonstrate their freedom by eating meat known to have been sacrificed to gods or goddesses.

One element in Paul's argument against eating sacrificed meat hints at women's participation. When he holds up Israel's experience in the desert as a warning against destructive use of spiritual resources he appeals to five different scenes from the Torah. Three refer to people in general: the craving for meat ending in the plague, the testing of God ending in the serpent bites, and the conspiring against God ending in a generation dying in the wilderness (Num. 11:1-35; 21:4-9; 14:1-45; 1 Cor. 10:6, 9-10). The other two stories are closest to Paul's theme of idol worship and have sexual overtones: the idolatry and dancing before the golden calf ending in slaughter and plague, and the sexual immorality and idolatry with the daughters of Moab, ending in the death of 24,000 (Exod. 32:1-35; Num. 25:1-18; Paul says 23,000 in 1 Cor. 10:7-8). Paul's choice of the quotation, "The people sat to eat and drink and stood up to play" (1 Cor. 10:7; Exod. 32:6), with the sexual implications of its last word, shows Paul is accentuating the link between idolatry and sexual immorality.

Of course this provides no direct mirror of Corinthian conduct. Not only are sexual innuendos standard in the repertory of Hellenistic Jewish polemic against idolatry and banqueting but, as we have seen, the Greek and Roman writers often question the respectability of women who appear at banquets.[9] Yet Paul's use of this polemic to invoke self-discipline will work as an argument only if there is some link between what he intimates and reality, and this link may be the presence of women at table. Such presence could be one of two kinds. Women seated where sacrificed meat is eaten could be connected with the temple or procured by the host with functions that in some way serve the men's worship or pleasure — cult prostitutes, priestesses, hetaerae, musicians, or other companions. If this is the image Paul has in mind, his charges here parallel his attack against men visiting prostitutes and would not implicate the women of the community whom he nowhere identifies as prostitutes. He could be warning the men, whose role in public life was broader, that eating at idol tables was likely to become a sexual offense as well.

On the other hand, the women at these tables could be guests themselves and could include the women of the community who are demonstrating their own freedom to eat everything without fear. Then Paul's sexual innuendos could suggest liaisons among the guests or simply a public presence of women and sociability across sexual lines outside the community, which Paul considers suspect. Paul's primary arguments against eating sacrificed meat are from harm to the community and from violation of God by worshiping non-gods, not from the danger of sexual immorality. Yet his allusions to this danger in the example of Israel in the desert suggest the possibility of Christian women's participation in such eating.

This possibility is supported by two first-century texts outside 1 Corinthians that show Christian women as significant participants in groups charged by other Christians with idolatry. Second Corinthians 6:14 – 7:1

instructs Christians not to be yoked with unbelievers, challenging, "What agreement has Christ with Beliar? . . . What peace can God's temple make with idols?" and reaffirming, "For you are God's living temple, as God said, . . . I will be father to you and you will be sons and daughters to me." This passage is loosely set in its literary context and has been identified as a fragment of the letter Paul wrote to Corinth before 1 Corinthians, as a part of Paul's later correspondence with Corinth now found in 2 Corinthians, or as an anti-Pauline fragment.[10] But it is widely recognized that the reference to "daughters" has been added to 2 Samuel 7:14 in some effort to draw Christian women away from a more inclusive theology and practice.[11] The polemic in Revelation 2:20-24 against a Christian woman prophet who "teaches and misleads my servants to be immoral and eat food sacrificed to idols" shows that in some locations and periods women were the primary leaders in this kind of early Christianity. The author of Revelation parallels Paul in 1 Corinthians, not only in charging Christians with immorality and idolatry and in restricting women prophets, but also in focusing on this as a "teaching" or "knowing" and in attacking strong self-confidence: "she does not want to repent." These two texts outside 1 Corinthians may address situations quite different from mid-first-century Corinth, but they increase the probability that, in a church with influential women prophets such as Corinth's, the authority to eat sacrificed meat was not claimed and exercised by men only.

Women's relation to meat sacrificed to gods and goddesses would be distinctive if they were purchasing and preparing it for community meals. But there are several indications that this was not the issue. Paul's warning that the Corinthians not offend a "brother" is set "in an idol temple" where the "brother" is watching, not in the community (8:10-12). In Paul's second example it appears to be at a nonbeliever's banquet where the meat is identified as sacrificial and therefore should not be eaten (10:27-29). Paul does not object to the purchase or preparation of the meat as he might if the issue were buying for a community meal where he knew that some had been offended. When Paul later attacks their community meals (11:21) there is no mention of people being offended by such sacrificed meat. Apparently the women in Corinth do not have any distinct relation to meat sacrificed to the gods. Nor is a link made between this meat and the prophets. Yet in so far as the women prophets are among the strong in the community who claim "All things are authorized" and "We all have knowledge" (10:23; 8:1), they may eat sacrificed meat as a mark of their authority as people of one God and as a challenge to others to participate at every table to God's glory.

The women prophets' behavior at the community's own meal and its meaning to them in particular is not specified in Paul's letter. Yet a good deal can be inferred from what Paul says when read in the context of other documents describing Greek women's culinary and food-serving roles. In the classical period of Greece women do all the food preparation, whether as housewives or slave women, with the exception of special anniversaries or weddings in well-off households when a professional cook can be hired. These cooks are free men who often appear in the old and new comedy, typically in leather apron with knife in hand, not only ready to sacrificially slaughter and cook but to supervise the serving of the meal.[12]

By the Hellenistic period the daily Greek meal of cooked cereal or bread with some vegetable relish, when possible with fish, was being elaborated by fruits from abroad, rabbit, even pork. The major meal of the day, now moved from noon to early evening, continued to be eaten with the hands, the men reclining but women and children still sitting in the ancient way.[13] In fact at the height of Macedonian power, the historian Theopompus of Chios is quoted as saying that "there is nobody, even among those in moderate circumstances, who fails to set an extravagant table, or does not own cooks and much other help, or does not lavish more for daily needs than they used to expend at the festivals and sacrifices."[14] Philo gives first-century CE evidence of this in his polemic against "Greek and non-Greeks who make their arrangements for ostentation rather than festivity, . . . serving varieties of baked meats, savoury dishes and seasonings produced by the labour of cooks and confectioners."[15] Both of these men lived among the wealthy and are speaking about them.

The greatest luxury in the Roman period is limited to the imperial circle, a few ranked families, and those considered ostentatious freedmen.[16] Corinth, destroyed by Rome in the second century BCE, was resettled with Roman freedmen when rebuilt by Julius Caesar[17] and could have had some kitchens with large staffs. But the existence of shops to buy baked goods, of hired cooks for banquets, as well as the proverbial high expense and great pretensions of a full-time male cook,[18] suggest that most homes hired a cook only on grand occasions. In the first century CE when Columella describes the careful preserving of each crop after harvests on a country estate, the work is done by the *vilica*—a female overseer or wife of the overseer.[19] Day-to-day cooking in all but the wealthiest families seems to be the uncontested sphere of women—of the wife or, where there are slaves, of the slave women whom she supervises.

The question of who is buying and preparing food in the Corinthian church when it gathers at one place is ambiguous. Is it possible that a person whose home is large enough to hold the full community has a professional cook or hires a cook to produce and supervise community banquets? Several aspects of Paul's argument make this unlikely. Paul says that not many of the Corinthian Christians come from powerful or well-known families (1:27-29), which means that those attending the meal would be unaccustomed to banqueting. Murphy O'Connor has proposed that up to nine people could be served in reclining positions in a good-sized dining room with up to fifty others fed in the covered courtyard,[20] but under these conditions a proper banquet would be difficult to serve, even to those inside. A professional cook could consider this work below his dignity, as would a cook hired to slaughter and bake for some days prior to a celebration. The expense for daily or weekly meals of this sort would be high as well. This kind of cooking and serving could be sustained only for an inner circle of guests. Recently, the differential feeding of guests has been proposed as a major cause of problems at Corinthian meals:[21] some (indoors) go ahead with their own meal, some are hungry (outside), others drunk (inside?). Paul's response gives no hint if a professional cook was involved. He does not ask the host to have the cook hold the meal until all are present. He does not assume that any centralized authority is responsible for serving of the meal. His final solution — that they should wait for each other and eat before they come if they are hungry — suggests that he does not think the host and his family are the problem, since they could hardly eat elsewhere.

Paul's charges and responses make more sense when the meal is conceived as cooked by women in the daily manner. This could have been in one of two ways (or by a combination or an alternation of them). Paul's words, "Each one goes ahead to eat his or her own meal," would seem to indicate that the food has been cooked in various homes and carried to a common place. If everyone has their own meal it would be difficult for people to wait for one another. Various ancient sources refer to a "meal from a basket."[22] Although this is more common among young people eating outdoors who do not have homes for exchanging of invitations, it is an available option for a group meeting too regularly in one home to expect full hospitality. If this was the case, Paul might be concerned about the meal breaking up into many private meals where those with nothing to bring are hungry and shamed into begging while others are drunk. Paul's advice to wait and eat together, or if too hungry for waiting to eat at home, would relieve the problem.

It is also possible that "Each one goes ahead to eat his or her own meal" could mean his or her own "portion." In that case the meal has been purchased and cooked centrally for all the people. But there is no central authority cooking and distributing the food to make it clear who is to be fed, what quantity and quality each receives, and who must arrive before the meal can begin. The feeding of widows causes questions of eligibility in various Christian contexts (Acts 6:1-6; 1 Tim. 5:1-16), as does the feeding of itinerant leaders (1 Cor. 9:4-6; Luke 10:8; 2 John 10; 3 John 5-8), perhaps because these people need constant feeding, but also because they cannot normally contribute to the food supply or the preparation, and are nonetheless considered eligible to be fed. If the same issue does not arise about other groups, it seems reasonable that they contribute to the community support in labor, money, or goods.

The lack of a definite system of food distribution in Corinth could be mechanical in nature, caused by the large number of people being fed, the many and irregular sources of money and food, or shifting responsibilities among the women doing the preparation. Or it could have to do with authority patterns in the community; those cooking, distributing, and interpreting the meal lacked the respect of others that was necessary for them to keep order. Or it could be that those preparing the meal were not interested in enforcing more structured patterns of community life.

The size of Corinth, coupled with the apparent growth of the community, might be evidence that technical problems of the first kind were responsible. But these could be overcome by increasing meal sites or times without disbanding a common hunger-satiating meal, if difficulties in respect for authority or in motivation were not present. Because Paul gives no indication that a faithful group serving the meal are frustrated by lack of general cooperation, it seems likely that those taking care of the meal are not focused on setting and maintaining orderly conduct. The women who arrive early to cook or distribute precooked meals are the only ones we can be sure are present when the food is ready to be eaten. They must be among those who "go ahead to eat their own meals."

Paul's complaint, "One is hungry, another drunk," does not necessarily prove an orgy. It does indicate that at least occasionally the food has run out before everyone arrives and this has caused conflict. Watered wine is the common drink with meals and must lead to enough high spirits that Paul can introduce the stock critique of common meals, drunkenness.[23] Paul's charges of hunger and drunkenness show that the church's meals, whether they are held daily or only on the Lord's Day (16:1), are not primarily symbolic or cultic acts. The church functions as the primary family by sharing the day's meal in which hunger is satisfied and companionship shared. Although women probably cook, there is no effective caste system that separates women and the male slaves from the meal's participants by making them responsible for others. On the contrary, the early arrival of women may give them a certain prominence. Women prophets may give thanks and bless the bread as is expected before the meal in the tradition Paul assumes that they know (11:24).

The question remains if women prophets would be taking part in the preparation of meals. This depends on whether prophecy is understood as a gift that gives its practitioners exemptions from other kinds of work, as Paul considers the apostles exempt from earning their living. Another key variable is the percentage of people who practice prophecy. This question is better addressed when taking up Paul's later discussion of prophecy. But the only mention of prophecy in this section — "Every man who prays and prophesies . . . every woman who prays and prophesies . . ." (11:4-5) — suggests in "every" and the link with prayer that these activities were a widely practiced function, not the basis for exemptions from other duties.

That women prophets in Corinth are unlikely to receive special ranking is supported by the contrast between Paul's picture of the meal in
Corinth and descriptions of meals in other non-temple-oriented Jewish
sects of the same century. Caution is necessary because the sketch of the
Qumran meal in the *Community Rule* is prescriptive and Philo's picture of
the contemplatives near Alexandria in *On The Contemplative Life* is eulo-
gistic. A critique of either group in the style of Paul's censure of Corinth's
meal would find some behavior amiss. Nonetheless it seems that these
groups put far more emphasis on rank, set order, and purity than Corinth's
church. *The Community Rule* of the Dead Sea Scrolls regulates what seems
to be a male celibate common life:

> Whenever there are ten men of the Council of the Community there shall not
> lack a Priest among them. And they shall all sit before him according to their
> rank and shall be asked their counsel in all things in that order. And when the
> table has been prepared for eating, and the new wine for drinking, the Priest
> shall be the first to stretch out his hand to bless the first-fruits of the bread
> and new wine.[24]

The celibate contemplatives near Alexandria whom Philo describes
include both men and women; most live alone and fast often, but assemble
every seventh day and hold a festal meal of bread and water every seventh
week:

> After the prayers the seniors recline according to the order of their admis-
> sion. . . . The feast is shared by women also, most of them aged virgins, who
> have kept their chastity not under compulsion like some of the Greek priest-
> esses, but of their own free will in their ardent yearning for wisdom. . . . The
> order of reclining is so apportioned that the men sit by themselves on the right
> and the women by themselves on the left . . . (on) plank beds of the common
> kinds of wood. . . . The President rises and sings a hymn composed as an
> address to God, either a new one of his own composition or an old one by
> poets of an earlier day. . . . After him all the others take their turn as they are
> arranged and in the proper order while all the rest listen in complete silence
> except when they have to chant the closing lines or refrains, for then they all
> lift up their voices, men and women alike. When everyone has finished his
> hymn the young men bring in the tables mentioned a little above on which
> is set the truly purified meal of leavened bread seasoned with salt mixed with
> hyssop.[25]

The precise ordering of persons and events in these descriptions contrasts
with Paul's picture of Corinth where people go ahead with their meals, get
different amounts of food and drink, are not silent, and apparently sit and
eat in no special ranking of seniority or office (16:15-18).

Paul's insistence that hunger be satisfied at home would mean the
greatest change in the life of women who prepare food. If they plan and
prepare food together, they would lose that shared responsibility and its

opportunities. Even if they prepare food at home to bring to the gathering, Paul's proposal to eat at home would reinstate the standard pattern of hot meals, requiring them to stay home until all the family members had arrived and eaten so as not to leave the hearth unattended. This would mean that the women who cooked would arrive last, not first, thus having fewer hours in the communal setting, and not being there initially to set the tone for the gathering and share in any "going ahead to eat." Instead, they would be spending additional hours within the family context in traditional roles of female and/or servile subordination. Finally they would lose what all community members lose when they stop eating the hunger-satiating meals together as a primary and physical act of common identity.

Paul's references to hunger and drunkenness indicate that this meal in Corinth was an informal feast, focusing on immediate and full participation rather than on one group serving others and watching to save food for latecomers. Such meals would not only have been the greatest innovation for those traditionally expected to cook and serve at home, but the same women would have reason to be most opposed to the reversal of the practice indicated by Paul's, "If any of you are hungry, let them eat at home."

Self-Understanding

The self-understanding underlying the women prophets' conduct in eating is reflected in the way Paul tries to persuade the Corinthians about sacrificed meat and the Lord's meal. Although we do not know definitely that the women prophets were among those eating sacrificed meat to demonstrate that there are no gods but one, there are reasons for assuming so, and we do know they were participants at the Lord's meal. They, among others, are apparent in the similar turn of Paul's argument in both cases to affirm God being one and their being one in Christ but to decry eating at the expense of the "weak brother" and proceeding with one's own meal without "discerning the body" and waiting for others. In neither case does Paul address the "weak" or "those who have nothing," but he consistently challenges the confident who are saying, "we all have knowledge," "all things are authorized," and who do not test themselves when they eat the bread and drink the cup. No women of Corinth are classified by Paul as victims of abuse, not even of the male sexual offenses he describes. That the women prophets are addressed among the strong is visible in Paul's ranking the prophets as second only to the apostles and in his efforts to regulate the dress and speech of the women who prophesy (12:28; 11:5; 14:34-38). It is appropriate to use what Paul indicates about the self-understanding of the strong throughout this section to explain why the women prophets act as they do.

Whereas Paul contrasts inadequate human knowledge with God's full knowledge, those he addresses apparently stress that the fullness of God is known in them—the one God who sets them free from all fears of pollution and invites them to sit at one table with all people. Their inclusive first-person plural, "We all have knowledge," shows that they see themselves as integral to the whole community that knows God is one, not as isolated individuals with special privileges. Yet this inclusiveness is not necessarily altruism. Those who are traditionally excluded have reason to claim, "We all have knowledge." Paul's correction of this principle by calling in practice for love that builds up the church indicates that they value their knowing not because it leads to benefits for others but because it illumines and strengthens all those who know as they speak together in the first-person. While conceding their knowledge, Paul challenges their confidence— "if any think they know anything, they do not yet know as they need to know"; "if any think they stand firm, let them watch not to fall" (8:2; 10:12). They apparently have no fear that the knowledge God gives is partial and will lead to a fall.

Paul tries to get the Corinthians to limit the use of the authority their knowledge of God gives them by appealing to their self-understanding using two examples. When he says, "Am I not free?" (9:1) and then says he chooses not to use his freedom, he implies that the woman who prophesies also says, "I am free," but chooses to act out her freedom. Paul concedes her claim to a free conscience, "For why should my freedom be judged by another person's conscience?" (10:29b) yet he wants her to restrain herself when it comes to eating. She sees both freedom of conscience and action at the core of her identity in Christ. These cannot be given up if the challenging power of the gospel is to be demonstrated. Paul's claim that he wins people by avoiding offense (9:19-22) would not be accepted in Corinth.

Paul's second example of the use of authority, the story of Israel in the desert, incorporates the Corinthian self-understanding in its description of the Israelites baptized by Moses in the cloud and the sea, eating the spiritual food and drinking the spiritual drink (10:1-4). In Corinth baptism and the meal play a constitutive role in their spiritual identity, mediating the necessary transformation and sustenance so that they stand and will not fall. There is no sign that these rites are accepted as physical acts mechanically ensuring immortality, any more than they think sacrificed food could pollute them physically. But on the other hand, baptism and the Lord's meal are not seen to work an ethical transformation in the sense of making the corporate body into a critical principle for self-judgment and self-discipline, as Paul would have it in his athletic and courtroom metaphors (9:24-27; 11:31-32; cf. 4:4-5). Rather, the food and drink are communal in a spiritual and liberating sense, drawing them into the new and inclusive identity in Christ where their own meals become the Lord's meal and celebration of life overcomes the memory of death. This releases the women prophets to know themselves positively and to demonstrate in their eating and drinking the authority of free people.

Theology

The Corinthian women prophets' behavior and self-understanding in eating can also be stated theologically. Knowing God has been the turning point for them (8:1, 4). God has set them free from the subordination to multiple divine and human jurisdictions and from the fears and dissipation of energy that they entail. Rather than putting the women in a new subordination by withholding certain knowledge and demanding instead their love and dependence (8:2, 3), the one God has given them all things. Their one obligation to God, if it can be called that, is to exercise this authority fully and not abdicate it in fear of offending others. Whether by bold eating of sacrificed meat or by uninhibited participation in the Lord's meal, they proclaim that "the world is the Lord's in all its fullness," they glorify God in their eating, and they challenge the world to know the one God and be free (10:26, 31; 11:21-22, 26). Paul is trying to modify this position when he claims to have the same full freedom and authority but exercises it by "enslaving himself" to win others (9:18-27) so as not to "use up" his authority in the gospel and lose God's reward. In contrast, the Corinthian women prophets would take this as a denial of the one God who gives authority to them without submission, without any measure that can be "used up," and without need to provide compensating rewards.

For Paul God is known in Christ, so his theology is developed christologically. Paul's life of adaption to others for the gospel's sake is that of a person subject to the law of Christ (9:21). Christ's death for the weak fellow-believer binds him to respect the scruples of the weak about eating idol food rather than to sin against Christ (8:7-13). Christ is the rock from which the Israelites drank and yet were lost in the wilderness as a warning to the Corinthians (10:4-5, 11). And the Lord's meal is a deathwatch in which the body Jesus gave "for you" is re-presented in the sober acts of self-judgment and waiting for others (11:20-34). In each case Christ means some restriction, some act of self-discipline.

Paul's repeated appeals to the authority of Christ to support the conduct he advises show that Christ is already the accepted standard of right conduct in the Corinthian church. Yet his long and many-faceted argument indicates that they support their views of right conduct with a different understanding of Christ. If Christ is not seen by Corinthian women prophets as an inner law guiding their adaption to others, in some contrasting way Christ is the freeing spirit who breaks through such restrictions; if Christ does not die to protect the scruples of the weak, he may be raised to make the weak strong; if Christ is not the dying body re-presented in patient waiting on others, he may be the raised body re-presented in the immediate joy of the feast; if Christ is not the rock in the wilderness whose "waters of contention" were a judgment on Israel and Moses (Exod. 17:1-7; Num. 20:2-13), he may be the spring that gives the unfailing spirit to drink.

By knowing the one God the women prophets of Corinth's church find themselves released from subjection, and Christ is the one who mediates this knowing to them. How this happens is suggested in Paul's polemic. His appeal to Christ, "The bread that we break, is it not a participation in Christ's body?" (10:16) is developed exclusively, as a participation that does not admit any rival participation. The Corinthians apparently see their participation in Christ to be as inclusive as the God who, being one over all, has no competitors and cannot be violated. Paul agrees that there are no divine competitors, but for him the human person has become the ultimate competitor. The one who makes and worships anything other than God is worshiping oneself, claiming to be stronger than God, provoking God to jealousy, and bearing the full weight of God's judgment. Participation in Christ is no assurance against this; it gives new power and authority that threaten greater idolatry unless accompanied by stringent self-restrictions.

In contrast, the Corinthians do not see their newfound participation in Christ as any threat to God. They see themselves called to live out this participation fearlessly by eating all things with all people. They may have defended this on the basis that the authority that comes from knowing God cannot threaten God, that participants in Christ cannot undermine Christ. Any less than full exercise of the authority God gives then becomes idolatry—the fear of other gods—and threatens the work of God and the presence of Christ in the world.

Idolatry and Immorality

It is only in light of this conflict between Paul and the Corinthians whom he wants to persuade concerning what constitutes idolatry that their differences concerning proper sexual practice can be understood. Paul advocates sexual abstinence because a spouse competes for devotion due to God, yet he concedes marriage—thus requiring it for partners—wherever immorality threatens. For Paul this dangerous immorality is not a question of physical pollution per se, just as idolatry is not a matter of any actual gods who compete against God. The pollution is personal and communal, a violation of God by violating God's temple, which they are corporatively, turning the community into a place of self-worship. Here an act of immorality is an act of idolatry. The link is explicit in the story of Israel in the desert. People claim power and sexual license, threatening the power of God whose gifts are sufficient but not—remembering the manna—excessive, and those who do not limit what they claim think themselves stronger than God and are destroyed. Conversely Paul commends the man who "has authority over his own desire" (7:37) and chooses not to marry, and concedes that he nonetheless does well if he chooses to "marry his virgin" to avoid immorality. The same self-restraint that is expected concerning sacrificed food to avoid idolatry is also expected of this man.

Paul does not ask the same control of the virgins' sexual impulses, nor of the married women. If necessary they are to give up freedom from sexual practice, not free practice of sexuality, to prevent immorality. Paul does not define the exact place of women within his view of human idolatry before God; what he does say could be read in one of two ways. Either women pose the same threat of idolatry through immorality as men but in a different way, or they pose no direct threat but are instrumental in men's sexually worked idolatry. Paul either sees women as full human beings in their sexuality vis-à-vis God, or he sees them as ancillary to males.

Throughout this section Paul's rhetoric of equality seems to speak for the former. Are women as well as men not being challenged to give up exercising their freedom in order to avoid claiming too much and worshiping themselves rather than God? If so, Paul sees women as full human beings in the sense of potential threats to God's power, although they may not exercise this threat by assertion of their sexuality but by assertion of freedom from it. Paul speaks of such withdrawal as a testing by Satan (7:5). But it is not evident that the idolatry that threatens to occur includes one partner's self-determination as well as the other's immorality. In fact, when Paul warns people against withdrawal from spouses and calls them to remain as they are, he does not appeal to the danger of idolatry but to God's calling and church practice (7:17). This suggests that choosing abstinence is not on the threshold of violating God. Paul himself prefers sexual self-determination by abstinence.

It is probably more accurate to say that in this argument Paul does not see women posing any direct threat to God through self-assertion. Women threaten God indirectly by withdrawing from availability for marriage and thereby allowing men to fall into immorality which is idolatry. This assumes that women are not full human beings in the sense of persons independently related to God, but they are instrumental in male humanity by which the good of the community is defined. Although full freedom to serve the Lord is best, freedom of women has no value where men are immoral, and restricted freedom is better. In spite of his rhetoric of equality, Paul presents women's sexuality neither as a possible reflection of God's glory nor as a direct counterclaim to glory. Immorality is explained as a male problem with theological significance because male sexuality can be a counterclaim to God's glory, and women are subsumed as the necessary, if not the ideal, solution.

The Corinthian women prophets may also understand immorality as a correlate of idolatry, or, put positively, they may make their sexual choices to glorify God. In contrast to Paul they do not see the strong human being as a threat to God's glory by usurping God's wisdom, defiling God's temple, and making the Lord's meal his or her own. They see the weak person as the threat to God's glory by rejecting God's gifts of wisdom and authority, and by withdrawing from full participation at the common table. Such faithless idolatry is overcome by the bold witness of those who eat sacrificed meat to show that God is one and has made the Lord's meal their own. In this way all eating is done to God's glory and there is no hesitation due to weak conscience or traditional roles. Sexually, this means that "a man is not to touch a woman" because "the woman has authority over her own body." Many married women no longer devote themselves to their husbands but to God in prayer, and the virgins and unmarried women are consecrated both in body and spirit.

Paul concedes that this devotion is ideal. Unless his concession is strictly for the purposes of argument as a base for the following demand to compromise — and his own sexual abstinence belies this — their view of the strong person glorifying God by using divine gifts is not an aberration in earliest Hellenistic Christianity but is a view he shares. It is more likely that Paul genuinely holds their principles but is redefining idolatry and immorality here in an effort to control behavior that has offended others, perhaps those Corinthians he had attracted from the synagogue with its pollution-sensitive morality, or other Christian Jews beginning to demand that the Gentile Christians "abstain from the pollution of idols and from unchastity" (Acts 15:20, 29). If Paul has learned since penning Galatians not to "oppose Peter to his face" but to "become like a Jew to the Jews," he now wants them to be "without offense both to Jews and to Greeks and to the church of God" (Gal. 2:11; 1 Cor. 9:20; 10:32; cf. 1 Thess. 2:14), possibly with a mind to furthering his forthcoming plans in Judea, Rome, and Spain (1 Cor. 16:1-4; Rom. 15:30-32). In contrast, the Corinthian women prophets do not restrict their conduct for fear of offending this group, who are peripheral to their experience, but continue to let their strength be a witness to God's glory.

6 | Women in the Image and Glory of God: 1 Corinthians 11:2-16

BETWEEN SPEAKING OF THE CORINTHIANS' eating sacrificed food and eating the Lord's meal, Paul insists on their proper head covering when praying and prophesying. This text is as difficult as it is important for understanding Corinthian women prophets. The best procedure is to consider all its arguments in turn to determine any implications for the women prophets. Then it should be possible to answer why he brings up head covering midway in an argument on eating and idolatry and what this means for women who prophesy.

Praise and a Definition with Corollary Statements

Where the passage begins is ambiguous. There is no sharp break after Paul's call for the Corinthians, whether eating or drinking, to imitate him as he imitates Christ (10:31–11:1). He continues, "And I praise you for remembering everything I said and keeping the traditions just as I passed them on to you" (11:2). This could be an acknowledgment that they already follow his traditions about the forthcoming topics of prayer and prophecy, but his extended critique in chapter 14 makes this unlikely. It cannot be praise for keeping his traditions about head covering because of the elaborate effort to persuade them to do so that follows. The praise must be a general approbation confirming that they are faithful receivers of traditions that have been handed down to them by a reliable transmitter. This may be necessary in order to successfully introduce them to a new tradition: "And I want you to know that . . ." (11:3). The conjunction introducing the new statement could be adversative, "But I want you to know . . ." and suggest a correction of what he has told them before, though it is presented as a friendly amendment. The following definition of "head," which they did not know before, is given by this introduction an aura of tradition that Paul has received and passed on to faithful receivers, all without requiring Paul—who may have just coined the definition—to make any explicit claims to this effect.

From this opening we learn several things about the Corinthian women prophets who were among those Paul is instructing about head covering. They must be Christians who have accepted the traditions of Jesus' death and rising from Paul (11:23-25; 15:3) or his praise would not be plausible. On the other hand, Paul's effort to begin by commending faithful receivers of tradition shows that they are not expected to accept the new instruction easily. Paul's highly personal approach — with nine first- or second-person pronouns or verbal suffixes in just over one sentence followed by seven sentences strictly in the third person — shows his effort at establishing a bond and the hesitancy of the Corinthians to be drawn into it.

Paul completes his statement in the form of a triple definition of "head," which as definition claims the authority of universal meaning without providing specific evidence: "But I want you to know that the head of every man is Christ, the head of woman is man, and the head of Christ is God." Christ's authority over the believer (here "man") opens the statement and cannot be contested in the context of Paul's gospel. The statement closes with Christ's subordination to God, a thesis distinctive to 1 Corinthians in Paul's letters, presented earlier to subordinate their leaders to them, "All things are yours . . . , and you are Christ's and Christ is God's," and developed at length in his closing argument that death will be the final power subordinated to Christ before Christ subordinates himself to God (3:21-23; 15:25-28). In this way, "the head of woman is man" is confirmed on two sides by being placed between the analogous claims of man's subordination to Christ and Christ's subordination to God in the triple definition of "head." It may also be supported by an allusion to Eve's punishment after the Fall, "He shall rule over you" (Gen. 3:16).

The reason Paul defines the word "head" to state this hierarchy of authority could be Paul's or the Corinthian's previous use of the term, whether in Hebrew or Greek. Paul uses the argument from Christ's subordination to God to confirm a reversal in his hearers' ordering of two lesser terms elsewhere (see chapter 2, Argument by Analogy to Christ's Subordination to God), and could be reacting here to the Corinthian use of the word "head" to claim some priority of women over men in Corinth.[1] A second possibility is that women could have claimed to possess "authority on the head" (11:10) in the literal sense of speaking with uncovered heads, an authority Paul contests by introducing the pun on "head" as "person with authority over."[2]

But Paul's own argument provides a reason for his pun on the word "head" — without appealing to the history of its use in Corinth. This becomes clear when he draws out two corollaries from his triple definition: "Every man who prays and prophesies with something on his head shames his head. And every woman who prays or prophesies with nothing on her head shames her head" (11:4-5). The second use of "head" in each sentence is the transferred meaning given in the definition. Man's head, meaning

Christ, is shamed when he prophesies with covered head, whereas
woman's head, meaning man, is shamed when she prophesies uncovered.
Paul's argument dissociating shame from honor later shows why the two
heads, Christ and man, are shamed in different ways. But it is already clear
that Paul's triple definition of "head" has been phrased to distinguish
woman's head from man's head and therefore legitimate opposite instructions for the two sexes on proper head covering when praying and prophesying. That some Corinthians do not agree with Paul and will not be easily
convinced is evident in the length of the following argument, which ends
with his challenge to those who "want to make an issue of this" (11:16). But
it is not obvious if Paul thinks that the appropriate clothing has been
neglected by both men and women or if he wants to change the conduct
of one sex and is introducing the equivalence of this conduct to the other
sex as an argument from equity or justice.

The men's situation is stated first and the women's second here and
at three other points in the immediate context (11:3, 4-5a, 7, 14-15a). This
might indicate that men's conduct is the issue in Corinth. But intervening
arguments between the four statements of equivalence address the women's
situation: she can shave her head but that is yet more shameful; she has
authority on her head due to the angels; is it proper for a woman to pray
to God uncovered?; her hair is given her for a covering (11:5b-6, 10, 13,
15b). These recurring asides on the women's conduct show that Paul
begins each statement of equivalence with what he expects of the men in
order to legitimate a corresponding duty of the women — a duty he stresses
in the following comment. What he expects of the women appears to be
"in line" with what is just stated and widely accepted for the men. The
repetition of equivalent statements suggests that the women whose conduct Paul wants to change are susceptible to an argument from justice.
Perhaps Paul knows that the women who prophesy uncovered are advocates or practitioners of a form of justice in the sexual distribution of
worship roles.

Argument from Genesis Dissociating
Shame from Honor and Human from Divine

The argument from shame has a key role in Paul's effort to persuade
the women prophets to cover their heads. First introduced in Paul's parallel
statements about how men and women shame their heads, it is intensified
for women by a shocking aside, "This is one and the same as shaving her
head." The following challenge to the woman to cut her hair is replaced by
what seems to them a reasonable concession, that she cover her head. To
understand these lines it is less important to determine why a woman's having short hair was considered shameful in Roman Greece[3] — whether

because short hair was the mark of slaves or prostitutes or women living like men—than it is to see how Paul uses what he considers to be an unthinkable alternative to appear flexible without giving anything away. His expectation that his challenge will be shocking shows that the women he wants to persuade are not social outcasts with no pretentions of honor but consider themselves worthy of respect in the community.

Paul turns to his other major rationale for head covering by alluding to the Genesis creation story: "For a man ought not to cover his head since he is God's image and glory, whereas the woman is a man's glory" (11:7). Paul profits from the authority of Genesis 1:27 on creation in God's image, but he does not quote it. This would involve using a Greek term with generic implications for the human being created in God's image rather than his term that means "the male." And a full quote would end inclusively, "male and female he created them." In fact Paul replaces the biblical narrative of God creating according to God's image with a description of the male as God's image and glory. Whatever credibility Paul receives from this interpretation of Genesis depends on its parallels to other interpretations of that time.

These interpretations differed greatly. Jacob Jervell distinguishes two major kinds of interpretation, an "ethical-anthropological" reading and a "historical-speculative" reading.[4] According to rabbis and other thinkers with "ethical-anthropological" interests, God's image is realized in the ethical choices made by all who know and keep the law. On the whole Paul is less interested in such thinking about human nature in its philosophical, generic sense than he is in figuring out how God's creation could have become this evil history, and what the time of origin can tell about the time of coming restoration. This issue motivates the "historical-speculative" readings of Genesis, both in rabbinical and non-rabbinical Judaism. In this tradition, the dominant motif is the glorious figure of Adam made in God's image to rule the earth as God does the heavens, sometimes pictured as a giant light-being and the semidivine model for the human creation. The hope that this Adam will be reconstituted in the final time is reflected in Paul's Christ, the second Adam, through whom comes life rather than death and who is God's brilliant image shining in our hearts (15:21-22; Rom. 5:12-21; 2 Cor. 4:3-6). This Adam typology often uses Eve to introduce the arrival of sin and the end of primeval glory (2 Cor. 11:3). Paul elsewhere contrasts Adam and Christ generically, Adam as the progenitor of all death and Christ as progenitor of all life, but here Paul contrasts the male who is God's image and glory—the Adamic light-being—and the woman who is man's glory.

Paul draws in Genesis 2 for further support, "For man was not created on woman's account but woman on man's account" (11:8-9). Thus the second creation story, in which God finds no match for man among the animals and makes woman to be bone of his bone and flesh of his flesh, becomes woman's humble tale of origin, leaving the first story about God creating male and female in the divine image as man's epic. Paul does not pursue the second story to name woman as the one leading man into sin but insinuates that her conduct could make man, who is her head, fall into shame.[5]

Paul develops his differentiated view of male and female shame by extending his description of man's creation to be God's image by calling him also God's glory. The word *glory* here comes from a tenuous translation of the last word in Genesis 1:26, "Then God said 'Let us make Adam (earth-one) in our image, after our likeness.'" These synonyms in the Hebrew text mean that this creation will be fashioned after God, as is a copy or imitation. But changes begin to happen when the Hebrew Scriptures are translated into Greek. A third word also normally translated into Greek as "likeness" is translated "glory" when referring to God.[6] Before Paul's time God's wisdom present at creation is being described as God's glory, as is the human creature God makes.[7]

Paul is not using "glory" to mean "copy" nor even "splendor" so much as "honor" in contrast to shame. If a woman is the glory of a man, her presence reflects honor on him and also makes the man vulnerable to shame through her. In the Jerusalem Talmud a story is told of Rabbi Jose the Galilean who was advised to divorce his wife because "she is not your glory."[8] If Paul knew this usage he may have applied what was used traditionally in Aramaic-speaking Roman Palestine to make a wife responsible for her husband's honor to make the women of Corinth's church responsible for the honor of its men.[9]

The argument from shame and what is written do not make complete sense here apart from Paul's underlying dissociation of human from divine. In Paul's definition of "head" the male has been linked with Christ and thereby with God, whereas the female has been linked with man. Then the attention shifts from the greater in each pair as head of the lesser, to the lesser as glory of the greater. The woman's uncovered head, taken to be the glory of man, is not allowed to compete for priority with man's uncovered head, which is the glory of God. The exclusive right of God to glory is the foundation of Paul's theology, so no other argument is more authoritative to him than the dissociation of human from divine. The assumption is that people seek their own glory at the expense of the glory of God. It follows that those who give up their own boast and share Christ's shame and suffering are promised to share in God's glory. This is realized in advance by the free gift of God's spirit that redounds to God's glory through human praise of God.[10]

Worship is a magnifying of God's glory. Therefore Paul is able to intensify his appeal to the dissociation of God's glory from all human competition when speaking of prayer and prophecy. Supported by his interpretation of Genesis 1 and 2 and popular assumptions about honor and shame, Paul argues that an uncovered woman leading in worship disrupts or dishonors the glory of God because she represents man's glory at the time and place where God alone is to be glorified.[11] Only the man, whose head represents Christ's glory, is to be uncovered in this setting.

The next cryptic sentence must be interpreted in this context: "Therefore the woman ought to have authority on her head on account of the angels." The phrase "the woman ought to" signals, by repeating the earlier "the man ought to" (11:7), an argument from justice. Here the disparity in what men and women ought to do because they have each been defined as the glory of a different "head" is disguised by their equivalence of responsibility. The logic is that of an enthymeme, a syllogism with one premise unspoken. Assuming the major premise that the head always exhibits glory in worship, the argument in the man's case proceeds from conclusion (a man ought not to cover his head) back to minor premise (being God's image and glory), whereas in the woman's case it proceeds from minor premise (but the woman is a man's glory) to conclusion (therefore the woman ought to have authority on the head). This comparison between men who ought not cover their heads and women who ought to have "authority on the head" presses toward a reading of "authority" as "cover." But why should a cover over a woman's head in worship to show that her head is not God's glory be described as the woman having authority in direct opposition to the lexical meaning of the term "authority"? Is Paul conceding on principle a claim by women to have "authority on the head" by challenging them not to use it? This difficult question will be returned to when reviewing all of Paul's and the Corinthians' authority claims in these chapters of 1 Corinthians.

The reference to the angels may be a fruitful lead. Why might a woman need "authority on her head on account of the angels"? In one possible reading these angels are the "sons of God" in Genesis 6:1-6, called "angels" in the retelling of 1 Enoch 6–16, who brought on God's retribution of the flood by marrying women and producing a race of giants. But Paul gives no other hint that woman's covering is meant as a protection from an angelic sexual attack. According to a second view, more widespread in Paul's contemporary Judaism, the angels are God's worshipers. They provide a permanent court for God, less for judicial consultation than to give God glory eternally. From this background come stories about the angels worshiping Adam when he is created because he reflects God's glory. God commands this worship in the Adam legends, but certain rabbis say that God puts Adam to sleep to expose his humanity and stop the angels' worship.[12]

If angels are to worship God, Paul may be arguing that woman must be covered to keep the heavenly host from a misplaced worship of man whose glory she reflects. This would mean Paul's demand that women have "authority on the head because of the angels" is not an added threat of a heavenly sexual attack on women, but strengthens Paul's underlying argument dissociating human from divine. The danger is not only that human males will be drawn away from the praise of God's glory toward their own glory reflected in women but even the angels will be enticed to defect. Sexual implications may not be completely absent, but Paul is more concerned with the unthinkable thought of mutiny in God's heavenly host than with angelic rape.

If Paul's arguments from Scripture and shame serve his dissociation of human from divine, then the whole edifice depends on the adequacy of the conflict model to interpret the relation of the divine and human. Is Paul's assumption that God's glory is under mortal threat from human claims to glory convincing? In this passage it is males who compete with God for glory, neglecting their intended function to be God's glory and cultivating their own glory as reflected in women. Woman is interpreted as a factor in the problem that man has with God, or God with man. It is because man experiences her as his own glory that Paul expects her to cover her head in worship. According to Paul what higher sanction could there be for the requirement than the defense of God's glory against man's boast?

Implications for the Women of Paul's Arguments from Genesis Dissociating Shame from Honor and Human from Divine

Paul assumes that the Corinthian women who prophesy consider themselves honorable and want to be considered for what they are. Though they prophesy without covering their heads, they do not live like the Cynics on the street to show their scorn for society. Better analogies would be to women in Jewish and Christian literature of the time, such as Aseneth or Thecla, who put aside women's dress or head covering when taking on new religious responsibility.[13]

The difficult task is determining from Paul's argument on Genesis what prophesying uncovered means to these women in Corinth. Does his use of Genesis suggest a contrary use of Genesis by them? Paul's collage of Genesis texts does not need to be explained as his side of an exegetical debate; witness the five stories of Israel's wilderness wandering in the previous chapter that warn the Corinthians against idolatry. But if it can be shown that Paul is trying to replace a certain Genesis interpretation in Corinth, these prophesying women can be understood in terms of their own exegetical rationale for not covering their heads.

There are indirect but significant signs that the Corinthians are appealing to tradition. If women prayed and prophesied uncovered because the custom of covering their heads was strange, or inconvenient, or seemed inappropriate in their home-based gatherings, it would have been counterproductive for Paul to make a *cause célèbre* of it. An argument from modesty, community benefit, or public conduct would suffice. The theological weight of Paul's argument makes it likely that the women who prophesied uncovered chose to do so for some purpose with social consequences and theological justification. This would explain an appeal to Christian tradition, if not necessarily to written Scripture.

The abbreviation and obscurity of Paul's arguments also suggest that he is not introducing certain language for the first time. If Paul's letter does not provide sufficient data to understand what he means by "having authority on her head" and "due to the angels" and he does not develop his thought further, these phrases probably are known in Corinth. So "the woman is the glory of a man," could be contesting some other interpretation of women's glory in Corinth.

I have already mentioned Paul's difficulties in using the Genesis passage on creation in God's image with its generic reference to "human being" and "male and female." Paul's choice of this text to make his point could have been constrained by a different use of this sentence in Corinth.

A more unmistakable clue that Paul is responding to a different interpretation of Genesis by Corinthian women prophets comes from comparing the way Paul interprets God's image here and elsewhere in his letters. This text breaks from Paul's consistent view that it is Christ who is God's image and that human beings see, reflect, or are transformed into the image of God in Christ.[14] In this situation it appears that Paul has reason to avoid speaking of all believers as persons reflecting God's image in Christ. Similarly, he delays human identification with Christ until the future in his defense of resurrection of the dead, distinguishing the earthly Adam or first human being whose image of dirt they have borne from the last, life-giving Adam or second human being whose heavenly image they will bear (15:45-49). This leaves the believer looking backward to Adam and forward toward the triumphant Christ with no present identity. It is possible that Paul is warding off a Corinthian view that the believer already embodies God's image in Christ. If so, this claim is most likely being made by women who prophesy, since Paul identifies men but not women who prophesy as God's image and glory.

It is this claim to be in God's image through Christ that is found in Galatians 3:27-28; 1 Corinthians 12:12-13, and Colossians 3:9-11. Because these three passages share a common structure, describe the new state of the baptized in Christ, and function in Paul's context as accepted traditions that can validate his arguments, they are widely thought to represent a pre-Pauline baptismal confession.[15] The fact that the three texts are not identical is standard for traditions that originate and spread orally.

Gal. 3:27-28

For those of you baptized into Christ have put on Christ.	There is neither Jew nor Greek;	there is neither slave nor free,	there is not male and female,	for all of you are one in Christ Jesus.

1 Cor. 12:13

For in one spirit we were all baptized into one body,	whether Jews or Greeks,	whether slaves or free,		and we were all given one spirit to drink.

Col. 3:10-11

. . . having put on the new human being that is remade for knowledge according to the image of the one who created him,	where there is not Greek and Jew, not cir-cumcision and uncir-cumcision, barbarian, Scythian,	slave, free,		but Christ is all and in all.

Apparently the confession had three parts: an opening statement in the first- or second-person plural affirming the baptism into Christ as putting on a garment, being integrated into one body, or putting on the new human being in God's image; second, a series of pairs representing basic social divisions that do not exist in the new identity; and finally a closing claim to all be one in Christ. The lack of reference to male and female in two of our three examples, along with its final position among the pairs, show that its place in the confession was somewhat tenuous. But this does not mean it was a secondary elaboration. Paul's Galatian letter that includes it focuses on Jew-Gentile issues and in that context he had no reason to add "male and female," though he could have promoted the Jew-Greek pair to first place. The fact that he uses words for "male" and "female" that apply to all species rather than his standard terms for human beings of each sex suggests that he is quoting the phrase in the Greek (LXX) text of Genesis 1:27, "male and female he made them." This is confirmed by the conjunction "and" between these words that breaks the "neither-nor" pattern Paul just used in speaking of Jew and Greek and slave and free.

That the pre-Pauline baptismal confession was a reworking of the Genesis story is put beyond doubt by a second quotation found in Colossians. It begins: "having put on the new human being that is new-made for knowledge 'according to an image' of the one who created him." (Here the final word, "him," refers to the "human being," which can have a generic meaning.) "According to an image" is an exact rendering of the prepositional phrase of Genesis 1:27 as it read in Greek.

A final sign that the baptismal confession reformulates Genesis is the way it mirrors Genesis 1:27-28 and 5:1b-2.

Gen. 1:27-28

And God made the human being; according to the image of God he made him;	male and female he made them.	And God blessed them saying, "Grow and multiply and fill the earth . . ."

Gen. 5:1b-2

In the day God made Adam he made him according to the image of God;	male and female he made them.	And he blessed them and named their name Adam on the day he made them.

Again, the first unit states the new identity in God's image, the second defines it in terms of the pair "male and female," and the third is a blessing and reaffirmation of their unity or common task. There is no direct quotation from this third unit found in the third unit of the Christian baptismal confession, but there is a parallel recapitulation of the first unit in an inclusive sense.

This evidence that the early Christian baptismal confession developed from Genesis as a new creation story clarifies its use by Paul and possible use by the Corinthian women prophets. For the women prophets it was important that the only pair mentioned in the Genesis sayings is "male and female." This must have been the initial pair Christians used and the model for the other pairs. Their confession of a new creation indicates a concern to state how male and female are related in the same way to Christ as God's image. This would make it congenial to the same people in Corinth whom Paul addresses repeatedly with the argument from justice.

In one way this confession of the new creation in Christ does not reaffirm but reverses the old creation story. In the place of "male and female he made them" appears "*not* male and female." Research has uncovered interesting speculation in Jewish and later Christian circles about an androgynous first creation.[16] Yet it may be overinterpreting this text to read that God's image in Christ, which is not male and female, is both male and female. Nearer clues to what could be meant by an identity that is not male and female can be found in Paul's usage. He, or the tradition before him, reduplicates "not male and female" in "neither Jew nor

Greek" and "neither slave nor free," indicating that "not male and female" was understood to mean overcoming in Christ a division cutting across the whole of society, which privileged one group at the expense of another (as Jews also understood the distinction between Jew and Greek).

Another clue is suggested in Paul's exegesis of the Genesis text in terms of the male being God's image and glory and the female the glory of the man (11:7). "*Not* male and female" may be a Christian reaction against a common Genesis interpretation that legitimates separate roles and a privileged position for the male. The newly baptized Christians, being untrained in exegesis of texts, may be less prone to reinterpret Genesis inclusively than they are to announce that the new creation in Christ, God's image, is *not* like the old creation. If God created the male first and then the female for the man, now in Christ, God creates an identity not male and female. The language is drawn from the creation story, but the meaning is not a new understanding of God's first act. Rather it is an announcement of God's new act to create in Christ, God's image, a new reality lacking the privilege of male over female.

Paul's changing use of the baptismal confession may be additional evidence of its meaning in Corinth. In Galatians, Paul quotes it to prove that all believers are Abraham's seed. Therefore he begins, "there is neither Jew nor Greek," and the final "not male and female" simply completes the citation (Gal. 3:1—5:12). But when he uses the confession to prove the variety of gifts in one body (1 Cor. 12:12-13), he omits "not male and female." This might be attributed to extraneous causes, such as the rhythm of the sentence, had not Paul in just the previous chapter abandoned his usual proclamation of Christ as God's image and set up the male as God's image and glory in explicit contrast to the woman as man's glory. This reverses the baptismal confession of a new creation "not male and female" and indicates that the later omission of this phrase has substantive meaning. He does not state explicitly that the woman is man's image rather than God's image, but he accomplishes the same thing, within the limits of the exegetical tradition, by calling her the man's glory.

Three aspects of the Corinthian women are reflected in Paul's arguments. In the first place, the impact of their knowing themselves to be a new creation in Christ, made in God's image "not male and female," has brought on Paul's narrowing of God's image to the male. They are not defined by how others are reading what is written in Genesis, but by the creation that has happened to them. Rejecting all social privilege and social disadvantage, they take on a single common identity in Christ and practice gifts of prayer and prophecy without regard to gender. The fact that Paul thinks it is necessary to redefine their identity in order to get the women prophets to cover their heads suggests that they have set aside a traditional covering because they are a new creation in God's image.

Second, Paul's argument dissociating shame from honor indicates that their conduct is no longer determined by the threat of shaming themselves and their husbands. Now their honor is based on their roles among those who have put on Christ. Seeing themselves recreated in Christ, God's image, and demonstrating God's glory, they would experience as shame anything that blocks, obscures, or denies this reality.

Finally, Paul's argument dissociating human glory from God's glory would surely be rejected by them as Paul introduces it, that is, in the demand for woman as man's glory to cover herself in order not to compete with God's glory reflected in man. But would they also reject this argument on principle? It presupposes that there is a war between humanity and God for glory, a revolt against God that will finally be put down to the praise of God's glory. They could take such an argument and turn it against those who deny God's glory in them. Yet the two functions we know they carried, prayer and prophecy, are not good weapons in a military scenario. When Paul intimates that their uncovered heads in prophecy might lead to mutiny against God among the angelic host, it does not prove that they see themselves as a feminine phalanx fighting among the heavenly host in defense of God's glory.

Their different view of human and divine is suggested in other Jewish traditions about the angels' role in creation. To the rabbis the greatest threat in the creation story was not that humanity seems to be made in the plural as male and female, but that God seems to be plural, "Let us make Adam (earth-one) in our image. . . ." To assure God's perfect uniqueness they brought angels on the scene whom God could consult in the plural. Then the equal threat that the one created could be like God was met by saying that the human being is like the angels. This led to various elaborations, the most prominent being that God's creature is like the angels in stature, in speech, in knowledge, and in the ability to see God.[17] Of course all this is a euphemism for people being made in God's image and like God, and as the stories grew and moved beyond rabbinical circles these elements were developed positively.

It is possible that the Corinthian prophets spoke of themselves as like the angels in speech or knowledge. Paul's only other reference to angels in the context of prophecy appears soon after chapter 11 in a critique of those who "speak in the tongues of humans and of angels but have no love" (13:1). Since the angels were sometimes pictured as mediators of the divine word, those who prophesied among the new creation might claim to understand, see, and speak like angels. To Paul the angels were potential mutineers against God's exclusive glory, so that "woman should have authority on her head because of the angels" who might turn to man's glory in her. But to the Corinthians the angels represented consummate knowing and speaking across a porous boundary between human and divine. Without fear of shame women may have claimed "authority on the head due to the angels" when they prayed and prophesied uncovered to glorify God in the company of the heavenly host.

Arguments from Justice, Shame, and Common Practice

Paul ends his argument from Scripture with what sounds like a concession or retraction of what he has said, "But woman is not independent of man in the Lord nor man of woman, for as the woman comes from the man so the man comes through the woman, and all things come from God" (11:11-12). This is an appeal to justice or equivalence in sexual roles. But it concedes less than appears. The interdependence is based on sexual differentiation: woman was made from man's rib and man is born from woman. This claim that woman's power is through birth does not yet say that salvation comes to her through childbearing (1 Tim. 2:15; 5:14), but it is a shift away from the identity in Christ that is "not male and female," particularly for any woman in Corinth practicing this identity through sexual abstinence. Paul's final phrase, "all things come from God," legitimates creation through the male and birth through the female as co-channels of divine life. The fact that this entire concession is introduced by the strong adversative, "but," reveals that up to this point Paul's statement on the head covering largely shows the *in*equivalence of the sexes—in spite of his two previous uses of equivalent language (11:3, 4-5). If any hearers are persuaded by Paul's talk of interdependence in the Lord that woman's role in childbirth can right the balance and make the head covering that he demands a sign of equivalence, this digression has been worth any momentum he lost.

Paul concludes his argument for women's head covering with three brief challenges: the first two return again to the dissociation of shame from honor. He puts it before them squarely, "Judge for yourselves, is it proper for a woman to pray to God uncovered?" Paul's role change—from bearer of authoritative tradition to sober friend—is disarming. Asking this question indicates that he is sure the Corinthians are used to seeing women pray with covered heads. If so, the women's uncovered heads are not standard Greek practice but are a statement demonstrating an understanding of their relation to God.

Paul's second question, asking if nature does not teach that long hair shames men and honors women, is in the same vein. A possible misreading that honorable hair should not be covered leads Paul to an awkward addendum, "for long hair is given her as a covering." The argument is by analogy: that nature gives a woman long hair as a covering teaching a woman to put something on her head as a covering. Presupposing that the women consider long hair an honor, Paul tries to draw them from this to considering its covering an honor. The opposite applies to men. The strength of these arguments in a society where assumptions about shame and honor are entrenched should not be underestimated.

Paul's two rhetorical questions show that the Corinthian women prophets function within an honor-oriented culture, so the fact that they have set aside the expected head covering indicates that they have some new basis of honor. The confession of the new creation suggests that their honor is no longer sought within the family unit, where woman's sexual vulnerability represents the threat of shame,[18] but within Christ, the image of God whom they have "put on."

Paul's final challenge dissociates their confidence as mere thought from the solid reality of his custom and church practice. "If any think they want to make an issue of this, we have no such custom, nor do the churches of God." The debate, he says, is closed. At the same time, his use of the present tense in the conditional phrase shows that he expects opposition. Women who do not cover their heads are the prime candidates to contend with him, but he does not choose a strictly feminine case to refer to those who "think they want to make an issue of this." This reflects Paul's practice of keeping his address broad, perhaps with the hope of generating the disciplines he wants within the whole Corinthian community as some put pressure on others. The phrase I translate "if any think they want to make an issue of this" could be read "if any think they can win out on this" or, more literally, "if any think they are victory-lovers." This suggests Paul could be picking up a positive self-designation of the women and using it ironically.[19] This is supported by the fact that in every other instance of this kind in this letter where Paul dissociates thought and reality, his challenges take up what seem to be their positive self-designations: they "think they are wise," "think they know something," "think they stand," and "think they are prophets or spiritual people" (see chapter 2, Argument Dissociating Thought from Reality). If the women who prophesy see themselves as "issue-makers," "victory-lovers," or "contenders," this is further indication that their heads are uncovered due to some assertion or claim, not simply by custom. The designation also suggests the possibility that they have overcome some opposition to their uncovered prayer and prophecy, that they found the contention a positive experience, and that they welcome other challenges as a chance to prove their gifts.

As in Paul's parallel arguments dissociating thought from reality, his rhetorical challenge turns into a rebuke in the name of reality, "we have no such custom, nor do the churches of God" (11:16). The custom referred to is the women's praying and prophesying without covering their heads. "We" stands for Paul who also appears in two other appeals to church practice (4:7; 7:17), which may therefore be appeals to practice in the churches he has founded. Though Paul does not propose any set custom or tradition — there may be none — he excludes their practice as unique. Perhaps someone like Apollos brought it from elsewhere. On the other hand, Acts has

women find new basis of honor [handwritten marginal note]

Apollos arriving suddenly in Ephesus "knowing only the baptism of John," and being instructed by Priscilla and Aquila, themselves recently of Corinth, before going on to Corinth himself (Acts 18:24-28). So the practice may have started in Corinth. That Corinth's women have been especially innovative might be gathered from the fact that Paul's last three appeals to church practice against the Corinthians explicitly mention women's conduct in sexual life, dress, and speech (7:17; 11:16; 14:34).

Social and Theological Implications for the Corinthian Women Prophets of Paul's Arguments on Head Covering

This passage indicates that in this community the important functions of prayer and prophecy are carried out by women as well as men and without any distinctive sign in their dress indicating a subordinate status. In spite of Paul's arguments from definition and divine subordination; from justice, Scripture, and church practice; and by dissociating shame from honor and human from divine, Paul still expects opposition to head covering. Apparently a great deal rides on this custom. Not only must the functions of prayer and prophecy be close to the personal identity of these individual women, but their social identity must also be threatened in order for them to oppose Paul as he anticipates. The covering may not be a physical block, such as a facial veil that would make the woman's speech-projection difficult, but it is at least a symbolic block that limits what others expect and what she sees to be her calling. When the woman decides not to cover herself against what "nature" and "custom" consider honorable, she is probably rejecting the roles associated with head covering that social history has yet to define precisely (see Appendix 8). It appears likely that public head covering is associated with women's subordination to males within traditional structures of marriage and family, whereas prophesying and praying with bare head signifies the independence of a woman consecrated to God. Paul's forceful move against opposition can only be seen as an effort to restrict her role in the community. Therefore it provides a measure of her considerable social power.

The ideological or theological position of the women in Corinth is also apparent in the practice of prophesying with heads uncovered. It puts them in direct contention with Paul's statement that God's glory reflected in the male, God's image, meets competition from the glory reflected in the female who is created from man and for man. What Paul experiences as a conflict between giving God glory in worship and receiving his own glory in woman's exposed head is apparently not experienced by the women. They lack the male viewpoint of themselves as originally created to be God's image or of the other sex as created to glorify them. Women may have been trained to see their original identity in a reversed form of Paul's view, with another sex as the ideal figure and themselves glorifying that figure. But Paul shows that these women claim to have undergone a new creation in no way like the old, and in "putting on Christ" to have been remade in the image and glory of God.

Their confession can be reconstructed in broad outline from Pauline references to an early Christian confession of a new creation (Gal. 3:27-28; 1 Cor. 12:13; Col. 3:10-11; cf. Gen. 1:26-27; 5:1b-2): We have put on Christ, the new human being remade in the image of the Creator, where there is no male and female, but Christ, all things and in all. This common identity of the Christ-image becomes expressed in praying and prophesying, widespread gifts practiced by both men and women but prominent among women in some way that Paul tries to restrict in his three-tiered definition of headship. It is in speaking that the Corinthian women prophets realize their full integration into Christ, God's image. They give God glory in praises and blessings and express God's glory for themselves and others in prophecy. This prayer and prophecy may be seen as a process of feeding and being fed, of circulation, aeration, or exercise of the new creation. Its purpose would be magnifying God's glory, not over against the glory of man, but as an end in itself experienced positively as life in Christ, God's image.

Glory and Idolatry:
1 Corinthians 11:2-16 in Context

The location of Paul's argument on head covering in a section on eating and idolatry appears arbitrary. After Paul speaks about sacrificed food he seems to go on to another issue of order in community worship. Yet it has been shown that what Paul says about the Lord's meal immediately after this passage is not simply a rule for orderly worship but a warning about the life-threatening danger of idolatry from not "discerning the body" and from eating what is "not the Lord's meal" as though it were. The question is how Paul's argument that women prophets be covered fits into a warning on idolatry. After responding to the topic of sacrificed food from their letter by appeal to his own positive example and Israel's negative example of self-restriction (9:1 — 11:1), Paul introduces two issues that they did not write about—women's head covering and the Lord's meal—and appeals beyond himself and Israel to the higher authority of Christ whose model he reflects and whose traditions he transmits (11:2-34). First he cites a new tradition in which Christ's subordination to God confirms man's to Christ and woman's to man. Second he cites a familiar tradition in which Jesus models ultimate self-restriction: "This is my body for you" (11:24). The first is offered with praise as an addendum to traditions they have kept, the second with blame as a tradition they have not kept. But both appeal beyond Paul's model to the Christ whom Paul models, both depict Christ in terms of his subordination, and both imply that not to imitate this Christ is to violate God.

Far from starting a new topic, Paul has continued his theme of the strong falling into idolatry, adroitly raising the stakes by a direct appeal to Christ. This brings home to the community the charge of idolatry in the form of a christologically based attack against those practices where the Corinthians are supremely confident—their unrestricted participation in prophecy and prayer and their joyful feasts.

On women's head covering Paul argues from definition, justice, and shame; the threat of violation against God appears only when he dissociates divine and human by appeal to what is written about God's image. Man as God's image and glory represents the divine side of the conflict, and woman as man's glory represents the human contention against God. The result is that woman must be covered to ensure the exclusive praise of God in worship. Instead of stressing God's threat of death in retribution, Paul praises them for having received everything he has passed on to them. He might have brought out the benefit of women's head covering to other group members but he does not, perhaps because it would not be credible or because it would have to be based on the weakness of the men. Having claimed for man the position of strength as woman's "head," Paul cannot integrate an argument from community benefit with his threat that God could be violated as he does in connection with the meal. Instead he intensifies the warning of idolatry by raising the specter of the worship of man in the angelic courts of God. Here Paul's argument seems to be predicated on a male experience of tension between self-glory associated with woman's uncovered head and God's glory associated with undistracted worship—an experience angels would unlikely share, let alone women, but one that sets his expectation for both.

The integral place of this text is further supported by noting how Paul's general understanding of authority helps to explain why he thinks a woman needs "authority on the head because of the angels" (11:10). In these chapters Paul uses "authority" to signify a recognized right or liberty that nevertheless ought not to be exercised, possibly in response to their claim that "all things are authorized" (6:12; 10:23). Paul and the Corinthians know that idols do not exist, but he warns them, "Watch out that your authority does not itself become a stumbling block to the weak" (8:9). Likewise he seeks recognition of his own right to their support in order to conclude "but we have not made use of this authority" (9:4, 12). And he advises them, "All things are authorized, but not all things are constructive. Seek not your own advantage but that of the other" (10:23b-24).

Could Paul be using his paradoxical view of authority as a privilege that one denies oneself when he tells the prophesying women that as the man's glory they "ought to have authority on the head on account of the angels," whereas men as God's image and glory ought to be uncovered? This does not seem to be indicated because Paul has not conceded that they have authority to be uncovered and then asked them not to use it. But it is possible that Paul could express his call to sacrifice as a true paradox: your self-covering is authority.[20]

Such rhetoric might be used if Paul is dealing with an authority claim by Corinthian women that he does not want to recognize directly, not even as a valid principle that they should not practice. If the women in Corinth are claiming authority to prophesy uncovered because everyone in God's image shares in worship with the angels, Paul could incorporate their entire claim "to have authority on the head because of the angels" into an argument requiring that man's glory in them be covered. If so, the fact that their own authority is being denied rather than freely set aside is disguised, and Paul's rhetoric co-opts the power of their positive claim "to have authority on the head on acount of the angels" against its intended purpose and practice.

Equally significant in understanding what Paul says about head covering is Paul's view of participation in the context of idolatry. Paul quickly denies any reality of idols and daemons. But there is one competitor left for God—the human being. Generally, Paul seems to use the word "human being" generically. The self-interest of the Israelites and those who go ahead with their own meals is pitted against the worship of God. In the case of the Lord's meal, respect for the Lord's body is identified with respect for the communal body, which includes all participants in Christ.

But in the case of the women's head covering, not only is the argument from community benefit not used to integrate all people into God's glory, but the threat to God's glory is located in woman as the glory of the male. She is the locus of the human offense against God, the aspect of the generic human that threatens to be a glory independent of God. Not by having any glory of her own that could threaten God, but by being called the glory of the man, woman is put in the position of bearing the restriction appropriate to human glory in Paul's theology of cosmic competition. She is not freed in Christ from this conflict because participation in Christ is held to be exclusive, not inclusive of the participation in self, which she represents on behalf of the male. Man requires that she cover herself because he takes her participation with full authority to be an idolatrous boasting of his glory against God.

Yet there is no indication that the conflict is internal within her. Having no glory of her own, she could glorify God without distraction. The conflict is in the male, between God's glory and his own glory, which he sees embodied in the woman. It is because of his participation in worship that Paul wants the woman's participation to be covered. There are no indications that the Corinthian woman prophet shares Paul's theology of cosmic competition. If she does not, she understands her participation as the glorification of God, not the assertion of the human glory that belongs to the male against God's glory. Those females and males who take issue with Paul will denounce his added tradition with its hierarchy of heads because it denies women's direct participation in Christ and blasphemes God's glory in the woman by calling it human glory belonging to the male.

Had Paul called for women prophets' head covering on the basis of custom alone, implications for these women would reveal their customs. But Paul takes up this issue in the context of warnings of idolatry and appeals to Christ as head of man and to God as head of Christ to sanction the headship of man over woman. This makes it possible to learn something about their Christology and theology. If they did not already understand Christ as the middle figure between God and the believer they would hardly understand Paul's appeal. The women prophets' mediating function for the people through prayer and prophecy suggests that they may understand Christ as mediator of God, the expression of God's initiative to people, and channel of human communication with God. Because their rejection of the male as image of God takes place in a debate about the meaning of the baptismal new creation, they are almost surely claiming with the pre-Pauline church of the Hellenistic cities an incorporation into Christ, God's image who is not male and female. This is lived out in at least three concrete social acts: eating at the same table with all people without fear of idolatry against the one God; prophesying uncovered whatever God says to the people; and praying uncovered whatever the people say to God. In this way they demonstrate that God is the new creator who sets one table for all people and remains in continual communication with them. Christ is God's image, the form of this new creation as a human identity that is not male and female. In speaking for God and to God they are full and authoritative participants in this new creation.

7 | Spiritual Women Speak for God and to God: 1 Corinthians 12–14

THIS UNIT OF PAUL'S LETTER maintains a single focus on the spiritual, from its opening line, "Concerning the spiritual, brethren, I do not want you to be ignorant," to its closing, "If any consider themselves to be prophets or spiritual, let them recognize the things I am writing you as the Lord's command" (12:1; 14:37). This recapitulation shows Paul is probably responding to a Corinthian letter topic concerning "spiritual people" he associates with prophets, rather than to a discussion of "spiritual things," which would also be grammatically possible. Yet midway in this section of the letter Paul directs his readers to seek spiritual things, above all to prophesy (14:1; cf 12:31). He assumes that his readers know that the spirit is God's and that its revealing makes spiritual people and the spiritual things they know and speak. As he says earlier, "We evaluate spiritual things among the spiritual" (2:13).

Corinth's Christian women prophets are among the spiritual Paul discusses in this section. Having been "baptized in one spirit into one body" (12:13), women now "pray and prophesy" (11:5), and in this argument about the spiritual Paul intends to shape their self-understanding, priorities, and behavior. Therefore, the way he argues to persuade them can be used to infer these women prophets' conduct and viewpoint to the best of Paul's knowledge. He may be persuading others as well—spiritual people who are not women and perhaps spiritual women who are not prophets—but his last and longest argument dissociating prophecy and tongues shows that he has people with these gifts in mind.

Their Common Identity or Paul's Differentiation of Gifts

Paul's first words in this section, "concerning the spiritual," reiterate the way he elsewhere refers to the Corinthians' letter to him (7:1, 25; 8:1; 12:1; 16:1, 12). In light of his earlier treatment of their letter topics, we anticipate that Paul is not answering questions addressed to an authority but questioning answers authoritatively delivered. In his opening words, "I don't want you to be ignorant" (12:1), Paul claims the rhetorical advantage of an instructor of the ignorant, as if they were waiting on his words. But to continue he must concede their knowledge. They know the great contrast between their present gifts of divine speech and their previous life at the mercy of gods who could not speak. On this basis Paul wants to make them understand that as sure as God's spirit cannot curse Jesus, no one can acclaim Jesus as Lord except in the spirit. Far from implying that Corinth's prophets are cursing Jesus, Paul uses the absurdity of this to secure them with all believers in a single confession. To get their assent he presents "Jesus is Lord," not as a required formula, but as an acclamation of the spirit. Yet his tight identification of the single phrase "Jesus is Lord" with the spirit of God suggests that the Corinthians' attention is on the freedom and creativity of the spirit in them, not this lowest common denominator—in which the spirit is confined to words of uniformity and subordination.

Yet Paul is not interested in pressing the phrase, and, confident that they do not oppose the single spirit, he launches into his major argument for the diversity of this spirit's functions. Three times he stresses the word "varieties" or "distinctions" of gifts, always tracing them to "the same" spirit/Lord/God active in many ways. Four times he repeats "to one this, to another that." His extended allegory of the interdependent parts of the body follows, explicated under the heading, "for the body is not one part but many" (12:14). The ultimate sanction given for this diversity is the divine will, explicitly appealed to three times as Paul summarizes each section of his argument: "the spirit distributing to each as it wills"; "God placed the parts, each single one of them, in the body as he wanted"; and "God placed these in the church, first apostles, second prophets, third teachers . . ." (12:11, 18, 28). In the last case the distinctions become a ranked list ending with tongues and their interpretation and with a call to "seek the greater gifts" (12:29-31).

It has been common to assume that Paul here extends his opening affirmation of unity. Yet his arguments are not for unity but diversity and develop a theological rationalization for division of labor and interdependence in the Corinthian community. Unity is also possible through common expectations and roles, especially within small groups of people who differentiate themselves more from outsiders than from each other. Because Paul's argument here is developed at length and with such care, it is probable that the Corinthians practice some form of this contrary option, taking themselves as "the spiritual" in a comprehensive sense, each being filled by God's spirit to speak divine mysteries in prophecy, prayer, wisdom, knowledge, revelation, and tongues. Paul's thanksgiving at the beginning of the letter, when he wants to affirm their best self-image, mentions no division of gifts, "You are rich in him in every way, in every act of speech and all knowledge . . . so that you lack no divine gift" (1:5, 7). The fact that Paul's language for these gifts remains flexible throughout the letter, defying schematization, indicates blurred rather than sharp lines in the common understanding of gifts. Each person in Corinth is probably not identified with a single gift and may not even be conscious of cultivating a variety of different gifts. Without a sharp definition of gifts, the Corinthians had no basis for thinking of certain persons having spiritual potential that others lack. Spirit-endowment was widely held to be the baptismal claim of every believer and its cultivation everyone's challenge.

This would not have excluded a competitiveness in the demonstration of the spirit, as in Paul's charge that they are "puffed up one over the other against each other" (4:6). Where each person expects to have the exercise of all gifts, people may not only be more ready to cultivate new gifts but also more prone to contest among themselves. Mary Douglas predicts this for societies where leadership is not ascribed in advance but achieved by some people exercising more effectively options open to all.[1] Although Paul argues against competitiveness by appealing to the single divine source of the spirit and to the common good for which different gifts are given to different members of the whole (3:3-5; 4:6-7; 12:14-27), the demonstration of gifts may be seen as highly beneficial in the open setting of Corinth's church. Here assertion is expected of participants and not taken as a revolt against given roles.

The linchpin in Paul's argument for diversity is his appeal to the baptismal confession midway in his argument: "For in one spirit we were all baptized into one body — whether Jews or Greeks, whether slaves or free — and we were all given one spirit to drink" (12:13). From their experience of this integration of different people in Christ Paul derives that "the body is not one part but many" (12:12-27). Paul has adapted the baptismal confession in two ways to make this point.

Most obvious is dropping any reference to male and female. Although this pair is also absent in Colossians 3:11, the phrase "male and female" cannot be seen as an arbitrary addition in Galatians alone, not only because it is not motivated by that context but because all indications are that the baptismal confession originated by a reworking of the Genesis claim that humanity is created in God's image "male and female" (Gen. 1:27-28; 5:1b-2; see chapter 6). Paul's freedom in Galatians to place the Jew/Greek and slave/free social distinctions before "male and female" and to develop only the first shows how much Paul's interests can influence his use of the baptismal formula. In 1 Corinthians where the omission of "not male and female" does not reflect lack of interest in women and men, it is best explained as Paul's conscious choice in the light of the Corinthian women not to evoke what "not male and female" means to them.[2] My analysis of Paul's argument that women who prophesy should cover their heads has shown that they claim to be a new creation in Christ who is God's image not male and female. Therefore they reject sex-specific practices and designated roles in the community, however complementary to those of others.

In his second adaption of the baptismal statement Paul drops its key negative particles. Whereas in Galatians and Colossians baptism is into Christ who is *not* Jew or Greek, *not* slave or free (Gal. 3:28; Col. 3:11), the Corinthians are called one in Christ *"whether* Jews or Greeks, *whether* slaves or free" (12:13). The social distinctions are not overcome in Christ but are accepted and integrated into Christ. The principle that distinctions between people are for the common good, which Paul has just claimed in connection with the spirit's differential distribution of gifts, is thus carried over to legitimate social distinctions. The extended body metaphor that follows lends itself as much to confirming the interdependence of naturally given as of spiritually acquired functions. This recalls the rule worked out earlier in the letter that all believers stay in the social situation in which they were called (7:17-24; 1:26-29), and could be read to imply that the spirit's gifts are given as appropriate for a person's social station.

Their Common Zeal or
Paul's Zeal for the Common Good

By the end of chapter 12, Paul's differentiation of gifts has allowed him to introduce a hierarachy from the apostle on down. Only on this carefully built foundation can Paul ask the rhetorical questions, "Are all prophets? . . . Do all speak with tongues?" (12:29-30) and control the negative answer that he wants to get. On the basis of this hierarchy of gifts Paul calls everyone who is not an apostle to seek the second highest gift of prophecy.

It is not clear how Paul can call people to seek certain gifts above others, since he has just argued that gifts are distributed "as the spirit wills" or "as God chose" (12:11, 18). The new argument is not consistent with the preceding one but moves toward the same goal. Just as he argued that one spirit gives different gifts to each for the common benefit, he now calls them not to seek inferior gifts but gifts that most benefit the community. His hierarchy of gifts exalting apostleship and prophecy is constructed to draw them toward the common good as he sees it and cannot be rationalized as a reversal of some Corinthian hierarchy favoring speaking in tongues. Yet Paul does try to enlist the Corinthians' zeal for the spiritual in his cause of making distinctions for the common good. His hierarchy of gifts culminates, "But be zealous for the greater gifts" (12:31), which is soon echoed, "Be zealous for spiritual things, especially that you might prophesy" (14:1). Finally he admits that they are already zealous and fits it to his aims, "So you yourselves, since you are zealots of the spirits, seek to build up the church that you may abound" (14:12).

What were they zealous for in Corinth? Paul seems to concede to their desires in one clause in order to get them to go his way in the next, providing clues of what they want: "Each of you when you gather has a song, a teaching, a revelation, a tongue, an interpretation—let all things be done constructively" (14:26). Apparently they are eager to be together where all can be stimulated by what each has to say. Again, "You are all able to prophesy—in turn, so that all may learn and be encouraged" (14:31). The context shows that speaking in turn is Paul's point, theirs being the freedom for all to prophesy. When Paul defends his wisdom at the start of the letter, he similarly claims to have what they recognize to be wisdom—"the depths of God," "the mind of Christ," "discerning spiritual things among the spiritual" (2:10-16)—again reflecting their communal process of stimulating each other in knowing God's spirit as if from within.

The best picture of the kind of zeal exercised in Corinth may be available in Paul's praise of love. The hymn to love seems to disparage all spiritual gifts including prophecy, and therefore not to belong in its present location where Paul has framed it between two calls to seek greater gifts. But love—life for the good of others—is being eulogized as the standard of greatness, and Paul will eventually argue that prophecy best serves this standard. Yet first Paul contrasts the exercise of all gifts to love's taking loss on behalf of others: "Love suffers long, love is kind and not zealous, love does not brag or boast, love is not improper, does not seek her own, does not provoke . . . love bears all things, believes all things, hopes all things, endures all things (13:4-7).

Paul's sharp contrast of this love to the exercise of all spiritual gifts suggests that the Corinthian prophets' highest value may be seen by reversing these verbs. They no longer suffer but zealously pursue a new life, not orienting themselves kindly on others' needs but rejoicing in what the spirit has done in them. They do not seek what others consider proper but provoke others to deal with God's spirit at work among them. Rather than bearing up hopefully and enduring faithfully, they dare to exhibit the spirit's creativity. Striving to embody positive divine forces is not alien to the Greco-Roman world or unique in early Christian theology. If we assume that Paul's position is uncontestable when reading 1 Corinthians 13, this is witness to the traditional authority of this text, the power of Paul's rhetoric, and perhaps to its appropriateness to our social situation. The women prophets of Corinth, on another social trajectory than Paul and with a different experience of Christ, are zealots for God's spirit in a way that seeks to realize a different social practice and theological integrity. Their watchword is probably not "love," which calls for self-sacrifice from a position of advantage, but more likely "spirit" or "wisdom" (14:37; 3:18), signifying a power divinely kindled among once inert people.

Their Integration of Prophecy with Speaking in Tongues or Paul's Dissociation

Paul is rhetorically well placed, coming out of his digression in praise of love, to dissociate prophecy from tongues on the basis that discourse benefiting all is to be preferred over ecstatic speech that benefits oneself. He pursues this dissociation for a full twenty-six verses, extending his argument from the common good by appeals to intelligibility, fruitfulness, maturity, scriptural authority, and community experience (14:1-26). Only his use of Isaiah is not completely clear. Isaiah proves for Paul that tongues are a sign for unbelievers, not meaning that ecstatic speech encourages belief, but that it is a "sign of stumbling" to test and prove unbelief, whereas prophecy induces belief.[3] The extended argument dissociating prophecy from tongues shows that Paul cannot assume that the Corinthians accept this negative function of ecstasy strictly to expose unbelief, nor the corresponding dissociation of tongues from prophecy.

But it is harder to determine how the Corinthians experience prophecy and tongues in an integrated way. The closest integration might be present where prophets move in and out of ecstatic speech in delivering prophecies. This movement into tongues could occur as the climax of prophecy when it reveals "unspeakable speech" (2 Cor. 12:4), or as a final sign confirming to believers that the prophecy is divine.[4] Yet would Paul choose to exalt prophecy as his way to curb ecstatic speech in the Corinthian church if tongues were accepted as the ultimate language of prophecy?

Paul's argument betrays one major distinction between prophecy and tongues that points in a different direction. The verbs Paul uses when referring to tongues — "speaking," "praying," "singing praises," "blessing," and "thanking" (14:2, 4-6, 9, 13-17, 23, 27, 39) — show that it is often described as a language of prayer or hymnic praise to God. So Paul argues that tongues edify oneself but not the church; they are addressed to God rather than to the people (14:2-4, 28). And elsewhere when Paul refers to the Spirit's speech welling up in the believer, he is talking about prayer to God (Gal. 4:6; Rom. 8:26-27). It cannot be assumed that all prayer in Corinth's churches is ecstatic, since certain acclamations of the divine name and some doxologies and hymns of praise would be traditional formulations. But that prayer is prone to become ecstatic speech might explain why Paul mentions praying along with prophesying as the functions for which women's heads are to be covered (11:5a).

If Paul's main argument here is to dissociate prophecy from tongues for the benefit of the church, and if tongues are widely understood as a language of prayer, what can be reconstructed of the way the Corinthians integrated prophecy and prayer? Three kinds of evidence contribute to such a reconstruction, and the picture will be clearest where they confirm each other. First, whatever integration of prayer and prophecy is practiced by Paul or other writers in the context is likely known and available for Corinthian use. Second, what Paul assumes about Corinthian practice as he tries to persuade the Corinthians probably reflects conduct in Corinth. Third, what is polemically advocated by Paul suggests contrary conduct in Corinth.

Paul's own practice of integrating prayer with prophecy, which was a tradition available for Corinthian use, is of two kinds. On the one hand are blessings and curses. Blessings to God (or reports of blessings) and the invoking of God's blessings on the hearers appear consistently at the opening of his letters, and God's blessings on hearers and curses on others appear in letter closings (Rom. 1:7-10; 15:33; 16:20; 1 Cor. 1:3-9; 16:22-23; 2 Cor. 1:2-4; 13:14; Gal. 1:3-5, 8-9; 6:18; Phil. 1:2-5, 9-11; 4:23; 1 Thess. 1:1-3; 5:23, 27-28; Phlm. 3-6, 25). The formal origin of such blessings is not the Greek letter but the Jewish liturgy, so they probably come to Paul as an accepted framework of Christian common life at the meal gathering (1 Cor. 10:16; 11:23-26), in which context the remainder of Christian speech, including prophecy, took place. This performative language invoking God's presence and power, which Paul uses to set off the writing and reading of his letters as holy time when prophecy may be anticipated, was likely used in opening and closing such time in Corinth.

Another of Paul's practices integrates prophetic speech and prayer. Twice Paul announces that he will tell his readers a mystery, once concerning resurrection and once concerning Israel's salvation. In each case the prophetic word is followed by an acclamation of God's greatness or shout of thanks to God (Rom. 11:25-36; 1 Cor. 15:51-57).[5] Such eruptions of thanks also happen when Paul tells some great news or some divine rescue in dire straits (Rom. 1:25; 2 Cor. 2:14; 8:16; 9:15). This means that the doxology in response to prophecy does not appear to be a formal element of a prophetic genre but is brought on when a speaker recalls God's extraordinary feats. In 2 Corinthians, Paul describes that such thanks for God's blessings magnify God's glory, and the petitions that plead for God's gifts and the good deeds that follow enter this circle of glorification (2 Cor. 1:9-11; 4:15; 9:11-15). If the prophecies of the women also reveal God's great mysteries and blessings, they could be accompanied by similar invocations and responses.

This study cannot analyze the relation between prophecy and prayer in other texts of the period, which might parallel Corinthian practice, but special attention should be given to the increasing prominence of prayer in the language of Colossians and Ephesians and the place of doxologies in the prophecy of the Apocalypse of John. Wider afield, but particularly interesting due to rows of vowels that probably represent ecstatic speech, are gnostic texts from the Nag Hammadi corpus. Some of these texts begin with exhortation and lead into a revelation narrative. The narrative tells the story of an ascent reaching its climax in an experience of God where recitation of divine names or other cries of acclamation give way to ecstatic sounds of praise.[6] If Corinthian prophecy parallels these ascent narratives, there could be something to learn here about their accompanying prayer.

Paul's argument in 1 Corinthians also suggests the way prophecy and prayer are integrated in Corinth. I see five other clues beyond the basic finding that tongues are taken as a prayer language. First, Paul assumes that prophecy and prayer both occur in the same gatherings of believers. They are not practiced in specialized sessions (14:6, 26), and neither is restricted to private practice before Paul proposes this for uninterpreted tongues. Second, the people who gather—adults, both female and male (13:11; 14:20; 11:4-5)—provide their own leadership through the many kinds of speaking that characterize the spiritual (14:6, 26). The general assumption is that "all speak in tongues" and "all prophesy," each believer being known for having received God's spirit (14:18, 23-24, 26, 31; 12:13; 2:12). Third, since the wealth of speaking gifts is more pronounced in Paul's letter than any uniform presentation of them (1:5-7; 4:8-10; 12:7-10, 27-30; 13:1-3, 8; 14:6, 26), the Corinthian practice must have been a broad and various demonstration of the spirit's power, not a ritual of spiritual exercises in a set order. The active gifts of miracle working, organizing, healing, and helping are also going on in this process, since Paul counts on the Corinthians recognizing these as well (12:9, 10, 28). Fourth, Paul assumes that tongues can be distinguished from prophecy because they are addressed by people to God, whereas prophecy is addressed to the people from God, suggesting a kind of circulation of the spirit in these demonstrations (14:2-5, 18, 26-28; cf. 2 Cor. 1:11; 9:13-15). The spiritual mediate God's insight to each other in wisdom, revelation, knowledge, prophecy, and teaching and in turn respond to God in hymns, blessings, and tongues.

Finally, Paul's words assume this is open to nonbelievers, who are attracted to come as well as take part vocally. Their reactions—"you're mad!" and "amen!"—show the responsive nature of the Corinthian community in which people audibly join in or dissociate themselves from each other's prayers (14:16, 23).[7] This interchange may explain why spiritual speech apparently occurs only as people gather and are stimulated by each other in the spirit but not in other settings (5:4; 14:23-26). Paul recounts one outsider's transition from unbelief to belief: he hears everyone prophesy and is convicted and exposed so that he falls on his face to worship God and calls out, "God is truly among you" (14:24-25). Here all the elements come together: communal prophecy, self-discovery, prayer that goes beyond words to a physical act, and a responding confession of God's presence among them, making this person part of the spirit-speaking community.

Beyond all that Paul's argument assumes about Corinth, what he directly and polemically advocates shows a contrary relation of prophecy to tongues. He insists at length on gifts distributed for mutual dependence. This indicates that the Corinthians differentiate gifts much less and are related by mutual stimulation in everything the spirit does, not by division of labor (12:4-13). Paul tries to channel this zealousness for spiritual things toward prophecy and its evaluation (12:31; 14:1, 12). He consistently lists speaking in tongues as the last of the gifts in the community or, with the same effect, he begins with tongues in his praise of love and raises the stakes to prophesying mysteries, miracle-working faith, and ultimately self-immolation (12:8-10, 27-30; 13:1-3). In chapter 14 Paul leaves behind the graduated list of gifts and sets up an antithesis between prophecy and tongues, disparaging the latter in a number of images. He associates tongues with self-development rather than community development, with barbarity, with immaturity, with barrenness, with madness, and perhaps with instruments used in pagan religious processions (14:4, 11, 14, 20, 23, 7; 13:1).

These arguments indicate a strong contrary valuation of ecstatic speech in Corinth. Rather than taking speaking in tongues as a distracting or even destructive force in common life, the Corinthians seem to experience such prayer as a heightening of whatever spiritual speech it accompanies, whether it serves to invoke and petition or acclaim and glorify God. It is possible that some of Paul's negative images for speaking in tongues are direct reversals of positive images used in Corinth: tongues seen as cultivated speech, as signs of maturity, as fruitful for the community, as a special intelligence, as a music particularly appropriate to the revealing of God in Christ. Earlier the women prophets have been approached by Paul to cover their heads "on account of the angels" (11:10), apparently on the basis that they see themselves worshiping among God's angelic host. When he discounts this, "although I speak in the tongues of humans and of angels but have no love," he may reflect what is their claim to be taking part in this most exalted community of praise.

Paul's polemic against public speaking in tongues is written as a defense of prophecy. He praises one sister to blame another, apparently drawing on the Corinthians' respect for prophecy to put speaking in tongues in question. If so, their view is not to be found in reversal of his antithesis but in rejecting the antithesis, based as it is on the argument that rational communication is the only socially constructive communication. Although Paul concedes that prayer in tongues may edify the speaker — that it may be retained with proper precautions of privacy or interpretation, possibly to sharpen and expose unbelief (14:2-5, 15-19, 21-22, 39) — the bottom line for Paul is that uninterpreted tongues are understood by no one but the speaker and do not build up the church.

Yet it is not accurate to say that Paul reduces the constructive social value of the spoken word to its rational content. He keeps his focus on communication. In this vein he might be expected to argue that in prophecy the speaker behind the speaker is God, whereas tongues are an inspired but merely human response. But Paul never makes this distinction. He takes the hearer rather than the speaker as his touchstone, rejecting tongues because the hearers do not understand them. This involves some arguing in Corinth, where it is only the outsiders who are expected to need tongues interpreted in order to understand and say "amen" (14:16). But with a proof text about God using foreign tongues to confirm Israel's disbelief, Paul claims tongues are not meant for believers — not even for those coming to believe who must be convicted by words of God's judgment and salvation (14:21-25). The hearers' need for a specific rational communication from God is the basis of Paul's argument for prophecy as the constructive spiritual gift.

For the Corinthian church and its women prophets this suggests not only a different experience of prayer in tongues as socially constructive but an underlying focus on speaking rather than hearing prophecy as well as tongues. Paul, being accustomed to speak to groups at length (or write if he must), knows that he must make his words fit the hearers to build up the church, but this model of one person's speech persuading multiple hearers appears not to be Corinth's practice. They speak rather than listen as the primary learning activity — "all speak in tongues," "all prophesy," as Paul concedes (14:23-24, 26, 31) — so their hearing of each other is a speaker's hearing, receiving it as something one could also speak, or joining in at any time, or overtaking it with another tone or message. Such speech has significant community-building power without taking the hearer's limitations as the touchstone for the speaker's persuasion. Instead it draws potential speakers into understanding through identification with (or opposition to) the speaker, through their own speaking, and through the impact of their speech on the speaking of others. This is not absence of rational content or of hearing. But the primary event, to put it socially, is the speaking community, or, to put it theologically, the spirit whose speaking builds the church. Where hearing is one element in a communal speaking process, the particular distinctions between what people say matter only as they take a speaking part in developing the affirmative stance of the group. And the spirit's ecstatic prayers to God in "sighs too deep for words" (Rom. 8:26) caution against closure, keeping the community open for new prophetic speech.

The above three probes to find out how the Corinthians integrate prayer and prophecy — searching the options visible in what Paul does, in what Paul assumes in Corinth, and in what Paul opposes in Corinth — produce some results that support each other. Most obviously, prophecy and ecstatic prayer appear to be ways that believers freely speak when they gather, expressing their own faith back and forth and drawing nonbelievers into participation and confession. In their understanding this human conversation of speaking and responding reflects a basic conversation in which God is speaking to people in their prophecy and people are responding to

God in their prayer, with this prayer to God appearing before, during, and/or after the prophetic word from God. Finally this divine speech and human response involves people in what is experienced as an inner-divine communication. It is God's spirit that inspires the ecstatic prayers that respond to the prophetic speaking of God in the people. This "knowing the mind of Christ" or sharing in the worship of angel voices is taken as an end in itself, the ultimate fruit of their common identity in Christ.

In light of such integration of ecstatic prayer and prophecy, it is possible to ask what forms of speech Corinthian prophecies may have taken. David Aune's recent form-critical study of surviving early Christian prophecy identifies six major forms,[8] several of which are improbable in Corinth. Oracles of assurance encourage people not to fear within contexts of lament and persecution, hardly the Corinthian situation—unless this "fear not!" might be spoken to those yet bound in the world's fixed social divisions. Prescriptive oracles warn and restrict in danger, such as Paul's "Keep away from immorality!" (6:18) and Ignatius' "Give heed to the bishop" (*Phld.* 7.1)—unlikely from people who claim freedom rather than make restrictions. Salvation and judgment oracles, which often appear together as words of blessing and curse, make categorical announcements as John of Patmos does against the prophet he calls Jezebel (Rev. 2:20-23). Although Paul describes how a judgment prophecy converts an unbeliever (14:24-25), and ends this chapter with something close to a judgment prophecy against any who do not recognize what he has said, the Corinthians are not interested in judging each other (6:1-8). If they judge Paul, it seems to be by ignoring him (4:1-13, 18). Oracles of blessing without woes of judgment seldom appear in early Christianity.

Aune's final two categories are more fruitful in locating the forms of the Corinthian prophecy. The first of these is legitimation oracles of two kinds: the self-commendation of the divine spirit in the first person, "I am the Alpha and the Omega" (Rev. 1:7), and the recognition oracle in which the spirit validates other human beings, "These people are the servants of the Most High God" (Acts 16:17). Paul uses the recognition oracle, "Jesus is Lord," as an acclamation the Corinthians know in order to argue from there to a differentiation of gifts (12:3). The Montanist prophet Maximilla speaks for both the divine and herself when she says: "I am chased like a wolf from the sheep. I am not wolf. I am word and spirit and power."[9] It is possible that the first-person claim of the Corinthians, "All things are authorized me" (6:12; 10:23), is not only a recognition of their own power but a divine self-commendation of the spirit in whose name they speak. It is unclear whether the dissension Paul mentions (1:11; 3:3; 4:6; 11:18) is limited to the first-person leadership struggle that does not claim inspiration—"I am Paul's"; "I am Apollos'"—or whether their oracular self-commendations also come in conflict with each other. Their use of the plural in "we all know" could speak against this (8:1; 2:6-16).

Aune's final category, the eschatological theophany oracle, is indicated for Corinth by Paul's description in different contexts of both their prophecy and tongues as a speaking of mysteries (13:2; 14:2), a term he uses elsewhere to introduce his own theophany oracles (Rom. 11:25-26; 1 Cor. 15:51-52). Earlier Paul thanked God that they lack no spiritual gift as they anticipate the Lord's revelation (1:7) and commended to them the sharing of revelations (14:6, 27, 30). This could mean that they tell their visions, as Stephen does when being stoned or as Quintilla or Priscilla tells of Christ appearing to her as a woman to say that Jerusalem will come down from heaven in Pepuza.[10] Yet they may speak less in narrative form than in first-person self-commendations of the depths of God so long hidden and now revealed through the spirit (2:6-16). Inspired interpretations of each other's revelations are also indicated for Corinth (12:10; 14:29). Finally, the Corinthians understand their ecstatic prayers to be inspired oracles of the divine spirit in them, even though in this passage Paul and more recently Aune do not classify them as prophecy.

Their Communal Speaking or Paul's Hearing of Individuals

In the second half of the chapter Paul asks what his argument adds up to — "What is it then, brethren?" — and answers with a series of regulations in the third-person imperative (14:26-33 or 35). He sets the scene by conceding their many gifts, but he sees them individually distributed[11] and leading up to his comprehensive regulation, "Let all things be done constructively." Under this rule he distinguishes two groups, speakers in tongues and prophets, giving each a charge and dealing with a possible difficulty in each case. He demands that not more than two or three of each group speak at any gathering, that no two speak at once, and that interpretation or evaluation always follow. This gives a remarkable picture of Corinth's church in contrast.

Paul's limitation to "two or at most three" speaking in tongues and "two or three" prophesying does not mean they are to make two or three permanent appointments but delays the speaking of others until another time (14:26-31). This rule shows that many people normally take part in prophecy and speaking in tongues at a single gathering. This is particularly stressed for speaking in tongues, which Paul restricts first and most sharply: "two or at most three."

Paul is not simply responding to practical problems of church growth. More complex and longer gatherings as the church grows need not be seen negatively, and external time limitations can lead to meeting in more places or more often. Paul's argument is that tongues are not publicly beneficial and, even when interpreted, a token number is enough. If his subsequent "let two or three prophets speak" is not included strictly to persuade the speakers in tongues by an argument from parity, it means that Paul wants more concentration on fewer voices in general. His priorities are hearing and dealing with what is said, and these do decline as the number speaking increases. However, the Corinthians' priority is speaking in the spirit, and it thrives on the expression and interaction of many voices.

Paul's second demand of each group, that those who speak in tongues do so "in turn" and those who prophesy speak "one by one," is evidence that people in Corinth speak in overlapping voices or all at once, as Paul reflects in his picture of "the whole church coming together at once and all speaking in tongues," and "all prophesying" (14:23-25). This cannot be dismissed as hyperbole. Paul insists that the first to prophesy be silent when the spirit inspires another who is still seated, defending this by his view of the common good — "so all may learn and all be encouraged" — and then by a maxim — "the prophets' spirits are subject to the prophets." The maxim may be his own coinage rather than an accepted tradition because it needs the heavy support he adds from the nature of God as God of peace and from universal church practice.

This provides some interesting details about Corinth: they apparently stand up to prophesy and expect the one already prophesying to give way to someone newly inspired rather than have the latter wait — showing the urgency of such expression. Paul appeals to the common good, prophetic practice, God, and the church to persuade them to prophesy one by one; they may use similar arguments to defend their multiple and often-simultaneous voices. That one prophecy multiplies into many could be acclaimed as good for all. The prophets' freedom could be defended by God's nature to give the spirit and by its life in all the churches. Or it may be that the flowering of prophecy and the freedom of the prophets' spirits are so widely prized that they need no defense.

Paul's third rule, calling for interpretation of tongues and evaluation of prophecy, shows that he has limited the number who speak and the time each one speaks in order to focus on what is being said. The listeners' reflection is being favored over the speakers' expression. This is to be fostered by a kind of speech that does not express anything new but reflects on the previous speaking to interpret or evaluate it.

In the case of interpreting tongues, the picture Paul gives is not consistent. Several times he lists interpretation as a separate person's gift after that of speaking in tongues, but then he charges speakers in tongues to pray to interpret (12:10, 30; 14:26; 14:5, 13). He repeats that tongues without interpretation do not benefit the church and should not occur when they gather (14:2-5, 16-19, 22, 26-28), but it is unclear how speakers in tongues can tell whether an interpretation will be given unless the speaker himself or herself is to interpret. But if so, how can one person interpret after many speakers as Paul stipulates? Moreover, how can prayers to God become information for people without ceasing to be prayers — are they translated as prayers being re-prayed? or are they spoken about as prayer topics?

These problems disappear if Paul is proposing a practice unknown in Corinth and therefore not conceived in a consistent way. Since he does not introduce interpretation as a new practice, it can only be new if he has reason to make it appear traditional, first listing it after the gift of tongues to introduce its role and legitimacy (12:10, 30; 14:26), then defending it as a way to salvage public speaking in tongues (14:5, 13-17, 26-27), and finally making its absence the reason for speakers in tongues to be silent in the churches (14:28, 39-40). But an innovation by Paul cannot be demonstrated conclusively. To take a middle road, I suggest there may be incidents of one speaker echoing in a more accessible way the ecstatic prayers of another that Paul then takes up and requires if tongues are to be legitimate in the church. At least it is obvious that tongues are not regularly interpreted in Corinth or Paul would not insist upon it.

Paul mentions the evaluation of prophecy only in one list (12:10), and calls on those not among the two or three prophets speaking to evaluate what they say (14:29). It is not clear if only prophets or all present are to evaluate. Paul's use of the definite article in calling "the others" to evaluate what two or three prophets have said shows that Paul means those who did not prophesy just before, thereby assuming that they might have done so. Far from indicating a narrowly defined group of those who prophesy and evaluate prophecy in Corinth, the implication is, as Paul elsewhere suggests, that all do so (14:24, 26, 31).

Paul seldom mentions evaluation of prophecy, so it is not possible to determine exactly what was done. An overly rationalistic view can be tempered by what Dautzenberg finds in many Jewish texts: one person's vision, revelation, or oracle is received by another and becomes the basis for an inspired interpretation.[12] Though the verb has a different suffix in Paul's earlier claim to "discern spiritual things among the spiritual" (2:13), this expansive "discerning" may be another way to speak of spiritual evaluation, perhaps closer to what goes on in Corinth under that heading than to what Paul wants to encourage there. His desire for second-order speech about previous speech, both among those who speak in tongues and those who prophesy, suggests that he wants to clarify meanings, narrow down options, and get a common mind. An example of this may be the evaluation Paul wants from them to confirm his spiritual judgment on the man living with his father's wife (5:3-5), or the spiritual recognition he soon demands for these regulations of their common life (14:37-38).

A pattern can be seen in the positions Paul takes about prayer and prophecy. He consistently favors a limited number of individuals speaking over an unlimited number and reflective speaking about earlier speech over the primary speech. Prophecy presents content for reflection that may convict a person to believe, so Paul accepts communal prophecy even when voices overlap (14:24-25). But two or three speaking in turn is preferred (14:29). And prophecy becomes more constructive when evaluated by others (12:10; 14:29). The same pattern is seen in Paul's position on public ecstatic speech. Spoken simultaneously, this speech is considered destructive (14:23). When just two or three speak one after another, it becomes tolerable (14:27). It becomes constructive only when its meaning is interpreted, at best when one person interprets what two or three say (12:10, 30; 14:5, 13, 27-28, 39-40).[13]

Paul wants the spiritual in Corinth to move away from communal and expressive leadership toward more individual and reflective leadership. Tongues have farther to go to become constructive by these canons, but prophecy is also being regulated in the same direction. If he has praised one sister to blame another, his restrictions fall on both.

EXCURSUS ON 1 CORINTHIANS 14:34-35

The presence of these two verses at the end of the chapter in several manuscripts rather than in their numerical order has been used as evidence of their secondary nature. The proposal is that a marginal gloss explaining Paul's restrictions on the spiritual in terms of women's silence was later inserted by copyists in two different places. But since no surviving manuscript lacks these words or puts them in a third place, such a gloss would have been very early, probably on the original letter either by the writer, an amanuensis, or possibly by the first person to copy the letter. Another explanation of the double location would be the displacement of an integral part of the text by an omission, corrected immediately by reinserting it at the end of the section. Since such an event would not happen more than once in the same way, a displacement theory requires demonstration that all the manuscripts sharing the displacement stem from one archetype. I will make this demonstration and consider possible reasons for the original displacement before returning to the interpretation of the text as it stands.

The manuscripts that place 14:34-35 at the end of the chapter are all either Greek-Latin bilinguals[14] or Latin texts, except for one miniscule from the twelfth century (signified by the number 88), which I shall take up last. Four Greek manuscripts of 1 Corinthians survive in bilingual form, signified by the letters D E F G, all with this variant placement of our verses. One of these (E) is a direct copy of the first mentioned (D), and the two remaining manuscripts are so close to each other that textual critics either consider the writer of F copied G or that both writers copied the same edited Greek text that the critics name X.[15] This means that there are only two Greek witnesses among the bilinguals, D and G (or X), and these two agree together against the Alexandrian text type in so many ways (six times departing from the Nestle-Aland 26th edition within our two verses, for example)[16] that the theory of a single common archetype of these two Greek texts — called Z — is well established.[17]

The Latin texts of these bilingual manuscripts of Paul's letters (signified by the same letters in small type: d e f g) also place our verses at the chapter's end. Yet they are not translations of their respective Greek texts, although there is occasional influence between the languages as they are copied, especially when they are written interlinearly as in Gg. Instead, the Latin texts come from a tradition that is already complex by the time the first of these bilinguals is made in the mid-fourth century. The Old Latin textual tradition, as it is called, apparently originated when the Greek text was read and translated orally into Latin as the gospel spread beyond the provinces, ethnic groups, and classes that spoke Greek well. Among the Old Latin texts the so-called "African" text type had a fixed form by the third century, with two "European" text types evolving soon after and becoming mixed in various ways. The Latin bilinguals are primarily of the second European type, but all extant Old Latin manuscripts of 1 Corinthians, whatever their type, agree with them in reading our verses at the end of the chapter.[18] Not until after Jerome's successor thoroughly corrected the Latin text of 1 Corinthians in light of an Eastern Greek text to form the Vulgate epistles about 400 CE, is there a Latin text type that reads 14:34-35 at the numbered location.[19] Although most Latin texts of the period have not survived, those we have do show the broadest possible early Latin evidence for locating 14:34-35 at the end of the chapter.

But this breadth is deceptive. Rather than pointing to independent witnesses that can corroborate each other, it indicates a common origin. There are so many places where a large part of the Old Latin tradition agrees against the Greek texts considered to be most reliable that the Latin readings are taken together as signs of a very specific, narrow base. The "African" and both "European" Latin text types are regularly traced back to a single original translation of a single Greek text. In addition, when the second of these European text types is later copied facing a Greek text, the single archetype of the Greek bilinguals (Z) is found to be "near to" the Greek text behind the Latin.[20] ("Near" here must mean that the Greek of the bilinguals is either an heir of the Greek text translated into Latin or a sibling with a common archetype.) This means that the entire tradition associated with Latin, often called "Western," is being traced back to one text. If it seems difficult to conceive that Paul's letters were available in Latin-speaking areas before the end of the fourth century only in one Greek text with its various copies and translations, it is more difficult to explain how else the "Western" tradition could have evolved so many widely held distinctive readings.

I could propose an alternative theory, that a Latin basic text evolving from multiple oral translations gradually became more and more uniform as ears got accustomed to certain readings and as the Latin was written and accepted as authoritative text. This theory would not put in question the single origin of each variant. It would argue that a variant rising from an oral translation (or an early scribal emendation of the Latin) could gain favor to become the accepted and single surviving text, and that meanwhile the Latin could influence the "Western" Greek text to make the bilinguals as parallel as they are. Yet even the scholars who allow for influence of Latin on Greek in this process continue to speak of a family relationship between the Greek and Latin.[21] The dominant hypothesis remains that of a distinctive Western Greek text giving rise both to the various Old Latin text types in the second and third centuries and to the Greek text behind the bilinguals by the fourth century.[22] On these grounds the late placement of 14:34-35 in all early "Western" texts demonstrates that it comes from the Greek ancestor text of this tradition. This makes it credible and highly probable that it originated from a single displacement.

The anomaly in the textual history of 14:34-35 is a Greek miniscule numbered 88 (Naples: Biblioteca Nazionale, II, A 7), which reads these two verses at the chapter's end. This might seem to be independent witness of an early Greek location, but several aspects of this manuscript speak against it. The twelfth-century date suggests a rebound from the "Western" tradition rather than a lone survival outside bilingual manuscripts of a pre-Old Latin Greek reading. It is also significant that the scribe, when finding the silencing at the end of the chapter being copied, immediately recognizes the error in its earlier omission and inscribes two short slashes on the line of writing to signify a necessary reversal of order before writing the words about the women. The scribe then puts similar marks some lines before to show where the words on the women belong, but these slashes must be squeezed in above the line. Evidently the scribe has both formats in hand and knows, once conscious of having followed one, that the other is correct. The Alands classify ms 88 in their Category III as a manuscript with only modest significance for determining the original text because its readings are largely from the Byzantine family.[23] A review of the 88 text of 1 Corinthians shows that it seldom parallels "Western" readings except where they also appear in the eighth-to-ninth-century Ψ manuscript and go on to become the majority reading.[24] This suggests that certain "Western" readings—especially ones that correct or clarify the meaning of a sentence—do survive and triumph for a time in the Byzantine ascendancy. In this context, the scribe's slashes and marginal marks in ms 88 represent the final demise of the "Western" placement of the women's silencing.

Although a displacement in the archetype of the "Western" tradition accounts for the double location of our text, there is no single, obvious explanation why such an inversion of sentences or omission and reinsertion took place originally. Perhaps an adequate solution can be found when the Beuron Old Latin edition of the Pauline corpus is complete. Meanwhile the following proposals are made strictly from the study of the Greek and Latin texts in the immediate context (14:29 – 15:5), on the assumption that drawing examples selectively from throughout this letter or from all Paul's letters without a full statistical study of the copyists' habits could prove whatever was wanted.

First, 1 Corinthians 14:34-35 could have been omitted by haplography as the copyist's eye skipped from the word "churches" (*ekklēsiais/ecclesiis*) in 14:33 to the same word in 14:35, which we find plural in a number of Greek and Latin texts (F C L d g b) and could also have stood at the end of a line. If so, a corrector immediately replaced 14:34-35 in the lower margin due to its length, possibly obscuring the sign marking where it should be inserted when replacing in the side margin the last word(s) of 14:33, "of the saints" (τῶν ἁγιῶν/*sanctorum*). The lower margin was probably the end of the chapter, or at least that place was marked as the point to insert the words, since they appear in no alternate location. The fact that 14:34-35 show about twice as many word reversals and other small variants as other verses in the context might stem from their having made the move to the lower margin on their way to becoming the "Western text." The weaknesses of this explanation are its dependence on an early appearance of the plural "churches" in 14:35 and its strictly literary nature.

A second explanation allows room for changes that could originate either in oral use or in copying. Harmonizations with parallel passages and other "improvements" for purposes of clarity or consistency are visible several places in the immediate context in the Old Latin and the bilingual texts. In 14:35 "woman" becomes plural either to follow the previous verse or perhaps in light of the broader plural pattern (Eph. 5:22, 24; Col. 3:18; 1 Pet. 3:1; 1 Tim. 2:9; 3:11). Verb forms are adjusted (14:31, 35; 15:1, 2 D F G). Most conspicuous is the addition of "I teach" in the phrase "as I teach in all the churches of the saints," completing 14:33 more clearly with this verb borrowed from the similar sentence in 4:17 (F G a f g Ambst and most Vulgate texts). A corrector with such freedom could conceivably, in the interests of clarity, delay the lines on women until after the instructions on prophecy, assuming perhaps, in light of later household codes, that what was said to women concerned household rather than church order.

A third option is that the passage is displaced due to the corrector's ideological point of view. A number of variants in the immediate context that appear consistently in the Old Latin and bilinguals show explicit corrections of the text's meaning. Least pointed may be the dropping of the word "command(s)" in 14:37 so that Paul's regulations are said to be "of the Lord" but not "the command(s) of the Lord" (14:37 D* F G b d f g Ambst). "The spirits of the prophets are subject . . ." becomes singular, "the spirit of the prophets is subject . . ." (14:32 D F G a b d g vgR Ambst), possibly due to a theological uneasiness with multiple spirits. Or this variant could have arisen from the more common use of the singular "spirit" in the passage, from the abbreviation of "spirit," or from the singular verb used with the Greek neuter plural noun. But there is clear moralizing when Paul's "if you hold on (to the gospel)" is replaced with "you ought to hold on" (15:2 D F G a b d g Ambst). And most blatant is the correction of the number to whom the risen Jesus appears from twelve to eleven in light of Judas's death (15:5 D F G a b d f g vg+ Ambst).

A tradition reflecting this much content editing in a short passage can also be credited with moving the lines about women to make a point. Did church order or household concerns make for independent use of the two verses restricting women? Or were the prophecy instructions used where women were active prophets? Either case could lead to the separation of the words on prophecy from the words about women. It is also possible that a scribe excised the two verses silencing women, and his/her omission was then corrected in the lower margin and read in the wrong location. Most New Testament copyists were conservative, and changing the text's meaning, or even clarifying it, were not common scribal practices. But in its earliest stage the Latin-related tradition experienced extensive adaptions, as this section of it demonstrates. In light of this, it is not scientific to exclude a priori the possibility of a translator's or scribe's ideological decision to displace or omit a passage silencing women. The context for such a decision could be the recurring second-century debates on women's proper Christian witness as seen in 1 Timothy, the Apocryphal Acts, the Montanist controversy, Tertullian, and the Acts of the Christian Martyrs.

Their Inspired Speech or Paul's Inspired Silencing

Because the transposition of 14:34-35 to the end of the chapter occurred in the Latin-related tradition, we can only accept that Paul wrote the chapter in the now familiar order. His regulation of women is close in structure and language to his previous regulations of speakers in tongues and prophets. Dautzenberg identifies three structural elements in each regulation: a third person imperative instruction, an explanatory sentence, and an example in conditional form telling what to do in a given case.[25] Words recur: "to speak," "to be subject," "to learn," "to be silent." And each regulation begins with reference to a particular group: "If anyone speaks in a tongue . . . ," "Prophets . . . ," "The women. . . ."

Yet these parallels do not disguise the significant differences between the three regulations. The regulation of speakers in tongues and prophets concerns people with the two spiritual gifts Paul has been distinguishing throughout the argument, and in each case he tells them how to speak and reflect on this speech. He commands silence only secondarily to prevent unlimited or uninterpreted speech. In the third case he introduces people not apparently under discussion and immediately requires silence, returning to speaking and learning only by way of concession in the concrete example. Above all, the arguments given for silence are different—in the first two cases the upbuilding of the church so that all may learn, in the third law and shame. How are these differences to be accounted for?

One option is to see Paul operating with a careful plan. He may recognize when he begins to write that women among the spiritual are leading the community in a new direction. If so, he is not in a position to attack directly, perhaps because they speak under the banner of Apollos, or because they have greatly expanded the community and make up its largest group, or because he does not question their spiritual experience but the way they express it. Therefore he begins by claiming equality and then priority to Apollos in order to recover his authority as architect and father of this church against those who are new and bold (1 Cor. 1–4). He uses this base to attack male sexual offenders in order to point behind them to a broader group of the spiritual whose freedom to leave spouses and eat sacrificed meat has led the others into temptation (1 Cor. 5–7). Immorality and idolatry are traced back to the uncovered heads of the women who pray and prophesy, and the disorderly eating to the people who think they participate in the Lord's meal (1 Cor. 8–11). Finally he insists that those who are spiritual find their unity in the interdependence of God's differently assigned gifts and focus their communal zeal on hearing and interpreting a few spiritual voices (1 Cor. 12–14). On this basis he can argue that others be silent, including women who by tradition and propriety should not be speaking. Paul may have constructed his argument aware that it was leading to this point, and that what could not be defended on the basis of the common baptism into Christ or the common good, could be defended by other arguments tenuously associated with them.

A second option is to read Paul as a less self-possessed persuader, one more subject to his own arguments and those of others, feeling his way toward solutions of problems only thereby defined. If so, the women prophets of Corinth may be largely on the margin of Paul's mind. They appear at key points in his arguments when he presses behind male sexual offenses for a solution the devout can bring off and when he probes the limits of his pleasure at Corinth's worship to discover his disturbance at the women's dress and at no one serving the meals. When he seeks order in their gatherings, he chooses prophecy over tongues, few speakers over many, reflection over expression — and male over female. He may not himself face the way his rhetoric points to the women as the solution on key issues to the problems he senses, if they will only return to their receptive role.

● Whether shaped by premeditation or intuition, Paul's arguments silencing women are clear and follow each other. Just before this silencing he has claimed the strongest sanctions from God's nature and church practice against overspeaking: "Even the prophets' spirits are subject to the prophets — for God is not God of disruption but of peace as in all the churches of the saints" (14:32-33). Coming after this, Paul's "Let the women be silent in the churches" associates women with such disruption of the divine peace without having to give sex-specific evidence. This prepares for the explanation, "for they are not permitted to speak but let them be subject," which is then confirmed — "as the law also says" (14:34). (Paul can appeal positively to the law: 7:19; Gal. 3:24; 4:21.) The concession of learning at home if they want appears to diminish the harshness of the regulation, but it actually specifies their household subordination. It also highlights the men to whom they could be subject at home, echoing Paul's earlier advice that the once-married return to their calling and that virgins marry if their suitors choose (7:10-38). Further explanation for the women not being permitted to speak in church is the shame involved, apparently the dishonoring of their husbands/fathers/masters through the sexual implications of public display. As in his argument on head covering, Paul has argued from nature (in this case God's nature), community practice, sexual subordination, the written tradition, and shame.

He concludes with two other kinds of argument and a threat. The rhetorical questions address the women just silenced — "Or did God's word originate from you? Or did it reach you people only?" — ridiculing any claims to essential speaking roles on their part. That Paul speaks to them directly here, even though he silenced them in the third person, follows his earlier juxtaposition of direct address and third-person commands when dealing with speakers in tongues and prophets (14:23, 28-31). The closing phrase in the last question, "Or did it reach you people only?" is written in an inclusive masculine form because "reach" is a territorial concept in Paul's mission thinking (2 Cor. 10:13-14; cf. Acts 13:51; 16:1). His point is that the gospel being carried from city to city by people like himself has reached not only the church in Corinth but people in many regions. The Corinthians are receivers of the tradition.[26]

Immediately Paul challenges any who think of themselves as prophets or spirituals to acknowledge the things he writes as the Lord's command, and he seals this with the threat, "Whoever does not recognize this is not recognized" (14:37-38). Because Paul has used the argument dissociating thought from reality at key points throughout the letter — "If any among you think they are wise . . . ," "If any think they know something . . . ," "If any think they want to make an issue of this . . ." (3:18; 8:2; 11:16) — it is clear that Paul is not conceding that they are prophets and spirituals but is reflecting their claim and challenging them to prove it by reversing their spiritual perception. The plural, "the things I write," must incorporate all the foregoing regulations of speech. But, as Dautzenberg demonstrates in his extended interpolation thesis,[27] the sharp tone and severe demands are rhetorically most appropriate to the categorical silencing of the women.

Or to put it differently, Paul's forcing a spiritual vote of confidence at exactly this point shows that the women's silencing is not a parenthetical matter but the turning point in his argument concerning the spiritual. Once he has called for their silence he has done all he needs to do. It is as if this move solves his problem concerning tongues and prophecy and now he only needs to ensure obedience. It is from the spiritual that he demands acknowledgment, so it can be assumed that "the Lord's command" refers to the Lord known in the spirit rather than to a traditional saying of Jesus. Yet this ambiguity only gives Paul's demand added authority.

The concluding threat, "Whoever does not recognize this is not recognized," means that one who denies this will not be recognized as a prophet or spiritual. The threat is given particular weight by being put in the *ius talionis* form in which divine retribution is implied by the passive of the same verb as the human act: "Whoever does not recognize this, God does not recognize."

This conditional curse is what makes Paul's demand that they recognize his silencings as the Lord's command into a spiritual vote of confidence. Paul thinks that he can get this recognition, perhaps understandably in the case of male prophets who need only wait their turn to speak, and with some credibility also in the case of men who must wait for an interpreter in order to speak out in tongues. But he seems to misgauge the women prophets by thinking they will demonstrate their status as prophets by agreeing they can never speak as prophets. Does not he force them into speaking as prophets against their own blanket silencing, and also against the more measured restrictions to which he has linked it? Either Paul underestimates the depth of his opposition in Corinth — as the continuing and intensifying struggle in 2 Corinthians suggests, or his sharp challenge and threat should not be read as signs of confidence on Paul's part but as signs of insecurity. When discussing head covering he suddenly cuts off his trailing arguments with the sharp, "If any think they want to make an issue of this, we ourselves have no such custom, nor do the churches of God."

The stonewalling here could also show that he senses he cannot get further by rational appeals.

The chapter's final two verses return without any transition except the fraternal "so then brethren" — disguising an exclusion of the women — to his previous stance of conceding their zealousness as long as they focus on prophecy, even warning them not to forbid speaking in tongues. On the basis of such a soft spirit he can then ask for a minimal thing, "But let everything be done decently and in order," and thereby throw the blanket of propriety over this attempted rape of the women's divine gifts.

When Paul claims the Lord's spiritual authority to silence the Corinthian women prophets at the culmination of his regulations for spiritual speech, his clarity gives us a corresponding clarity about the people he is dealing with. That he demands silence shows it is not general behavior or appearance that is the issue but the women's speaking, which occurs, as he says, "in the gatherings" or "churches." That he demands this silence after he has silenced uninterpreted tongues and simultaneous prophecy shows that it is not a peripheral disturbance he refers to but some kind of spiritual speaking. That he follows this silencing with sharp rhetorical questions and a spiritual counterclaim, putting his authority with them to the test, shows that the women's speech is the heart of the alternative spiritual authority to his own. The concrete data this argument yields may be considered under three headings: which women speak? what kind of speech is it? and what does it mean for themselves and their society?

As to which women are speaking, Paul's regulation refers to women generally. The Greek term with which the sentence begins, "the women," could mean "wives" in a conjugal context, but there is no indication of that here. In a separate sentence six clauses later he does refer to "their own men" of whom they should ask questions, and this is often read "husbands." Yet the phrase is appropriate not only for wives, since daughters, widows, and women slaves are just as subordinate to the man of the house. Nor can we assume that Paul excludes from his restrictions the exceptional woman who lives alone or with other women just because he concedes that women may ask men questions at home.

His reference to women is a good indication that it is not a select few who speak in the church but women in general, or at least women of various stations. His earlier instruction to "any woman who prays and prophesies" (11:5) is again broad, as are his repeated statements that all can prophesy (14:5, 24, 31) and his effort to get all to be zealous for the higher gifts (12:31; 14:1, 12, 39). The women prophets of Corinth are probably not a self-conscious band of three or eight or even fifteen, but are the women at large as the spirit moves them to prophesy. This does not make it a misnomer to call them "women prophets" rather than "prophesying women," since the same freedom of the spirit to speak through many voices is assumed among men and Paul speaks of all with this gift interchangeably as "prophets" and "those who prophesy."

The kind of speaking the women do is indicated primarily by the location of the women's silencing at the apex of the argument "concerning the spiritual," and specifically at the end of Paul's concerted effort to dissociate prophecy from ecstatic speech. The women's speech will be spiritual in a way that closely integrates what Paul wants to dissociate, the oracles of God to the people and the inspired responses of the people to God. They may be particularly gifted in what he wants to exclude from public worship. This is a broad range of speech: the speaking of the whole group when prophesying God's word to each other in overlapping voices, all extended sessions of inspired speech of any kind, and all prophecies and praise not interrupted by reflection.[28]

It has been proposed that women's speech takes the form of questions because after silencing them Paul concedes that they may ask questions at home. This is prefaced with the phrase, "but if they want to learn anything," which implies that they want "to learn." But previously Paul insisted that prophets speak one by one "so that all might learn," betraying that such learning by listening is his agenda, not theirs. If Paul quickly concedes that they can still "learn" elsewhere in order to counter objections to his silencing the women, this tells nothing about the women except that they have a wide following that needs to be appeased.

What the Corinthian women's prophecies and prayers mean to themselves and their society is not indicated here in terms of discursive content but mutual relation, in terms of their confidence in themselves and the respect that others accord them. The fact that they are singled out for restriction shows that Paul does not expect them to be effectively limited by his regulations of speakers in tongues and prophets. He must either think that their prophecy is so dynamic as to disrupt his plan for a listening community, even if it limits itself to a few speaking seriatim, or he thinks that they will not so limit themselves. Perhaps he prefaces his silencing of the women with the statement that the prophets' spirits are subject to the prophets in all the churches because he knows that their speech is not determined by what he considers standard conduct in the churches nor by subordination to other prophets.

An extraordinary measure of their confidence appears in Paul's two rhetorical questions that follow their silencing, "Or did God's word originate from you? Or did it reach as far as you people only?" (14:36) Paul wants to expose their initially receptive role and strictly local impact in comparison to his active, worldwide role in bringing the gospel to Corinth and carrying it further. His geographical mission boast has been provoked by a parallel spoken or unspoken boast on their part to be the point of origin and point of destination of God's speaking in Corinth. Their confidence is such that some see no need for the itinerant apostle to return (4:18).

This confidence is evidence of the respect in which others hold them and their prophecies. If ammunition is indicative of the enemy's forces, the three-chapter argument about the spiritual that moves through divine distribution of gifts, praise of self-abnegating love, exalting of the gift that edifies listeners to the silencing of certain ecstatics and prophets and the suppression of women's public voices is no small tribute to the social influence of those upon which its weight falls. Paul's specific appeal to propriety, legality, and proper subordination in his directive concerning them also shows the respect accorded these women. He is not dealing with a marginal group who provide comic relief in the assemblies but with people who have reputations to consider, who can be challenged not to let go the good name they have acquired and make themselves vulnerable to charges of shameful conduct or lawlessness. Other sources indicate that for a woman to live without sexual relations with men and to begin to have visions or spiritual knowledge only enhances her reputation in Hellenistic-Jewish and Christian communities of this time.[29] But this conduct makes her susceptible to charges of immorality as perpetrator of religiously cloaked seduction, and such charges have to be meticulously guarded against by her and her supporters, the more so the greater her reputation becomes.[30]

Finally and most indicative of the Corinthian women prophets' social influence is the fact that Paul appeals to the Spirit against the spirit in them. In other contexts Paul has challenged those who think they are wise, knowing, standing firm, or competitive to guard themselves, even using the same third-person imperative in two cases to counsel them rather to "become foolish" and "watch not to fall" (3:18; 10:12; cf. 8:2; 11:16). But only in this final argument dissociating thought from reality does Paul challenge those who "think they are prophets or spiritual" to recognize something he has just said as coming from the Lord. Paul does not run risks without reason, so we can assume this is a counterclaim to a strong spiritual claim.

Paul seems to write with confidence in his own victory, yet his argument indicates an equal confidence on the part of the women and other people he has restricted, raising Paul's response to such high stakes. And because he not only appeals to offenders to judge, but to any prophets or spiritual people in Corinth, the issue becomes one of community respect, not merely only one of self-confidence. It must be to challenge some of the most respected in the community that Paul puts his spiritual authority on the line, confident that God's spirit will vindicate him. His final conditional curse in its form of apodictic divine retribution, "Whoever does not recognize this is not recognized," is an oracle in its own right and puts the case beyond any human court. Paul's gauntlet is down. But due to the way God's authority functions in the Corinthian church, he must leave it to God's spirit in them to determine whether that same spirit has or has not spoken in him.

8 | Women Risen to New Life in Christ: 1 Corinthians 15–16

AFTER PAUL'S RULES SILENCING uninterpreted tongues, simultaneous prophecy, and all women in the churches, he defends the resurrection of the dead against Corinthians who deny it, then ending the letter with plans and greetings. Barth was right that this section, considering its position and length, must culminate Paul's entire argument in some way.[1] If Barth was wrong to depict Corinth's small group of believers as cultural Christendom in triumph over God, he does press us to determine what this concluding argument tells about the people that Paul seeks to persuade.

Paul's Resurrection Witness to Corinth against the Corinthians' Resurrection Witness to Paul

The first issue is why Paul does not begin this section in his usual way with "But concerning resurrection . . ." (cf. 7:1, 25; 8:1; 12:1; 16:1, 12) or "I have heard . . ." (cf. 1:11; 11:18) and then counter their letter or voice with his view of resurrection. Instead he prefaces his charge against those who deny resurrection of the dead (15:12) with a full paragraph introduction (15:1-11).[2] It may be too soon after his demand that all the spiritual recognize his silencings or not be recognized for him to make additional demands. Apparently this matter of resurrection is not a rider that can be carried on momentum left from the previous argument—whether there is no such momentum or whether the new weight is too great—and a base for agreement must be rebuilt.

Paul returns to his role of bringing the gospel to them. By recalling the event of his having announced a gospel to them, that they received, he claims the authority to instruct them (cf. 4:14-17; 11:2, 23; Gal. 1:6-9; 1 Thess. 4:1). Because this is not his first telling of this gospel, there is a seriousness, even a rebuke, in the opening verb: "I make known to you, brethren, the gospel which I announced to you." And he does not settle for this reassertion of their original relationship but adds six clauses: "which you also accepted, on which you also stand, through which you also are saved, in such terms as I announced it—if you keep your grasp, unless you

159

have believed for nothing." This wild redundancy highlights their receiving role as the full foundation for their faith and insinuates that they have been incapable of fulfilling it. Paul has just restricted the spirit speaking in them, addressing his last words to the women: "Did God's word come forth from you?" (14:36) and now he asserts a one-way communication, "I make known . . . I announced . . . I announced" and "you received . . . you stand . . . you are saved . . . you grasp . . . you believed" (15:1-2). He is claiming to be the true authority over against the voices of God's word coming forth from Corinth despite the fact that he has not silenced all the people there in every way.

The content of the tradition as he tells it follows, framed by words about its transmission that link Paul modestly but inseparably to previous authorities: he received the tradition from them (15:3a), and all that matters is that he or they proclaimed it and "you believed" (15:11). This framework shows that Paul is still working to be recognized as one of these authorities. The tradition as he presents it includes four events—that Christ died, that he was buried, that he is risen, and that he appeared. The latter verb is repeated four times to recount successive appearances to Peter and the Twelve, to the 500, to James and the apostles, and "last of all as to a miscarriage" to Paul (15:3-8).

Of course Paul no more received a gospel that included his own seeing Christ than Moses described his own death at the end of Deuteronomy. Paul has written himself into the authoritative tradition, and commentators look away delicately and ask if he also added James and the apostles, or at least the 500 "of whom . . . some have died." The tradition could not have been a fixed creed yet, or Paul could not have adapted it. It is even possible that Paul, under pressure in Corinth, is first to take these reports—these various sources of the "good news" that followed Jesus' death—and present them as a single authoritative tradition received and passed on. But that he has had to move carefully to incorporate himself as the final witness of the climactic event is clear in the self-deprecations and explanations with which he describes Christ's appearance to him (15:8-10)—"a miscarriage," "least of the apostles," "not worthy to be called an apostle because I persecuted God's church," "I labored more than they all, though not I but God's grace with me."[3] Paul is working hard to show that he not only received and passed on authoritative tradition, but that his witness is an accepted, if anomalous, part of the tradition itself.

This way of beginning to discuss that some Corinthians deny resurrection of the dead shows that they do not yet accept Paul as a resurrection witness. But Paul's next major argument assumes they do think Jesus is risen (15:12-19). They may only recognize witnesses within the first weeks as Luke does, in which case Paul is not so much proposing a new view of resurrection as claiming to share the authority already granted to witnesses. But this would not explain why many champion Apollos, who was not an early witness, or how they claim primary authority for their own speech in the spirit. Therefore it is more probable that they do not see Paul as the final resurrection witness because they themselves know the living Christ in the spirit. In this case, Paul's emphatic introduction of Christ's appearance to him with the words, "Last of all . . ." refers only initially to his being the last of all the apostles, as an expression of his modesty, but more significantly refers to being the last of all believers, as a denial that Corinthian spiritual experience can be a primary source for knowledge of the risen Christ. The Corinthians may not think of their experiences as resurrection appearances strictly in Paul's sense, since it is Paul's interest, not theirs, to make resurrection appearances function as a list to validate past events.

But if Paul wants to validate past events, why does he stretch the concept of resurrection to include Christ's appearance to him? This seems to open the gate to similar claims in Corinth. Perhaps Paul does not begin to think of Christ's resurrection with a short list of witnesses to which he adds himself but begins closer to where the Corinthians are with a view of all believers knowing the risen Christ in the spirit, which he has constricted in his debate with them. In any case he now sees his experience not as one among other evidences of the spirit but as the closing event in a resurrection canon, an event that he calls a "miscarriage" because it is somehow mistimed or misshapen, but by God's grace is a witness to Christ and not to himself.[4]

The Corinthians, who do not see their own glory in the spirit as a threat to God but as the sign of Christ's new life among them, would not have shared this kind of self-deprecation, nor would they have settled for word-of-mouth proof of Christ's resurrection from Peter or James, let alone from Paul. They expect to see Christ themselves, or to hear Christ in their own speaking, to know Christ is alive because they are living a new identity in Christ that they have not lived before. If they do not say that "he appeared" to them, it would only be because their experience of Christ's rising is broader than this term Paul chooses from apocalyptic and Christian tradition to establish these validating past events.

Paul's "narrative of the facts" concerning resurrection not only bars all the spiritual in Corinth from being primary witnesses to Christ's life but has particular implications for the women prophets. In his previous argument, after silencing the women and challenging any who consider themselves prophets or spiritual to take this as the Lord's command, Paul says, "So my brethren, be zealous to prophesy," in such a way that "brethren" cannot be taken as inclusive of the women (14:34-39; cf. 1 Thess. 4:1-8). But two sentences later when a new topic is introduced, "Now I want you to know, brethren, the gospel that I announced to you" (15:1), there is no sign that women are not also intended as "brethren." One major function of this chapter's introduction may be to try to reincorporate into Paul's audience all those who once received what he taught. Yet, in spite of this inclusiveness, he gives no ground to the women prophets' claim that God's word comes forth from them. The gospel he makes known is passed on to them by a one-way communication from him, or from others through him (15:1-3). Even their role in further transmission, already excluded in church speaking, is not suggested in any way.

A more difficult question concerns the absence of the women witnesses to the resurrection in Paul's list. If commentators notice this at all, they treat it as evidence that the empty tomb story was a late construction unknown to Paul, recorded first in the Gospel of Mark and later elaborated into stories of Christ appearing to women.[5] But all Gospel appearance stories are recorded later than Mark's original ending (Mark 16:1-8), and it is doubtful that stories of appearances to women would have been constructed after the tradition had "more reliable" accounts. The stories of appearances to women are old, though it cannot be proven that Paul knew and rejected them. But scholars willing to consider that Paul may have omitted the phrase "not male and female" when he quotes the baptismal confession in this letter (12:13; cf. Gal. 3:28)[6] need to consider the possibility that he omitted the women's resurrection witness.

In spite of great differences, all the Gospel resurrection narratives begin with the women, and the two Gospels that speak of an appearance to women tell that before other appearance stories. This suggests that from the beginning there was some expectation to hear about the women first, especially in an account stressing sequence as Paul does. This could cause Paul, in an effort to give prior place to Peter, not to tell of an appearance to the women. Paul could see the women adequately incorporated among the "brethren" in the appearance to the larger group, as Luke does when inserting an appearance to Peter in his narrative (15:6; Luke 24:10-11, 33-36).

A second reason for omission might be the question of women's admissability or credibility as witnesses. This might particularly concern a writer such as Paul who lists "sightings" to magnify proof.

A third possible cause for omission could be Paul's desire not to provide support for women who prophesy in Corinth from the news that women's word was the genesis of the resurrection faith.

The first explanation begs the question of why Paul should be interested in Peter's primacy. In Galatians, Paul stresses how he took issue with Peter (Gal. 2:11-14); in 1 Corinthians an element of competition is implied between Peter and Paul (1:12; 3:22; 9:5). Therefore, the fact that Jesus appears first to Peter in Paul's narrative is more likely traditional than Paul's doing. If the women are absent because their witness is less credible, this would also point to a pre-Pauline omission, since in the Corinthian context Paul could expect women's voices to be relatively persuasive. Only the third reason for omission, to discourage women's speech, fits into the context of Paul's own argument. This indicates that if Paul did not find the appearance to women already missing for either of the first two reasons, he omitted it for the third reason.

But the scales may weigh more in the latter direction than this suggests. A total omission of the story of the women would demand more reasons than provided by Petrine primacy or women's lack of credibility as witnesses, since other writers such as Luke adjust for both problems and still begin with the women. If Paul is working with multiple traditions to consolidate one "received tradition" over against an appeal in Corinth to present an expanding experience of Christ, it is no less likely that he omit offending appearance stories as that he add Christ's appearance to him.

Paul begins his defense of resurrection of the dead with this narrative of past events — his past announcement of a received tradition to them, the past events concerning Christ so announced, and his own past experience of Christ. But the foundation he builds for his argument is not uncontroversial. The apparent neutrality of an appeal to past events and received tradition functions to legitimate the perspective from which it recounts the past.[7] Paul uses the familiar tradition of Christ's dying and rising to legitimate his claim to be the final member in a select, formally transmitted list of witnesses to Christ's resurrection, witnesses whose reports are said to be the basis of the Corinthians' faith and part of its content. For the women prophets this means that their present experience and communication of the risen Christ are being challenged by another gospel based strictly on the witness of certain male apostles and a single large group. This other gospel is restricted to the claim that Jesus was once alive in the early days — or in Paul's case, years — after his resurrection.

The Corinthians' Denial of Resurrection of the Dead Met by Paul's Denial of Resurrection of the Living

At this point Paul charges that some of them deny the resurrection of the dead. He presents their denial as an outright and complete rejection of life beyond the grave, and he intensifies and dramatizes this characterization of them throughout the chapter (15:12, 19, 32-34, 35). However, there is some problem in the exact fit of this skeptic's persona that he lays upon them, as can be seen in his loose attributions, "some of you say," and "but someone will say" (15:12, 35), and in his resort to the conditional first-person plural to describe them, "If we have hope only in this life, we are of all people most pitiful," and "if the dead are not raised, let us eat, drink and be merry, for tomorrow we die" (15:19, 32). Yet the impressive length and location of this chapter weigh against its being meant for a marginal group. The best solution is to identify this as a characterization that stereotypes the nature of their denial in order to give Paul a better foil for his argument.[8] This means that the reason and aim of his argument extend beyond demolishing the obvious opponent, who rejects all life beyond death, to some more difficult effort to persuade.

Before Paul states their denial he has already framed it as an absurdity in light of the witness given to Jesus' resurrection: "Now if Christ is proclaimed risen from the dead, how can some of you say that there is no resurrection of the dead?" (15:12) Then he reverses the point, refuting the denial from its consequences, "If there is no resurrection of the dead, then Christ is not risen" (15:13).[9] To see every particular case excluded when a generalization is denied confuses logical and historical necessity, but Paul goes on to dismantle their faith and his proclamation to show what would follow Christ not being risen. The way this argument hangs on Christ being risen shows that Paul is sure he has the support of the Corinthians for Christ's resurrection, if not on the basis of the appearances he has listed, then on the basis of their own experience of Christ.

When Paul repeats the argument, he threatens that if the dead are not raised then Christ is not risen and three dire consequences take place that preoccupy Paul throughout the chapter. He warns that, without a vindicating resurrection of the dead, everything he and they do in the gospel will be in vain (15:2, 10, 14, 17, 30-32, 58). Sin will plague them in spite of Christ's death for their sins unless Christ destroys death (15:3, 17, 32-34, 54-57). And Christians who die will be lost if his resurrection does not guarantee theirs (15:6, 18, 20, 51). These three problems—unrewarded work, sin, and death—are expected to be solved by the resurrection of the dead. This suggests that those Paul charges with denying resurrection of the dead may lack preoccupation with these problems.

Paul brings to a climax the negative consequences of their denial of the dead's resurrection with a final logical conclusion in the tone of a cry, "If our only hope in Christ is in this life, we are of all people most pitiful" (15:19). This bifurcation of present and future hope is Paul's argument against the stereotyped skeptic in order to exclude the option of a more inclusive view. Yet his argument assumes that they believe in the living Christ as their life. How they combine believing a risen Christ and denying resurrection of the dead must be drawn from Paul's positive arguments that follow. The first argument defends the resurrection of the dead directly (15:20-28), ending with renewed appeals to their experience and his (15:29-34). The second argument answers an objection to his argument (15:35-49), and again is followed by appeals (15:50-58).[10]

Because Paul has been describing the blight if there was no resurrection and Christ had not risen, he begins his first positive argument with an emphatic, "But now Christ is risen from the dead, the first fruit of the sleeping." So the believing dead are called (1 Thess. 4:13-15; 1 Cor. 11:30; 15:6, 18, 20, 51). This image of the first fruit defines Christ in terms of his benefit for the dead, he being the first resurrected of a now sure harvest to life of the dead. Corinthians who reject resurrection of the dead would probably not characterize Christ as first fruit or assurance for the dead. Their confession about Christ's dying and rising might be spoken in terms of his impact on the living, in images signifying not an outstanding promise but some kind of present fulfillment, not first fruit but harvest. They could use Paul's next contrast, "Since through a human being comes death, so through a human being comes resurrection," but they would have to delete Paul's last word, "of the dead," which defines Christ's life in terms of the dead (15:20). The same would apply to the future tense that ends the following, "As in Adam all die, so in Christ all will be made alive" (15:22). In other contexts Paul applies the Adam/Christ typology to the present before he extends it to the future (15:44b-49; Rom. 5:12-21), so it is probably inaccurate to speak of the Corinthians deleting his reference to the future and the dead. Their present-tense reading is probably the common one and includes the future by implication, whereas in defending resurrection of the dead Paul is narrowing his use to the future. This may seem an understandable tactic on Paul's part. But it also makes understandable why the Corinthians might deny the resurrection of the dead. Here it functions to make death (or, for survivors, Christ's return 15:23, 51-52) the entry to life in Christ and meanwhile leaves them as good as dead in Adam, dependent on the indirect word of certain early witnesses that Jesus was once raised and therefore has become the first fruit assuring resurrection for the dead. They will not give up their claim that the decisive transformation has already taken place in Christ and that they are fully alive.

The remainder of Paul's first argument explains how "all will be made alive in Christ" (15:22-28). The key is his first line "Each in its own order," meaning nothing ahead of its time, as the sequence of temporal clauses that follows shows. Christ is first fruit until his coming on behalf of those in Christ, which is followed by what is described on the authority of two psalms as a military victory over all his enemies, including the last which is death. But, we are assured, God is not among "all things put under his feet." Instead Christ finally submits himself to God, who had put all things under Christ's feet, so that God becomes "all in all."

This conclusion of Paul's first argument puts the Corinthians in question in three ways. First, it undermines their present claims to life in Christ by delaying Christ's "making alive" to a future time that begins at his coming and is incomplete until death is overthrown and Christ submits himself to God. Second, it depicts this "making alive" as Christ's destruction of all competing powers and their subjection under his feet, with no reference to the participation, liberation, or rejoicing of others in this victory. This leaves no room, even in the future, for positive Corinthian claims to fulfillment and ruling in Christ (4:8).

Third, it envisions the consummation of Christ's "making alive" as Christ's own subjection to God, thereby exalting such subordination as the highest possible act for a human being, and defining God in terms of exclusive and isolated power over all others. This must have a special impact on women in Corinth who are told to "be subject" in an absolute use of the same verb at the close of Paul's previous argument concerning the spiritual (14:34). There Paul also appeals to God's nature to justify subordination among the prophets, "for God is not a God of disruption but of peace" (14:32-33). A God of disruption in this context seems to imply a God who fosters the tensions involved in broad communal participation, a God of zeal (12:31; 14:1, 12, 39). In contrast, Paul stresses a communal life of "decency and order" (14:40) and a future with each event "in its order" (15:23). In Corinth, Paul's God might be described as God of peace and order.

Paul's appeals that follow his first argument express again how absurd the Corinthians' denial is, this time not because it excludes Christ's resurrection and their faith but because it conflicts with what believers do (15:29-34). In rhetorical questions he demands to know why people baptize on behalf of the dead if the dead won't be raised, and why he puts himself through danger each hour if there is no vindication. He does not say they are the ones who baptize for the dead, but his argument assumes that they respect this rite and probably practice it (15:29). If entering into Christ's life happens for them at the time of baptism, it is possible that they have tried to confer this blessing on new believers who die. (A preparation period can be required in groups who stress initiation rites.) If so, Paul's argument proves that the Corinthians consider the dead to have a certain life in Christ, however their state after death is understood. But the event of being made alive is apparently intended to happen in baptism as they confess Christ or speak in the spirit, not after death. The suddenly dead are somehow dependent on the living, not the living dependent on an eventual resurrection of the dead.

Paul's second point, that his suffering must be vindicated, probably goes right by them as his more aroused rhetoric suggests, reaching its climax in the scriptural invitation, "If the dead are not raised, 'Let's eat, drink and be merry, for tomorrow we die'" (15:30-32). Then he berates them. "Don't be deceived, 'Bad company ruins good character.' Sober up . . . some have no knowledge of God, I must say to your shame" (15:33-34).[11] However exaggerated his diatribe against their sin, it is apparent that they do not see death as a time of judgment for sin or of vindication for sacrifices made during life. To them life in Christ must be its own judgment and reward, a relation to God with others that lacks this legal framework or already gives vindication in Christ's life.[12]

In this argument Paul says nothing directly about what resurrection means to the Corinthians beyond the fact that some deny the resurrection of the dead. It can be filled in to some extent by reading their views as the reverse side of Paul's argument with the guidance of the rest of the letter.

But this approach suffers from lack of precision. Baptism for the dead, however it was practiced, can provide one clear piece of evidence. It suggests that baptism is understood by them as the key event in which believers receive Christ's life. This is confirmed by the way Paul uncharacteristically distances himself from baptism in 1 Corinthians, dissociating himself from any intention to baptize in Corinth (1:13-17), warning them not to be like those who were baptized into Moses and died in the wilderness (10:1-12), and finally citing the practice of baptizing the dead against their profession that the dead are not raised (15:29). This letter as a whole also gives evidence that the Corinthians draw on at least three traditions of Christian baptism, and these provide a base for reading why they oppose Paul concerning resurrection of the dead.

The most widely attested baptismal tradition in the New Testament (which itself may be composite) associates baptism with water and the descent or receiving of the spirit, and sometimes speaks of repentance, fire, a divine-sent voice, and consequent speaking in tongues, prophesying, or witnessing (Mark 1:10-12; Matt. 3:1-17; Luke 3:1-22; John 1:19-28; 3:5-7; Acts 1:8; 2:1-4, 38; 8:15-17, 36-39; 10:44-48; 19:5-6; 1 Cor. 12:13; Eph. 4:1-6). This tradition is evident in the way the Corinthians identify themselves as the spiritual who speak in tongues and prophesy, and in Paul's recognizing this spirit as the initiator of faith, "In one spirit we were all baptized . . . and we all drink one spirit" (12:13; 2:10-12; 12:1-13; 14:2-5, 12, 37). That they receive this spirit sacramentally is confirmed in Paul's warning them about the Israelites who died in the wilderness although they were "baptized into Moses in the cloud and in the sea and all ate the same spiritual food and drank the same spiritual drink, for they drank from the spiritual rock that followed and that rock was Christ" (10:2-12). (Spiritual food and drinking the spirit are not usual parts of this baptismal tradition but have apparently become linked with it in Corinth.[13]) At the end of this warning Paul says, "Let those who think they stand, watch out not to fall" (10:12), a sign that the Corinthians may claim to "stand" or be fearless and invulnerable due to the spirit given in baptism. If so, when Paul claims that it is the gospel he announced "in which you stand" (15:1), he substitutes his list of witnesses, which assure resurrection of the dead, for their confidence in the spirit given to each in baptism.

In a second baptismal tradition, Christians claim to take off the old humanity as the pre-baptismal garment and put on Christ, God's image who cancels out the social privilege and oppression that cut across the old humanity (see chapter 6). The believer's new identity is not ordered as Jew or Greek, slave or free, male or female, but is one in Christ (Gal. 3:27-28; 1 Cor. 12:12-13; Col. 3:9-11). All elements of this tradition seem to be known in Corinth, as indicated by Paul's reversal of their interpretation of Christ as God's undifferentiated image who is not male and female (11:7) in favor of the male as God's image in a context where different people have interdependent gifts "whether Jews or Greeks, whether slaves or free" (12:13). When Paul uses the tradition of two forms of humanity to contrast Adam in whom all *have* died, and Christ in whom all *will be* made alive (15:22), he is supplanting another Christian use of Adam and Christ to signify baptismal transformation — Adam as each person's death and Christ as each person's new life (cf. Rom. 5:18).

In a third and equally distinct baptismal tradition the believer participates in Christ's dying and rising to new life. The initial impetus for this interpretation may have been the challenge to share in Jesus' death (Mark 10:38-39) as ritualized in a burial under the water of baptism and a rising to life (Rom. 6:4; Col. 2:12). By linking dying and rising with Christ to baptism, Paul suggests a recognized tradition, "Don't you know that we who were baptized into Christ Jesus were baptized into his death?" (Rom. 6:3) And there is considerable indirect evidence that the Corinthians take their baptism to be a death and resurrection with Christ.

One sign is that Paul avoids mentioning dying and rising with Christ in this long letter, although it is a major unifying theme in his thought (Gal. 2:19-20; 2 Cor. 4:7-14; 5:14-15; Rom. 5:3-11; 7:6; 8:10-11; Phil. 3:10-11). In these other texts Paul always speaks of new life with Christ as a present reality, going on to affirm its future fulfillment only in some cases. Yet in 1 Corinthians he withholds all encouragement of a deeper present experience of Christ's dying and rising, as if not to evoke what dying and rising with Christ mean in Corinth. In telling the resurrection tradition Paul reduces Jesus' death and rising to little more than necessary conditions for Jesus' past appearances (15:3-8); and when Paul says "I die daily" (15:31), it is to prove that there must be vindication after death, not to display Christ's life already present in his.

A second sign they claim to be resurrected is that some of them deny resurrection of the dead. We know no other doctrine they deny. On the contrary they speak affirmatively: "We all know," "All things are authorized," "All can prophesy" (6:12; 8:1; 10:23; 14:12, 31). They might ignore death, but they would only deny the resurrection of the dead if this teaching threatened to supplant their own life, the resurrection of the living.

To these may be added a third sign of their resurrection claim — the many ways Paul describes them living an exalted state of wisdom, power, and honor; standing beyond judgment; speaking in angels' tongues (4:10; 2:15; 13:1). This is most clear in his complaint, "You are already complete! You are already rich! Without us you have begun to rule!" (4:8) The messianic rule that Paul sharply limits in this argument to a time after Christ comes and triumphs over death — and in a way that leaves all power in God's hands alone (15:24-27) — is claimed here as a present reign in which believers fully participate. Only in what is probably the post-Pauline letter to the Colossians does the New Testament express a present resurrection triumph as bold as that attributed to the Corinthians: "Being buried with him in baptism, you were also raised through confidence in the empowering by God who raised him from the dead. Even you, who were dead people in the transgressions and uncircumcision of your flesh, God made alive with Christ. . . . Having stripped the armour off the principalities and powers, God has exposed them in open view, publicly triumphing over them in Christ" (Col. 2:12-15).

Against the Corinthian Claim to Live in the Spirit
Paul Reserves Spiritual Life until the Dead Are Raised

These baptismal traditions continue to provide a way of identifying the Corinthians' affirmations and watching what is happening to them in Paul's second argument for resurrection of the dead (15:35-58). Paul has just quelled the mutiny staged by his own distraught, "Let's eat, drink and be merry, for tomorrow we die," with a stern charge that they not sin, "for some have no knowledge of God, I must say to your shame" (15:32-34). The same berating tone continues, "But someone will say, how are the dead raised? With what body do they come? You fool!" Those who have no knowledge of God are now coalesced into this single fool who mocks Paul over the resurrection of the dead by asking how decayed bodies can rise.

But it is not necessarily the Corinthians speaking. His opening words, "But someone will say," suggest that he is writing both sides of the dialogue, constructing a stereotyped interlocutor who sees the body decay and is sure there is only this life in which to eat, drink, and be merry. Paul can use this interchange to teach the Corinthians, somewhat in the way that his attacks on incestuous and promiscuous men help him stir the devout into action (see chapter 4). On the affective level the Corinthians will not want to be classified with fools and may be provoked into considering Paul's contrary views. In terms of content, Paul shows them that he is no more a literal reductionist than they, that he is not advocating a physical reconstitution of the body but assumes with them and all the "enlightened" that the human body is mortal and the divine alone is immortal and gives life. They may have their own view of how the wise receive life — whether through the mind or soul that knows immortal reality, through an immortal spirit that pervades all reality, or, as I have argued and the baptismal confession suggests, by divine creative acts that make life out of death. But knowing that he does not mean the worst can open them up to listen. And conversely, his beginning this way assures them that he knows they are not really "fools" either.

The fool who asks how the dead are raised is answered with an earthy analogy. In mock patience Paul informs the farmer that a seed must dry up and die in order to germinate and is a naked thing nothing like the "body that will come to be" (15:36-38). While he hopes the Corinthians are dissociating themselves from such a fool by recognizing the obvious—thereby accepting Paul's disjunction between a dead body and another body to come—Paul explains the new body, which its necessary but dead predecessor cannot explain: God creates the body, "each according to its kind" (Gen. 1:11). This allows Paul to stretch the word "body" to include not only earthly but heavenly bodies in all their glory. So Paul gets the sanction from God's will, from Scripture, and even—if they know it—from the Platonists' view of stars as immortal persons made of pure light to help to break down the popular stereotype of the body as by definition perishable.[14]

The seed analogy with its scriptural explanation is then applied to the resurrection of the dead in a series of antitheses: "What is sown perishable is raised imperishable. What is sown in dishonor is raised in glory. What is sown in weakness is raised in power. What is sown a body of soul is raised a body of spirit" (or "What is sown an ensouled body is raised a spiritual body") (15:42-44). The final comparison is not quite parallel to the preceding ones, and its meaning remains in suspense until the following exegesis of Genesis 2:7. But its setting among the antitheses shows that Paul rejects any positive reading of "soul" and identifies it with that which is sown in decay (cf. 2:14), whereas that which rises is the "body of spirit" or "spiritual body."[15]

The question opening the section, "How do the dead rise? with what body do they come?" has been answered: "it is raised a spiritual body." The spiritual in Corinth find that Paul has nudged the word "body" up to meet them by doing everything possible, including a rerun of astral creation, to assure them that the body raised is not the body sown, the "spiritual body" is not the "ensouled body." Or it is possible he could be correcting their tendency to consider the soul impervious to the decay of the body by classifying the soul as part of what decays. In any case they share the broad Christian tradition of receiving the spirit in baptism and probably assume that they have the spiritual body he speaks of. They may hear themselves already "sown" and raised as spiritual bodies in Christ, parallel to their being dead and raised in Christ according to the third baptismal tradition. Paul has encouraged them to make this identification by describing what is raised in contrast to what is sown in terms of the virtues they claim in contrast to their past—though in this context he substitutes imperishability for wisdom—so that their past selves are what is sown, perishable, dishonored, and weak, and their present selves are what is raised, imperishable, glorified, and powerful (1:26-29; 4:10).

But Paul is not finished. His second argument for the resurrection climaxes in an interpretation of Genesis. It is prefixed with the often unnoticed statement, "If there is an ensouled body, there is also a spiritual body" (15:44b). Paul has reversed his opening conclusion from effect to cause—to use his image, there is no live plant without a dead seed (15:36)—into a conclusion from cause to effect—if there is a seed there will be a plant. The lack of proof would be more obvious if he had not abandoned his seed image and switched to speaking of the ensouled body and the spiritual body—allowing him to cover for lack of necessity with expected sequence. It might seem that he had given up proof from cause and effect when he declared that the old body is dead and the new body is God's creation. But divine agency is apparently intended as a distinct sanction from Scripture (Gen. 1:11) for the possibility of a heavenly body, an argument not compatible with but parallel to the cause and effect argument that comes to the conclusion, "If there is an ensouled body, then there is a spiritual body."[16]

Paul immediately supports this vulnerable conclusion by an explicit appeal to God's creating the male human being in the garden. Paul takes up the words of Genesis 2:7 LXX: "And God shaped the man of dirt from the earth and he breathed into his face a breath of life, and the man became a living soul." Paul uses the end of the verse first to characterize Adam as a living soul and contrasts this Adam with the life-giving spirit that he identifies as the second Adam, then repeating this contrast by telling the origin of the two: "Even as it is written, 'The first man Adam became a living soul, the last Adam a life-giving spirit. . . . The first man was of dirt from the earth, the second man was from heaven'" (15:45, 47). The Genesis text's authority is thus extended to affirm two Adams, the second as "life-giving spirit" apparently found hidden in the two cognate words describing God's spirit, "breath of life."[17] The point that Paul emphasizes in this reading of Genesis that Adam, as the living soul, comes first, while Christ, as the life-giving spirit, comes last—is present in Genesis only tenuously in God's shaping the earth-man before breathing life into it. Paul stresses this sequence, even interrupting his quotation of Genesis, with the sentence, "Yet the spiritual is not first but the ensouled, then the spiritual" (15:46).

What is the meaning of this sequence, for Paul and the Corinthians? One explanation sees Paul reacting to a tradition in Hellenistic-Jewish wisdom exegesis that speaks of two different divine creations of humanity associated with the two creation stories in Genesis.[18] In this tradition God first creates the idea of humanity in God's own image—immortal, unchanging, and supremely real in the Platonic sense, not limited by body or sexuality (Gen. 1:27). Then God creates—in the story Paul is reading—the physical, living, male and female persons (Gen. 2:7, 21-25). The fact that Paul tells of two Adams at all may come from this tradition or from a common source. But he finds them both in the second story: one in "he became a living soul" and the other in God's "breath of life," and in *that* order, as if to reverse the temporal priority of the ideal Adam over the physical Adam, presumably on behalf of an ultimate resurrection in the last Adam, Christ.

This could be intended to reverse a Platonizing exegesis of Genesis in Corinth,[19] one developed under the influence of Hellenistic-Jewish wisdom but as a Christian theology identifying the ideal humanity made in

God's image with Christ. Corinthians with such a theology could be expected to consider Christ an ideal image rather than a sense-perceptible, sexual body. When putting on Christ as God's image according to the baptismal tradition, they would see themselves as heavenly humans, made before Adam's time and directed to spiritual wisdom rather than physical desire. This is an attractive proposal because it provides a unifying focus for understanding Corinthian thought from Paul's emphatic reversal of wisdom's two Adams. If they took Christ as the original humanity, they would have seen their baptisms as the recollection or recovery of their essential nature in the Platonizing sense, not as the constituting act of a new creation. Their withdrawal from sexuality and the relative independence of women could then be accounted for as consequences of an identity that precedes sexual differentiation. Yet the prominence of communal prophecy, baptism, and other physical demonstrations of the spirit are more difficult to integrate into a Platonist anthropology.

The greater difficulty of this explanation for Paul's stress on sequence is that it draws on the first story of creation in God's image, which Paul is not discussing here, and ignores more obvious explanations from within Paul's argument. Paul has introduced the story of creation in the garden to support his final antithesis, "What is sown an ensouled body is raised a spiritual body," and in this antithesis is already using language from the story (15:45). The problem is that this Genesis passage, ". . . he breathed into his face a breath of life, and the man became a living soul," threatens to make God's breath or spirit into that which is sown and the living soul into the resulting crop, throwing off the entire demonstration that the spiritual body follows the death of the ensouled body (Gen. 2:7 LXX). Paul's previous conclusion from cause to effect, "If there is an ensouled body, there is also a spiritual" (15:44b), would not be supported but undermined by such Scripture proof.

Why does Paul choose this text if it does not suit his purposes? It does give Paul the chance to answer his question, "With what body do they come?" in terms of a "spiritual body" distinct from Adam's human life. All Paul needs to do is apply the word "body" to both the "living soul" and the "life-making spirit" to show that the Scripture anticipates two kinds of humanity, a mortal body and a spiritual body—assuming that the sequence can be held firm. But this question of his fictive interlocutor is insufficient explanation for choosing a Genesis sentence *ending* with the "living soul" to prove that the living soul comes *first*. However, a Corinthian use of this story could explain why Paul reworks it. They may use the early part of this Genesis passage to stress that God first formed Adam from the earth and then gives the breath of life in Christ. Thus the Corinthians could see themselves among the spiritual bodies, sown perishing and raised imperishable, sown in dishonor and raised in glory, sown merely formed and raised spiritual (15:35-44b). If so, Paul intensifies their sequence: the Adam who dies gives way to the Adam who generates life, the earthly one to the heavenly one, and—at last they hear themselves named—those of earth to those of heaven (15:45-48). Thus Paul draws them into this mirror by fine threads woven together from all their baptismal traditions—the spirit that gives life, the new human being from the old, the life that comes out of death.

Only his last sentence reveals that the threads have formed a web, "Just as we have borne the image of the earthly one, so we *will* bear the image of the heavenly one" (15:49). Their reaction to the future tense is palpable. It is not that Paul's point of view has changed since he introduced the two Adams in the first argument: "For just as in Adam all die, so also in Christ all will be made alive" (15:22). But the second argument for the heavenly body has been so carefully kept in the present tense that the spiritual have confirmed it from their own exegesis and experience. This rhetorical strategy is the best evidence that Paul would not have broken the spell in mid-spin by an attack on their reading of the two Genesis stories.

Now Paul makes it clear that he has been talking about a transformation that has not yet happened to the Corinthians. This means that his use of explicit baptismal language for what is by definition beyond their reach takes on a sharp edge. They "will bear the image of the heavenly one" only at some future time. Whether they still bear the image of the earthly one or live in a limbo between the image "we have borne" and the image we will bear" is clarified in Paul's next appeals. He no longer allures them with argument but applies personal pressures and sanctions to support his stand.

First he speaks from Christian tradition and then rephrases in the language of the present discussion: "But I tell you, brethren, that flesh and blood cannot inherit God's kingdom, nor can what perishes inherit imperishability" (15:50; 6:9-10, 13; John 3:5-6; 1:12-13). They are unmistakenly taken as flesh that perishes (cf. 3:1-4), as those now bearing the image of Adam. This is confirmed by prophecy (15:51-52; cf. 1 Thess. 4:15; Rom. 11:25), an irony that would not be lost on those baptized in the spirit that is presently speaking in them. Paul recounts his vision of the last moment when "the dead will be raised incorruptible, and we will be changed" (15:51-52). This excludes the possibility that the change in the believer has already taken place. Paul then explains why the surviving will need to be transformed just as those whose bodies have fully perished, because "this perishability must put on imperishability and this mortal must put on immortality" (15:53). They remain defined by their perishability. Their baptismal "putting on" of Christ is fully co-opted for the time of his ultimate coming. Finally the cry of victory over death, spoken by Isaiah in the future tense and apparently claimed by believers as an accomplished fact in this past tense, is again thrown into the future by Paul's introduction, "But when this perishability has put on imperishability and this mortal has put on immortality, *then* will be the word which is written, 'Death has been swallowed up in victory'" (15:54-55).[20]

The chapter closes with a warning on sin and the law, with thanks to God "who gives us the victory in Jesus Christ" and with a call, "So, my loved brethren, be firm, unshakable, excelling in the Lord's work always, knowing that your labor in the Lord is not in vain" (15:57-58). These words promise that those who hold on to the past tradition and work hard will receive a future reward after the dead are resurrected and the surviving are changed to join in immortality.

The women prophets are hit by Paul's second argument for the dead's resurrection in two ways. First, Paul has displaced their putting on Christ as God's image from the baptismal confession, dropping its qualification as not male and female and projecting it into the ultimate future. Meanwhile it is the image of Adam (or that of Eve made from his rib? [11:8]) that the women are to go on carrying until the time when mortal puts on immortality. So they are suspended between one male image and another, both claiming universality in their own period but neither offering a present life of full humanity to women.

Second, Paul indicates that the spiritual bodies of the resurrected dead are to be differentiated in glory on analogy to the astral heavenly bodies according to God's choice (15:39-41), as Paul earlier said the gifts are distributed in the church (15:38; 12:11, 18, 28). This final ordering is expected to solve the questions arising from some people believing more firmly than others, working harder, suffering more, being instrumental in the faith of others, not bearing false witness; that is, it will provide the retribution stressed by Paul, in order that nothing be done in vain (15:2, 10-11, 14-15, 17, 31-32, 58). This might seem to be a benefit to the women prophets who appear to have much to be requited for. But the women reading Paul's closing admonition to his beloved brethren to be firm, knowing their work will be rewarded, would still have in mind Paul's parallel admonition to his brethren to prophesy and do everything decently and in order, spoken by Paul just after silencing their prophecy (15:58; 14:39-40; cf. 11:33-34). If it is Paul's God of peace and order who will assign the spiritual bodies, they must know that their wrongs will not be righted. Their God, on the other hand, would not be reserving and assigning at all, but would give all gifts immediately and across every boundary to the joyful disruption of their common life.

In summary, Paul's first argument in this chapter centers on the image of Christ as first fruit of the resurrection of the dead, a resurrection that takes place not in this life but after Christ comes and triumphs over death. Paul's second argument claims that as the plant does not appear before the seed is sown, nor the last Adam before the first, so the imperishable body—which is their immortality, victory, and inheritance in the kingdom— cannot come until the imperishable body dies or, surviving, is changed into an imperishable spiritual body at the end. The remaining question is whether Paul neglects the believers' present life in Christ simply because his focus here is on the dead and on ultimate survival, or whether he intends this radical shift from present to future in the temporal location of life in Christ.

In the first argument he consistently collapses the present life of the believer. The tradition cited about Christ's dying "for our sins" is quickly corrected so that "you are still in your sins" if the dead are not raised and Christ is not risen (15:3, 18). Beyond this there are no benefits of Jesus being alive except a past list of appearances; even Paul's own work is due to God's grace and not Jesus' presence. Believing the gospel is identified with believing the resurrection of the dead (15:2, 11, 14, 17). The function of being "in Christ" is to be first at the time of his coming (15:23). In the second argument all life is reduced to two realities, the perishable and the imperishable, earthly bodies and heavenly bodies, first Adam and last Adam (15:36-37, 40, 42-48). "We have borne the image of the one of dirt and will also bear the image of the heavenly one," but meanwhile the change is still ahead and "flesh and blood cannot inherit."

All these arguments could conceivably be defended as Paul's pruning away of every limb of the tradition to revive the resurrection of the dead, but he is not able do this without making the dead's resurrection the core confession on which everything depends. In the context of 1 Thessalonians this might be understood in terms of his concern for the bereaved (1 Thess. 4:13-18). But Paul's charge that some Corinthians have died for their conduct at the Lord's meal (11:30) shows that here his defense of the resurrection is not on behalf of the bereaved. In 1 Corinthians he consistently challenges the believers to limit the use of their authority in matters of wisdom, sexuality, meat eating, and spiritual leadership—often proposing specific restrictions, and his final pruning in this setting cannot be seen as an isolated case. Even where the argument for the common good plays a role—he claims their eating idol food may "destroy the brother for whom Christ died"—his overriding argument is that they must not make God jealous or claim to be stronger than God (8:11; 10:1-22). This letter is written on behalf of the God whom Paul serves, to defend God from their bold claims on God's gifts. All indications are that Paul reduces the gospel to proof that Jesus was alive shortly after his death, which guarantees resurrection beyond the grave and vindication of sacrificial work. This undermines the Corinthians' assurance that Christ is alive in their prayer and prophecy and in the authority of those God sets free.

It is difficult for those of us raised in a world where resurrection is reserved for the dead to understand what resurrection in Christ might have meant for the Corinthian women prophets. Different parts of Paul's argument give us footholds for a tentative reconstruction. In the first place, to these prophets resurrection is not subjection to an external tradition secured by a few authoritative past witnesses but is a present and communal experience of themselves coming to life in Christ. As communal, it probably incorporates some memory of the women and men who experienced Christ's presence from the beginning. Nor is the resurrection an anticipation of future subjection by telling a narrative of God's coming defeat of multiple claims to life by the claims of Christ alone, followed by the subordination of Christ's claim to God. Rather, life in Christ is generative and creative so that death is not defeated by capture and destruction of an evil life-force but death's weakness and pain are overpowered with health and life.

Second, Christ's resurrection is not a guarantee or first fruit of something not yet experienced; this first fruit begins the harvest immediately and only thereby secures the harvest to come. God is not identified with peace and order, withholding life until some proper sequence of events occurs, but God is identified with disruption that overwhelms the structures that ossify life.

Third, Christ's resurrection is not a retribution, either as reward for good work or punishment for past sin, but an initiation that liberates people from an old humanity bound in the structures of sin, stratified as male or female, slave or free. The new humanity that puts on God's image is not split between privilege and deprivation or reward and punishment but is a single identity in Christ where people mediate God to each other in prophecy and each other to God in prayer.

Fourth, the resurrection is not the preserve of the dead. It must be conceded to Paul against the skeptic that God can bring life out of death, honor from shame, and immortality to what is mortal. The practice of baptism for the dead suggests that the Corinthians think life continues in some way when people die, but what matters to them is that God expects and gives a full and present exercise of that resurrection life. Not restricted to the world of the dead, God is now meeting death in Adam with life in Christ. Paul's argument defending resurrection of the dead and of those who survive until Christ's coming, an argument apparently directed against the skeptic, is in fact seeking to persuade those who live in Christ that God has not raised them to life.

Paul's Quick Memos Show His Network of Commitments in Tension with a Different Corinthian Network

The precision of Paul's final notes and instructions in 1 Corinthians 16 makes them as revealing as their brevity makes the picture fragmentary. The following comments will be limited to basic points and their implications for the Corinthian women prophets.

The Corinthians know about Paul's collection for Jerusalem and apparently mentioned it in their letter, as Paul's short instructions headed "concerning the collection" indicate. There was apparently no objection in principle that he must contest, but some lack of response or effective method of collection makes him propose a new approach. On the first day of the week (before any shopping? before coming together?) all of them are to set aside what they can and keep it for when Paul comes. The fact he says he has given these instructions in Galatia's churches cannot be strictly for historical interest or interchurch ties. He probably wants them to hear that this system is not being tailor-made to avoid problems in Corinth.

However, the problems are obvious. Funds in these homes are probably used up each week for food and other expenses, some of it communally, and Paul cannot raise money quickly when he comes, nor is there a person in the community everyone will trust to keep it for a distant time and place associated with Paul. Very possibly, those few who would give to Paul's project do not do so because they doubt that those who gather common money would keep these funds separate. As has been previously proposed in discussing common meals, women who cook, women who have a church in their homes, women without families to serve, and/or women known for single devotion to the community and leadership in it may handle food donations including food or money for the hungry. Would it be strange if people accustomed to the order of a synagogue did not want to lose sight of their money in this informal system with minimal allegiance to Paul? His instruction that persons of their choice carry the gift to Jerusalem would assure major donors that they could help choose these people or be chosen, as well as attract gifts from others who do not want to send Paul to Jerusalem rich. Yet Paul leaves the door open to going himself, which he later does. One wonders if other itinerant leaders have private collections the Corinthians support, or whether they use up their own resources in local outreach and resent such procedures.

Paul's travel plans and recommendation of Timothy echo his earlier demand that they learn from Timothy what Paul teaches in all the churches and his earlier warning that he is coming soon to test if there is any action behind their boasts (4:16-21). He also charged that some of them act as if he will never return (4:18) and now explains why he will not be there soon—he wants to stay with them so he must pass through Macedonia first, and there is too much to do in Ephesus to leave before Pentecost. He is trying to be everywhere at once. And he tells them, almost pathetically, not to make Timothy afraid when he comes, not to despise him, to send him back as soon as possible. Thinking of Timothy taking the reaction to this letter, he pleads for mercy—hardly a strong recommendation, but maybe safer for Timothy. So the women prophets will not attack Timothy as Paul's full representative, yet he can pick up their reactions and report quickly to Paul. Apparently Timothy is not part of their own communication network.

Word about Apollos probably follows because, as Paul's "And concerning Apollos" suggests, they have spoken about him in their letter and Paul's response shows they wanted him to come—yet Timothy is on the way as Paul writes and they are offended. Paul insists that he urged Apollos "many times to come to you with the brethren." He claims he did his very best. But "the brethren" almost surely applies to the group, to be named next, who are carrying this letter to Corinth. One can see why Paul would like Apollos to accompany the letter and thus support the recovery of Paul's leadership in Corinth and the restructuring of their life. It is therefore not surprising that Apollos has not come, though it is unclear if Paul is saying, with some blame, that Apollos was in no way willing to come now, or if more likely Paul disguises Apollos' refusal to come by stressing that God has him engaged elsewhere.[21] The indirect message that he will come when he can is probably meant to show that Apollos and Paul are on good terms and in general agreement on Corinth. But the lack of any greeting to the Corinthians from Apollos makes this doubtful.[22] Paul's rather cryptic sentence about Apollos suggests, in spite of Paul's efforts to the contrary, that the Corinthian women prophets may still have allies with whom they maintain communication.

Paul's closing admonition shows that his memos are done. After writing this sentence there may be some lapse until the delegation arrives that will carry the letter, at which time their commendation and the last greetings are appended. The admonition is consistent with the letter as a whole, "Watch, stand in faith, be manly, be strong, do everything with love" (16:13). For the women prophets it cuts across the grain at every point: watch for the transformation yet to come, stand not in the spirit's confidence but in the faith transmitted to you, be like men unflinching in your duty, strong at your assigned post, and be ready to sacrifice yourself for others.

Paul highly recommends the household of Stephanas who will apparently carry his letter. But the tone is not so much enthusiastic about them as monitory to the hearers, beginning "I entreat you, brethren. You know the household of Stephanas . . . ," and continuing with witness to their seniority and devotion, "so you also would well be subject to such people and to each coworker and laborer" (16:15-16). This verb, used for the right attitude for women in the churches and still more recently hallowed by the ultimate subjection of the world to Christ and Christ to God, is recommended toward this household of Stephanas, Paul's first baptized converts in Corinth (14:34; 15:27-28; 1:16). No women in this household are mentioned. Some are doubtless at least marginally intended, but subjection to his household is unlikely to mean subjection to its subject members.

Paul's next announcement of joy at the arrival of Stephanas, Fortunatus, and Achaicus suggests that these three may represent the household he has been discussing, the later two being either slaves, freedmen, sons, brothers, or simply fellow artisans in a house workshop of Stephanas.[23] In any case, Paul's point in conclusion is that these three have made up for the Corinthians' absence and have put his spirit to rest concerning them and their spirits concerning him (16:17-18). Apparently they have carried news and letters both ways—hardly restful letters, but the assumption is that ignorance or rumors are put to rest by direct communication and those who are faithful make it known (2 Cor. 2:12-13; 7:5-13; Phil. 2:28). They may travel regularly because Paul expects Timothy to come back with them. He ends the commendation, "Therefore recognize such people" (16:18b). After the opening reminder that this household is "firstfruit of Achaia" and the intervening call to be subject to them, this closing does not confirm so much Paul's respect for these men as the Corinthians' lack of respect. It is likely the women prophets among others in Corinth do not share Paul's enthusiasm for his early converts, whether due to these converts' lack of the newer wisdom, their earlier training as God-fearers or Jews, their more patriarchal household structure, their higher economic or social status, their conservative influence in the community, or their allegiance to Paul. They may have encouraged a Corinthian letter to Paul when business took them to Asia, hoping for a response that could recoup Paul's influence in Corinth and theirs as well. Paul is returning the favor and disclosing the problem.

The final greetings are few and general except that Aquila and Prisca and the church in their house ask "many times" to be remembered to them (16:19). This couple appear in Paul's letters here, perhaps in or near Ephesus where Paul is writing (15:32; 16:8), and again in Rome where Paul sends them effusive thanks as fellow workers who have risked their lives for him and the Gentile churches (Rom. 16:3-5). Second Timothy 4:19 suggests that they returned to Asia later. By Luke's account they were first expelled from Rome with the Jews during Claudius' reign, moved their tent-making business to Corinth where Paul lived and worked with them, and later moved with Paul to Ephesus, teaching Apollos about baptism when he arrived from Alexandria and sending him on to Corinth (Acts 18:2-3, 18, 26-27). Because Aquila is never mentioned without Prisca, and she usually first, she was unmistakably a key Christian leader, with churches in their home in Ephesus and Rome and a highly mobile economic base. As previously suggested, she may have taught Apollos baptismal traditions known to the women in Corinth (see chapter 3) and yet remained in close working relations with Paul across many provinces. Whether she prophesied is unknown but is not unlikely, considering Paul's concession to the Corinthians that all may prophesy. Paul's greeting from Aquila and her to Corinth indicates that she has continuing relations to women in Corinth, possibly fostered by letters and visits.

After calling on the Corinthians to greet each other with a holy kiss, Paul's final greeting is his own and in his own hand. He probably also writes out the curse on any who do not love the Lord, the call on the Lord to come, and the blessing of the Lord's grace and his own love. Such curses, calls, and blessings go beyond argument to performative speech—the kind practiced by the spiritual. Prophets will recognize that God has been invoked and will invoke God to support their response in return.

9 | Conclusion

THE AIM OF THIS STUDY has been to reconstruct what can be known of the women prophets in Corinth's mid-first-century church from the significant role they play in the rhetorical situation of Paul's 1 Corinthians. To conclude I first draw together some of the findings about these women as Paul projects them—their conduct, self-understanding, and theology. Second, I test one proposal I have made on the basis of these findings, the proposal concerning the social status of the Corinthian women prophets and of Paul (see Excursus on Social Status after chapter 3 and Appendix 7). I do this by building on the work of people using other methods, specifically Bruce Malina and Jerome H. Neyrey who use Mary Douglas's "group/grid" analysis and E. A. Judge and Peter Marshall who analyze Greco-Roman social conventions. In each case the last-named person has applied the method fruitfully to 1 Corinthians; I will propose some implications of their methods concerning the women prophets' social status, an issue they do not address. The assumption is that different methods should not produce contrary results but confirm and broaden other findings.

Conduct and Functions of the Corinthian Women Prophets

In a society where women are in short supply due to female infanticide and death at childbirth and are therefore married young and remarried quickly when widowed, many Christian women have withdrawn from sexual relations (7:1-40). Slave women normally have no such option. But since this might also be said in a different sense of free women, slave women are probably making similar attempts where age, influence, or a Christian mistress make it possible.

Those who withdraw from sexual relations are not under the authority of another person in the same sense as before. This is evident in the fact that some of them do not continue to live with husbands but are separated and live with relatives or other women. They may no longer take care of their own children if the father, whose children they legally are, has relatives or slaves to care for them. Other women continue to live in the same home with husbands, perhaps due to children. Some remain with parents. All these women cease—or do not begin—to bear children, moving the focus of their commitment to the new community. They cook together or carry food to common meals daily or weekly, thereby being present early and late to make the Lord's meal their own meal. The creative force of the communal home is shown by Paul's extended effort to separate the common life as a public domain from private life, relegating to individual homes not only the hunger-satisfying meal but uncovered heads in prophecy, ecstatic prayer that is not interpreted, collecting of money, and all women's speech, thereby confirming the household system with its subordination.

Paul describes the unmarried women and virgins as "consecrated both in body and spirit" (7:34). From this one might infer that they take abstinence from sexual relations as the essential act that transfers loyalty from husband or betrothed to God in the mode reflected in the second- to fourth-century Apocryphal Acts.[1] Their confidence in baptism and spiritual food and drink could be seen as other signs that the physical is to them the guarantor of the spiritual (10:1-4). But then one would expect them to construct a closed social world, with tight boundaries against pollution in matters of food, clothing, and social contact. Instead, the Corinthian women are known for flexibility and freedom — eating at temples, putting off head covering, supporting a young couple whom Paul considers incestuous — and it is Paul who cries out "flee idolatry," "flee immorality."

In Corinth, Paul is the wary one, fearing that the free gift of God's spirit will be co-opted for human gain unless there is a radical discipline of the body. This is best understood from Paul's experience of sin as competition for God's glory. Therefore he sees that the body, without separating itself from the world, which is destined ultimately for life, must close itself off from every temptation to learn from the world the way of human glory, which is death. This reading gives Paul the benefit of the doubt at several points where his restrictions come perilously close to stifling the spirit. But to speak on his behalf, he leaves even his most extreme pronouncements expelling the man living with his father's wife and silencing the women to the adjudication of the spirit at work in the communal body (5:4-5; 14:37). Without this concession of the spirit's ultimate freedom, Paul's restrictions of believers in matters of wisdom, sexuality, eating, speaking, and rising from present death would be exposed as external restrictions on the spirit and not as the spirit's peculiar self-discipline in face of a mutiny against God's glory.

In contrast to Paul, the women prophets in Corinth's church do not experience in themselves a struggle against God that requires radical restrictions of the body. Instead, the danger seems to be that the spirit poured out might be wasted if fearful people do not allow its exercise in themselves and the community. Many reject sexual relations that involve the authority of one person over the body of another in order to devote themselves to prayer and prophecy. But this does not exclude their support of the sexual bonds of others not ruled by such authority (7:3-5; 5:2, 6).

True authority is that of the spirit, exercised physically both in feasting on sacrificed food to show that all food is the one God's gift or in joyful celebration of the Lord's meal to share Christ's living presence (8:1-6; 11:20-34). No one regulates the meal or judges sexual conduct. Apparently the spirit is trusted to overpower and cleanse itself of every weakness through its free expression in the community. Whether in speech or acts of authority, the spirit animates a people once scattered and dead, raising them as a communal demonstration of Christ's resurrection.

The best picture of their common life comes from Paul's response to their prayer and prophecy. Because Paul expects prayer to be heightened by sexual abstinence (7:5), and because the Hellenistic world anticipates women prophets will be chaste,[2] it may be the participation in prophecy and prayer that draws women to become "consecrated both in body and spirit." Prophecy and prayer are practiced by women with their heads uncovered, the common dress in their own and each others' homes, but not necessarily in public as Paul tries to impress upon them (11:13-16). The fact that Paul expects contention rather than compliance on the issue shows their practice is deliberate. They retain the house-church as their own space and signify that they are no longer determined by shame through sexual subordination but are determined by honor through the spirit as persons who have put on Christ, God's image not male and female, and mediate God to each other. They do not see this as competing for glory against God, let alone as representing man's glory in the male competition against God that absorbs Paul. Rather they glorify God by being glorified in communal speaking to and for God.

Prophecy and prayer are practiced (14:1-40) by rising from any seated position in the gathering and speaking in the Spirit, not necessarily waiting for another to finish. Such speaking stimulates others to speak and extended sessions are common. Learning in the community takes place less by hearing a few people and weighing what they say than by many people speaking what they are all beginning to see. In Corinth, the two kinds of speech that Paul contrasts, prophecy and speaking in tongues, are not sharply differentiated as gifts belonging to different people or as appropriate in different contexts. Prophecy speaks for God, most likely either directly in first-person divine self-commendations, announcements, and blessings or in accounts of revelations and words of divine wisdom. Ecstatic speech is the language of prayer in response, appearing when praises, acclamations, and pleas to God have exhausted discursive speech. There may also be a teaching of wisdom particularly associated with baptism, an instruction in "the depths of God," "the mind of Christ," and the new life "not male and female" such as Apollos receives from Priscilla and Aquila according to Luke (Acts 18:26).

In the interaction of these voices, leadership is determined functionally by actual influence in the community. Many people strive to lead others in these ways, and the authority of a prophecy or prayer is apparently not taken as less the spirit's authority because it is also the authority of the person who speaks. Where conflict appears it is open and, at least on the issue of itinerant leaders, brings on counter-affirmations from others (1:12). Paul's objection to their speech is not that an elite group withdraws in body or spirit but that they exceed and, he thinks, overwhelm others who do not participate as fully. Because the community is not careful to avoid offending others, its outreach is probably taking place less among those established in religion or society than among those who lack position and stand to gain from new claims. The ethics fostered are release from external authorities and communal expression of divine authority, not the ethics of self-discipline and community order. The fact that Paul's regulating of tongues and prophecy climaxes in demanding the women's silence and then in putting this to a spiritual vote of confidence shows the women prophets' key role in his opposition.

Theology and Self-Understanding of the Corinthian Women Prophets

The basic outlines of the Corinthian women prophets' theology are familiar: God freely chooses to recreate humanity by raising Christ from the dead so that all who put on Christ, God's image, are no longer male and female, free and slave, Jew and Greek, but are people filled with God's spirit—that alone knows God—and become channels of this spirit to others. This is familiar not only because we retrieve their theology through Paul's and therefore in his idiom, but because faith in Christ took this shape in the Hellenistic cities before Paul. But within this language-world significant theological differences could be expressed, and the tension between Paul and the Corinthians represents only one possible axis of such conflict. Paul and the Corinthians had different interpretations of the several traditions in which this confession is made: God's resurrection of the crucified Christ, God's new creation of the believer in Christ, and the spirit of God working in those who believe.

The fact that Paul argues from Christ's resurrection to prove resurrection for the dead shows that the Corinthians and Paul agree that God has raised the crucified Christ from the dead (15:12-19). The Corinthians apparently share the early view that the crucifixion was an act of violence committed by the world's rulers who did not know God's intent (2:8). But God raised Christ to expose their ignorance, overcame their death-dealing power, and revealed Jesus as the Lord of Glory. From the Old Testament the church takes up acclamations in the completed past tense of what God has accomplished, "He has put all things under his feet"; "Death has been swallowed up in victory" (15:25-28, 54). God's raising of Christ is demonstrated by pointing, not to a past event, but directly to those who are transformed by the triumph of the Lord of Glory over death. They may express this by stating that they have passed from death into life, that they have been crucified and raised up in Christ, or that they have died and they live with Christ in God (15:21; Rom. 6:4; Col. 2:9-15; 3:1-4).

In 1 Corinthians, Paul pulls back from this present claim to make a sharply different interpretation of Christ's resurrection, securing it as an event in the past by selected early witnesses, with his own experience of Christ taken as the final authoritative witness (15:1-11). Although Paul calls the raised Christ the "first fruit," this resurrection harvest is restricted to the dead—he is the "first fruit of those who have fallen asleep" (15:18, 20). A partial exception is made to include a transformation of living believers who survive until that future time when Christ appears and triumphs over the powers, the last of which is death (15:23-28, 51-54). This makes certain witnesses of the past event of Christ's resurrection the guarantors of a future resurrection for those in Christ, allowing no present access to Christ's life.

Paul's aim is to protect the imperishable spiritual life from claims to inheritance by perishable flesh and blood. Since the Corinthians agree that only those who receive God's spirit can inherit this life, it is evident that he does not accept the spirit they have received. In a world where Paul suffers losses and his work threatens to be in vain (15:2, 10, 14, 17, 30-31, 58), he cannot believe that death has yet been overcome. God may promise and guarantee life in Christ's resurrection, but God is not permitted to give the spirit that can receive life in a world where there is death. By restricting the field of God's power in raising Christ to past witnesses and the future dead, Paul makes believers dependent on the word of selected witnesses concerning what kind of present conduct God will reward in the future resurrection.

In contrast, the Corinthian women prophets claim direct access to resurrected life in Christ through God's spirit. Being thus filled, rich and ruling, they take part in Christ's joyful meal and God's word goes forth from them to each other in ever-widening circles (4:8; 14:36). They must still contend against contrary powers, as Paul demonstrates (11:16; 14:34-38). But they experience Christ to be alive in that contention, demonstrating to them that God will not be restricted to the past or future for purposes of human reassurance or control.

A second early Christian affirmation, that God creates a new humanity in Christ, also leads to conflict between Paul and the women prophets in Corinth. In other letters Paul stresses that people in Christ no longer know each other in the old terms as Jew and Greek but have been made a new creation according to God's image (Gal. 6:15; 2 Cor. 5:16-17; Gal. 3:27-28; Col. 3:9-11). But in 1 Corinthians the canceling of privilege in a new creation "neither Jew nor Greek, slave nor free, not male and female" (Gal. 3:28) becomes an integration of parts with different degrees of honor into a functioning whole "whether Jews or Greeks, slaves or free" (1 Cor. 12:12-31). Male and female are not included in this integration but are confirmed in the old mold, the privileged male being identified as God's image and glory and the female as man's glory (11:8). This is at such odds with the Christian tradition that Paul quickly concedes a certain interdependence in Christ—but not to cancel out required symbols of male privilege (11:11-16). Finally Paul says, "Just as we have borne the image of the earthly one, so we will bear the image of the heavenly one" (15:49). He thus removes the old and new humanities into the past and future, disqualifying the people already created as God's image in Christ.

This many-faceted attack indicates that the Corinthians see themselves as a new humanity created in Christ, God's image, a new creation nothing like the old. With Paul they see that the old creation in Adam was strictly earthly and bound to sin and death (15:22-23, 45-50), whereas only the new creation is in God's image. This is specified, not individually in terms of purity from sins or excellence in virtues, but communally or socially in terms of there being "neither Jew nor Greek, slave nor free, not male and female." The baptismal confession quotes phrases in Genesis 1:27 and 5:1-2 and derives its Jew/Greek and slave/free pairs from an original "male and female" in these texts. The Corinthians stress that a one-time privilege of male over female is supplanted by a single identity in Christ, which is the new creation in God's image. No one has headship or authority over another in body or spirit but all are consecrated to God. The positions of domination and shame based on old roles are gone and a new reality of divine honor has taken their place. The Corinthians demonstrate their authority in Christ by eating, speaking, and working together without fear that they could be competing with God's glory. Their only obligation is to withhold nothing in realizing God's image among themselves so that all might see and come to participate in the new humanity in Christ.

The third affirmation, that God's spirit of wisdom and power is poured out on the foolish, is above all a bone of contention. Paul, offended by what he sees as Corinthian foolishness that claims to be wisdom, can only affirm the Spirit's gifts by qualifying them with internal checks, warnings, and calls to self-discipline or by carrying his claims into paradox and exposé. Sacrificed food may be eaten, but only with one eye on a brother who could be offended and the other on God who could be made jealous (8:9-13; 10:14-22). Paul's own right to be fed in exchange for preaching is dramatized at length in order to be renounced (9:1-18). Paul tells them in Christ's words to eat the bread and drink the cup, but "whoever eats and drinks without discerning the body, eats and drinks judgment" (11:23, 29). Christ is the power and wisdom of God for believers, but strictly as the crucified, not the resurrected one. This is demonstrated in God's sending the trembling apostle and calling the powerless and ignorant Corinthians (1:24—2:6). The wisdom Paul does claim to speak to the mature he cannot speak to the contentious in Corinth (2:6–3:4). It seems that the spirit is being poured out only to be sucked back like a receding tide. If the demand exceeds the gift, Paul considers it for their own good. Or it may be God whom Paul wants to protect from squandering gifts on them.

In stark contrast, the Corinthians are confident in the spirit. They who were once ignorant, weak, and shamed have now become wise, strong, and honored through the gifts God has given them (1:26; 4:10). Once dependent on the powerful and controlled by fear, now they are nourished continually with spiritual food and drink and have become filled, rich, and ruling (10:3; 4:8). Furthermore, these gifts are not given externally or exercised mechanically, making the Corinthians into divine slaves. God's own spirit, which alone knows God, has been given to them so that they are able to understand God as if from within, to discern God's gifts, and to exercise them in fitting ways (2:6-16). By the work of God's spirit in them they become mediators to others of what God gives. This may happen in acts of healing, helping, administering, believing, and teaching (12:8-11, 28-30).

But most prominently the women are known for speaking God's thoughts to the people in prophecy and responding for the people to God in prayer (11:5; 14:1-38). In both cases it is God's spirit that inspires them, drawing them—and others through them—into a divine communion that moves beyond speech into "tongues of angels" (13:1). These gifts and the spirit by which they are exercised are not given sparingly so as to make the many dependent on a few to speak and explain what is spoken. Apparently anyone may receive the spirit, and prophecy becomes a communal experience where voices pile up and are extended so that people inspire each other to express what they had not before known and thus discover that God is present among them (14:24-36).

In all this, God is known through the Spirit as the Giver without reserve, one whose resources are never limited, one never wary of being misused or upstaged but always pouring forth insight and power and blessing wherever humans are open to receive. This understanding of God also seems to determine the Corinthians' experience of Christ as life from death and as new humanity replacing the old. Far from knowing Christ as one who possesses, rules, or judges them as regent for a God who is the ultimate ruler and judge (3:21-23; 11:3; 15:25-28), they know Christ as life-bringer, as the new creation in God's image. Christ reveals a God who is Wisdom, she who cannot be overcome by rejection but always finds a way to make herself at home and be fruitful among the people. Christ mediates this Wisdom who speaks and listens to her people constantly and makes them mediators of God. Therefore the ethical life is not conceived as duty but as expression. God's glory is not an exclusive prerogative always to be guarded against seizure but an endless effulgence or a circulation into which God draws all those who pass it on. The model of God is parent rather than patron, not one who seeks humble renunciation from others out of fear of being upstaged, but one whose glory is only to give, and, were it possible, to be surpassed in the giving and glory of those who follow.

Social Status Findings Tested by a "Group/Grid" Analysis and by an Analysis of Greco-Roman Social Conventions

In an excursus at the end of chapter 3, I propose, on the basis of the preceding rhetorical study of 1 Corinthians 1–4, that this community's women prophets achieve a rising social status in the church, which brings them into conflict with Paul whose social status is falling. The issue is not whether the conflict is caused by theological or social factors. It could be said that their faith and Paul's put each through the social change that leads to conflict between them. But the event has a measurable reality as social status change and consequent social conflict which has not been recognized and which in turn affects their conflicting theologies. The question being tested is whether the women prophets do or do not experience a significant rise in social status through participation in this community with a consequent impact on Paul's writing of 1 Corinthians.

The evidence I develop for the change in social status of these Corinthians and of Paul in the excursus to chapter 3 is near the surface of Paul's argument in 1 Corinthians 1–4. Though his primary aim here is self-presentation and self-defense, he supports this by exposing their change in social status as a triple betrayal. They have betrayed their calling by God as the foolish, weak, and shamed; they have betrayed the gospel of Christ crucified that he preached to them; and they have betrayed his own shamed apostolate through which he has paternal authority over them (1:26; 2:2; 4:6-21). I use the categories of wisdom, power, and honor from 1 Corinthians 1–4 and ethnic status, condition of servitude, and gender from succeeding chapters to gauge the social status of the Corinthian women and of Paul before and then after entering the church (1:26; 4:10; 7:12-28; 12:13). I find that the women's status has risen across many factors while Paul's has fallen, though his status is probably still higher than theirs in absolute terms. This direction of movement parallels a difference in their theologies and ethics, his oriented on Christ's sacrifice and crucifixion, which he imitates in his own self-discipline and accepting loss (1:17−2:5; 5:7; 8:11; 9:22-27; 10:32−11:1; 14:2-4, 19), theirs on Christ once a victim but now risen and already living and speaking in them as Lord of Glory (2:6-16; 4:8-10; 6:12; 8:1; 10:23; 11:5; 14:26-36). Finally, I indicate that this takes place in the Roman East of the early empire where men who are well-placed Hellenistic Jews may experience tension between religious integrity and continued social advancement, while at the same time people once without status are gaining skills, connections, and money with which to compete.

Because the question is one in social history, it should be possible to test this proposal built on the findings of a rhetorical analysis by the results of other methods now being applied to the social conflict seen in 1 Corinthians. If history is the effort to reconstruct and interpret the human past in its unremitting particularity, social analysis looks for the repeated patterns that human life takes in a certain period, recently showing special interest in ways of life that characterize not only the writing elite but also the wider population. Today, social scientists and anthropologists are adapting certain models used in studing comparative social organization to the study of ancient Mediterranean culture.[3] Mary Douglas's "group/grid" model has been among the most fruitful of these for cross-cultural social analysis.[4] At the same time social historians are working to identify the relevance for New Testament study of specific social conventions of Greco-Roman life, drawn from literary texts and surviving buildings, pottery, coins, art works, and inscriptions.[5]

The problem in testing my thesis by the findings of these two methods is that the people using "group/grid" and social convention analysis to study 1 Corinthians have not focused on either Corinth's women prophets or changes in social status. Therefore there can be no direct confirmation from their work. However, they do discuss the social status of Paul's opponents in 1 Corinthians and address many of the relevant texts and problems. I will summarize their findings concerning the conflict and see if the methods they use can be extended to deal with possible changes of status in this community and the Roman East, and with the women prophets among Paul's hearers. This might encourage those skilled in these methods to address the questions of the women prophets' role in Corinth's opposition to Paul and the function of changing social status in this conflict.

"Group/grid" Analysis Applied to Social Status Changes in the Corinthian Church

For purposes of cross-cultural comparison Mary Douglas distinguishes between "strong group" societies where social control is strongly enforced on all members within group boundaries and "weak group" societies where individuals move in and out of groups freely. A primary sign of strong group formation in the body politic is strong control exerted over the physical bodies of persons in the society. "Grid" varies independently of "group" and measures how tightly or loosely people are programmed by society's symbol systems and social classifications in such a way that they are insulated from others in set roles and patterns of life, as by age and sex. Jerome H. Neyrey documents both "grid" and "group" in his essay on 1 Corinthians. Paul calls for "strong group" boundaries by regulating all apertures of the body in their eating, sexual conduct, and speaking, whereas his opponents insist on freedom of individual decision and expression.[6] Neyrey also identifies Paul's advocacy of defined classifications and roles as "high grid" whereas the Corinthians reject differentiation and discipline. Neyrey notes how Paul's social program is reduplicated cosmologically so that the church, with its ranked membership, is the body of Christ and the believers' ultimate hope is the resurrection of the body in which woman's subordination to man and man's to Christ is incorporated in Christ's subordination to God. Neyrey concludes that for Paul "the order of God's creation will not be abolished in heaven,"[7] whereas for Paul's opponents in Corinth resurrection is found in noncontrolled spirit and individual freedom.

Neyrey's detailed analysis confirms much of what I have argued in contrasting the positions of Paul and the Corinthian women prophets, although he gives only passing attention to the Corinthian stance as a foil for Paul's and in closing argues that Paul's position is found throughout his letters and, one infers, is normative for the believing interpreter. I am more interested in using the "group/grid" model to describe the culture in the Corinthian church when Paul is writing. Therefore I use rhetorical analysis to see how Paul's argument reveals the situation in which he is trying to persuade. This is in no sense a "strong group/high grid" situation where firm group boundaries are combined with tight social classification into an unquestioned moral and ritual order—although that may be Paul's point of spiritual origin in an ideal Israel and his hope for God's ultimate kingdom to come. Rather he finds himself in a "semi-weak group/low grid" situation where a distinctively identified but not tightly bound group, which programmatically rejects given symbolic classifications, is expected to ignore his warnings of schism within and pollution from without. Not that Paul is the only one interested in changing the group's life. Some early converts from the synagogue may join him in fighting for recovery of stronger boundaries between holy and profane and sharper classification in sexual roles and social customs, but others in Corinth apparently continue their journey away from traditional classifications, encouraging even ousiders to speak in response to their prophecies through increasingly porous boundaries.

In this way social conflict and social change may become better understood through Douglas's model, once initial focus is put on what a text's rhetoric can tell us about the social situation that provokes the text. If a group is part of a larger society, it is also essential to consider its relation to the whole society and ask whether changes in the group reflect wider social changes. Douglas generated her model on the basis of research in small and insulated societies in Africa and Melanesia. But she did this in order to bring these societies into cross-cultural comparison with societies today. This has thrown her into complex societies, societies within societies, little societies dominated by big ones, or old ones giving way to young ones—what we might call an imperial configuration whether in the modern world or the Roman East. A radically "strong group/high grid" imperial society tolerates no independent arenas of significant power but

swallows others into its firm boundaries, making them subject to its classifications—in Rome's case to a patriarchal slave-holding system gathering
wealth to serve a legally privileged class. A case in point is Rome's razing
of Corinth almost two centuries before Paul, when it resisted Rome's
advance by mobilizing a league of Greek cities. A century later Rome built
a colony and provincial capital in Corinth's place. But lasting empires are
not held together by force alone. Republican Rome strengthened its "grid"
by operating under the fiction that it was making alliances with free cities,
semi-independent groups, and even kingdoms who welcomed its armies.
By such alliances Jews in Hellenistic cities were able to maintain their own
relatively "strong group/high grid" system of councils, courts, and synagogues—the social structures in which Paul was reared.

Piecing together evidence from first-century texts reveals two broad
social changes occurring, one in the ruling society and a corresponding one
in Judaism and its offspring such as the Christian church.[8] Douglas's model
suggests links between these changes and the changes Paul attests in
Corinth. A century before Paul, Rome's republican system collapsed from
growing corruption and the emptiness of its fictions into civil war, after
which the Senate was willing to hand over all but the central, pacified
provinces of the north Mediterranean to the imperial rule of one individual,
a rule at first carried out by Augustus who possessed some skill in maintaining old alliances. But emperors became more arbitrary and senatorial
power further weakened, so that by mid-first century one can almost characterize the central urban empire as a "weak group/low grid" society. In
provincial cities like Corinth if taxes were paid external controls were
basically absent, and honor fell on whoever could generate wealth and connections. Achieved status bypassed attributed status in importance, and
people with influence either accepted the new media of exchange and
began to compete as individuals for money and friends, or they withdrew
into the aristocrat's memories of the past. People with no influence became
the victims of the competition for wealth. Peasants and slaves who worked
the land bore on their bodies the force exerted by both taxes and rents. The
"free-market" in power was confirmed at the top level in the year 69 CE
when four different people declared themselves emperor at Nero's assassi-
nation and the prize was won by Vespasian who led the strongest legions.

Groups like the Jews found their situation changing, but not all of
them in the same way. Rural Palestine, misruled by the emperor's legions
and friends, became the base for movements of reform, apocalyptic hope,
or revolt. Palestinian Jews tried to carry into the Hellenistic cities these
reform movements that defended Torah and temple. But life in the urban
centers was different. Here established Jews and Jewish Christians were
more interested in recovering the stability and respect traditionally theirs
by alliance with Rome. This was both assisted and complicated by the fact

that their religious communities had become attractive to non-Jews looking for integrity and solid connections in a turbulent time.

As traditional classifications faltered across the empire the women prophets are rising in Corinth's church. Paul comes from the class among Jews with education, family influence, and Roman citizenship, so he rejects the way honor now floats on the open exchange. He makes virtue out of the losses he has taken to keep his integrity in an unstable world, first as a Jew and even more as a servant of Christ. In Corinth he moves toward new "high grid" classifications, at least of men and women, and tries to strengthen "group" boundaries and secure discipline and group order modeled after his own apostolic sacrifices in the name of the cross of Christ. Perhaps to keep people of privilege in Corinth's church from reverting to Torah reform or opting for private gain, he tries to limit their undeniable loss of traditional privileges at the expense of rising groups in the society by calling all believers to remain in the positions they had when called.

To the Corinthian women and other more marginal people, the changed values in the cities would not have been seen as vulgar respect for money and power but as breakdown of rank and privilege, allowing a wider group to compete for some measure of self-development and social influence. It is not necessarily the case that they gained new social standing before entering this community and now use the church to confirm their new wealth, knowledge, or emancipation. Religious life is a service with value in open exchange, and all evidence suggests that the power they offer to others in prayers and prophecies was gained in this community. Functioning as part of a relatively "weak group/low grid" community within a society moving in the same direction, they find no grounds in their social or religious experience to succumb to Paul's reorganization of Corinth's church into a more "strong group/high grid" structure.

Douglas's model is useful in integrating the display of three levels of social reality. The first is the conflict in this small group between Paul's defense of the church against pollution and the confidence and aggressiveness of his Corinthian opponents. Second is the social change taking place in this conflict. It might seem necessary to chart social change as a separate dimension on the "group/grid" model, a "before" and "after" diagram showing what has happened between. But because people perceive their advantage in comparison to their own past, social change may be evident in the intense identification with new "grid" positions. The Corinthians' perceived prospects are rising as the grid that locks them in gives way, making them programmatically "low grid," while Paul, by not using his rights, solemnly chooses the "higher grid" that he cannot avoid since times have changed. Third, this does not happen in an insulated group but as part of society at large, in this case not only that—since Paul's position still has more advantages than theirs—but as part of the broader social situation as people perceive it changing. In society as a whole the advantage of people like Paul has fallen in contrast to the relative advantage of people like the women prophets.

The problem with this analysis for the student of religious values comes both from its emphasis on perceived advantage and its ignoring of distinctive religious practices and classifications. But "advantage" should not be taken as a negative word. Some people need a fair advantage they have not had before, and others like Paul can choose not to use their advantage only because they have it. And distinctive Christian practices and beliefs are alive and well in Corinth. But they replicate strikingly different social realities for distinct people in a time of social change.

The Analysis of Social Conventions Applied to Social Status Changes in the Corinthian Church

This investigation will be restricted to a single pattern of social life in the Roman East, the conventions of friendship, patronage, and enmity as they have been reconstructed and applied to the understanding of 1 Corinthians by Peter Marshall.[9] My purpose is to present his thesis briefly and try to expand it to incorporate the women prophets in Corinth in order to test my proposal concerning the Corinthian women's changing social status. I work from Marshall in the absence of a parallel study of the conventions of Greek women in imperial cities and in the Corinthian church.[10] My assumption is that in a society dominated by men, male friendship and patronage conventions will have some influence on women and will be able to illuminate the way women function, especially in relation to men outside their own families.

Marshall begins with detailed studies of the friendship and enmity conventions in Greco-Roman society, a world where doctors and lawyers were not paid by social equals but received the benefits of friendship — gifts, permits, honors — without which one could not take full part in society. Patronage was a kind of fictive friendship for social inferiors in which benefits that could not be returned stored up honor and personal support for the patron.[11] Enmity arose from a breakdown in the reciprocities of friendship and patronage. Failing to respond as expected was taken as a betrayal, and in place of gifts the two parties hurled invectives and tried to shame each other.

Marshall proposes that Paul has been offered the friendship of certain wealthy people in the Corinthian church through a gift that he refuses, apparently because he sees himself as their benefactor — their father, their patron — since it was he who brought the gospel to them. When they see that he accepts gifts from Christians in Philippi but not from them, they caricature him as a flatterer who is a different person in every new situation. He responds by charging them with insolence and empty boasts. Marshall identifies this rhetoric as the kind of enmity that comes when a friendship between equals is rejected and concludes that Paul has refused support from Corinthians of his own privileged class. Marshall does not make it clear why Paul wants to keep the patronal upper hand in this relationship when he has been willing to accept hospitality and gifts from other people of means, including some in Corinth, on the assumption that the gospel he brought has more than filled his obligation to them.[12]

Perhaps the difference between those Paul depends on and those he refuses to depend on can be understood by considering status changes. Marshall provides an opening for this analysis when he says that Paul accuses Corinthian opponents of boasting or "hubris," which implies youth, flaunting wealth, insulting others for pleasure, and generally making a "breach of one's assigned status."[13] They are not destitute, but they may not be respected equals either.

It is possible that Marshall's characterizations of friendship and enmity, drawn from earlier or more aristocratic authors such as Homer, Aristotle, Cicero, and Seneca do not adequately describe the volatile social situation of the post-Augustan Roman East. As people of senatorial rank diminished in number and power, other people were rising, whether through emancipation, military service, commercial interactions, trade, by serving in the imperial household, or by skills in speaking, writing, and other services. People might have money or valuable talents without having become socially respected. If Paul's opponents come from these groups rather than from more established families, charging them with "hubris" may be part of a general reaction among longer-established people like Paul to rising groups. Paul may accept support from his equals at the same time as he refuses dependence on these "social arrivals" who commit a "breach of their assigned status" in presuming to become his patrons. This could explain why his refusal is couched in reminders of their humble origins and remonstrances of not wanting to become a burden on them but only to love them (1:26; 9:12; 11:7-11; 12:14-16).

In contrast, those Paul recognizes as friends and coworkers in Corinth and Philippi come from the synagogue or have homes near it, are known for their households, provide hospitality for the churches and Paul, and are shocked by unruly behavior (Acts 16:11-15; 18:1-8; Rom. 16:1-5; 1 Cor. 1:11-16; 16:15-19; Phil. 4:14-20). I suggest it is these people that Paul would recognize as social equals in Corinth, and from them he accepts hospitality. These Jews and God-fearers have, like Paul, taken social losses on entering the Christian community and are now bound tightly together with Paul in friendship through his losses for them and theirs for him, in both cases generated and justified by Christ's primary sacrifice.

But people whose status is rising in the church would not have shared Paul's ethos. The stoic self-denial respected in more established society during a time of retrenchment would seem to be weakness among those whose status is not ascribed but achieved. They would have been eager to establish friendships, especially with the church's founder, but not friendships characterized by dependence on him as their father and patron through his gift of the gospel. It is unclear whether they intended to become Paul's patrons in a way that he could not reciprocate in their eyes or whether they looked for a friendship exchange with mutual gain. In any case Paul rejects their entire experience of gain in Christ, and his rejection of their aid may come before they make any offer (9:1-18).

Women prophets who participated in all aspects of the church's life could not have been immune to this interest in friendship. Since gifts of money were less the issue than food, drink, and lodging when Paul was present (9:3-14; 2 Cor. 11:9; 12:14-18), women would have had a close connection to such gift-giving and particular sensitivity to refusals of such service. Paul's extended defense of his rights to their hospitality, coupled with refusal to use these rights in order not to lose his divine reward by achieving any present gain from them (9:1-18), could only be heard by these women as a rejection of friendship between equals.

Paul and his Corinthian opponents operate in the same community, so their status cannot be completely disparate. But much is explained if Paul's status has changed for the worse and he has interpreted this as a voluntary loss congruent with the self discipline characteristic of his class and his theology of Christ crucified. His friends are those who share this experience and theology. In contrast, the status of many Corinthians, including the women Paul is regulating, has improved. They interpret this as achieved gain congruent with their social experience and their theology of Christ raised and ruling. Throughout his letters Paul avoids using explicit friendship language to interpret Christian life. Instead he speaks about work, becoming a slave, and serving. His opponents seem intent on avoiding servile subordination and gaining friendship in Christ built on independence and achieving mutual advantage. When Paul refuses their hospitality—whether offered or not—and refuses to join them in mutual gain, they are offended, rejecting a friendship based on mutual loss and self-denial. As Marshall shows, the result is enmity.

Unfinished Postscript

The fitting ending for a reconstruction from rhetoric would be a reconstruction in rhetoric, that is, a clear voice from the other side of the argument. Fiorenza names "historical imagination" as the final step in exegesis because it is not enough to get the mind informed if the lost voice has not been recovered. She concludes her chapter, "Toward a Feminist Critical Method," with her student's apocryphal letter from Phoebe.[14] Rosemary Ruether begins her "Sexism and God-talk" with Mary Magdalene's story, and Dory Previn gives us the eyes and mind of the Queen of Sheba as she visits Solomon.[15] Our liturgy and preaching are, at their best, just such works of historical imagination.

But the task is not easy. It is a long way from an outline of the Corinthian women prophets' theology or a sketch of their behavior to a speaking voice. Women's language will be practical, but will it be coarse or cultivated? And to whom are they speaking? Is it to be a debate with Stephanas? a sharp letter back to Paul? an allegory for Apollos? Most likely it will be a message sent to Prisca, a warning for the virgins. One day there must be a story of it all for the children. But first there will be a prophecy to the community, and prayer to God.

Unfortunately I am not a debater, a storyteller, or a prophet. But I do hear voices in the distance coming closer.

Appendix 1:
Rhetorical Criticism*

IT IS COMMONLY GRANTED that rhetorical analysis must go beyond simple identification and classification of rhetorical figures to a comprehensive understanding
of texts as acts of persuasion. Yet the "rigorous methodology" that George Kennedy
and others have demanded in modern rhetorical criticism has yet to be worked out.
At least four approaches to rhetorical criticism of the Pauline letters are being tested.

Some research has taken its lead from early work of Bultmann on the diatribe
and of Johannes Weiss on Pauline rhetoric. Those provoked by Bultmann compare
Paul's style to that of other writers of his time, with particular interest in how and
why Paul favored certain rhetorical devices. Stanley Stowers and Thomas Schmeller
respond directly to Bultmann in their recent studies of the diatribe. Norbert
Schneider takes up antithesis in Paul, Karl Plank irony, and J. T. Fitzgerald the
catalogue of hardship. Following the lead of Weiss, others analyze selected Pauline
texts to describe the interaction of various stylistic devices in his writing. Aída
Besançon Spencer compares his style in three different passages and Josef Zmijewski
analyzes the "fool's speech" in 2 Corinthians 11–12. Still others such as Chan-Hie
Kim and John L. White clarify Paul's letters through analysis of ancient Greek letter
writing. All these studies focus on stylistic analysis, but this moves them toward questions about the function of stylistic features in the text and the situation of writing.

At the other end of the spectrum from literary style to the rhetorical situation
come studies that focus primarily on the social world constituted by Paul's letters.
Norman Petersen's study of kinship constructions in Philemon and Peter Marshall's
work on friendship and enmity conventions in Corinth both become studies of
Paul's rhetoric at the point where they focus on linguistic means by which Paul
shapes the relation he wants with his hearers. This research promises to be important for rhetorical criticism of NT texts, although it is not yet clear how it will
contribute to a comprehensive methodology for analyzing a text's rhetorical
situation.

The primary methodological options of those attempting a comprehensive
rhetorical analysis of Paul's letters are illustrated in recent monographs by Hans-
Dieter Betz and Folker Siegert. Betz applies all facets of classical rhetorical analysis
in order to determine the species of a particular text as deliberative, judicial, or
epideictic—his Galatians commentary identifies the letter as judicial apology—and
to show how all aspects of its topics, arrangement, and style serve that purpose. This

---

*Names of authors in each appendix refer to their works listed at the end of that
appendix.

has the advantage of requiring him to specify at every point the function of Paul's rhetoric, provoking other practitioners of this method to challenge his results and show why the letter is deliberative or epideictic. George Kennedy's recent introduction to the use of rhetorical criticism in New Testament studies outlines the three species of argument and, when considering Paul's letters, proposes against Betz that Galatians is deliberative rhetoric. Recent interpreters of 1 Corinthians are reacting against emphasis on Paul's self-defense and forensic speech, Wüllner and Humphries arguing that Paul seeks through epideictic speech to confirm views already held, Kennedy and Fiorenza (1988) that he writes 1 Corinthians as deliberative speech to press for decision and action.

The advantage of using Hellenistic rhetoric to analyze Paul's writing is obvious: these are the conventions he most likely heard and used if he spoke about rhetoric and they help us read his letters in light of other texts of the period. Bünker and Forbes as well as others apply different aspects of classical rhetorical analysis to 1 Corinthians. Nevertheless, the fact that ancient rhetoric was taught as a prescriptive as well as descriptive discipline can raise problems for its use today if what Paul said is subordinated in any way to what rhetorical handbooks considered appropriate for that unit or species of speech — as if production could be explained by training. This raises major questions, such as whether the classical three species of speech are adequate for the analysis of letters, even letters that were intended to be read aloud to persuade a group.

The other comprehensive approach to Paul's rhetoric is represented by Folker Siegert's study of Romans 9–11. He practices the "new rhetoric" of Chaim Perelman and L. Olbrechts-Tyteca, which is not "new" in any sense of imposing modern categories of analysis on classical texts. The classical species, topics, arrangements, and figures all reappear here, and the most important new designation of "argument by dissociation of concepts" clarifies a way of persuading documented in classical texts. What is new is the thorough-going focus on argument as the proper subject of rhetoric, with argument interpreted broadly to include all efforts to persuade in a situation with common assumptions, and an insistence on classifying every element of rhetoric in terms of its argumentative function even though this function can vary with use. This means the description of a text as an argument in a rhetorical situation takes priority over questions about what should appear in this kind of speech, what order is expected, or how well trained this rhetor was.

Siegert does not use Perelman and Olbrechts-Tyteca's division of all argument into four kinds because he thinks their nomenclature has metaphysical connotations. Instead he organizes arguments very loosely in terms of their predominantly formal, content, or interactional characteristics. This could reduce the new rhetoric to the strictly analytical function of identifying the multiple arguments as they structure a particular text rather than determining what Paul's persuasive goal is in that rhetorical situation. It would seem more appropriate to move toward a stronger emphasis (correcting nomenclature if necessary) on Perelman and Olbrecht-Tyteca's middle-range classification of arguments: "arguments from the structure of reality," "arguments constructing reality," "quasi-logical arguments," and "arguments by dissociation." Though there may be infinite varieties of rhetorical situations, some typology of arguments should be possible that shows the weight of different kinds of arguments in a text and indicates, within a certain range, the rhetorical situation. For example, the arguments in a text could be located on a two-dimensional chart that measures the relative weight of arguments from deduction and induction (arguments from reality and arguments constructing reality) on one gauge and on the other gauge the relative weight of arguments from identification and dissociation (quasi-logical and dissociative arguments). This would provide four quadrants in which the argumentative strategy of different passages or even texts could be located relative to each other with possible implications about rhetorical situation. Classical rhetoric's three species of speech should reappear here in a way more structurally integrated with the analysis of arguments, and the typology could encourage comparative and theoretical work on how speech persuades in different situations.

Recent articles by Wilhelm Wüllner and Andreas H. Snyman analyze problems and possibilities of New Testament rhetorical criticism. Wüllner suggests that the practical purpose of rhetoric to persuade extends the meaning of rhetorical criticism beyond the text to wider questions of practice and persuasion. This is clarified in the programmatic statement of a rhetorical paradigm for biblical studies in Elisabeth Schüssler Fiorenza's 1987 Society of Biblical Literature presidential address. By understanding discourse rhetorically, she incorporates the New Testament texts as historical and literary events of persuasion, including the long history of their readings, within our accountability to reconstruct our world ethically through yet better readings. Her recent article on the rhetorical situation of 1 Corinthians is an example of that kind of reading. We did not come to similar conclusions independently but have been in conversation for some time with converging readings.

The fruit we can expect to see from rhetorical analysis of 1 Corinthians is indicated by three papers read at one recent meeting of the Society of Biblical Literature. Margaret M. Mitchell drew on classical literary parallels to identify the anti-factionalism in chapter 10 as Paul's rhetorical choice, Troels Engberg-Pederson reinterpreted Paul's exhortation on dress in worship as a concession to the contentious by one who prefers to teach concession by example, and Dale Martin traced Paul's repeated appeals for concord addressed to probably high-status speakers in tongues as a sign of the letter's unified rhetorical strategy.

Betz, Hans Dieter. *Galatians: A Commentary on Paul's Letter to the Churches in Galatia*. Philadelphia: Fortress Press, 1979.

————. "The Problem of Rhetoric and Theology according to the apostle Paul," *L'apôtre Paul, personalité, style et ministère*. A Vanhoye, ed. Leuven: Leuven University Press, 1986, 16-48.

Bünker, Michael. *Brief Formular und rhetorische Disposition im 1 Korintherbrief*. Göttingen: Vandenhoeck & Ruprecht, 1984.

Bultmann, Rudolf. *Der Stil der paulinischen Predigt und die kynisch-stoische Diatribe*. Göttingen: Vandenhoeck & Ruprecht, 1910.

Engberg-Pedersen, Troels. "I Corinthians 11:16 and the Character of Pauline Exhortation," unpublished paper read at the Society of Biblical Literature 1989 Annual Meeting.

Fiorenza, Elisabeth Schüssler. "The Ethics of Interpretation: De-Centering Biblical Scholarship," *JBL* 107 (1988), 3-17.

———. "Rhetorical Situation and Historical Reconstruction in I Corinthians," *NTS* 33 (1987), 386-403.

Fitzgerald, J. T. "Cracks in an Earthen Vessel: An Examination of the Catalogues of Hardship in the Corinthian Correspondence." Ph.D. dissertation, Yale University, 1984.

Forbes, Christopher. "Comparison, Self-Praise and Irony: Paul's Boasting and the Conventions of Hellenistic Rhetoric," *NTS* 32 (1986), 1-30.

Humphries, Raymond. "Paul's Rhetoric in I Corinthians 1-4," Ph. D. dissertation, Graduate Theological Union, 1979.

Kennedy, George A. *New Testament Interpretation through Rhetorical Criticism.* Chapel Hill and London: University of North Carolina Press, 1984.

Kim, Chan-Hie. *Form and Structure of the Familiar Greek Letter of Recommendation.* Missoula, Mont.: Scholars Press, 1972.

Marshall, Peter. *Enmity in Corinth: Social Conventions in Paul's Relations with the Corinthians.* Tübingen: J. C. B. Mohr (Paul Siebeck), 1987.

Martin, Dale. "Tongues of Angels and Other Status Indicators," unpublished paper read at the Society of Biblical Literature 1989 Annual Meeting; monograph on 1 Corinthians forthcoming from Yale University Press, 1990.

Mitchell, Margaret M. "Factionalism in 1 Corinthians 10," unpublished paper read at the Society of Biblical Literature 1989 Annual Meeting, an excerpt from "Paul and the Rhetoric of Reconciliation: An Exegetical Investigation of the Language and Composition," Ph.D. Dissertation, University of Chicago, 1989.

Perelman, Chaim, and L. Olbrechts-Tyteca. *The New Rhetoric: A Treatise on Argumentation.* Notre Dame and London: University of Notre Dame Press, 1969.

Petersen, Norman. *Rediscovering Paul: Philemon and the Sociology of Paul's Narrative World.* Philadelphia: Fortress Press, 1985.

Plank, Karl A. *Paul and the Irony of Affliction.* Atlanta: Scholars Press, 1987.

Schmeller, Thomas. *Paulus und die "Diatribe": eine vergleichende Stilinterpretation.* Münster: Aschendorff, 1987.

Schneider, Norbert. *Die rhetorische Eigenart der paulinischen Antithese.* Tübingen: J. C. B. Mohr (Paul Siebeck), 1970.

Siegert, Folker. *Argumentation bei Paulus, gezeigt an Römer 9–11.* Tübingen: J. C. B. Mohr (Paul Siebeck), 1985, 181–254 on 1 Corinthians.

Snyman, Andreas H. "On Studying the Figures (schēmata) in the New Testament," *Biblica* 69 (1988), 93-107.

Spencer, Aída Besançon. *Paul's Literary Style: A Stylistic and Historical Comparison of II Corinthians 11:16—12:13, Romans 8:9-39, and Philippians 3:2—4:13.* Jackson, Miss.: Evangelical Theological Society, 1984.

Stowers, Stanley Kent. *The Diatribe and Paul's Letter to the Romans.* Chico, Calif.: Scholars Press, 1981.

Weiss, Johannes. "Beiträge zur paulinischen Rhetorik," *Theologische Studien,* B. Weiss zu seinem 70. Geburtstag dargebracht. Göttingen: Vandenhoeck & Ruprecht, 1897, 165-247.

White, John L. *The Form and Structure of the Official Petition: a Study in Greek Epistolography.* Missoula, Mont.: Society of Biblical Literature, 1972.

Wüllner, Wilhelm. "Hermeneutics and rhetorics: from 'truth and method' to 'truth and power.'" *Scriptura* 53 (1989), 1–54.

———. "Where is Rhetorical Criticism Taking Us?" *CBQ* 49 (1987), 448–63.

Zmijewski, Josef. *Der Stil der paulinischen "Narrenrede." Analyse der Sprachgestaltung II Kor 11,1-12,10 als Beitrag zur Methodik von Stiluntersuchungen neutestamentlicher Texte.* Köln-Bonn: Verlag Peter Hanstein, 1978.

Appendix 2:
Early Twentieth-Century
Research on Women

ALTHOUGH ADOLF VON HARNACK WROTE no extended monograph on women in the early church, his chapter on women in *The Mission and Expansion of Christianity in the First Three Centuries* and his essay proposing that Prisca wrote Hebrews are in the best tradition of the scholarship in the history of religions school. He is critical of dogmatic readings and ready to let the evidence speak for itself. His proposal that women were a primary channel for the spread of early Christianity and his list of women's names and roles are developed further by his student Leopold Zscharnack in *Der Dienst der Frau in den ersten Jahrhunderten der Christliche Kirche*. By reading directives against women's conduct as evidence of it, Zscharnack provides what may be the first careful reconstruction of women's leadership in the early church. He also proposes and tests broad theories, arguing, for example, that heresy made women prophets and teachers suspect, then clericalism made the widows' ministries seem inferior, and finally monasticism made the deaconesses' administration appear worldly, leaving only the cloistered virgins with primary religious roles after the fourth century.

Among scholars who carry on this tradition of careful and creative scholarship of the twentieth-century's early decades are Herbert Preisker and Gerhard Delling. Preisker ranges broadly, contrasting the women ascetics among the first proclaimers of God's apocalyptic kingdom with those Luke depicts as virginal mediators of divine power. Intermediate, but not quite like either, he finds the obsessive practical missioners of Paul's letters, filled by the mystic indwelling of Christ. Delling documents in detail Paul's alienation from marriage and sexuality. Although he tries to explain too much by Paul's Jewish horror of cultic practices that seem pagan, he generally does not fall into blaming the Corinthian women for the religious inferiority attributed to them by Paul. We need good translations of all these studies to extend the influence of their critical viewpoint and broad knowledge of ancient sources.

Delling, Gerhard. *Paulus' Stellung zu Frau und Ehe.* Stuttgart: Kohlhammer, 1931.

Harnack, Adolf von. *Die Mission und Ausbreitung des Christentums in den ersten drei Jahrhunderten*, Vol 2. 3d revised and extended edition. Leipzig: T. C. Hinrichs, 1915, 58–78 (4th ed., 1924). English translation of the shorter 2nd ed.: *The*

Mission and Expansion of Christianity in the First Three Centuries, Vol 2. Trans. and ed. by James Moffatt, 2d rev. ed. New York: Putnam's and London: Williams and Norgate, 1908, 64–84.

———. "Probabilia über die Adresse und den Verfasser des Hebräerbriefs," *ZNW* 1 (1900), 16–41.

Preisker, Herbert. *Christentum und Ehe in den ersten drei Jahrhunderten.* Berlin: Trowitzsch & Sohn, 1927.

Zscharnack, Leopold. *Der Dienst der Frau in den ersten Jahrhunderten der christliche Kirche.* Göttingen: Vandenhoeck & Ruprecht, 1902.

Appendix 3:
Apology for Paul

A SECOND KIND OF TWENTIETH-CENTURY STUDY still widely practiced takes Paul as the standard for sexual mores and religious roles today. Although much that is useful can be culled from this work, its apologetic purpose pervades every interpretation and can contort Paul's meanings to get readings it wants to validate.

Among apologists are a long line of scholars who seek to defend traditional roles for women in various ways. Alfred Juncker's *Die Ethik des Apostels Paulus* highlights Paul's struggle against "every religiously motivated emancipation movement." Writing after mid-twentieth century, Ludwig Hick stresses Paul's view of women's equality in the Lord, but warns that equal worth does not cancel out the natural distinctions between men and women in rank, rights, and duties based on their different natures. The bugaboo is "Gleichmacherei," which might be translated "playing at being alike," or "putting on airs of identity." Franz Leenhardt finds in Paul a metaphysical interdependence of man and woman who are both made in God's image, but this interdependence is not reversible since woman is also man's glory and is always tempted to seek emancipation. He adds an aside, "Moreover the disciplinary measures directed against women (to silence disruptions) are inexpendable and the woman of any time who wants them to be forgotten has only to watch out that they do not become necessary." A recent classic in this vein is James B. Hurley's *Man and Woman in Biblical Perspective*, which manages to show the entire Bible culminating in the 1 Timothy exclusion of women from religious authority.

But the same approach can also serve the opposite cause. As early as 1915, H. Wienel in *Paulus, der Mensch und sein Werk* proposed that from Jesus' preaching to Revelation and throughout Paul's letters, Christendom was a revolt against state power and social subordination. An extensive interpolation theory is needed to explain the parts of the text that dilute this radical message. An example of the apologetic tendency in recent study of Paul on women is Robin Scroggs's article, "Paul and the Eschatological Woman." He follows the widely accepted interpolation theory excising women's silencing from Paul's letter (see Appendix 11 and the Excursus on 1 Cor. 14:34-35 in chapter 7), and interprets the women's veiling by arguing that Hebrew and Greek usage of the word "head" indicate that Paul saw man as "source" but not as "ruler" of woman.

Hick, Ludwig. *Stellung des hl. Paulus zur Frau im Rahmen seiner Zeit*. Köln: Amerikanisch-ungarischer Verlag, 1957.

Hurley, James B. *Man and Woman in Biblical Perspective.* Grand Rapids: Zondervan, 1981.

Junker, Alfred. *Die Ethik des Apostels Paulus.* Halle: M. Niemeyer, 1904–1919, 175.

Leenhardt, Franz. "Die Stellung der Frau in der christlichen Gemeinden," *Die Stellung der Frau in Neuen Testament und in der alten Kirche.* Zurich: Zwingli-Verlag, 1949, 43 (quotation my translation).

Scroggs, Robin. "Paul and the Eschatological Woman," *JAAR* 22 (1972), 283–303.

Wienel, H. *Paulus, der Mensch und sein Werk.* 2d ed. Tübingen: J. C. B. Mohr (Paul Siebeck), 1915.

Appendix 4:
Ideological Reconstruction of
the Corinthian Conflict

A THIRD KIND OF STUDY may or may not bear marks of apology, but makes its primary task the reconstructing of the situation in Corinth that provoked 1 Corinthians.

The still-reigning thesis of a spiritual or wisdom-oriented movement in Corinth was developed by Johannes Weiss in his 1910 Meyer Series commentary, *Der erste Korintherbrief,* following work by predecessors such as C. F. Georg Heinrici, Wilhelm Lütgert, and R. Reitzenstein. Rather than taking the four contending parties as the key to understanding the conflict in Corinth, Weiss interpreted the parties in light of Paul's general struggle against confident, spirit-filled "perfect ones" whose "gnosis" told them no physical act of eating, idol sacrifices, or immorality could threaten their spiritual union with Christ. Women putting off veils and slaves seeking emancipation were probably part of this movement. In 1914, Adolf Schlatter proposed instead that the spiritual group in Corinth was primarily ascetic and prophetic, including many women who claimed authority over their own bodies in the service of the Spirit. Schlatter's effort to explain this movement by Jewish rather than broader Hellenistic influence was not convincing, nor was his accent on the ascetics' selfishness in order to justify Paul's reaction, but his working through the texts with the question about ascetic women in mind was fruitful.

The thesis of Corinthian spirituality in some hands became overdoctrinaire. H. D. Wendland among others used gnostic disparaging of the body to explain libertinism and asceticism equally and simultaneously. Walter Schmithals made gnostic dualism the measure of the Corinthians at every point.

Recent treatments by scholars such as Hans Conzelmann and Helmut Köster remind one more of Weiss's original care to work inductively from the texts to reconstruct what it is that unifies the Corinthians' high spirituality, resurrection Christology, and radical ethics. But the question concerning women's possible roles in this movement is not developed. For example, Conzelmann's evidence that cult prostitution is more fable than fact in first-century Corinth brings up a question he does not address: are the charges of immorality in 1 Corinthians less social history than a rhetorical strategy to get ascetic spiritual women, where Paul thought necessary, to concede marriage?

Recent research on women in the Corinthian church (see following appendices) seldom integrates its findings into a comprehensive picture of the conflict with Paul. Klaus Thräde's 1977 study of women in Greek, Roman, and Jewish society and in the early church recognizes women prophets among leading figures in the Corinthian church. But by reading the veiling debate as a cultural conflict over clothing and taking the silencing as an interpolation, he dissociates the Corinthian women from any particular role in the moralistic and ascetic movement that Paul opposes. In 1978, Elisabeth Schüssler Fiorenza recognizes the key place of Paul's admonitions concerning women at the start and finish of his treatment of the church's spiritual life (1 Cor. 11–14). Yet here and in her comprehensive study of early Christian women of 1983, *In Memory of Her. A Feminist Theological Reconstruction of Christian Origins*, she minimizes the conflict between Paul and the women in Corinth. They equally affirm the spiritual gifts of the divine Spirit-Sophia. Paul restricts the full practice of these gifts to curb an orgiastic impression given by loosened hair and to prevent wives of Christian men from participating with other women in public spiritual demonstration. The focus here is on women participating with Paul in spiritual leadership rather than on women in a spiritual movement at odds with Paul (see my critique at that time), though she recognizes that Paul opens the door for increasing restriction of women in the churches. In 1987, Fiorenza identifies Paul's rhetorical appeal to unity and patriarchal authority in 1 Corinthians as a strategy for persuading well-placed men in the community to discipline those, including the women, whose authority is new and spiritual.

Conzelmann, Hans. *I Corinthians: A Commentary on the First Epistle to the Corinthians*. Philadelphia: Fortress Press, 1975 (German, 1969).

Fiorenza, Elisabeth Schüssler. *In Memory of Her: A Feminist Theological Reconstruction of Christian Origins*. New York: Crossroad, 1983.

———. "Rhetorical Situation and Historical Reconstruction in I Corinthians," *NTS* 33 (1987), 386–403.

———. "Women in the Pre-pauline and Pauline Churches," *USQR* 33 (1978), 153–66.

Heinrici, C. F. Georg. *Der erste Brief an die Korinther*. 8th ed. Göttingen: Vandenhoeck & Ruprecht, 1896.

Köster, Helmut. "Review of Ulrich Wilkins, Weisheit und Torheit," *Gnomon* 33 (1961), 590–95.

Lütgert, Wilhelm. *Freiheitspredigt und Schwärmgeister in Korinth. Ein Beitrag zur Charakteristik der Christuspartei*. Gütersloh: C. Bertelsmann, 1908.

Reitzenstein, Richard. *Die hellenistischen Mysterienreligionen, ihre Grundgedanken und Wirkungen*. Leipzig and Berlin: Teubner, 1910.

Schlatter, Adolf. *Die korinthische Theologie*. Gütersloh: C. Bertelsmann, 1914.

Schmithals, Walter. *Gnosticism in Corinth*. New York and Nashville: Abingdon, 1971 (German, 1956).

Thräde, Klaus. "Ärger mit der Freiheit. Die Bedeutung von Frauen in Theorie und Praxis der alten Kirche," *"Freunde in Christus werden . . ." Die Beziehung von Mann und Frau als Frage an Theologie und Kirche*, by Gerta Scharffenorth and Klaus Thräde (Gelnhausen/Berlin: Burckhardthaus-Verlag, 1977), 35–128.

Weiss, Johannes. *Der erste Korintherbrief.* Göttingen: Vandenhoeck & Ruprecht, 1910.

Wendland, H. D. *Die Briefe an die Korinther.* Göttingen: Vandenhoeck & Ruprecht, 1962.

Wire, Antoinette Clark. Contribution to "In Memory of Her: A Symposion on an Important Book," ed. Susan Setta, with response by Elisabeth Schüssler Fiorenza, *Anima* 10 (1984), 105–9.

Appendix 5:
Apollos

ALTHOUGH THE REFERENCES to Apollos in 1 Corinthians and Acts are relatively few, his prominence and ambiguous origins in both texts have attracted recurring interest. Research has been of three kinds. Apollos has appeared marginally in the study of Paul's purposes in 1 Corinthians, likewise in the study of Luke's purposes in Acts. Occasionally Apollos has been studied as a representative of an otherwise little-known branch of earliest Christianity.

The study of Paul's rivals in 1 Corinthians developed in the context of F. C. Baur's thesis of an early Christianity polarized between Pauline and Jerusalem factions. C. K. Barrett and recently Gerd Lüdemann see Peter as Paul's major rival in Corinth, primarily because Paul insists on the right to the financial support due all the apostles who have seen the Lord, and because Paul claims the church has no other foundation than the one he has laid down which is Christ (9:1-18; 15:1-11; 3:10-11; cf. Matt. 16:16-18). In contrast, they note that Apollos is taken as Paul's coworker (3:5−4:6).

Johannes Munck denies that there is any leadership conflict in Corinth due to the weakness of this evidence for conflict with Peter. Wilhelm Lütgert proposed early that Paul is facing an extreme form of his own spiritual gospel, and C. F. Georg Heinrici, Johannes Weiss, and Birger Pearson (1975) developed the thesis of a strong Apollos faction in Corinth. All these agree that the letter is a unified argument, not for freedom against Jerusalem-based tradition and law, but for self-discipline against spiritual confidence and bold expression. The groundwork for this spirituality may have been laid by Paul's gospel as John C. Hurd shows and Conzelmann supports. But its mobilization is reasonably attributed to Apollos whose name Paul lists first, and often alone, of all his contenders in the argument against this world's wisdom (1:12−4:8).

How much can be read from this argument about Apollos depends on the caution or boldness of the modern exegete. Apollos has remarkable success when he waters what Paul plants in Corinth, and the Corinthians want him to return and continue his work (3:5; 16:12-13). He may also do some new planting. Almost a century ago Heinrici proposed that it is Apollos' baptismal initiations that make Paul reticent about his own baptizing in Corinth (1:14-16). The language of wisdom, mysteries, and certain persons as "spirituals" has often been traced to Apollos. Pearson (1973, 1975) suggests that Apollos carries to Corinth an Alexandrine exegetical tradition by which the "spirituals" claim to have received the breath of God at creation, making them fit to know divine wisdom. The question is whether there is sufficient evidence in Paul's creation argument (15:45-46) and in Luke's reference to the exegete Apollos from Alexandria to justify using this reading of Genesis from Philo to interpret Paul's opponents in Corinth.

Scholarship on the Apollos account in Acts 18:24 – 19:7 has focused on the question of why this dynamic proclaimer of Jesus knows only John's baptism. Many commentators have credited Luke with inserting the instruction by Priscilla and Aquila in order to legitimate Apollos' ministry, which comes from nonapostolic circles. Alfred Loisy, Ernst Käsemann, and Ernst Hänchen see Luke excluding alternative Jewish-Christian or speculative traditions of his time by disparaging this Christian from Alexandria as one who knew only John's water baptism. Since Luke is not so bold as to construct a baptism by Aquila (exegetes haven't mentioned the possibility that he could be suppressing a baptism by Priscilla), he simply tells of Apollos being instructed by them. Then he adds the next story of Paul baptizing the other followers of John to underscore the need for all to come into the one holy church. In a different vein, Eduard Schweizer reads Apollos as a competing Hellenistic-Jewish missionary "seething with the spirit" and teaching the "way of the Lord," whom Luke with his narrower experience can only understand as a Christian. But because Apollos needs further instruction, Luke classifies him as a semi-Christian in the mold Luke has made for John the Baptist.

In all these interpretations Luke's theology is the focus rather than Apollos. But since association with John the Baptist and instruction by Paul's coworkers are not Luke's standard means to identify and initiate deviants into the apostolic fold, it seems more likely that these are elements of pre-Lukan tradition adapted to this use and available for reconstructing who Apollos was. I turn then to the minority who focus their study on the peculiar kind of Christianity represented by Apollos.

Martin Dibelius's important study of John the Baptist in 1911 proposed that Apollos represents a stream of Christianity outside the one Luke knows. In this world that Luke considers half-Christian, which is possibly influenced by the Galilee Jesus traditions, a man with John's baptism who has the spirit that proclaims Christ as Messiah apparently has no need of a second baptism. Preisker saw this as the golden age of the spirit in the church before precedence is given to cult and office. Dibelius took it as positive evidence for multiple simultaneous Christian traditions, including Paul's, which Luke alternately ignores and co-opts into his picture of the single tradition flowing from Jerusalem to Rome.

Recent studies of early Egyptian Christianity by Colin H. Roberts, Birger Pearson, and A. F. J. Klijn piece together brief New Testament and second-century Christian papyri texts that suggest that first-century Christianity in Egypt is an integral part of Judaism. It probably comes to Alexandria from Palestine or Syria along well-traveled sea routes. Pearson (1986) shows how the rich store of materials on Jews in first-century Egypt (see also Victor Tcherikover and Aryeh Kasher) can be mined for signs of many varieties of Judaism — including the Christian — and for the geographical, social, and intellectual locations of Jews in Alexandria. Working from second-century texts linked to Egypt, Roberts discusses the first-century Christians' names for God. Klijn notes Egyptian Christians' fondness for polemic, for Jesus' sayings and deeds, for Jesus as a revealer of knowledge who is impervious to death, and for Christianity as a movement rather than as a church. The fuller understanding of first- and second-century Christian Judaism in Egypt offers our best hope of providing a wider context for improved reading of 1 Corinthians and Acts on Apollos.

Barrett, C. K. *A Commentary on the First Epistle to the Corinthians.* New York: Harper & Row, 1968.

Bauernfeind, Otto. *Kommentar und Studien zur Apostelgeschichte.* Tübingen: J. C. B. Mohr (Paul Siebeck), 1980, 227–29.

Baur, F. C. *Paul, the Apostle of Jesus Christ, his Life and Work, his Epistles and his Doctrine: A Contribution to a Critical History of Primitive Christianity.* 2d ed. London and Edinburgh: Williams & Norgate, 1873–1875.

Conzelmann, Hans. *I Corinthians: A Commentary on the First Epistle to the Corinthians.* Philadelphia: Fortress Press, 1975 (German, 1969).

Dibelius, Martin. *Die urchristliche Überlieferung von Johannes dem Täufer.* Göttingen: Vandenhoeck & Ruprecht, 1911, 87–98.

Hänchen, Ernst. *The Acts of the Apostles: A Commentary.* Philadelphia: Westminster, 1971 (German, 1956, revised 1965).

Heinrici, C. F. Georg. *Das erste Sendschreiben des Apostel Paulus an die Korinther.* Berlin: Wilhelm Hertz, 1880, 35–44.

Hurd, John C., Jr. *The Origin of I Corinthians.* New York: Seabury Press, 1965.

Käsemann, Ernst. "Die Johannesjünger in Ephesus," *Zeitschrift für Theologie und Kirche* 49 (1952), 144–54.

Kasher, Aryeh. *The Jews in Hellenistic and Roman Egypt: The Struggle for Equal Rights.* Tübingen: J. C. B. Mohr (Paul Siebeck), 1985.

Klijn, A. F. J. "Jewish Christianity in Egypt," *The Roots of Egyptian Christianity.* Philadelphia: Fortress Press, 1986, 161–75.

Loisy, Alfred. *Les actes des apôtres.* Paris: Emile Nourry, 1920.

Lüdemann, Gerd. *Paulus, der Heidenapostel, Vol. II: Antipaulinismus im frühen Christentum.* Göttingen: Vandenhoeck & Ruprecht, 1983.

Lütgert, Wilhelm. *Freiheitspredigt und Schwärmgeister in Korinth. Ein Beitrag zur Charakteristic der Christuspartei.* Gütersloh: C. Bertelsmann, 1908.

Munck, Johannes. *Paul and the Salvation of Mankind.* Richmond, Va.: John Knox Press, 1959 (German, 1954).

Pearson, Birger A. *The Pneumatikos-Psychikos Terminology in I Corinthians: A Study in the Theology of the Corinthian Opponents of Paul in its Relation to Gnosticism.* Missoula, Mont.: Society of Biblical Literature, 1973.

———. "Hellenistic-Jewish Wisdom Speculation and Paul," *Aspects of Wisdom in Judaism and Early Christianity.* Ed. by R. L. Wilken. Notre Dame: Notre Dame University, 1975.

———. "Earliest Christianity in Egypt: Some Observations," *The Roots of Egyptian Christianity.* Philadelphia: Fortress Press, 1986, 132–59.

Preisker, H. "Apollos und die Johannesjünger in Act 18,24-19,6," *ZNW* 30 (1931), 301–4.

Roberts, Colin H. *Manuscript, Society, and Belief in Early Christian Egypt.* London: Oxford University Press, 1979.

Schweizer, Eduard. "Die Bekehrung des Apollos, Ag. 18,24-26," *Evangelische Theologie* 15 (1955), 247–54.

Tcherikover, Victor. *Hellenistic Civilization and the Jews.* Philadelphia: Jewish Publication Society of America, 1959.

Weiss, Johannes. *Der erste Korintherbrief.* Göttingen: Vandenhoeck & Ruprecht, 1910.

Appendix 6:
Wisdom

THE STUDY OF WISDOM in 1 Corinthians occurs within a ferment of debate on what wisdom meant in Hellenistic Judaism and early Gnosticism. Post-exilic Jews praise wisdom as the invaluable treasure established from creation itself, yet experienced as distant and alien. They speak of wisdom so exalted or deep that it is inaccessible to those who seek it (Job 28) or of wisdom as a street woman rejected by those she is seeking to attract (Prov. 1–9). Greek-speaking Jews later extend these images. One general tradition speaks positively of wisdom, the divine partner in creation, who chooses Israel for her dwelling (Wis. 7–9; Sir. 1; 24; Philo, *On Flight and Finding* 50–52, *On the Cherubim* 49–50). Another tradition is pessimistic about history and in its apocalyptic visions and prophecies gives us glimpses of the rejected one who must take refuge where she can or disappear completely from the earth (*Bar.* 3:9 — 4:4; *1 Enoch* 42; 4 Ezra 5; Matt. 11:16-19/Luke 7:31-35; Matt. 23:24-39/Luke 11:49-51; 13:34-35). Felix Christ provides a brief introduction to these texts. How they variously function to reaffirm one God in a world foreign or hostile to God is sounded out by Gerhard von Rad and Burton Lee Mack.

A third tradition of Hellenistic wisdom religion combines a radical pessimism about the known world and its Creator with supreme confidence in a spiritual enlightenment of those with higher heavenly origins. It describes a female wisdom figure who is the preeminent divine wisdom or who explains in her own story the fall of spiritual reality into this world, indicating the reverse path for the believer (see Hans Jonas, Kurt Rudolph, Rose Arthur, and Deirdre Good).

Certain questions have dominated recent research in this area—wherever scholars have moved beyond description of wisdom's role within any single tradition. What is the origin of wisdom's multiform, largely feminine characterization? In what way and under what influences does Jesus Christ become identified as God's wisdom? And how does Jewish wisdom speculation become transposed into Gnosticism?

On the origin of wisdom few people today choose either Rudolf Bultmann's thesis of a single original myth of wisdom created, appearing on earth, rejected, and returning to heaven, or the counter-proposal by Ringgren that wisdom rises strictly from a personification of Yahweh's attributes. Jewish wisdom is a creature of many myths as they come into the same cultural solution with the worship of Yahweh. In an article called "The Mother of Wisdom," Hans Conzelmann shows how the years of research by R. Reitzenstein and others indicate the Jewish texts' dependence on Egyptian Isis hymns. Christa Kayatz has found in certain Jewish wisdom passages the myths of the Egyptian goddess of order, Maat; and G. Böstrum (as summarized by Leo Perdue) finds the myth of the Canaanite fertility goddess Ishtar-Astarte. Conzelmann speaks of an extended process of "reflective mythology" as motifs from many myths are adapted to preserve and enhance Yahwism in different multicultural settings. Burton Mack traces this process through the Hellenistic-Jewish wisdom hymns; and Elisabeth Schüssler Fiorenza shows Christians drawing on similar traditions, perhaps including the Isis myth and cult, in forming christological hymns. From these studies a question rises concerning how "reflective" this mythology is. If the borrowing appears initially in hymns, it is more probable that community worship gives birth to this syncretism, as people who know many traditions speak in praise of Christ, provoking some among them to reflect on what can hardly be rejected in their own worship practice.

A second research interest, the relation of Jewish wisdom traditions to the beginnings of Gnosticism, is too little answered to summarize. Groundwork has been laid by Jacob Jervell, Birger Pearson, and Th. H. Tobin on the exegesis of Genesis texts in Jewish and Gnostic wisdom speculation; by James M. Robinson (1971) on genres used in Jewish and gnostic writing; and by many others working on individual Gnostic texts that may hold the data needed to answer this question.

The third research interest is wisdom Christology, with particular concern to locate the point at which Jesus Christ becomes identified with God's wisdom. Felix Christ's broad proposal of a Sophia Christology in the synoptics, Matthew and Luke's sayings source (Q), and even perhaps by Jesus, is sharpened in Jack Suggs's demonstration that Matthew uses a source in which Jesus is an emissary or child of wisdom (Q from Luke 7:31-35; 11:49-51) and writes a gospel in which Jesus is God's wisdom speaking and acting (Matt. 11:2, 19; 23:34-39; see also James M. Robinson, 1975, and a critique by Marshall Johnson, 1974). The relation of these synoptic wisdom traditions to 1 Corinthians 1-4 has been probed by James M. Robinson (1971), B. Fjärstedt, and Elisabeth Schüssler Fiorenza, but without precise literary or historical results.

When Paul says, "We preach Christ crucified . . . , God's power and wisdom," and tells the Corinthians that Christ is "wisdom to us from God," his identification of Christ as God's wisdom is unmistakable. But this characterization is not developed mythically and appears in Paul's undisputed letters only here in 1 Corinthians 1-2. Those who propose a key role for wisdom theology in Paul either attribute Colossians and Ephesians to him as well (J. B. Lightfoot and Hans Windisch), or propose with Conzelmann that Paul began a "wisdom school" that flowered in these writings later attributed to him. Conzelmann and Scroggs explain that Paul did not elaborate his wisdom theology because he considered wisdom an advanced study for those fully transformed into Christ's death, hence not yet appropriate for the Corinthians. Gerd Theissen is now using psychological categories to describe this wisdom. He proposes we may best understand it as a higher subconscious consciousness of the divine from within through God's spirit given in the crucified Christ, a spirit violently rejected by the ruling human consciousness.

These writers insist on a positive reading of Paul's wisdom claims. But the primary trend in scholarship has been to explain Paul's intense focus on wisdom in 1 Corinthians 1-4 as his reaction to alternate wisdom claims in Corinth. Scandinavian and English-speaking research tends to limit itself to a minimal description of Corinthian wisdom built on Paul's explicit charges about strife, boasting, and overconfidence (see Nils A. Dahl). However, similar accusations in other letters with different issues at stake suggest Paul's charges are more polemical than descriptive. German research on the wisdom texts has been able to build on an extended debate about Paul's Corinthian opponents (see Appendix 4), in this century dominated by Lütgert's and Schlatter's thesis of a spiritualist movement. In 1959, Ulrich Wilkins took the wisdom claims in 1 Corinthians as his key and proposed that Paul was in a christological controversy with Jewish-Christian Gnostics who identified the risen Christ as God's wisdom personified and experienced through baptismal initiation as a spiritual identity with Christ. In 1965, Walter Schmithals proposed the presence of a Jewish-Christian Gnosticism in Corinth, combining the myth of the Iranian primal human with the Messiah figure. He thinks this led to a sharp body-spirit dualism in Corinth—for which the letters give little direct evidence.

In response Luise Schottroff cautioned that the traditional wisdom motifs Paul uses are common to Gnostic, Jewish, and Christian dualism. The way they function in Paul's self-understanding shows that his dualism in 1 Corinthians 1–4 is not primarily a Jewish apocalyptic in-breaking of God's righteousness into an evil age but a radical cleft between those filled with God's spirit and those who side with the world's rulers. But Paul breaks from this Gnostic-type dualism he shares with his opponents by pointing to the exposure of the world's ignorance in Christ's death. This death is God's foolish wisdom at work in history to overcome worldly wisdom. She leaves open, though not explicitly, the possibility that the Corinthian Christians may also be innovating their own genuinely Christian self-understanding from a distinct dualistic experience.

American scholars tend to find insufficient evidence of cosmic and anthropological dualism to convince them that Paul's opponents in Corinth are Gnostics. Instead they draw on Hellenistic-Jewish sources to explain Corinthian theology on the one hand, and on the more apocalyptic Jewish tradition to interpret Paul's opposition to them on the other. This brings us back to the optimistic and pessimistic strands of Jewish wisdom thought. For example, in reviewing Ulrich Wilkins, Helmut Köster describes Christ functioning for the Corinthians, not as a revealer identified with divine wisdom, but as an inspired mystagogue who mediates God's spirit and wisdom to the initiated, much as Moses functions for Philo. In reaction against this instrumental view of Christ, Paul presents Christ as God's wisdom in order to show Jesus' historical death as the point of deliverance for all who hear. Köster's unburdening the Corinthians of excess Gnostic cosmologies is a welcome relief, though there is something of a literary bias suggested, both in Suggs on Matthew and in Köster on Paul, reserving to the New Testament writers the key christological move of identifying Christ as God's wisdom.

Birger Pearson interprets the Corinthians in terms of Hellenistic-Jewish wisdom's distinction between the natural and spiritual person as seen in Philo's exegesis of Genesis 2:7, which describes God's in-breathing of life into Adam. He argues that the Corinthians take the story anthropologically to explain the difference between what is natural or corruptible—including human life—and those few who exhibit the divine spirit that enjoys immortality and wisdom. The evidence is clearer for Pearson's view that Paul reads Genesis 2:7 temporally or apocalyptically, in a way also found occasionally in Qumran and the rabbis, to contrast people of the present world marked by sin and death with the incorruptible people of the coming resurrection age. Köster and Pearson are not as persuasive that the optimistic wisdom strand is best defined by comparison with Alexandrine philosophy and not with the praises of wisdom that also incorporate symbols of apocalyptic reversal in the spirit.

Arthur, Rose Horman. *The Wisdom Goddess: Feminine Motif in Eight Nag Hammadi Documents*. Lanham, New York, and London: University Press of America, 1984.

Böstrum, G. *Proverbiastudien. Die Weisheit und das fremde Weib in Spr. 1–9*. Lund: C. W. K. Gleerup, 1935.

Bultmann, Rudolf. *The Gospel of John: A Commentary*. Philadelphia: Westminster Press, 1971, 21–31 (German, 1941).

———. *Theology of the New Testament*, Vol I. New York: Charles Scribner's Sons, 1951, 164–83 (German, 1948).

Christ, Felix. *Jesus Sophia. Die Sophia-Christologie bei der Synoptikern*. Zürich: Zwingli Verlag, 1970.

Conzelmann, Hans. "The Mother of Wisdom," *The Future of our Religious Past*. Ed. by James M. Robinson. New York: Harpers, 1964, 230–43.

———. "Paulus und die Weisheit," *NTS* 12 (1966), 231–44.

Dahl, Nils A. *Studies in Paul: Theology for Early Christian Mission*. Minneapolis: Augsburg Publishing House, 1977, 40–61.

Fiorenza, Elisabeth Schüssler. *In Memory of Her: A Feminist Theological Reconstruction of Christian Origins*. New York: Crossroad, 1983, 105–241.

———. "Wisdom Mythology and the Christological Hymns of the New Testament," *Aspects of Wisdom in Judaism and Early Christianity*. Ed. by R. L. Wilken. Notre Dame: University of Notre Dame Press, 1975, 17–41.

Fjärstedt, B. *Synoptic Tradition in I Corinthians: Themes and Clusters of Theme Words in I Corinthians 1–4 and 9*. Uppsala: Uppsala Teologiska Institutionen, 1974.

Good, Dierdre J. *Reconstructing the Tradition of Sophia in Gnostic Literature*. Atlanta: Scholars Press, 1987.

Jervell, Jacob. *Imago Dei. Gen 1, 26f. im Spätjudentum, in der Gnosis und in der paulinischen Briefen*. Göttingen: Vandenhoeck & Ruprecht, 1960.

Johnson, Marshall D. "Reflections on a Wisdom Approach to Matthew's Christology," *CBQ* 36 (1974), 44–64.

Jonas, Hans. *The Gnostic Religion: The Message of the Alien God and the Beginnings of Christianity*. 2d rev. ed. Boston: Beacon Press, 1963.

Kayatz, Christa. *Studien zu Proverbien 1–9*. Neukirchen: Neukirchener Verlag, 1966.

Köster, Helmut. Review of U. Wilkens, *Weisheit und Torheit. Gnomon* 33 (1961), 590–5.

Lightfoot, J. B. *Notes on Epistles of St. Paul from Unpublished Commentaries*. London: Macmillan & Co., 1895.

Lütgert, D. W. *Freiheitspredigt und Schwärmgeister in Korinth. Ein Beitrag zur Charakteristik der Christuspartei*. Gütersloh: C. Bertelsmann, 1908.

Mack, Burton Lee. *Logos und Sophia. Untersuchungen zur Weisheitstheologie im hellenistischen Judentum.* Göttingen: Vandenhoeck & Ruprecht, 1973.

Pearson, Birger. *The Pneumatikos-Psychikos Terminology in I Corinthians.* Missoula, Mont.: Society of Biblical Literature, 1973.

Perdue, Leo. *Wisdom and Cult.* Missoula, Mont.: Scholars Press, 1977, 142–55.

Rad, Gerhard von. *Wisdom in Israel.* Nashville: Abingdon Press, 1972, 144–76.

Reitzenstein, Richard. *Die hellenistischen Mysterienreligionen, ihre Grundgedanken und Wirkungen.* Leipzig and Berlin: Teubner, 1910.

Ringgren, H. *Word and Wisdom: Studies in the Hypostatization of Divine Qualities and Functions in the Ancient Near East.* Lund: Hakan Ohlsson, 1947.

Robinson, James M. "Jesus as Sophos and Sophia: Wisdom Tradition and the Gospels," *Aspects of Wisdom in Judaism and Early Christianity.* Ed. by R. L. Wilken. Notre Dame: Notre Dame University Press, 1975, 1–16.

———. "Logoi Sophōn: On the Gattung of Q," *Trajectories through Early Christianity.* Philadelphia: Fortress Press, 1971.

Rudolph, Kurt. *Gnosis: The Nature and History of Gnosticism.* San Francisco: Harper & Row, 1983.

Schlatter, A. *Die korinthische Theologie.* Gütersloh: C. Bertelsmann, 1914.

Schmithals, Walter. *Gnosticism in Corinth.* Nashville: Abingdon Press, 1971.

Schottroff, Luise. *Der Glaubende und die feindliche Welt. Beobachtungen zum gnostischen Dualismus und seiner Bedeutung für Paulus und das Johannesevangelium.* Neukirchen: Neukirchener Verlag, 1970.

Scroggs, Robin. "Paul: Sophos and Pneumatikos," *NTS* 14 (1968), 33–55.

Suggs, Jack. *Wisdom, Christology and Law in Matthew's Gospel.* Cambridge: Harvard University Press, 1970.

Theissen, Gerd. *Psychological Aspects of Pauline Theology.* Philadelphia: Fortress Press, 1983.

Tobin, Th. H., S.J. *The Creation of Man: Philo and the History of Interpretation.* Washington, D.C.: The Catholic Biblical Association of America, 1983.

Wilkins, Ulrich. *Weisheit und Torheit.* Tübingen: J. C. B. Mohr (Paul Siebeck), 1959.

Windisch, Hans. "Die göttliche Weisheit der Juden und die paulinische Christologie," *Neutestamentliche Studien*, Georg Heinrici zu seinem 70. Geburtstag. Leipzig: Hinrichs, 1914, 220–35.

Appendix 7:
The Social Location of
the Corinthian Christians

RECENT RESEARCH IN THIS AREA is characterized by a reaction against the opinion, dominant from Christianity's aristocratic second-century critics to the twentieth-century papyri scholar G. Adolf Deissmann, that the first city Christians were from the lowest social classes. From his study of Roman history in texts, inscriptions, and papyri, E. A. Judge is developing a picture of Paul's congregations in the context of the client systems, voluntary associations, and friendship conventions of the literate Roman East. Because Paul's associates show a frequency of Latin names ten times higher than in public inscriptions in the Roman East, he suggests that many come from freedmen's and veterans' families. But the rank of Roman citizenship does not give them the status of well-established local families, and this may be what they are seeking when they join voluntary associations such as the house-churches in Corinth, thus running afoul of Paul who deliberately abandons social status for tentmaking and a harsh itinerant life style. Paul's insistence on self-support in Corinth is not read as an indication of the Corinthians' poverty but as Paul's own effort to maintain independence among the strong. Hans Dieter Betz interprets Paul's self-support in the context of anti-sophistic polemic, Ronald Hock in the rabbinic artisan and Greek gentle philosopher traditions, Gerd Theissen in contrast to a strictly charismatic legitimation, and Peter Marshall as Paul's evasion of restricting Greco-Roman friendship bonds between equals.

What then of the Corinthians as "not many wise . . . , not many powerful, not many of ranking families" (1:26)? Wilhelm Wüllner (1973) goes so far as to read the clause interrogatively, "Are not many wise . . . ?" But this grammatical form for a question is less common in Paul and does not make as good sense of the accompanying phrase "according to the flesh," nor of the paragraph as a whole. Another proposal by Wüllner that the triad "wise, powerful, noble" refers not to social station but divine favor has been weakened by his later determination that such a set formula for divine favor cannot be confirmed for this period (1982). Theissen is satisfied that "not many wise" shows that some were wise. His study of those in Corinth who are named as leaders, homeowners, providers of hospitality, or travelers yields a list of sixteen people of some means who seem to be the most active in the congregation (1982, 69–119). He sees such people providing the space, food, and leadership for the meeting of both major Corinthian factions, displaying their wisdom, power, and status in mobilizing the common people (1982, 54–57). The fact that all sixteen people other than Apollos appear to be in Paul's camp suggests that Theissen should have asked whether those claiming Apollos might not have lower social status—though Marshall argues that rhetorical convention and not low status prevents enemies from being named (341–48). Abraham Malherbe's study of the social level in Paul's churches emphasizes Paul's writing style as a key indication of his considerable culture and that of his intended audience.

Wayne Meeks's comprehensive study cautions against using any one standard of social status, or even Judge's double categories of rank and status, proposing instead distinct scales for education, wealth, sex, etc. This practice, which I adopt, also encourages awareness of whose view of status is being considered at any one point and highlights those people with significant inconsistency between the various kinds of status they hold. Their social position is likely to be unstable and they may generate social change, as "the strong" apparently do in Corinth. My chief adaption has been to consider the social status of a particular group in Corinth and to observe how entering the community has changed their social status and how this change is reflected in their theology. Paul's "Consider your calling, brethren, not many were wise according to the flesh, not many powerful, not many of ranking families" (1:26), turns out to be significant not only for revealing the many who were without these advantages when called and the "not many" who were relatively privileged, but also for showing that most hearers have left behind their earlier social station so that Paul is stirred up to evoke their "calling" (see chapter 3 excursus and chapter 9).

Meeks's use of the sociological model of status inconsistency shows that the social sciences are increasingly informing New Testament study. Bengt Holmberg's more traditional Weberian analysis of power within the Pauline communities must now be compared with Bruce Malina's anthropologically informed study of honor, dyadic personality, and kinship in the New Testament; Walter Rebell's application of the social-psychological categories of cognitive balance, reactance, and the double bind to Paul's congregations; Aloys Funk's use of a sociological quantitative content analysis to study roles and status in these churches; and Richard Rohrbaugh's effort to use relational concepts such as creditor/debtor and worker/non-working-user-of-workers to get beyond describing to explaining the interests that maintain Greco-Roman class structures. Recently Jerome Neyrey has applied Bruce Malina's adaption of Mary Douglas's "group/grid" model to 1 Corinthians, distinguishing Paul as "strong group" from his opponents as "weak group" and showing how each demonstrates the appropriate differences in cosmology and approach to the body (see chapter 9).

Betz, Hans Dieter. *Der Apostel Paulus und die sokratische Tradition*. Tübingen: J. C. B. Mohr (Paul Siebeck), 1972.

Deissmann, G. Adolf. *Light from the Ancient East: The New Testament Illustrated by Recently Discovered Texts of the Graeco-Roman World*. London: Hodder & Stoughton, 1910, 403.

Douglas, Mary. *Cultural Bias*. Occasional Paper No. 35 of the Royal Anthropological Institute, 1978; reprinted in *In the Active Voice*. London, Boston, and Henley: Routledge & Kegan Paul, 1982, 183–254.

———. *Natural Symbols: Explorations in Cosmology*. 2d rev. ed. Harmondsworth, England: Penguin Books, 1973.

Funk, Aloys. *Status und Rollen in den Paulusbriefen. Eine inhaltsanalytische Unter-suchung zur Religionssoziologie.* Innsbruck: Tyrolia-Verlag, 1981.

Hock, Ronald. *The Social Context of Paul's Ministry: Tentmaking and Apostleship.* Philadelphia: Fortress Press, 1980.

Holmberg, Bengt. *Paul and Power: The Structure of Authority in the Primitive Church as Reflected in the Pauline Epistles.* Philadelphia: Fortress Press, 1978.

Judge, E. A. "Cultural Conformity and Innovation in Paul: Some Clues from Contemporary Documents," *Tyn Bul* 35 (1984), 3–24.

——. "The Early Christians as a Scholastic Community," *Journal of Roman History* 1 (1960), 4–15, 125–37.

——. *Rank and Status in the World of the Caesars and St. Paul.* University of Canterbury Publications 29, University of Canterbury, 1982.

——. "The Social Identity of the First Christians: A Question of Method in Religious History," *JRH* 11 (1980), 102–17.

Lenski, Gerhard. "Status Crystallization: A Non-Vertical Dimension of Social Status," *American Sociological Review* 19 (1954), 405–11.

Malherbe, Abraham. *Social Aspects of Early Christianity.* Baton Rouge: Louisiana State University Press, 1977, 29–59.

Malina, Bruce. *Christian Origins and Cultural Anthropology: Practical Models for Biblical Interpretation.* Atlanta: John Knox Press, 1986.

——. *The New Testament World: Insights from Cultural Anthropology.* Atlanta: John Knox Press, 1981.

Marshall, Peter. *Enmity in Corinth: Social Conventions in Paul's Relations with the Corinthians.* Tübingen: J. C. B. Mohr (Paul Siebeck), 1987.

Meeks, Wayne A. *The First Urban Christians: The Social World of the Apostle Paul.* New Haven: Yale University Press, 1983, 54–55 and 70.

——. "The Social Context of Pauline Theology," *Interpretation* 37 (1982), 200–77.

Neyrey, Jerome, H., S.J. "Body Language in 1 Corinthians: The Use of Anthropological Models for Understanding Paul and his Opponents," *Semeia: The Social-Scientific Criticism of the New Testament and its Social World* 35 (1986). Ed. by John H. Elliott, 129–70.

Rebell, Walter. "Paulus—Apostel im Spannungsfeld sozialer Beziehungen: Eine socialpsychologische Untersuchung zum Verhältnis des Paulus zu Jerusalem, seinen Mitarbeitern und Gemeinden." Ph.D. Disseration, Bochum, 1982.

Rohrbaugh, Richard. "Methological Considerations in the Debate over the Social Class Status of Early Christians," *JAAR* 52 (1984), 521–46.

Theissen, Gerd. "Legitimation and Subsistence: An Essay on the Sociology of Early Christian Missionaries," *The Social Setting of Pauline Christianity: Essays on Corinth.* Ed. by John H. Schütz. Philadelphia: Fortress Press, 1982, 27–67.

——. "Social Stratification in the Corinthian Community," *The Social Setting of Pauline Christianity: Essays on Corinth.* Ed. by John H. Schütz. Philadelphia: Fortress Press, 1982, 69–119.

Wüllner, Wilhelm. "The Sociological Implications of I Corinthians 1:26-28 Reconsidered," *Studia Evangelica,* Vol 6. Ed. by E. A. Livingstone. Berlin: Akademie-Verlag, 1973, 666–72.

——. "Tradition and Interpretation of the 'Wise-Powerful-Nobel' Triad in I Cor 1, 26," *Studia Evangelica,* Vol 7. Berlin: Akademie-Verlag, 1982, 557–62.

Appendix 8:
Women's Head Covering

ALTHOUGH 1 CORINTHIANS 11:2-16 is obscure at several points, it has unquestionably been the modern reader's difficulty with Paul's position that has focused recent attention on this text. The difficulty is approached either by addressing it directly as a hermeneutical problem, by interpolation theories, by reconstruing Paul's meaning, or by using the text as evidence for views other than Paul's.

The hermeneutical studies are of course less interested in historical reconstruction than in the interpreter's approach. Linda Mercadante shows how women's changing social role has influenced the discussions of this text available in English in such a way that Paul is now seen as placing no restrictions on the women. Krister Stendahl defends a "realistic exegesis" of Paul's meaning for his time, in spite of its difficulty for us, turning us from 1 Corinthians 11 to Galatians 3:28 as the cutting edge of his thought. Madeleine Boucher argues that Paul's view of woman's full and yet subordinate integration into Christ is not strange in his world and yet presents an intolerable contradiction to us. This presses us to review the way we understand biblical authority. Similarly John Maier's sensitive exegesis of this text challenges the Catholic church, which has dropped the veils Paul defended on grounds of apostolic tradition, Scripture, and reason, to reconsider whether it can hold the line against women priests on the same grounds.

The offense of this text to readers today has also led to interpolation theories. G. W. Trompf gives as good an argument for interpolation from this passage as can be made where there is no manuscript evidence for it. Robert Jewett and Winsome Munro show the complex maze one enters when reorganizing the textual history of a correspondence or an entire tradition to get a consistent development of thought from charismatic equality to doctrinaire subordination. Murphy O'Connor argues convincingly against an interpolation.

The majority of recent studies work to reinterpret what Paul meant in this text against the traditional reading of the veil as a symbol of subordination. Particularly influential has been Robin Scroggs's revival of Bedale's hypothesis that "head" in Greek means "source" (as in "headwaters") rather than "ruler" and hence indicates only a temporal priority of the man at creation, which Paul then balances with woman's priority in the birth process. Two important articles propose new readings of women's having "authority on the head because of the angels." J. A. Fitzmyer takes "authority" to signify the similar Aramaic term "veil" and proposes that the angels, who are to be shielded from all things unnatural or defective at Qumran, are here shielded from women's uncovered heads. Hooker notes that it is man's glory represented by women's heads, which are to be covered when God is being glorified, giving women positive authority to praise God without disturbing the natural order guarded by the angels. A few scholars such as Jerome Murphy-O'Connor take requirements concerning women's clothing as a complement to equal strictures against male dress associated with homosexuality. Others like A. Feuillet settle for women's special "dependence in equality." In each case the efforts to clear Paul of advocating women's subordination seem to deal inadequately with the text as a whole argument.

A more indirect reinterpretation of Paul's meaning is made by those studying what head covering meant in Corinth as a background for understanding Paul. Klaus Thräde's analysis claims that because women in Greece went uncovered for the most part, Paul was forced to draw on heavy theological artillery to institute a tradition that was probably Jewish in the Corinthian church. But he does not explain why Paul continues with arguments that appeal to custom and nature. On the other extreme, Fitzmyer thinks Paul is defending what any Greek woman would have thought to be decent behavior. But he does not explain why there is an elaborate theological argument. A third position represented by Stefan Lösch and Elisabeth Schüssler Fiorenza points to inscriptions, literature, and artistic representations showing Greek women putting aside veils and/or loosening their hair in mystery cult worship, giving some reason for both Paul's argument from the modesty of daily hair covering and his theological barrage. Attention to the significance of clothing and hairstyles in all available sources by Cynthia Thompson and Richard Oster may eventually settle this particular issue.

Finally, this passage can be read as evidence for views other than Paul's. Initially this was done to justify Paul for not consistently affirming equality in Christ: Walter Schmithals says Paul was forced to it by Gnostics who claimed a mythical spiritual equality of men and women and immunity from demonic threat. Jacob Jervell's key study of how creation in God's image was interpreted in this period recognizes that mythical and/or androgynous readings of God's image appear in Judaism and Christianity apart from Gnosticism — and even in Gnosticism at times apart from radical dualism. So the focus of research begins to shift from Paul against the background of a dualistic Gnostic heresy to the variety of sometimes conflicting Jewish and Christian religious experiences and accompanying biblical interpretations. Jervell is convinced that Paul does not develop his usual theology of Christ as God's inclusive image when writing to Corinth, substituting instead the male as God's image and glory and the woman as man's glory, because others are interpreting Genesis 1:27 in a baptismal rite that ends all sexual distinctions in Christ. De Merode stresses the pre-Pauline nature of the primitive Christian theology expressed in Galatians 3:28 within its Greek and Jewish context. Meeks and MacDonald suggest that the image of God as androgyne, which was later influential in Gnostic communities and individual asceticism, may already be present in the realized eschatology of women in Corinth who enact baptismal reunification by uncovering their heads like men, seeing themselves to be beyond sexuality, and equal to the angels in an androgynous Christ. Betz not only recognizes that Galatians 3:27-28 is pre-Pauline, but that Paul argues in the opposite direction in 1 Corinthians 11:12. Thus Meeks, MacDonald, and Betz join Pagels and Fiorenza in conceding that the conservative reaction to the radical Christian experience of baptism in the image of God that is not male and female begins in Paul's reaction to the Corinthian women who did not cover their heads.

Betz, Hans Dieter. *Galatians: A Commentary on Paul's Letter to the Churches in Galatia.* Philadelphia: Fortress Press, 1979, 181–85, 199–201.

Boucher, Madeleine. "Some Unexplored Parallels to I Cor. 11,11-12 and Gal. 3,28: The New Testament on the Role of Women," *CBQ* 31 (1969), 50–58.

Fiorenza, Elisabeth Schüssler. *In Memory of Her: A Feminist Theological Reconstruction of Christian Origins.* New York: Crossroad, 1983, 218–236.

Fitzmyer, J. A. "A Feature of Qumran Angelology and the Angels of I Cor. XI. 10," *NTS* 4 (1957–58), 48–58.

Feuillet, A. "La dignité et le rôle de la femme d'après quelques textes pauliniens: comparaison avec l'ancien testament," *NTS* 21 (1975), 157–91.

——. "Le signe de puissance sur la tête de la femme, I Cor. 11,10," *NRT* 9 (1973), 945–54.

Hooker, M. D. "Authority on her Head: An Examination of I Cor. XI. 10," *NTS* 10 (1963–64), 410–16.

Jervell, Jacob. *Imago Dei: Gen 1, 26f im Spätjudentum, in der Gnosis und in den paulinischen Briefen.* Göttingen: Vandenhoeck & Ruprecht, 1960, 293–312.

Jewett, Robert. "The Redaction of I Corinthians and the Trajectory of the Pauline School," *JAAR* Supplement 46 (1978), 389–444.

Lösch, Stefan. "Christliche Frauen in Corinth (1 Cor. 11:2-16)," *TQ* 111 (1947), 216–61.

MacDonald, Dennis Ronald. *There is No Male and Female: The Fate of a Dominical Saying in Paul and Gnosticism.* Philadelphia: Fortress Press, 1981.

Meeks, Wayne A. "Image of the Androgyne: Some Uses of a Symbol in Earliest Christianity," *HR* 13 (1973–74), 165–208.

Meier, John "On the Veiling of Hermeneutics (I Cor. 11:2-16)," *CBQ* 40 (1978), 212–26.

Mercadante, Linda. *From Hierarchy to Equality: A Comparison of Past and Present Interpretations of I Cor. 11:2-16 in Relation to the Changing Status of Women in Society.* Vancouver: G-M-H Books for Regent College, 1978.

de Merode, Maria. "Une théologie primitive de la femme?" *RTL* 9 (1978), 176–89.

Munro, Winsome. *Authority in Paul and Peter: The Identification of a Pastoral Stratum in the Pauline Corpus and I Peter.* Cambridge: Cambridge University Press, 1983.

Murphy-O'Connor, Jerome. "The Non-Pauline Character of 1 Cor. 11:2-16?" *JBL* 95 (1976), 615–22.

——. "Sex and Logic in 1 Cor. 11:2-16," *CBQ* 42 (1980), 482–500.

——. "1 Corinthians 11:2-16 Once Again," *CBQ* 50 (1988), 265–74.

Oster, Richard E. "When Men Wore Veils to Worship: The Historical Context of I Corinthians 11:4," *NTS* 34 (1988), 481–505.

Pagels, Elaine. "Paul and Women: A Response to a Recent Discussion," *JAAR* 42 (1974), 538–49.

Schmithals, Walter. *Gnosticism in Corinth.* Nashville: Abingdon Press, 1971, 237–43.

Scroggs, Robin. "Paul and the Eschatological Woman," *JAAR* 41 (1972), 283–303; see also 43 (1974), 532–37.

Stendahl, Krister. *The Bible and the Role of Women: A Case Study in Hermeneutics.* Philadelphia: Fortress Press, 1966.

Thompson, Cynthia L. "Hairstyles, Head-coverings, and St. Paul: Portraits from Roman Corinth," *BA* 51 (June, 1988), 99–115.

Thräde, Klaus. "Ärger mit der Freiheit. Die Bedeutung von Frauen in Theorie und Praxis der alten Kirche," *"Freunde in Christus werden . . ." Die Beziehung von Mann und Frau als Frage an Theologie und Kirche* by G. Scharffenorth and K. Thräde. Gelhausen/Berlin: Burckhardthaus-Verlag, 1977.

Trompf, G. W. "On Attitudes Toward Women in Paul and Paulinist Literature: I Cor 11:3-16 and its Context," *CBQ* 42 (1980), 196–215.

Appendix 9:
Concerning the Virgins

MOST OF THE ANCIENT CHURCH read that here Paul is speaking about virgin daughters living in single devotion to the Lord — daughters whose fathers were considering whether to have them marry. A strong defense of this interpretation with the patristic citations was written in 1905 by J. Sickenberger. His purpose was to refute an alternative hypothesis by H. Achelis and A. Jülicher arguing that Paul is dealing with something like the institution of spiritual marriage, the cohabitation of an ascetic pair, which is clearly attested by the third century. In support of the spiritual marriage reading it can be argued that the early interpretation, in terms of a father-daughter relationship, could have arisen from the church's strong opposition to ascetic cohabitation. And it makes more sense that the man who "thinks he may act improperly toward his virgin" because he does not "have authority over his own desire" be the virgin's suitor and not her father.

Scholarship was split between the paternal and spiritual marriage readings until W. G. Kümmel gained wide support for a third thesis in 1957. Not finding sufficient evidence of a father's struggle nor of asceticism in marriage, Kümmel proposes an engagement Paul considered to be binding according to Jewish tradition, but one not yet consummated due to an intervening commitment to the Lord. Some difficulties remain. Would the Corinthians be consulting Paul about a problem that rises from Jewish custom, binding engagement not being a Greek tradition? Is not Paul using a causative verb, "He who causes his own virgin to marry does well?" Why is she called his "virgin," not his "betrothed"? And why is she not consulted? In chapter 5 I adopt a modified form of Kümmel's view, suggesting an engagement or courtship in which the young woman's interest in virginity is not shared by the man. Paul then gives the man authority to cause the virgin to marry him so that he will not be tempted to immorality. A recent article by Margaret Y. MacDonald considers what it meant for the virgins to be "holy in body and spirit."

The crucial broader questions about the significance of sexual abstinence for Christian women in the imperial world have only recently begun to be addressed (Brown, Burrus, Countryman, Pagels, Wire), with some of these studies focusing particularly on the church in Corinth (Dennis R. MacDonald, Margaret Y. MacDonald.).

Achelis, H. *Virgines subintroductae. Ein Beitrag zum VII Kapitel des I. Korintherbriefs.* Leipzig: Hinrichs, 1902.

Brown, Peter. *The Body and Society: Men, Women and Sexual Renunciation in Early Christianity.* New York: Columbia University Press, 1988.

Burrus, Virginia. *Chastity as Autonomy: Women in the Stories of Apocryphal Acts.* Lewiston, N.Y.: E. Mellen Press, 1987.

Countryman, L. William. *Dirt, Greed, and Sex: Sexual Ethics in the New Testament and their Implications for Today.* Philadelphia: Fortress Press, 1988.

Jülicher, A. "Die geistliche Ehen in der Alten Kirche," *Archiv für Religionswissenschaft* 7 (1904), 373–86.

———. "Die Jungfrauen im ersten Korintherbrief," *Protestantische Monatshefte* 22 (1918), 97–119.

Kümmel, W. G. "Verlobung und Heirat bei Paulus (I Cor 7:36-38)," *Neutestamentliche Studien für Rudolf Bultmann zu seinem siebzigsten Geburtstag.* 2d ed. Berlin: A. Töpelmann, 1957.

MacDonald, Dennis Ronald. *There Is No Male and Female: the Fate of a Dominical Saying in Paul and Gnosticism.* Philadelphia: Fortress Press, 1987.

MacDonald, Margaret Y. "Women Holy in Body and Spirit: The Social Setting of 1 Corinthians 7," *NTS* 36 (1990), 161–81.

Meeks, Wayne. "The Image of the Androgyne: Some Uses of a Symbol in Earliest Christianity," *HR* 13 (1974), 165–208.

Pagels, Elaine. *Adam, Eve and the Serpent.* New York: Random House, 1987.

Sickenberger, J. "Syneisaktentum im ersten Korintherbrief?" *BZ* 3 (1905), 44–69.

Wire, Antoinette C. "The Social Functions of Women's Asceticism in the Roman East," *Images of the Feminine in Gnosticism.* Ed. by Karen L. King. Philadelphia: Fortress Press, 1988, 308–23.

Appendix 10:
Prophecy in Hellenistic Churches

AT PRESENT THERE IS no scholarly consensus on the nature or extent of prophecy in the early Hellenistic house-churches, witness the variety of views represented in a recent essay collection by J. Panagopoulos. One broad position takes Paul's advocacy of intelligible prophecy in 1 Corinthians 12–14 as the model for how prophets acted. J. D. G. Dunn and David Hill each develop a homogenous picture of the normative teacher-prophet on this basis. Although Ellis recognizes the roots of Christian prophecy among the visionaries of the Jewish apocalyptic tradition, and therefore might seem to belong to a second group of interpreters who stress the mystery in prophecy, he conceives this influence in terms of intelligible wisdom and inspired exegesis. Christian prophets appear in the image of the Hebrew prophets—predicting, judging, and above all exhorting the church to live out its calling. Cothenet puts it in this way: prophecy may be more spontaneous and occasional than other teaching in the church, but it is essentially guidance by interpreting Scripture. All recent writers on prophecy are indebted to two earlier exegetical studies of the prophetic role in the New Testament by G. Friedrich and G. Greeven, and to a broader investigation of ancient prophecy by E. Fascher.

The most ambitious recent study of New Testament prophecy as exhortation is Ulrich B. Müller's *Prophetie und Predigt im Neuen Testament*. Müller's aim is to determine the form, content, and historical tradition of the prophecy that Paul wants to dissociate from ecstatic speech in Corinth. He sees Paul rejecting the adequacy of the Corinthian speaking of God's mysteries "in the tongues of angels" — probably a Pythian or Dionysian tradition mediated through Hellenistic-Jewish views of divine ecstacy—and instituting in its place the prophetic challenge to repent and return to God. This is traced back to the deuteronomistic history and also seen in the prophecy of John the Baptist and of Jesus in Matthew's and Luke's common sayings source. From the messages to the seven churches in Revelation Müller develops criteria to locate this kind of parenesis in Paul's letters—its major forms being the challenge to repentance, the salvation oracle, and judgment teaching. Müller makes a major contribution to our understanding of Paul's proclamation within its historical tradition, but the question remains whether Paul's speech is not being taken too much as the gauge of normative early Christian prophecy. Paul's elaborate work in 1 Corinthians to untangle prophecy and tongues witnesses to their full and far more complex integration in church practice.

The second group of studies take as their subject the hidden divine mysteries that may be received in visions, dreams, or possession experiences and may not be expressible in human language. Whereas New Testament research has often tended, as we see in H. Bacht, to see Corinthian tongues as an aberrant phenomenon, a "pollution" from Greco-Roman ecstatic prophecy, recent studies like T. Callan's ask how Judaism and Christianity come to marginalize ecstatic prophetism, or H. Kraft and J. Reiling find evidence of a significant revelatory prophecy tradition in Christian communities into the second century.

Two studies stand out in this connection, Gerhard Dautzenberg's *Urchristliche Prophetie* for seeking the Jewish roots of this tradition and David Aune's *Prophecy in Early Christianity and the Ancient Mediterranean World* for attempting a comprehensive form-critical analysis. Dautzenberg locates a two-stage process of prophecy in Jewish apocalyptic sources — Daniel, Qumran, *1 Enoch*, 4 Ezra — and in reports of prophecy from Josephus and Philo. First the mystery or vision is received, and second there is an interpretation of its immediate, often apocalyptic, significance. In Jewish worship the law was taken to be the formative mystery, interpreted by inspired speech among the Essenes and Therapeutes; in Jewish-Christian worship the prophetic vision often took the law's place as God's voice that prophets then interpreted to the community.

As for women's prophecy, Dautzenberg argues that the silencing of women in 1 Corinthians 14:33b-38 was first added to the letter near the time of 1 Timothy. In the century after Paul a society-wide reaction against Hellenistic women's emancipation first led to household subordination of Christian women, then to direct efforts to silence them in worship, so that by the early third century reports that God was speaking through prophets in Christian worship die out. It is Dautzenberg's interpolation thesis that allows him to read 1 Corinthians, not as the first surviving Christian attempt to regulate prophecy by dissociating it from ecstacy, requiring interpreters, and denying women the right to prophesy, but as the apostolic advocacy of a normative orderly speaking and interpreting of mysteries by men and women in all churches. The practices Paul criticizes are largely taken to be local aberrations.

David Aune's study of early Christian prophecy in its Mediterranean setting is distinctive for its form-critical study of Greek oracles, followed by an equally complex typology of Hellenistic-Jewish prophecies. On this foundation, not on Old Testament prophecy, he develops criteria to locate 107 prophecies that have survived from early Christianity. These are identified by their attribution to a divine source, provision of special knowledge, traditional prophetic formulas, reference to inspiration experiences, and/or loose integration into their literary contexts. He finds that most of these are oracles of assurance, salvation, judgment, and legitimation. Although Aune is exemplary in not confusing Paul's arguments with descriptions of the situations he is addressing, the results are relatively meager for understanding the function of prophecy in earliest Christianity including Paul's Corinth. This is partly due to the fact that oracles survive in numbers only in the later periods of Revelation, the *Odes of Solomon,* and the *Shepherd of Hermas.* It is also the case that Aune's detailed analysis of forms of speech is not matched by a parallel comprehensive investigation of the social functions of these forms.

Some new methods are beginning to be applied in the study of early Christian prophecy that may change the face of future research. Gerd Theissen proposes that the modern psychological theory of the unconscious can contribute to the understanding of Corinthians speaking in tongues. Jerome Neyrey is applying to

1 Corinthians Mary Douglas's anthropological model that interprets efforts to restrict the bodily orifices including the speaking mouth as evidence of tightening structures of social control. Thomas Overholt uses a cross-cultural study of prophecy today in order to understand the prophecy of Israel, but his recent collection of mediation accounts in modern traditional societies are equally suggestive for those developing hypotheses concerning early church prophecy.

Aune, David E. *Prophecy in Early Christianity and the Ancient Mediterranean World*. Grand Rapids: Wm. B. Eerdmans, 1983.

Bacht, H. "Wahres und falsches Prophetentum," *Biblica* 32 (1951), 237–62.

Callan, T. "Prophecy and Ecstacy in Greco-Roman Religion and in I Corinthians," *NovT* 27 (1985), 125–40.

Cothenet, Edouard. "Les prophètes chrétiens comme exégètes charismatiques de l'écriture," *Prophetic Vocation in the New Testament and Today*. Ed. by J. Panagopoulos. Leiden: E. J. Brill, 1977, 77–107.

Dautzenberg, Gerhard von. "Zur Stellung der Frauen in den paulinischen Gemeinden," *Die Frau im Urchristentum*. Ed. by G. Dautzenberg, H. Merklein, and K. Müller. Freiburg, Basel, and Vienna: Herder, 1983.

————. *Urchristliche Prophetie: ihre Erforschung, ihre Voraussetzungen im Judentum und ihre Struktur im ersten Korintherbrief*. Stuttgart: Kohlhammer, 1975.

Douglas, Mary. "Social Preconditions of Enthusiasm and Heterodoxy," *Forms of Symbolic Action, Proceedings of the 1969 Annual Spring Meeting of the American Ethnological Society*. Ed. by R. F. Spencer. Seattle: University of Washington Press, 1969, 69–80.

Dunn, J. D. G. *Jesus and the Spirit*. London: SCM Press, 1975.

Ellis, E. Earle. *Prophecy and Hermeneutic in Early Christianity: New Testament Essays*. Tübingen: J. C. B. Mohr (Paul Siebeck), 1978, Chaps. 2, 6. 8.

Fascher, E. *Prophētēs: Eine sprach- und religionsgeschichtliche Untersuchung*. Giessen: A. Töpelmann, 1927.

Friedrich, G. "prophētēs," *TDNT*, Vol VII. Ed. by G. Friedrich. Grand Rapids: Wm. B. Eerdmans, 1968, 828–61.

Greeven, D. H. "Propheten, Lehrer, Vorsteher bei Paulus: Zur Frage der Ämter im Urchristentum," *ZNW* 44 (1952–53), 1–43.

Hill, David. *New Testament Prophecy*. Atlanta: John Knox Press, 1979.

Kraft, H. "Die altkirchliche Prophetie und die Entstehung des Montanismus," *TZ* 11 (1955), 249–71.

Müller, Ulrich B. *Prophetie und Predigt im Neuen Testament: Formgeschichtliche Untersuchungen zur urchristliche Prophetie*. Gütersloh: Gerd Mohn, 1975.

Neyrey, Jerome H., S.J. "Body Language in I Corinthians: The Use of Anthropological Models for Understanding Paul and his Opponents," *Semeia* 35 (1986), 129–70.

Overholt, Thomas W. *Prophecy in Cross-Cultural Perspective*. Atlanta: Scholars Press, 1986.

Panagopoulos, J. *Prophetic Vocation in the New Testament and Today*. Leiden: E. J. Brill, 1977.

Reiling, J. *Hermas and Christian Prophecy: A Study of the Eleventh Mandate*. Leiden: E. J. Brill, 1973.

Theissen, Gerd. *Psychological Aspects of Pauline Theology*. Philadelphia: Fortress Press, 1987 (German, 1983).

Appendix 11:
1 Corinthians 14:34-35

ISSUES OF INTERPRETATION CANNOT BE EVADED in dealing with these sentences, so modern scholars have generally responded in one of three ways: they hold that Paul does not say these lines, that he does not mean them, or that the Corinthian women ask for them. To take these up in reverse order, the latter approach was sufficient in 1839 when H. A. W. Meyer concluded: "Regarding gifts of the Spirit . . . Corinthian women, with their freer mood inclined towards emancipation, must have presumed on this. . . . Paul is decided against all undue exaltation and assumption on the part of women in religious things, and it has been the occasion of much evil in the church" — leaving a delightful ambiguity about whether it might be Paul's decision that has been the long-term evil. More recently, others have studied Greek religion to find orgiastic tendencies that justify Paul's restrictions of Corinthian women (Kröger and Kröger). Apology on Paul's behalf is unnecessary, but not the basic research on the religion of women in Greece that can make multiple contributions to the study of the Christian women prophets in mid-first-century Corinth (Krämer, Lefkowitz and Fant, Heyob).

A second more broadly pursued approach has been to argue that Paul does not mean it, that he does not intend the silencing of the Corinthian Christian women. Since he has already instructed women to cover their heads when praying and prophesying (11:5), he can only be restricting women in other roles, in other kinds of meetings, or women of another marriage status. The role forbidden to women is often taken to be didactic rather than inspired, based on Paul's concession that those who want learning should ask at home (Moffatt, Kümmel in Lietzmann and Kümmel). But because teaching is not specified, others say only interrupting with questions is forbidden (Wendland, Wolff). Or the type of assembly may account for Paul's different instructions, women's prophecy and prayer being permitted in private groups but not "in the gatherings" (Schlatter). Or only those with husbands are required to question them in private rather than public, but other women may speak (Barrett, Ellis 1978, Fiorenza 1983). Against these various proposals remain the univocal words to Corinth, "Let the women be silent in the churches," spoken in a passage restricting spiritual, not didactic gifts, to a community not split between public and private space but meeting in homes, in a society where not only wives, but children, slaves, and widows are subordinate to men in their households. A recent suggestion that in 14:34-35 Paul is quoting and in 14:36 refuting men in Corinth who want to silence women is not convincing because this silencing is one of three in a sequence, and because Paul does not attribute it to others as he does elsewhere when quoting in order to refute another position rather than to build on it (1:12; 15:12; cf. 6:12, 13; 7:1; 8:1-7; 10:23; Flanagan and Snyder).

A third proposal is that Paul does not write 14:34-35 but that it is a later interpolation. Some say Paul added it in the margin while rereading (Ellis 1981). The lapse in time and context between his first writing and this correcting explains how Paul can conflict with his own instructions on head covering in 11:5 and insert words about women into a chapter on spiritual gifts. The gloss is then seen to have been incorporated into the text at different places. Others date the marginal gloss at the turn of the century, attributing it to the collector of Paul's letters or to a copyist sharing the views and vocabulary of the writer of 1 Timothy (Bousset; Barrett as alternative view; Fee, the best defense of interpolation to date). Yet 1 Corinthians is in circulation across the Mediterranean before Paul's letters are collected, as *1 Clement*, Ignatius, and probably the *Didache* already show, and no copy survives without this passage in some location. This presses the date of the interpolation back and puts in question if we can solve the problems of this text by finding a time band between the unambiguously spiritual days of Paul and the beginning of the letter's circulation when someone proscribed women's speech in the margin.

The problem becomes more acute for the extended interpolation theory favored by many Western scholars today and reflected in the paragraph structure given the Nestle-Aland 26th edition of the Greek New Testament (Weiss 1910; Conzelmann; Dautzenberg 1975, 1983). Here the interpolation is said to begin earlier with 14:33b, "As in all the churches of the saints" — in spite of awkward repetition in the next phrase, "let the women be silent in the churches," and in spite of Paul's consistent practice in 1 Corinthians to make this kind of appeal to universal church conduct at the end of sentences rather than at the beginning (4:17; 7:17; 11:16). When Weiss proposed this longer interpolation, he attributed each of these four appeals to universal church conduct—as well as the letter's opening lines, "to all those called . . . in every place" (1:2) — to a redactor using 1 Corinthians to introduce the first churchwide edition of the Pauline corpus (Weiss 1900, 1910). Conzelmann drops the theory that the entire letter was edited for the church at large, yet at the same time adds to the interpolation Paul's next sentence, "Or did God's word originate from you? Or did it reach you people only?" as an interpolator's claim to churchwide validity. He does not explain how the final masculine phrase, "you people only," can be addressed to women.

In 1975, Gerhard Dautzenberg published the first extensive study of the authenticity and meaning of this passage in the context of his monograph on early Christian prophecy. His further elaboration of the interpolation theory is carefully done, and yet it exposes what I consider its two greatest problems.

If the interpolation is longer than the two verses found differently located in the manuscripts (14:34-35), it cannot be explained as a marginal gloss variously inserted into the text. Instead, the dislocation must arise from a later correction of the interpolation. This means that between Paul's writing of 1 Corinthians and the first circulation of the "Western" text a more complex series of intervening events is being proposed: the origin of a rule silencing women in Christian churches; the interpolation of that rule here (14:34-35) along with a churchwide authority claim (14:33b and 36) and a sharp challenge to spiritual recognition (14:37-38); the subsequent elimination of the lines silencing women (14:34-35) by a scribe "for whatever reasons, perhaps in connection with the Montanist movement" (Dautzenberg 1975, 269–71); the restoration of these lines in the margin (by a third corrector!); and finally the insertion of the lines in the wrong place by the next copyist. In a later publication Dautzenberg also concedes a possible influence of the Eastern form of the text (in the traditional order) on the writer of 1 Timothy (Dautzenberg 1983; Trummer), which would require at least the first two of these stages to have occurred before 1 Timothy was written.

The second question to Dautzenberg is whether the gradual extension of the interpolation theory from 14:34-35 (Heinrici 1880) to include first 14:33b (Weiss 1000), then 14:36 as well (Conzelmann 1060), and now also 14:37-38 (Dautzenberg 1975, 253–57), does not indicate that the two verses are more tightly welded to their context than at first appears. The rhetoric builds on itself consistently without loss of power. What seems to keep the interpolation theory alive for Dautzenberg, without positive manuscript evidence nor a radical disjunction in the immediate context, is his sense of a wider contradiction between women covering their heads to prophesy where all prophecy is done so as to be constructive, and women being silent where a leadership caste has been established. This evaluation comes from reading the head covering in 1 Corinthians 11 as the permission to prophesy that it purports to be rather than as an initial restriction on women's prophecy, which the rhetoric shows that it is (Lietzmann). More broadly, it comes from reading 1 Corinthians as a description of a spiritual movement being fostered by Paul rather than as an argument to change the Corinthians' conduct and reshape their spiritual experience.

Dautzenberg does not have a naive view of the church moving in single file from freedom under Paul to a monarchic episcopacy. For example, he suggests that the rule silencing women may be developing simultaneously with Paul in another place (Dautzenberg 1975, 257–61, 300). But Dautzenberg and his predecessors in the interpolation theory do not read this letter as concrete evidence of this leadership struggle. Too quickly taken in by Paul's arguments from the common good, they amplify them to justify regulations such as the head covering that even Paul does not defend in this way. And they weaken or excise from the text restrictions that the common good cannot be stretched to cover.

Barrett, C. K. *A Commentary on the First Epistle to the Corinthians.* London: Adam & Charles Black, 1968, 330–33.

Bousset, Wilhelm. "Der erste Brief an die Korinther," *Die Schriften des neuen Testaments.* Ed. by J. Weiss. Göttingen: Vandenhoeck & Ruprecht, 1908, 141–42.

Conzelmann, Hans. *I Corinthians: A Commentary on the First Epistle to the Corinthians.* Philadelphia: Fortress Press, 1979 (German, 1969), 33, 246.

Dautzenberg, Gerhard von. *Urchristliche Prophetie, ihre Erforschung, ihre Voraussetzungen im Judentum und ihre Struktur im ersten Korintherbrief.* Stuttgart, Berlin, Köln, and Mainz: Kohlhammer, 1975, 257–74, 290–300.

———. "Zur Stellung der Frauen in den paulinischen Gemeinden," *Die Frau im Urchristentum.* Ed. by G. Dautzenberg, H. Merklein, and K. Müller. Freiburg, Basel, and Vienna: Herder, 1983.

Ellis, E. Earle. "The Silenced Wives of Corinth (I Cor. 14:34-5)," *New Testament Textual Criticism: Its Significance for Exegesis. Essays in Honour of Bruce M. Metzger.* Ed. by Eldon Jay Epp and Gordon D. Fee. Oxford: Clarendon Press, 1981, 213–20.

———. *Prophecy and Hermeneutic in Early Christianity: New Testament Essays.* Tübingen: J. C. B. Mohr (Paul Siebeck), 1978, 27.

Fee, Gordon D. *The First Epistle to the Corinthians.* Grand Rapids: Wm. B. Eerdmans, 1987, 699–708.

Fiorenza, Elisabeth Schüssler. *In Memory of Her: A Feminist Theological Reconstruction of Christian Origins.* New York: Crossroad, 1983, 230–31.

Flanagan, Neal M., and Edwina Hunter Snyder. "Did Paul Put Down Women in 1 Cor. 14:34-36?" *Biblical Theology Bulletin* 11 (1981), 10–12.

Heinrici, C. F. Georg. *Der erste Sendschreiben des Apostle Paulus an die Korinther.* Berlin: William Hertz, 1880, 457–61.

Heyob, Sharon Kelly. *The Cult of Isis among Women in the Greco-Roman World.* Leiden: E. J. Brill, 1975.

Krämer, Ross S. "Ecstatics and Ascetics: Studies in the Functions of Religious Activities for Women in the Greco-Roman World," Ph.D. dissertation, Princeton University, 1976.

———, ed. *Maenads, Martyrs, Matrons, Monastics: A Sourcebook on Women's Religions in the Greco-Roman World.* Philadelphia: Fortress Press, 1988.

Kröger, Catherine Clark, and Richard Kröger, "Pandemonium and Silence at Corinth," *The Reformed Journal,* June 1978, 6–11.

Lefkowitz, Mary R., and Maureen B. Fant, eds. *Women's Life in Greece and Rome: A Source Book in Translation.* Baltimore: Johns Hopkins University Press, 1982.

Lietzmann, Hans. extended by W. G. Kümmel. *An die Korinther I and II.* 5th rev. ed. Tübingen: J. C. B. Mohr (Paul Siebeck), 1969, Lietzmann 75; Kümmel 190.

Meyer, Heinrich August Wilhelm. *Critical and Exegetical Handbook to the Epistles to the Corinthians.* New York and London: Funk & Wagnalls, 1890 (from 5th German ed., 1870), 333–35.

Moffatt, J. *The First Epistle of Paul to the Corinthians.* London: Hodder & Stoughton, 1938; New York and London: Harpers, n.d.

Nestle, Eberhard, and Kurt Aland et al. *Novum Testamentum Graece.* 26th rev. ed. Stuttgart: Deutsche Bibelstiftung, 1979, 466.

Schlatter, A. *Paulus, der Bote Jesu.* Stuttgart: Calwer Verlag, 1969 (German 1st ed. 1934).

Trummer, P. *Die Paulustradition der Pastoralbriefe.* Frankfurt: Lang, 1978, 144–49.

Wendland, Paul. *Die Briefe an die Korinther.* Göttingen: Vandenhoeck & Ruprecht, 1968, 132.

Wolff, Christian. *Der Erste Brief des Paulus an die Korinther, Zweiter Teil: Auslegung der Kapitel 8–16.* Berlin: Evangelische Verlagsanstalt, 1982, 140–46.

Weiss, Johannes. "Der Eingang des ersten Korintherbriefes," *TSK* 37 (1900), 125–30.

———. *Der erste Korintherbriefe: Kritisch-exegetischer Kommentar über das Neuestestament.* Göttingen: Vandenhoeck & Ruprecht, 1910, 4, 120, 184, 277, 342–43 n. 3.

Appendix 12: Resurrection

THE PRIMARY ISSUE IN INTERPRETING RESURRECTION in 1 Corinthians is no longer whether Paul tries to prove it by citing witnesses (Bultmann 54–55; Barth) but how best to understand the Corinthians who say, "there is no resurrection of the dead" (15:12), since everything Paul says is counteracting them. (For summaries of the debate on this issue see Wilson 90–98; Becker 69–76; Sellin 17–37, 261–69; and Wedderburn, 1987, 6–37.) Commentators agree that the Corinthians did not expect their spiritual life to end in death. When Paul implies this in 15:12, 19, 32, it is more likely a misrepresentation that serves Paul's argument or an exposé of what their position leads to rather than evidence of Paul's ignorance as Bultmann postulated (Wedderburn, 1987, 36; Sellin 19; Bultmann). Because Paul addresses the Corinthians differently than the Thessalonians (1 Thess. 4:13 – 5:1), only a few scholars think the people in Corinth simply expect Christ to return before they die (Spörlein 190–98).

The two major contending explanations of why some Corinthians say "there is no resurrection of the dead" are that they think resurrection is of the living not the dead, having already overcome death at baptism, or that they think, in line with Hellenistic-Jewish wisdom texts, that the spirits of the wise are not threatened by the corruption of the flesh. The early advocates of an already present resurrection (Von Soden 259 n. 28; Schniewind; Käsemann) linked the heightened sacramentalism in Corinth (10:1-13) with baptismal dying and rising with Christ (Rom. 6:1-11; Col. 2:9-15; 3:3-4) and the claim to be already resurrected (2 Tim. 2:18). Schniewind also cited gospel traditions of graves opening on Easter to show early identification of Jesus' resurrection with a general resurrection. By 1962, Käsemann had sketched a full theological history of early Christian apocalyptic in which the Corinthians, due to the influence of mystery initiations, understood themselves to be raised in Christ at baptism to rule with him over the powers of this world. This spiritualization of apocalyptic resurrection was also linked with the Hellenistic-Jewish myth of the divine Sophia leading her own into an ascetic and ultimately angelic life. In contrast to this, Paul insisted on Jesus' resurrection as "the great exception" and held the line in Corinth against any present resurrection of overconfident believers.

During the 1960s and 1970s this thesis was developed and clarified. Jervell's *Imago Dei* provided groundwork in Jewish texts and did not focus on the contrast of Paul and the Corinthians but on the continuity between early Hellenistic-Christian hymns acclaiming death, resurrection, and enthronement at baptism, the Corinthian realization of the image of God in Christ as a new creation beyond all earthly distinctions, and Paul's ethical and eschatological modifying of these views. Whether Paul at first preached the realized eschatology in Corinth (Thrall) or the Corinthians adopted a primitive baptismal dying and present rising with Christ as first attested in Colossians 2:12 and 3:3 (Jervell 257, 261; Tannehill 10), or whether the Corinthians generated this death and resurrection rite that Paul later modified (Becker 63), when Paul wrote this letter the "center of gravity" for the Corinthians was on realizing Jesus' resurrection and for Paul on embodying Jesus' death (Thistelton). Becker's *Auferstehung der Toten im Urchristentum* set this view of the Corinthian controversy into a broader picture of the developing Christian understanding of believers' resurrection.

The second position that defines the Corinthians primarily by their anthropological dualism began from the general thesis that the Greeks considered the soul immortal, suggesting that Christians in Corinth might expect that the soul of the dying would be exalted (Lietzmann 79, quoting Justin, *Dial.* 80). Proposals were then made that Paul's opponents in Corinth maintained the radical dualism found later among the Gnostics. After Schmithals's thoroughgoing application of Gnostic categories and mythology to Corinth showed that the fit had to be forced at a number of points, attention turned to Hellenistic-Jewish wisdom texts. In Philo were found very striking parallels to terminology apparently used by the Corinthians to characterize themselves as spiritual, wise, perfect, pure, incorruptible, glorious, and royal—all in the context of a strong mind-body dualism (Horsley 1978). More specifically, the dichotomy Paul reflects in Corinth between spiritual people and those who are mere "psychics," found directly only in Gnostic texts, was traced in Pearson's *The Pneumatikos-Psychikos Terminology* back to its possible roots in Hellenistic-Jewish exegesis of Genesis 2:7. Study of this exegesis, begun by Lietzmann and Jervell, and also pursued by Wedderburn 1973, has been clarified recently by Tobin's *The Creation of Man: Philo and the History of Interpretation*, which sorts out the various pre-philonic stages in Philo's exegesis. It seems that before Philo, Jewish wisdom speculation was distinguishing the man shaped from earth of Genesis 2:7 from the heavenly and immortal idea of humanity created in God's image in Genesis 1:27. So when Paul insists that the earthly, "psychic" Adam is first, and juxtaposes to this one a last Adam, Christ, who is a life-giving spirit (15:45), he reverses the traditional order of immortal Adam before mortal Adam. This could be a direct polemic against a Corinthian claim that Christ reveals a spiritual, immortal identity prior and superior to earthly humanity (Pearson 24–26; Sellin 101–14). Or Paul could be reversing wisdom's two Adams to subordinate the Corinthian naive new humanity to the ultimate triumph of the last Adam over death (Wedderburn 1973, 302).

Hellenistic-Jewish wisdom texts can be used in a number of different ways to provide insights about the Corinthians who deny resurrection of the dead. Sandelin in *Die Auseinandersetzung mit der Weisheit in 1. Korinther 15* works through 1 Corinthians 15 comparing the various functions of Christ with the functions of Sophia in Philo and Wisdom of Solomon. Though this leaves much of Philo (and Paul) unexplored and the parallels perhaps two sharply drawn, Paul's heavy debt to wisdom thought is clear. Sandelin proposes that Paul presses wisdom thought into reversed modes to counter what is seen as a Corinthian proclamation of Sophia incarnate in all the righteous dead—including Christ—whose souls rest in heaven until Christ judges. Brandenburger's most recent work in this area, *Fleisch und Geist*, is a wide-brush study of that wisdom dichotomy that allowed Paul to elaborate his divine-human dualism in wisdom's substance categories alongside apocalyptic's temporal terms. Sellin centers his *Der Streit um die Auferstehung der Toten* on a thorough exploration of the wisdom traditions behind Paul's Genesis 2:7 exegesis in 1 Corinthians 15. He finds the Corinthians rejecting "resurrection" — which they understood strictly as physical reconstitution—in favor of receiving the primal spiritual identity of the wise, which lifts a person from earthly to heavenly life.

Finally, Wedderburn's *Baptism and Resurrection* attacks the thesis of a present resurrection with Christ in Corinthian baptism by demonstrating the lack of any precise or complete parallels to this practice in the initiations of the mystery religions (90–163). He concludes that life in the spirit with Christ is better traced to Jewish identification with representative figures and to Hellenistic ecstatic prophetism, neither of which is transmitted through initiation rites (233–68). Yet his own careful review of Dionysian and Eleusinian myths and of initiation to new life in the wisdom story of Aseneth suggests that Judaism could draw on mystery traditions in a way that he will not admit (181–232). Above all he does not succeed in isolating the Corinthians from the Pauline tradition of resurrection with Christ when arguing that Romans 6 does not draw dying and rising from baptism traditions, that Colossians 2:12 is a literary development of Romans 6, and that Philippians 3:20 is not written until Paul is in Rome (37–89). It is clear that the Christian mix of resurrection kerygma, apocalyptic, wisdom, and identification rituals could, and very soon did, generate a confession of present resurrection. Only a positive reconstruction from Paul's arguments of a Corinthian wisdom theology that fully accounts for these Christians denying resurrection can compete with an explanation this close at hand.

Barth, Karl. *The Resurrection of the Dead. University Lectures on I Cor. 15.* New York: Fleming H. Revell Company, 1933 (German, 1924).

Becker, Jürgen. *Auferstehung der Toten im Urchristentum.* Stuttgart: KBW Verlag, 1976.

Brandenburger, Egon. *Fleisch und Geist: Paulus und die dualistische Weisheit.* Neukirchen-Vluyn: Neukirchener Verlag, 1986.

Bultmann, Rudolph. "Karl Barth, 'Die Auferstehung der Toten,'" *Glauben und Verstehen. Gesammelte Aufsätze,* Vol. 1. Tübingen: J. C. B. Mohr (Paul Siebeck), 1964, 38–64.

Horsley, Richard A. "'How Can Some of You Say that There is No Resurrection of the Dead?' Spiritual Elitism in Corinth," *NovT* 20 (1978), 203–31.

Jervell, Jacob. *Imago Dei. Gen 1,26f. im Spätjudentum, in der Gnosis und in den paulinischen Briefen.* Göttingen: Vandenhoeck & Ruprecht, 1960.

Käsemann, Ernst. "Zum Thema der urchristliche Apokalyptik." *ZTK* 59 (1962), 257–84.

Lietzmann, Hans. *An die Korinther I/II. Handbuch zum Neues Testament.* 5th ed. extended by Werner Georg Kümmel. Tübingen: J. C. B. Mohr (Paul Siebeck), 1969.

Pearson, Birger A. *The Pneumatikos-Psychikos Terminology in 1 Corinthians. A Study in the Theology of the Corinthian Opponents of Paul and its Relation to Gnosticism.* Missoula, Mont.: Society of Biblical Literature, 1973.

Sandelin, Karl-Gustav. *Die Auseinandersetzung mit der Weisheit in 1 Korinther 15.* Meddelanden Fran Steftelsens for Abo Akademi Forskningsinstitut 12. Abo: Abo Akademi, 1976.

Schmithals, Walter. *Gnosticism in Corinth: An Investigation of the Letters to the Corinthians.* Nashville: Abingdon Press, 1972.

Schniewind, J. "Die Leugner der Auferstehung in Korinth." *Nachgelassene Reden und Aufsätze.* Ed. by E. Kähler. Berlin, 1952, 110–39.

Sellin, Gerhard. *Der Streit um die Auferstehung der Toten: Eine religionsgeschichtliche und exegetische Untersuchung von 1 Korinther 15.* Göttingen: Vandenhoeck & Ruprecht, 1986.

Soden, H. von. "Sakrament und Ethik bei Paulus. Zur Frage der literarischen und theologischen Einheitlichkeit von 1 Kor. 8-10," *Das Paulusbild in der neueren deutschen Forschung.* Ed. by K. H. Rengstorf. Darmstadt: Wissenschaftliche Buchgesellschaft, 1964, 338–79. Tr. in abridged form in *The Writings of St. Paul.* Ed. by Wayne A. Meeks. New York: W. W. Norton, 1972, 257–68.

Spörlein, Bernard. *Die Leugnung der Auferstehung.* Regensburg: Verlag Friedrich Pustet, 1971.

Tannehill, Robert C. *Dying and Rising with Christ: A Study in Pauline Theology.* Berlin: Verlag A. Töpelmann, 1967.

Thistelton, Anthony C. "Realized Eschatology at Corinth." *NTS* 24 (1977–78), 510–26.

Thrall, Margaret E. "Christ crucified or second Adam? A Christological Debate between Paul and the Corinthians," *Christ and Spirit in the New Testament.* Ed. by Barnabas Lindars and Stephen S. Smalley. Cambridge: Cambridge University Press, 1973.

Tobin, Th. H., S.J. *The Creation of Man: Philo and the History of Interpretation.* Washington, D.C.: The Catholic Biblical Association of America, 1983.

Wedderburn, A. J. M. *Baptism and Resurrection: Studies in Pauline Theology against its Greco-Roman Background.* Tübingen: J. C. B. Mohr (Paul Siebeck), 1987.

———. "Philo's 'Heavenly Man.'" *NovT* 15 (1973), 301–26.

Wilson, J. H. "The Corinthians Who Say There Is No Resurrection of the Dead," *ZNW* 59 (1968), 90–107.

Women Who Speak for the Divine—
Selected Texts from the Early Empire[1]

ALL TEXTS QUOTED in this collection appear to be written by men and need to be read with the same care about the rhetoric of the author that 1 Corinthians demands. This selection of excerpts on women's prophecy are meant to guide the reader to the full texts in which they appear and must be interpreted.[2] Recommended English translations, quoted by permission, are acknowledged by immediate reference in parentheses to the major series or collections,[3] or by specific reference in the notes.

I. Women Prophets of Past Renown
in the Early Roman Empire

The Sibyls

1. It is said that during the reign of Tarquinius another very wonderful piece of good luck also came to the Roman state, conferred upon it by the favour of some god or other divinity; and this good fortune was not of short duration, but throughout the whole existence of the state it has often saved it from great calamities. A certain woman who was not a native of the country came to the tyrant wishing to sell him nine books filled with Sibylline oracles; but when Tarquinius refused to purchase the books at the price she asked, she went away and burned three of them. And not long afterwards, bringing the remaining six books, she offered to sell them for the same price. But when they thought her a fool and mocked at her for asking the same price for the smaller number of books that she had been unable to get for even the larger number, she again went away and burned half of those that were left; then, bringing the remaining three books, she asked the same amount of money for these. Tarquinius, wondering at the woman's purpose, sent for the augurs and acquainting them with the matter, asked them what he should do. These, knowing by certain signs that he had rejected a god-sent blessing, and declaring it to be a great misfortune that he had not purchased all the books, directed him to pay the woman all the money she asked and to get the oracles that were left. The woman, after delivering the books and bidding him take great care of them, disappeared from among [human beings].[4] . . . There is no possession of the Romans, sacred or profane, which they guard so carefully as they do the Sibylline oracles. They consult them, by order

of the senate, when the state is in the grip of party strife or some great misfortune has happened to them in war, or some important prodigies and apparitions have been seen which are difficult of interpretation.

Dionysius of Halicarnassus (late first century BCE).
The Roman Antiquities IV 62. 1-5 (LCL)

2. Now is come the last age of the song of Cumae; the great line of the centuries begins anew.

Virgil (70 BCE–19 BCE), *Eclogue* IV 4-5[5] (LCL)

3. There is a rock rising up above the ground. On it, say the Delphians, there stood and chanted the oracles a woman, by name Herophile and surnamed Sibyl. The former Sibyl I find was as ancient as any; the Greeks say that she was a daughter of Zeus by Lamia, daughter of Poseidon, that she was the first woman to chant oracles, and that the name Sibyl was given her by the Libyans. Herophile was younger than she was, but nevertheless she too was clearly born before the Trojan war, as she foretold in her oracles that Helen would be brought up in Sparta to be the ruin of Asia and of Europe, and that for her sake the Greeks would capture Troy. The Delians remember also a hymn this woman composed to Apollo. In her poem she calls herself not only Herophile but also Artemis, and the wedded wife of Apollo, saying too sometimes that she is his sister, and sometimes that she is his daughter. These statements she made in her poetry when in a frenzy and possessed by the god. Elsewhere in her oracles she states that her mother was an immortal, one of the nymphs of Ida, while her father was a human. These are the verses—

I am by birth half mortal, half divine;
An immortal nymph was my mother, my father an eater of corn;
On my mother's side of Idaean birth, but my fatherland was red
Marpessus, sacred to the Mother, and the river Aïdoneus. . . .

Herophile became the attendant of the temple of Apollo Smintheus, and . . . on the occasion of Hecuba's dream she uttered the prophecy which we know was actually fulfilled. This Sibyl passed the greater part of her life in Samos, but she also visited Clarus in the territory of Colophon, Delos and Delphi. Whenever she visited Delphi, she would stand on this rock and sing her chants. . . .

The next woman to give oracles in the same way according to Hyperochus of Cumae, a historian, was called Demo, and came from Cumae in the territory of the Opici. The Cumaeans can point to no oracle given by this woman, but they show a small stone urn in a sanctuary of Apollo, in which they say are placed the bones of the Sibyl. Later than Demo there grew up among the Hebrews above Palestine a woman who gave oracles and was named Sabbe. They say that the father of Sabbe was Berosus, and her mother Erymanthe. But some call her a Babylonian Sibyl, others an Egyptian.

Phaënnis, daughter of a king of the Chaonians, and the Peleiae (Doves) at Dodona also give oracles under the inspiration of a god, but they were not called by [people] Sibyls. . . . The Peleiades are said to have been born still earlier than Phemonoë, and to have been the first women to chant these verses:—

Zeus was, Zeus is, Zeus shall be; O mighty Zeus.
Earth sends up the harvest, therefore sing the praise of earth as Mother.

... These are the women ... who, down to the present day, are said to have been the mouthpiece by which a god prophesied. But time is long, and perhaps similar things may occur again.

> Pausanias (second century CE), *Description of Greece* X, 12 (LCL)

4. The sibyl regarded him [Aeneas] and, sighing deeply, said: "I am no goddess, nor do thou deem any mortal worthy of the honour of the sacred incense. But, lest you mistake in ignorance, eternal, endless life was offered me, had my virgin modesty consented to Phoebus' love. While he still hoped for this and sought to break my will with gifts, he said: 'Choose [*sic*] what you will, maiden of Cumae, and you shall have your choice.' Pointing to a heap of sand, I made the foolish prayer that I might have as many years of life as there were sand-grains in the pile; but I forgot to ask that those years might be perpetually young. He granted me the years, and promised endless youth as well, if I would yield to love. I spurned Phoebus' gift and am still unwedded. But now my joyous springtime of life has fled and with tottering step weak old age is coming on, which for long I must endure. . . . Though shrunk past recognition of the eye, still by my voice shall I be known, for the fates will leave me my voice."

> Ovid (43 BCE–18 CE), *Metamorphoses* XIV 129–46, 151–53 (LCL)

5. When we halted as we reached a point opposite the rock which lies over against the council-chamber, upon which it is said that the first Sibyl sat after her arrival from Helicon where she had been reared by the Muses (though others say that she came from the Malians and was the daughter of Lamia whose father was Poseidon), Sarapion recalled the verses in which she sang of herself: that even after death she shall not cease from prophesying, but that she shall go round and round in the moon, becoming what is called the face that appears in the moon; while her spirit, mingled with the air, shall be for ever borne onward in voices of presage and portent. . . .

The foreign visitor remarked, "And these recent and unusual occurrences near Cumae and Dicaearcheia [Vesuvius' eruption, 79 CE], were they not recited long ago in the songs of the Sibyl? and has not Time, as if in her debt, duly discharged the obligation in the bursting forth of fires from the mountain, boiling seas, blazing rocks tossed aloft by the wind. . . ."

Thereupon Boëthus said, . . . "These prophets of the type of the Sibyl and Bacis toss forth and scatter into the gulf of time, as into ocean depths with no chart to guide them, words and phrases at haphazard, which deal with events and occurrences of all sorts; and although some come to pass for them as the result of chance, what is said at the present time is equally a lie, even if later it becomes true in the event that such a thing does happen."

> Plutarch (c 50 CE–120 CE), *The Oracles at Delphi*, 398C–399A (LCL)

6. Marcus Varro—and there was no one among the Greeks more learned than he—when he spoke about the *quindecimviri* in *Divine Things*, which he wrote to

Caius Caesar, says: "The Sibylline Books were not the work of one Sibyl, but are called by the name, Sibylline, because all women seers of the Sibyl have been [so] called by the ancients, either from the name of the one at Delphi, or from the announcing of the councils of the gods."

> Lactantius (c 300 CE) citing Marcus Varro (late first and early second century CE), *The Divine Institutes* I 6[6]

Women of Jewish Scripture Remembered as Prophets and Visionaries

7. For the helpmeets of these men are called women, but are in reality virtues. . . . Zipporah, the mate of Moses, whose name is "bird," speeding upwards from earth to heaven and contemplating there the nature of things divine and blessed. . . .

Without supplication or entreaty did Moses, when he took Zipporah the winged and soaring virtue, find her pregnant through no mortal agency (Exod. ii. 22).

> Philo (mid-first century CE), *On the Cherubim* 41 and 47 (LCL)

8. For at the command of God the sea became a source of salvation to one party and of perdition to the other. As it broke in twain . . . the people marched under guidance right on until they reached the higher ground on the opposite mainland. But when the sea came rushing in with the returning tide, and from either side passed over the ground where dry land had appeared the pursuing enemy were submerged and perished. This wonderful sight and experience, an act transcending word and thought and hope, so filled with ecstasy both men and women that forming a single choir they sang hymns of thanksgiving to God their Saviour, the men led by the prophet Moses and the women by the prophetess Miriam.

> Philo, *On the Contemplative Life* 86–87 (LCL)

9. What I say is vouched for by that prophetess and mother of a prophet, Hannah, whose name is in our tongue "Grace." For she says that she is giving as a gift to the Holy One her son Samuel (1 Sam. i. 11), not meaning a human being but rather an inspired temper possessed by a God-sent frenzy.

> Philo, *On Dreams* I 254[7] (LCL)

10. Now Reu took as his wife Melcha the daughter of Ruth, and she bore to him Serug. And when the day of his delivery came, she said, "From him there will be born in the fourth generation one [Abraham] who will set his dwelling on high and will be called perfect and blameless; and he will be the father of nations, and his covenant will not be broken, and his seed will be multiplied forever."

> Pseudo-Philo (first century CE?), *Biblical Antiquities* 4:11 (OTP)

11. And this man [Amram] had one son and one daughter; their names were Aaron and Miriam. And the spirit of God came upon Miriam one night, and she saw a dream and told it to her parents in the morning, saying, "I have seen this night, and behold a man in a linen garment stood and said to me, 'Go and say to your parents, "Behold he who will be born from you will be cast forth into the water; likewise through him the water will be dried up. And I will work signs through him and save

my people, and he will exercise leadership always."'" And when Miriam told of her dream, her parents did not believe her.

Pseudo-Philo, Biblical Antiquities 9:9-10[8] (OTP)

12. And Saul said to the people, "Let us seek out some medium and inquire of him what I should plan out." And the people answered him, "Behold now there is a woman, Sedecla by name, and this is the daughter of the Midianite diviner who led the people of Israel astray with sorceries, and behold she dwells in Endor." . . . And when she saw Samuel rising up. . . . Saul said to her, "What is his appearance?" She said, "You are asking me about divine beings. For behold his appearance is not the appearance of a man. For he is clothed in a white robe with a mantle placed over it, and two angels are leading him. . . ."

Pseudo-Philo, Biblical Antiquities 64:3-6 (OTP)

13. Dabora then summoned Barak and charged him to select ten thousand of the youth and to march against the foe: that number would, she said, suffice, God having prescribed it and betokened victory. . . . The Israelites and Barak were dismayed at the multitude of the enemy and resolved to retire, but were restrained by Dabora, who ordered them to deliver battle that very day, for they would be victorious and God would lend them aid. . . .

The enemy fell, many being crushed to death beneath the chariots. But Sisares, having leapt from his chariot when he saw that the rout was come, fled till he reached the abode of a woman of the Kenites named Iale; she, at his request to conceal him, took him in, . . . and took an iron nail and drove it with a hammer through his mouth and jaw, piercing the ground; and when Barak's company arrived soon after she showed him to them nailed to the earth. Thus did this victory redound, as Dabora had foretold, to a woman's glory.

Josephus (c 37–c 100 CE), Jewish Antiquities V 202-4, 202-9[9]
(LCL)

14. As she [Abigaia] was descending the defiles of the mountain, she was met by David coming against Nabal with his four hundred men. . . . "Wherefore pardon me," she said, "and render thanks to God who has prevented thee from soiling thy hands with human blood. For if thou remainest clean, He Himself will avenge thee on the wicked; and may the evil that awaits Nabal fall likewise on the heads of thy foes. But be gracious to me in deigning to receive these presents from me, and, out of regard for me, dismiss thy indignation and wrath against my husband and against his house. For it becomes thee to show mildness and humanity, especially as thou art destined to be king." And David accepted. . . . Ten days and no more did Nabal remain alive and then departed this life.

Josephus, Jewish Antiquities VI 301-6 (LCL)

15. When the king [Josiah] heard [the books of the law] read, he rent his garments and, calling the high priest Eliakias, sent him and the scribe himself and some of his closest friends to the prophetess Oolda. . . . she told them to go back to the king and say that the Deity had already given His sentence against them and that no one could make it ineffective even by supplications; this sentence was to destroy the

people and drive them out of their country and deprive them of all the good things which they now had, because they had transgressed against the laws and during so long an interval of time had not repented, although the prophets exhorted them to act thus wisely and foretold the punishment for their impious deeds, which, she said, He would certainly inflict on them in order that they might believe that He was God and was not speaking falsely about any of the things which He had announced to them through the prophets. However, she said, for the sake of Josiah, who was a righteous man, He would put off these calamities for a time, but after his death would send down on the multitude the sufferings He had decreed against them.

Josephus, Jewish Antiquities X 59-61 (LCL)

16. For her faith and hospitality Rahab the harlot was saved. For when the spies were sent to Jericho by Joshua. . . . she said to the men, "I know assuredly that the Lord God is delivering to you this land; for the fear and dread of you has fallen on those who dwell in it. When therefore it shall come to pass, that ye take it, save me and my father's house." And they said to her, "It shall be as thou hast spoken to us; when therefore thou knowest that we are at hand, thou shalt gather all thy folk under thy roof, and they shall be safe; for as many as shall be found outside the house shall perish." And they proceeded to give her a sign, that she should hang out a scarlet thread from her house, foreshowing that all who believe and hope on God shall have redemption through the blood of the Lord. You see, beloved, that the woman is an instance not only of faith but also of prophecy.

1 Clement 12:1-8 (end of first century CE) (LCL)

17. And when Aseneth had ceased making confession to the Lord, behold, the morning star rose out of heaven in the east. And Aseneth saw it and rejoiced and said, "So the Lord God listened to my prayer, because this star rose as a messenger and herald of the light of the great day." And Aseneth kept looking, and behold, close to the morning star, the heaven was torn apart and great and unutterable light appeared. And Aseneth saw (it) and fell on (her) face on the ashes. And a man came to her from heaven and stood by Aseneth's head. And he called her and said, "Aseneth, Aseneth. . . . Rise and stand on your feet, and I will tell you what I have to say. . . ."

And she went to the man . . . and stood before him. And the man said to her, "Remove the veil from your head, and for what purpose did you do this? For you are a chaste virgin today, and your head is like that of a young man." And Aseneth removed the veil from her head.

And the man said to her, "Courage, Aseneth, chaste virgin. Behold, I have heard all the words of your confession and your prayer. Behold, I have also seen the humiliation and the affliction of the seven days of your want. . . . Behold, from today, you will be renewed and formed anew and made alive again, and you will eat blessed bread of life, and drink a blessed cup of immortality, and anoint yourself with blessed ointment of incorruptibility. Courage, Aseneth, chaste virgin. Behold, I have given you today to Joseph for a bride, and he himself will be your bridegroom for ever (and) ever.

And your name shall no longer be called Aseneth, but your name shall be City of Refuge, because in you many nations will take refuge with the Lord God, the Most High, and under your wings many peoples trusting in the Lord God will be sheltered, and behind your walls will be guarded those who attach themselves to the Most High God in the name of Repentance. For Repentance is in the heavens, an exceedingly beautiful and good daughter of the Most High. And she herself entreats the Most High God for you at all times and for all who repent in the name of the Most High God. . . ."

And the man smiled at Aseneth's understanding, and called her to himself, and stretched out his right hand, and grasped her head and shook her head with his right hand. And Aseneth was afraid of the man's hand, because sparks shot forth from his hand as from bubbling (melted) iron. And Aseneth looked, gazing with her eyes at the man's hand. And the man saw (it) and smiled and said, "Happy are you, Aseneth, because the ineffable mysteries of the Most High have been revealed to you, and happy (are) all who attach themselves to the Lord God in Repentance, because they will eat from this [honey]comb. For this comb is (full of the) spirit of life. And the bees of the paradise of delight have made this from the dew of the roses of life that are in the paradise of God. And all the angels of God eat of it and all the chosen of God and all the sons of the Most High, because this is a comb of life, and everyone who eats of it will not die for ever (and) ever."

And the man stretched out his right hand and broke a small portion off the comb, and he himself ate and what was left he put with his hand into Aseneth's mouth, and said to her, "Eat." And she ate. And the man said to Aseneth, "Behold, you have eaten bread of life, and drunk a cup of immortality, and been anointed with ointment of incorruptibility. . . ."

And the man said to the comb, "Come." And bees rose from the cells of that comb, and the cells were innumerable, ten thousand (times) ten thousand and thousands upon thousands. And the bees were white as snow, and their wings like purple and like violet and scarlet (stuff) and like gold-woven linen cloaks, and golden diadems (were) on their heads, and they had sharp stings, and they would not injure anyone. And all those bees encircled Aseneth from feet to head.

And other bees were great and chosen like their queens, and they rose from the damaged part of the comb and encircled Aseneth's mouth, and made upon her mouth and her lips a comb similar to the comb which was lying before the man. And all those bees ate of the comb which was on Aseneth's mouth. And the man said to the bees, "Go off to your place." And all the bees rose and flew away into heaven. And those who wanted to injure Aseneth fell to the ground and died. And the man stretched out his staff over the dead bees and said to them, "Rise you, too, and go away to your place." And the bees who had died rose and went into the court adjoining Aseneth's house and sought shelter on the fruit-bearing trees.

And the man said to Aseneth, "Have you seen this thing?" And she said, "Yes, Lord, I have seen all these (things)." And the man said to her, "So will be all my words which I have spoken to you today. . . ."

And Levi was on Aseneth's right (side) and Joseph on (her) left. And Aseneth grasped Levi's hand. And Aseneth loved Levi exceedingly beyond all of Joseph's brethren, because he was one who attached himself to the Lord, and he was a prudent man and a prophet of the Most High and sharp-sighted with his eyes, and he used to see letters written in heaven by the finger of God and he knew the unspeakable (mysteries) of the Most High God and revealed them to Aseneth in secret. . . .

> *The Confession and Prayer of Aseneth* 14:1-4, 8; 15:1-3, 5-7;
> 16:14-15; 16:17 – 17:2; 22:12-13, commonly called *Joseph and*
> *Aseneth* (first century CE?) (OTP)

18. And Eve said to Adam, "My lord, while I was sleeping I saw a vision – as if the blood of our son Abel was in the hand of Cain (who was) gulping it down in his mouth. That is why I am sad." And Adam said, "God forbid that Cain would kill Abel! But let us separate them from each other and make separate places for them." And they made Cain a farmer and Abel a shepherd, that in this way they might be separated from each other. After this Cain murdered Abel.

> *Life of Adam and Eve* 23:2-5 (first century CE?) (OTP)

19. [Job] motioned to his daughter called Hemera, and he said to her, Take this ring and go to the strong-room and fetch the three little golden urns, so that I may give you your inheritance. She went away and fetched them. And he opened them and took out three cords of many colours, such as no person could possibly describe; for they were not of earth but of heaven, flashing with sparks of fire like the rays of the sun. And he gave one cord each to his daughters, saying, Take them and gird them round you, that they may keep you safe all the days of your life and fill you with every good thing.

The other daughter, called Cassia, said to him, Father is this the inheritance you were saying was better than our brothers'? What is the use of these strange cords? How can we live on them? And their father said to them, Not only will you be able to live on them; but these cords will lead you to the greater world – to life in the heavens. . . .

Accordingly, the one called Hemera got up and wound her rope about her, just as her father had said. And she assumed another heart, no longer minding earthly things. And she gave utterance in the speech of angels, sending up a hymn to God after the pattern of the angels' hymnody; and the Spirit let the hymns she uttered be recorded on her robe.

And then Cassia girded herself, and she too experienced a change of heart, so that she no longer gave thought to worldly things. And her mouth took up the speech of the heavenly powers, and she lauded the worship of the heavenly sanctuary. So if anyone wants to know about the worship that goes on in heaven, he can find it in the hymns of Cassia.

And the remaining one, the one called Amaltheias-Keras, put on her girdle; and she likewise gave utterance with her mouth in the speech of those on high. Her heart too was changed and withdrawn from worldly things; and she spoke in the language of the cherubim, extolling the Lord of Virtues, and proclaiming their glory. Anyone who would pursue the Father's glory any further will find it set out in the prayers of Amaltheias-Keras.

After the three had finished singing their hymns, I, Nereos, Job's brother, sat down beside him as he lay upon his bed; and I listened to my brother's three daughters as they discussed together the heavenly mysteries. And I wrote down this book, except for the hymns and the signs of the word, for these are the mysteries of God.

So Job lay ill in bed, yet without pain and suffering, for pain was no longer able to affect him because of the sign of the girdle that he wore. And after three days he saw the holy angels who came for his soul. And he got up immediately and took a lyre and gave it to his daughter Hemera; to Cassia he gave a censer; to Amaltheias-Keras he gave a tambourine; that they might give praise to those who had come for his soul. And as they took them, they saw the shining chariots which had come for his soul. And they gave praise and honour, each in her special tongue. And after this, he who sat in the great chariot got out and greeeted Job (this the three daughtere saw, ac did aloo thoir fathor, but no onc clac). Hc took Job's ɔoul, went off with it in his arms, and placed it in the chariot and journeyed to the east. But Job's body was made ready for burial and carried to the grave. His three daughters led the way, with their girdles around them, singing hymns of praise to the father.

The Testament of Job 46-52 (first or second century CE?) (AOT)

20. R. Eliezer says, "This refers to Rahab the whore, who kept an inn. Eight priests and eight prophets descended from Rahab the whore, and these are they: Jeremiah, Hilkiah, Sariah, Menassiah, Baruch, Neriah, Hanamel, and Shallum."

R. Judah says, "Also Huldah the prophetess descended from the descendants of Rahab the whore, as it is said, 'So Hilkiah the priest, Ahikam, Akbor, Shaphan, and Aɛiah went to Huldah the propheteɛɛ, wife of Shullum ɛon of Tikvah, ɛon of Harhas, the keeper of the wardrobe, and consulted her at her home in the second quarter of Jerusalem' (1 Kgs. 22:18).

"And it further says, 'Lo, when we come to the land, you shall tie a red thread . . .' (Joshua 2:18).

"Now it is an argument a fortiori: here is someone who comes from a people of whom it is said, 'You shall not keep alive a single soul' (Deut. 20:16). But because she brought herself near, the Omnipresent brought her near, if an Israelite carries out the Torah, all the more so."

Sifre to Numbers (Tannaitic Midrashim, possibly late second century), 78. I 1[10]

21. "And an angel of the Lord said unto her [Hagar]: Return to thy mistress, etc. . . . and an angel of the Lord said unto her: I will greatly multiply thy seed, etc." (Gen. XVI, 9f). How many angels visited her? R. Hama b. R. Hanina said: Five, for each time 'speech' is mentioned it refers to an angel. The Rabbis said: Four, this being the number of times 'angel' occurs. . . . R. Isaac quoted: "She seeth the ways of her household (Prov. XXXI, 27): Abraham's household were seers, so she [Hagar] was accustomed to them [angels]."

Genesis Rabbah (Early Amoraic Midrashim, probably not in writing before 400), 45. 7[11]

Other Early Women Prophets and Visionaries

22. The Pelasgians, when the war was still going on, went to consult the oracle, as did also the Boeotians. Now Ephorus is unable, he says, to tell the oracular

response that was given to the Pelasgians, but the prophetess replied to the Boeotians that they would prosper if they committed sacrilege; and the messengers who were sent to consult the oracle, suspecting that the prophetess responded thus out of favour to the Pelasgians, because of her kinship with them (indeed, the temple also was from the beginning Pelasgian), seized the woman and threw her upon a burning pile, for they considered that, whether she had acted falsely or had not, they were right in either case, since, if she uttered a false oracle, she had her punishment, whereas, if she did not act falsely, they had only obeyed the order of the oracle.

Now those in charge of the temple, he says, did not approve of putting to death without trial—and that too in the temple—the men who did this, and therefore they brought them to trial, and summoned them before the priestesses, who were also the prophetesses, being the two survivors of the three; but when the Boeotians said that it was nowhere lawful for women to act as judges, they chose an equal number of men in addition to the women. Now the men, he says, voted for acquittal, but the women for conviction, and since the votes cast were equal, those for acquittal prevailed; and in consequence of this prophecies are uttered at Dodona by men to Boeotians only.

Strabo (64 BCE–24 CE), Geography 9. 2. 4 (LCL)

23. When the Phocaeans were setting sail from their homeland an oracle was delivered to them, it is said, to use for their voyage a guide received from the Ephesian Artemis; accordingly, some of them put in at Ephesus and inquired in what way they might procure from the goddess what had been enjoined upon them. Now the goddess, in a dream, it is said, had stood beside Aristarcha, one of the women held in very high honour, and commanded her to sail away with the Phocaeans, taking with her a certain reproduction which was among the sacred images; this done and the colony finally settled, they not only established the temple but also did Aristarcha the exceptional honour of appointing her priestess.

Strabo, Geography 4. 1. 3-4 (LCL)

24. When Philomelus had control of the oracle he directed the Pythia to make her prophecies from the tripod in the ancestral fashion. But when she replied that such was not the ancestral fashion, he threatened her harshly and compelled her to mount the tripod. Then when she frankly declared, referring to the superior power of the man who was resorting to violence: "It is in your power to do as you please," he gladly accepted her utterance and declared that he had the oracle which suited him. He immediately had the oracle inscribed and set it up in full view, and made it clear to everyone that the god gave him the authority to do as he pleased.

Diodorus of Sicily (first century BCE), The Library of History XVI 27. 1[12] (LCL)

25. When a certain oracle bade them [the Athenians] bring the priestess of Athena from Clazomenae, they sent and fetched the woman, and lo! her name was Peace. And this, as it seemed, was the advice which the divinity would give the city at that time, namely, to keep the peace.

Plutarch (c 50 CE–120 CE), Lives: Nicias 4 (LCL)

26. [Caius Marius and his soldiers] used to carry about ceremoniously in a litter a certain Syrian woman, named Martha, who was said to have the gift of prophecy, and he would make sacrifices at her bidding. She had previously been rejected by the senate when she wished to appear before them with reference to these matters and predicted future events. Then she got audience of the women and gave them proofs of her skill, and particularly the wife of Marius, at whose feet she sat when some gladiators were fighting and successfully foretold which one was going to be victorious. In consequence of this she was sent to Marius by his wife, and was admired by him. As a general thing she was carried along with the army in a litter, but she attended the sacrifices clothed in a double purple robe that was fastened with a clasp, and carrying a spear that was wreathed with fillets and chaplets. Such a performance as this caused many to doubt whether Marius, in exhibiting the woman, really believed in her, or was pretending to do so and merely acted a part with her.

> Plutarch, *Lives: Caius Marius* 17. 1-3 (LCL)

27. Gordius, they said, was a poor man of the Phrygians of old, who tilled a scanty parcel of earth and had but two yoke of oxen: with one he ploughed, with the other he drove his wagon. Once, as he was ploughing, an eagle settled on the yoke and stayed, perched there, till it was time to loose the oxen; Gordius was astonished at the portent, and went off to consult the Telmissian prophets, who were skilled in the interpretation of prodigies, inheriting — women and children too — the prophetic gift. Approaching a Telmissian village, he met a girl drawing water and told her the story of the eagle; she, being also of the prophetic line, bade him return to the spot and sacrifice to Zeus the King. So then Gordius begged her to come along with him and assist in the sacrifice; and at the spot duly sacrificed as she directed, married the girl, and had a son called Midas. Midas was already a grown man, handsome and noble, when the Phrygians were in trouble with civil war; they received an oracle that a chariot would bring them a king and he would stop the war. True enough, while they were discussing this, there arrived Midas, with his parents, and drove, chariot and all, into the assembly. The Phrygians, interpreting the oracle, decided that he was the man whom the gods had told them would come in a chariot; they thereupon made him king, and he put an end to the civil war. The chariot of his father he set up in the acropolis as a thank-offering to Zeus the King for sending the eagle.

> Arrian (second century CE), *Anabasis of Alexander* II 3. 2-6 (LCL)

28. When the turn of keeping guard by night fell to Antipater, it was resolved to assassinate Alexander by attacking him in his sleep.

It so fell out that Alexander, not from any outside suggestion, as some say, kept on drinking till daylight. Aristobulus, however, says that a Syrian woman with a spirit of divination followed Alexander, and that she was at first a laughing-stock both to Alexander and his friends; but when everything in her divination seemed to come true, Alexander no longer made light of her, but the Syrian had access to the King day and night and often watched over him as he slept. On this occasion then when Alexander rose from his potations she met him, while under the spell

of her inspiration, and begged him to return and continue drinking all night long;
Alexander therefore, believing this warning to be prophetic, returned and continued, and so the plot of the squires came to nothing.

Arrian, Anabasis of Alexander IV. 13. 4-6 (LCL)

29. Beside this Pan [in Arcadia] a fire is kept burning which is never allowed to go
out. It is said that in days of old this god also gave oracles, and that the nymph Erato
became his prophetess, she who wedded Arcas, the son of Callisto. They also
remember verses of Erato, which I too myself have read.

Pausanias (second century CE), Description of Greece VIII 37. 11
(LCL)

II. Prophecies and Visions Attributed to
Women of the Early Roman Empire[13]

The Sibyl

30. However much wealth Rome received from tribute-bearing Asia,
   Asia will receive three times that much again
   from Rome and will repay her deadly arrogance to her.
   Whatever number from Asia served the house of Italians,
   twenty times that number of Italians will be serfs
   in Asia, in poverty, and they will be liable to pay ten-thousandfold.
   O luxurious golden offspring of Latium, Rome,
   virgin, often drunken with your weddings with many suitors,
   as a slave will you be wed, without decorum.
   Often the mistress will cut your delicate hair
   and, dispensing justice, will cast you from heaven to earth,
   but from earth will again raise you up to heaven,
   because mortals are involved in a wretched and unjust life.
   Samos will be sand, and Delos will become inconspicuous,
   Rome will be a street. All the oracles will be fulfilled.
   Smyrna will perish and there will be no mention of it. There will be an avenger,
   but for the bad counsels and the wickedness of its leaders . . .
   Serene peace will return to the Asian land,
   and Europe will then be blessed. The air will be good for pasture
   for many years, bracing, free from storms and hail,
   producing everything—including birds and creeping beasts of the earth.
   O most blessed, whatever man or woman will live to that time! . . . .

   (I say) these things to you, having left
   the long Babylonian walls of Assyria, frenzied, a fire sent to Greece,
   prophesying the disclosures of God to all mortals,
   so that I prophesy divine riddles to men.
   Throughout Greece mortals will say that I am of another country,
   a shameless one, born of Erythrae. Some will say that
   I am Sibylla born of Circe as mother and Gnostos as father,

a crazy liar. But when everything comes to pass,
then you will remember me and no longer will anyone
say that I am crazy, I who am a prophetess of the great God.

> *Sibylline Oracles* III 350-71, 809-818.[14] (OTP)

31. Thrice-wretched one, I am weary of putting an utterance of disaster in my
      heart
and the inspired chant of oracles, I who am the familiar friend of Isis.
First, indeed, around the steps of your much-lamented temple
maenads will dart, and you will be in bad hands
on that day, when the Nile traverses
the whole land of Egypt up to sixteen cubits,
so as to flood the whole land and drench it with streams.
The beauty of the land and glory of its appearance will disappear. . . .
You, too, Corinth, bewail the mournful destruction within you.
For when the three sister Fates, spinning with twisted threads,
lead the one who is (now) fleeing deceitfully
beyond the bank of the isthmus on high so that all may see him,
who formerly cut out the rock with ductile bronze,
he will destroy and ravage your land also, as is decreed. . . .
But why does my clever mind suggest these things to me?
Now, wretched Asia, I bewail you piteously
and the race of Ionians, Carians, and Lydians rich in gold.
Woe to you, Sardis, woe lovely Trallis,
woe Laodicea, beautiful city, how you will perish
destroyed by earthquakes and changed to dust.

> *Sibylline Oracles* V 52-59, 214-219, 286-291 late first century
> (OTP)

The Pythia of Delphi

32. God forgives all uncontrollable acts. [In response to an inquiry about absolution from a young celibate priest who became drunk and had intercourse with a woman.]

> Plutarch (c 50–120 CE), *The Oracles at Delphi* 404A[15]

33. His residence was Ithaca; Telemachos was his father and Epikaste Nestor's daughter was his mother, who bore him to be a very wise man. [In response to Hadrian who asked Homer's home and parentage.]

> *Certamen Homeri et Hesiodi* 37-40; Anthologia Palatina 14.102

34. In the sanctuary of Demeter Chloie and Kore, beside the propylaion on the acropolis, where grain first grew, it will be better to. . . . [Incomplete response to an unknown question from the Athenians.]

> *Inscriptiones Graecae* 2, second edition, 5006

Christian Women

35.   . . . the perfect Virgin stood,
Who was preaching and summoning and saying:
O you sons of men, return,
And you their daughters, come.
And leave the ways of that Corruptor,
And approach me.
And I will enter into you,
And bring you forth from destruction,
And make you wise in the ways of truth.
Be not corrupted
Nor perish.
Obey me and be saved,
For I am proclaiming unto you the grace of God.
And through me you will be saved and become blessed
I am your judge;
And they who have put me on shall not be falsely accused,
But they shall possess incorruption in the new world.
My elect ones have walked with me,
And my ways I will make known to them who seek me;
And I will promise them my name.
    Hallelujah.
      Odes of Solomon 33 (second century?)[16]

36.   A cup of milk was offered to me,
And I drank it in the sweetness of the Lord's kindness.
The Son is the cup,
And the Father is He who was milked;
And the Holy Spirit is She who milked Him;
Because His breasts were full,
And it was undesirable that His milk should be ineffectually released.
The Holy Spirit opened her bosom,
And mixed the milk of the two breasts of the Father.
Then She gave the mixture to the generation without their knowing,
And those who have received (it) are in the perfection of the right hand.
The womb of the Virgin took (it),
And she received conception and gave birth.
So the Virgin became a mother with great mercies.
And she laboured and bore the Son but without pain,
Because it did not occur without purpose.
And she did not require a midwife,
Because He caused her to give life.
She brought forth like a strong man with desire,
And she bore according to the manifestation,
And acquired with great power.
And she loved with redemption,

And guarded with kindness,
And declared with grandeur.
    Hallelujah.
       Odes of Solomon 19[17]

37. A number of young catechumens were arrested, Revocatus and his fellow slave Felicitas, Saturninus and Secundus, and with them Vibia Perpetua, a newly married woman of good family and upbringing. Her mother and father were still alive and one of her two brothers was a catechumen like herself. She was about twenty-two years old and had an infant son at the breast. (Now from this point on the entire account of her ordeal is her own, according to her own ideas and in the way that she herself wrote it down.)

. . . I got permission for my baby to stay with me in prison. At once I recovered my health, relieved as I was of my worry and anxiety over the child. My prison had suddenly become a palace, so that I wanted to be there rather than anywhere else.

Then my brother said to me: 'Dear sister, you are greatly privileged; surely you might ask for a vision to discover whether you are to be condemned or freed.'

Faithfully I promised that I would, for I knew that I could speak with the Lord, whose great blessings I had come to experience. And so I said: 'I shall tell you tomorrow.' Then I made my request and this was the vision I had.

I saw a ladder of tremendous height made of bronze, reaching all the way to the heavens. . . . At the foot of the ladder lay a dragon of enormous size. . . . 'He will not harm me,' I said, 'in the name of Christ Jesus.'

Slowly, as though he were afraid of me, the dragon stuck his head out from underneath the ladder. Then, using it as my first step, I trod on his head and went up.

Then I saw an immense garden, and in it a grey-haired man sat in shepherd's garb; tall he was, and milking sheep. And standing around him were many thousands of people clad in white garments. He raised his head, looked at me, and said: 'I am glad you have come, my child.'

He called me over to him and gave me, as it were, a mouthful of the milk he was drawing; and I took it into my cupped hands and consumed it. And all those who stood around said: 'Amen!' At the sound of this word I came to, with the taste of something sweet still in my mouth. I at once told this to my brother, and we realized that we would have to suffer, and that from now on we would no longer have any hope in this life. . . .

The day before we were to fight with the beasts I saw the following vision. Pomponius the deacon came to the prison gates and began to knock violently. I went out and opened the gate for him. He was dressed in an unbelted white tunic, wearing elaborate sandals. And he said to me: 'Perpetua, come; we are waiting for you.'

Then he took my hand and we began to walk through rough and broken country. At last we came to the amphitheatre out of breath, and he led me into the centre of the arena.

Then he told me: 'Do not be afraid. I am here, struggling with you.' Then he left.

I looked at the enormous crowd who watched in astonishment. I was surprised that no beasts were let loose on me; for I knew that I was condemned to die by the beasts. Then out came an Egyptian against me, of vicious appearance, together with his seconds, to fight with me. There also came up to me some handsome young men to be my seconds and assistants.

My clothes were stripped off, and suddenly I was a man. My seconds began to rub me down with oil (as they are wont to do before a contest). Then I saw the Egyptian on the other side rolling in the dust. . . .

We drew close to one another and began to let our fists fly. My opponent tried to get hold of my feet, but I kept striking him in the face with the heels of my feet. Then I was raised up into the air and I began to pummel him without as it were touching the ground. Then when I noticed there was a lull, I put my two hands together linking the fingers of one hand with those of the other and thus I got hold of his head. He fell flat on his face and I stepped on his head.

The crowd began to shout and my assistants started to sing psalms. Then I walked up to the trainer and took the branch. He kissed me and said to me: 'Peace be with you, my daughter!' I began to walk in triumph towards the Gate of Life. Then I awoke. I realized that it was not with wild animals that I would fight but with the Devil, but I knew that I would win the victory. So much for what I did up until the eve of the contest. About what happened at the contest itself, let him write of it who will.

> Perpetua (c 182–202 CE), as quoted in *The Martyrdom of Perpetua and Felicitas* 3-4, 10[18]

38. They are flesh, and they despise flesh.

> Prisca, Montanist Prophet (late second century), as quoted by Tertullian (c 50–120 CE), *On the Resurrection of the Flesh* 11. 2, with the following introduction: The Paraclete speaks brilliantly through the prophetess Prisca about these people [those who live carnally and deny resurrection of the flesh]:[19]

39. When the heart gives purification, they see visions and, lowering their faces, also hear unmistakable voices, as health-giving as they are hidden.

> Prisca, a Montanist Prophet, as quoted in Tertullian, *On Exhortation to Chastity* 8

40. In the form of a woman dressed in shining armour Christ came toward me and put wisdom in me and revealed to me that this place is holy and that here Jerusalem will come down from heaven.

> Prisca or Quintilla, Montanist Prophets (late second century), as quoted by Epiphanius (fourth century), *Panarion* 49, 1, 2-3, with the following introduction: For the Quintillians or the Priscillians in Pepuza say—or Quintillia or Priscilla (I don't know exactly)—but, as I said above, one of these women in Pepuza had laid down to sleep when Christ came to her and put in her mind this dream. Being thus deceived she spoke:

41. After me there will not be yet [another] prophet, but the completion.

> Maximilla, a Montanist Prophet (late second century), quoted in
> Epiphanius, *Panarion* 48. 2. 4

42. Do not hear me, but hear Christ.

> Maximilla, as quoted in Epiphanius, *Panarion* 48. 12. 4

43. The Lord has sent me as a partisan, an informer and an interpreter of this work and covenant and promise, compelled, willing or not willing, to know the knowledge of God.

> Maximilla, as quoted in Epiphanius, *Panarion* 48. 13. 1

44. I am chased from the sheep like a wolf. I am not a wolf. I am word and spirit and power.

> Maximilla, as quoted in Eusebius, *History of the Church* V 16. 17

III. Women Prophets at Holy Sites in the Early Roman Empire

General Descriptions of Women Prophets at Oracular Sites

45. There is a chasm at this place where now is situated what is known as the "forbidden" sanctuary, and as goats had been wont to feed about this because Delphi had not as yet been settled, invariably any goat that approached the chasm and peered into it would leap about in such an extraordinary fashion and utter a sound quite different from what it was formerly wont to emit. . . . For some time all who wished to obtain a prophecy approached the chasm and made their prophetic replies to one another; but later, since many were leaping down into the chasm under the influence of their frenzy and all disappeared, it seemed best to the dwellers in that region, in order to eliminate the risk, to station one woman there as a single prophetess for all and to have the oracles told through her. And for her a contrivance was devised which she could safely mount, then become inspired and give prophecies to those who so desired. And this contrivance has three supports and hence was called a tripod. . . .

It is said that in ancient times virgins delivered the oracles because virgins have their natural innocence intact and are in the same case as Artemis; for indeed virgins were alleged to be well suited to guard the secrecy of disclosures made by oracles. In more recent times, however, people say that Echecrates the Thessalian, having arrived at the shrine and beheld the virgin who uttered the oracle, became enamoured of her because of her beauty, carried her away with him and violated her; and that the Delphians because of this deplorable occurrence passed a law that in future a virgin should no longer prophesy but that an elderly woman of fifty should declare the oracles and that she should be dressed in the costume of a virgin, as a sort of reminder of the prophetess of olden times.

> Diodorus of Sicily (first century BCE), *The Library of History* XVI
> 26. 2-6 (LCL)

46. The oracle at Delphi never would have been so much frequented, so famous, and so crowded with offerings from peoples and kings of every land, if all ages had not tested the truth of its prophecies. For a long time now that has not been the case. Therefore, as at present its glory has waned because it is no longer noted for the truth of its prophecies, so formerly it would not have enjoyed so exalted a reputation if it had not been trustworthy in the highest degree. Possibly, too, those subterraneous exhalations which used to kindle the soul of the Pythian priestess with divine inspiration have gradually vanished in the long lapse of time; just as within our own knowledge some rivers have dried up and disappeared, while others, by winding and twisting, have changed their course into other channels. But explain the decadence of the oracle as you wish, since it offers a wide field for discussion, provided you grant what cannot be denied without distorting the entire record of history, that the oracle at Delphi made true prophecies for many hundreds of years.

Cicero (first century BCE), *Concerning Divination* I 19. 37-38 (LCL)

47. At the outset, it is true, those who uttered the prophecies [at Dodona] were men . . . , but later on three old women were designated as prophets after Dione also had been designated as temple-associate of Zeus. Suidas, however, in his desire to gratify the Thessalians with mythical stories, says that the temple was transferred from Thessaly . . . and also that most of the women whose descendants are the prophetesses of to-day went along at the same time.

Strabo (64 BCE–24 CE), *Geography* 7. 7. 12 (LCL)

48. [Serapion:] "Before long we shall be finding fault with the prophetic priestess because she does not speak in purer tones than Glaucê, who sings to the lyre, and because she is not perfumed and clad in purple when she goes down into the inner shrine, and does not burn upon the altar cassia or ladanum or frankincense, but only laurel and barley meal. Do you not see," he continued, "what grace the songs of Sappho have, charming and bewitching all who listen to them? But the Sibyl 'with frenzied lips,' as Heracleitus has it, 'uttering words mirthless, unembellished, unperfumed, yet reaches to a thousand years with her voice through the god.'"

[Theon:] . . . "If these verses be inferior to Homer's, let us not believe that the god has composed them, but that he supplies the origin of the incitement, and then the prophetic priestesses are moved each in accordance with her natural faculties. . . . The voice is not that of a god, nor the utterance of it, nor the diction, nor the metre, but all these are the woman's; he puts into her mind only the visions, and creates a light in her soul in regard to the future; for inspiration is precisely this."

Plutarch (c 50–120 CE), *The Oracles at Delphi* 397A-C (LCL)

49. The maiden who now serves the god here was born of as lawful and honourable wedlock as anyone, and her life has been in all respects proper; but, having been brought up in the home of poor peasants, she brings nothing with her as the result of technical skill or of any other expertness or faculty, as she goes down into the shrine. On the contrary, just as Xenophon believes that a bride should have seen

as little and heard as little as possible before she proceeds to her husband's house, so this girl, inexperienced and uninformed about practically everything, a pure, virgin soul, becomes the associate of the god.

Plutarch, *The Oracles at Delphi* 405CD (LCL)

50. For my part, I am well content with the settled conditions prevailing at present, and I find them very welcome, and the questions which [people] now put to the god are concerned with these conditions, . . . like the hypothetical questions in school: if one ought to marry, or to start on a voyage, or to make a loan; and the most important consultations on the part of States concern the yield from crops, the increase of herds, and public health—to clothe such things in verse, to devise circumlocutions, and to foist strange words upon inquiries that call for a simple short answer is the thing done by an ambitious pedant embellishing an oracle to enhance his repute. But the prophetic priestess has herself also nobility of character, and whenever she descends into that place and finds herself in the presence of the god, she cares more for fulfilling her function than for that kind of repute or for people's praise or blame.

Plutarch, *The Oracles at Delphi* 408B-D (LCL)

51. When Greece, since God so willed, had grown strong in cities and the place was thronged with people, they used to employ two prophetic priestesses who were sent down in turn; and a third was appointed to be held in reserve. But to-day there is one priestess and we do not complain, for she meets every need.

Plutarch, *Obsolescence of Oracles* 414B (LCL)

52. Wherever in Greece a perpetual fire is kept, as at Delphi and Athens, it is committed to the charge, not of virgins, but of widows past the age of marriage. . . . Some, moreover, are of the opinion that nothing but this perpetual fire is guarded by the sacred virgins; while some say that certain sacred objects, which none others may behold, are kept in concealment by them.

Plutarch, *Lives: Numa* 5 and 8[20] (LCL)

53. [The Epicureans say,] "The gods do not exist, and even if they do, they pay no attention to [people]." . . . And then those who talk thus . . . get themselves appointed priests and prophets! Priests and prophets of whom? Of gods that do not exist! And they themselves consult the Pythian priestess—in order to hear lies and to interpret the oracles to others! Oh what monstrous shamelessness and imposture!

Epictetus (c 50–120 CE), *Discourses* II 20. 23 and 27 (LCL)

54. As you go up the citadel [of Corinth] you come to the sanctuary of Hera of the Height, and also a temple of Apollo. . . . Oracular responses are still given here, and the oracle acts in the following way. There is a woman who prophesies, being debarred from intercourse with a man. Every month a lamb is sacrificed at night, and the woman, after tasting the blood, becomes inspired by the god.

Pausanias (second century CE), *Description of Greece* II 24. 1 (LCL)

55. But as to the pronouncements of the priestesses at Pytho, when they are ecstatic, both Plato and all people declare that the Pythian has said these things. What art do these priestesses know who are incapable of preserving and memorizing their predictions? . . . These women neither have any deeper knowledge than other people, nor, if they do know anything, do they speak from training and prescience. But, as they are moved each time by the God, they dispatch [people] throughout the earth, to Ionia, Pontus, Cyrene, to the ends of the world. . . . What will you say of the priestesses in Dodona, who know as much as the God approves, and for as long as he approves? Yet neither had they any such knowledge until they entered into communion with the God, nor afterwards do they know anything which they have said, but all inquirers understand it better than they. So those who were ignorant and made inquiry have learned from them, but those who told what must be done do not even know the very fact that they have spoken at all.

Aelius Aristides (second century CE), *In Defense of Oratory* 34-35, 40, 42-43 (LCL)

56. Plague take all philosophers who say that bliss is to be found only among the gods! If they but knew all that we endure for the sake of [people], they would not envy us our nectar and ambrosia. . . . Apollo . . . has taken up a very active profession, and has been deafened almost completely by people besetting him with requests for prophecies. One moment he has to be in Delphi; the next, he runs to Colophon; from there he crosses to Xanthus, and again at full speed to Delos or to Branchidae. In a word, wherever his prophetess, after drinking from the holy well and chewing laurel and setting the tripod ashake, bids him appear, there is no delaying—he must present himself immediately to reel off his prophecies, or else it is all up with his reputation in the profession.

Lucian (second century CE), *The Double Indictment* 1 (LCL)

Specific Women's Prophecies at Holy Sites

57. When Appius came to consult the Oracle, intent on learning the secrets of Rome's destiny, no priestess had occupied the sacred tripod for many years and silence therefore reigned on the towering crag. However, he ordered the priest to open the Temple and usher the Pythoness into Apollo's sacred presence. Her name was Phemonoë, and she was strolling idly from the Castalian Spring towards the laurel grove when he seized her, dragged her to the shrine and pushed her inside; but being afraid to enter the innermost sanctuary, she tried to discourage Appius's curiosity by prevarication. 'Appius,' she said, 'why do you take it upon yourself to demand the truth? Responses no longer come from the chasm. . . .'

Phemonoë was clearly not telling the truth; her very agitation suggested that the god must still be at work. So the priest tied one laurel wreath, bound with white wool, above her brow in the form of a fillet, and used another to secure the long tresses behind. But Phemonoë, as yet unwilling to seat herself on the tripod in the innermost sanctuary, came to a sudden halt just beyond the Temple threshold, pretending to be possessed. What she said was uttered neither wildly nor incoherently, as it would have been had the god taken possession of her. . . . He shouted angrily: 'You impious creature, I have come to inquire about the fate of this distracted world. Unless you stop speaking in your natural voice and go down at once to the chasm for true inspiration, the gods whose Oracles you are taking in vain will punish you—and so will I!'

Appius's violence terrified her into action. She approached the lip of the great chasm and seated herself on the tripod. Then for the first time she experienced the divine afflatus, still active after so many centuries, and Apollo genuinely possessed her at last. He forced his way into her heart, masterful as ever, driving our her private thoughts and draining her body of all that was mortal, so that he could possess it wholly. She went blundering frantically about the shrine, with the God mounted on the nape of her neck, knocking over the tripods that stood in her path. The hair rose on her scalp and when she tossed her head the wreaths went flying across the bare floor. Apollo's fury was so fierce that fire seemed to boil from her mouth. He whipped her, goaded her, darted flames into her intestines; but at the same time kept her on the curb and prevented her from disclosing as much as she knew. Countless centuries crowded tormentingly in her breast. . . . Phemonoë went through a distressing search among the fates of far more important men than Appius before she finally came upon his own. As soon as she recognized it, her mouth foamed frenziedly; she groaned, gasped, uttered weird sounds, and made the huge cave re-echo with her dismal shrieks. In the end Apollo forced her to use intelligible speech and here is the response she gave:

'Appius, you shall avoid the tremendous perils of warfare,

Taking your lonesome ease in Euboea, that haven of refuge.'

This was all, because Apollo cut short the prophecy. . . .

The Priestess ran full tilt against the Temple doors, broke them open and rushed out. She was still in an ecstasy, not having been able to expel the god; who continued to prevent her from telling Appius the full story. Her eyes rolled wildly as she gazed at the sky, and her expression changed continuously; never placid, but varying between alarm and menace. Her cheeks were alternately scarlet and deathly pale, and this was a paleness which induced rather than registered fear. As yet she felt no relief after her labours, but was shaken by heavy sobs. . . . Phemonoë collapsed on the floor, and was revived with difficulty.

Lucan (39–65 CE), Pharasalia or The Civil Wars V 120-225[21]

58. To the memory of Ammias, priestess of the gods, her children, the disciples of the gods, dedicate this altar and funerary urn. Let he who would learn from me the truth pray before this altar, and whatever he may ask of me I will impart to him, whether in daylight or in darkness.

An epitaph found at Thyatira in Lydia (Roman period)[22]

59. And when the parents brought the child Jesus to carry out the practices of the law concerning him, . . . there was a prophetess, Hanna, a daughter of Panouel of the tribe of Asher. She had become advanced in years, having lived with a man seven years from her virginity and as a widow until she became eighty four. She had not left the temple where she served in fasting and prayer night and day. And approaching at that hour she was praising God and she was speaking about him [Jesus] to all the people awaiting the redemption of Jerusalem.

Luke 2:27, 36-38 (late first century CE)[23]

60. I lost my direction, and at high noon was quite astray. But noticing on a high knoll a clump of oaks that looked like a sacred grove, I made my way thither in the hope of discovering from it some roadway or house. There I found blocks of stone set roughly together, hanging pelts of animals that had been sacrificed, and a number of clubs and staves — all evidently being dedications of herdsmen. At a little distance I saw a woman sitting, strong and tall though rather advanced in years, dressed like a rustic and with some braids of grey hair falling about her shoulders. Of her I made full inquiry about the place, and she most graciously and kindly, speaking in the Dorian dialect, informed me that it was sacred to Heracles and, regarding herself, that she had a son, a shepherd, whose sheep she often tended herself. She also said that the Mother of the Gods had given her the gift of divination and that all the herdsmen and farmers round about consulted her on the raising and preservation of their crops and cattle.

"And you too," she continued, "have come into this place by no mere human chance, for I shall not let you depart unblest." Thereupon she at once began to prophesy, saying that the period of my wandering and tribulation would not be long, nay, nor that of mankind at large. The manner of her prophesying was not that of most men and women who are said to be inspired; she did not gasp for breath, whirl her head about, or try to terrify with her glances, but spoke with entire self-control and moderation. . . .

Dio Chrysostom (c 40–c 120 CE), *The First Discourse on Kingship* 52-56 (LCL)

61. As it happened, a deputation from abroad had arrived to consult the oracle. The [sacrificial] victim remained unmoved and unaffected in any way by the first libations; but the priests, in their eagerness to please, went far beyond their wonted usage, and only after the victim had been subjected to a deluge and nearly drowned did it at last give in. What, then, was the result touching the priestess? She went down into the oracle unwillingly, they say, and half-heartedly; and at her first responses it was at once plain from the harshness of her voice that she was not responding properly; she was like a labouring ship and was filled with a mighty and baleful spirit. Finally she became hysterical and with a frightful shriek rushed towards the exit and threw herself down, with the result that not only the members of the deputation fled, but also the oracle-interpreter Nicander and those holy men that were present. However, after a little, they went in and took her up, still conscious; and she lived on for a few days.

Plutarch (c 50–120), *Obsolescence of Oracles* 438A–C (LCL)

IV. Women Prophets and Visionaries not Located at Holy Sites in the Early Roman Empire

Women with Predictions, Dreams, and Recognitions

62. Writers report a custom of the Cimbri [a German tribe] to this effect: Their wives, who would accompany them on their expeditions, were attended by priestesses who were seers; these were grey-haired, clad in white, with flaxen cloaks fastened on with clasps, girt with girdles of bronze, and bare-footed; now

sword in hand these priestesses would meet with the prisoners throughout the camp, and having first crowned them with wreaths would lead them to a brazen vessel of about twenty amphorae; and they had a raised platform which the priestess would mount, and then, bending over the kettle, would cut the throat of each prisoner after he had been lifted up; and from the blood that poured forth into the vessel some of the priestesses would draw a prophecy, while still others would split open the body and from an inspection of the entrails would utter a prophecy of victory for their own people; and during the battles they would beat on the hides that were stretched over the wicker-bodies of the wagons and in this way produce an unearthly noise.

Strabo (64 BCE–24 CE), *Geography* 7. 2. 3 (LCL)

63. Munius Lupercus, commander of a legion, was sent, among other gifts, to Veleda. This maiden of the tribe of the Bructeri enjoyed extensive authority, according to the ancient German custom, which regards many women as endowed with prophetic powers and, as the superstition grows, attributes divinity to them. At this time Veleda's influence was at its height, since she had foretold the German success and the destruction of the legions. But Lupercus was killed on the road.

Tacitus (40–120 CE), *The Histories* IV 41 (LCL)

64. Further, [the Germans] conceive that in woman is a certain uncanny and prophetic sense: they neither scorn to consult them nor slight their answers. In the reign of Vespasian of happy memory we saw Velaeda treated as a deity by many during a long period; but in ancient times also they reverenced Albruna and many other women—in no spirit of flattery, nor for the manufacture of goddesses.

Tacitus (40–120 CE), *Germany* 8[24] (LCL)

65. A similar thing happened also to his wife Glaphyra, the daughter of King Archelaus, to whom, as I said before, Alexander, the son of Herod and the brother of Archelaus, had been married when she was still a virgin. For when Alexander was put to death by his father, she married Juba, the king of Libya, and when, after the death of the Libyan king, she was living as a widow with her father in Cappadocia, Archelaus divorced his wife Mariamme to marry her, so overwhelming was his love for Glaphyra. And while she was the wife of Archelaus, she had the following dream. She seemed to see Alexander standing before her, and in her joy she embraced him warmly. But he reproached her and said, "Glaphyra, you certainly confirm the saying that women are not to be trusted. For though you were betrothed and married to me as a virgin, and children were born to us, you let yourself forget my love in your desire to marry again. But not content even with this outrage, you had the temerity to take still a third bridegroom to your bed, and in an indecent and shameless manner you again became a member of my family by entering into marriage with Archelaus, your own brother-in-law and my own brother. However I will not forget my affection for you but will free you of all reproach by making you my own, as you were (before)." A few days after she had related these things to her women friends she died.

Josephus (c 37–c 100 CE), *Jewish Antiquities* XVII 350-53 (LCL)

66. While he [Pilate] was seated on the judgment stand, his wife sent word to him saying, let nothing happen between you and that righteous man. For I have suffered many things on his account today in a dream.
Matthew 27:19 (late first century CE)

67. [Galba] was encouraged too, in addition to most favourable auspices and omens, by the prediction of a young girl of high birth, and the more so because the priest of Jupiter at Clunia, directed by a dream, had found in the inner shrine of his temple the very same prediction, likewise spoken by an inspired girl two hundred years before. And the purport of the verses was that one day there would come forth from Spain the ruler and lord of the world.
Suetonius (75–140 CE), *The Lives of the Caesars* VII 9. 2

68. And in those days Mary got up and went hurriedly into the hill country to a city of Judah, and she entered the house of Zachariah and greeted Elizabeth. And it happened that when Elizabeth heard Mary's greeting, the baby jumped in her womb. Elizabeth was filled with the Holy Spirit and shouted with a great cry, "Blessed are you among women and blessed is the fruit of your womb! And where has this come from, that my Lord's mother should come to me? For behold, as the sound of your greeting entered my ear, the baby jumped in my womb with joy! And blessed is she who believed that there will be a fulfillment of the things spoken to her by the Lord!"
Luke 1:39-45 (late first century)

69. And it happened when we were going into prayer that a certain slave girl who had a divining spirit met us. She provided her owners a good profit by prophesying. Following Paul and us she cried out, "These people are servants of the most high God who announce to you the way of salvation!"
But she did this for many days. Paul became annoyed and turned on the spirit and said, "I command you in Jesus Christ's name to come out of her." And it came out at that moment. But when her owners saw that their hope of profit was gone, they seized Paul and Silas and dragged them into the market square before the rulers. . . .
Acts of the Apostles 16:16-19

Women Known as Prophets

70. And on the next day we left and came to Caesarea and we entered the house of Philip the evangelist, one of the seven, and stayed with him. And he had four virgin daughters who prophesied.
Acts 21:8-9 (late first century)

71. To the angel of the church in Thyatira write: Thus says God's Son, the one who has eyes like a flame of fire and feet like forged gold. I know your works and your love and faith and service and endurance, and that your later works are greater than your first. But I have this against you, that you tolerate the woman Jezebel who calls herself a prophetess and teaches and leads my servants astray to act immorally and

to eat what is sacrificed to idols. And I have given her time to repent, but she does not want to repent of her immorality. Behold, I am throwing her down flat in bed and those who commit adultery with her I am throwing into tribulation — if they do not repent of her works — and her children I will strike dead. All the churches will know that I am the one who searches heads and hearts, and I will give each of you according to your works.

But I say to the rest of you in Thyatira, those who do not share this teaching and have not known what they call the "depths of Satan." I will not put any other burden on you, but hold to what you have until I arrive.

And to the one who is victorious and keeps doing my works until the end I will give authority over the nations. That one will herd them with an iron rod the way ceramic pots are shattered, as even I have received [rule] from my Father. And I will give that one the early morning star. Let those who have ears hear what the spirit says to the churches.

Revelation of John 2:18-29 (late first century)

72. But there is another among these heretics, Marcus by name. . . . It appears probable enough that this man possesses a demon as his familiar spirit, by means of whom he seems able to prophesy, and also enables as many as he counts worthy to be partakers of his Charis themselves to prophesy. He devotes himself especially to women, and those such as are well-bred, and elegantly attired, and of great wealth, whom he frequently seeks to draw after him, by addressing them in such seductive words as these: "I am eager to make thee a partaker of my Charis, since the Father of all doth continually behold thy angel before His face. Now the place of thy angel is among us: it behoves us to become one. Receive first from me and by me Charis. Adorn thyself as a bride who is expecting her bridegroom, that thou mayest be what I am, and I what thou art. Establish the germ of light in thy nuptial chamber. Receive from me a spouse, and become receptive of him, while thou art received by him. Behold Charis has descended upon thee; open thy mouth and prophesy."

On the woman replying, "I have never at any time prophesied, nor do I know how to prophesy;" then engaging, for the second time, in certain invocations, so as to astound his deluded victim, he says to her, "Open thy mouth, speak whatsoever occurs to thee, and thou shalt prophesy." She then vainly puffed up and elated by these words, and greatly excited in soul by the expectation that it is herself who is to prophesy, her heart beating violently, reaches the requisite pitch of audacity, and idly as well as impudently utters some nonsense as it happens to occur to her, such as might be expected from one heated by an empty spirit.

Henceforth she reckons herself a prophetess, and expresses her thanks to Marcus for having imparted to her of his own Charis. She then makes the effort to reward him, not only by the gift of her possessions (in which way he has collected a very large fortune), but also by yielding up to him her person, desiring in every way to be united to him, that she may become altogether one with him.

But already some of the most faithful women . . . have withdrawn from such a vile company of revellers. This they have done, as being well aware that the gift of prophecy is not conferred on [people] by Marcus, the magician, but that only those to whom God sends His grace from above possess the divinely-bestowed power of prophesying; and then they speak where and when God pleases, and not when Marcus orders them to do so.

Irenaeus (c 130–202 CE), *Against Heresies* I 13. 1-4 (ANF)

73. Others again, that they may set at nought the gift of the Spirit, which in the latter times has been, by the good pleasure of the Father, poured out upon the human race, do not admit that aspect presented by John's Gospel, in which the Lord promised that He would send the Paraclete; but set aside at once both the Gospel and the prophetic Spirit. Wretched [people] indeed! who wish to be pseudo-prophets, forsooth, but who set aside the gift of prophecy from the Church; acting like those who, on account of such as come in hypocrisy, hold themselves aloof from the communion of the brethren. We must conclude moreover, that [this kind] cannot admit the Apostle Paul either. For, in his Epistle to the Corinthians, he speaks expressly of prophetical gifts, and recognises men and women prophesying in the Church.

Irenaeus, *Against Heresies* III 11. 9[25] (ANF)

74. Some like poisonous reptiles crawled over Asia and Phrygia, and boasted that Montanus was the Paraclete and that the women of his sect, Priscilla and Maximilla, were the prophetesses of Montanus. . . . Against the so-called Cataphrygian heresy the power which champions the truth raised up a powerful and invincible weapon at Hierapolis in Apolinarius . . . and with him many others. . . . One of these at the beginning of his treatise against the Montanists indicates that he had also taken part in oral controversy against them. He writes . . . "But when I had just come to Ancyra in Galatia and perceived that the church in that place was torn in two by this new movement which is not, as they call it, prophecy but much rather, as will be shown, false prophecy, I disputed concerning these people themselves and their propositions so far as I could, with the Lord's help, for many days continuously in the church. . . .

"In Phrygian Mysia there is said to be a village called Ardabav. There they say that a recent convert called Montanus, when Gratus was proconsul of Asia, in the unbounded lust of his soul for leadership gave access to himself to the adversary, became obsessed, and suddenly fell into frenzy and convulsions. He began to be ecstatic and to speak and to talk strangely, prophesying contrary to the custom which belongs to the tradition and succession of the church from the beginning. . . . He raised up two more women and filled them with the bastard spirit so that they spoke madly and improperly and strangely, like Montanus. The spirit gave blessings to those who rejoiced and were proud in him, and puffed them up by the greatness of its promises. . . . The Christians of Asia after assembling for this purpose many times and in many parts of the province, tested the recent utterances, pronounced them profane, and rejected the heresy, — then at last the Montanists were driven out of the church and excommunicated."

"Since then they called us murderers of the prophets because we did not receive their chattering prophets (for they say that these are those whom the Lord promised to send to the people), let them answer us before God . . . was any one of the women ever scourged in the synagogues of the Jews or stoned? Never anywhere. It was a different death that Montanus and Maximilla are said to have died; for the story goes that each of them was inspired by a mind-destroying spirit to commit suicide, though not together, and there was much gossip at the time of the death of each . . . perhaps Montanus and Theodotus and the above mentioned woman died in this way, but perhaps they did not."

Again in the same book he says that the sacred bishops of that time tried to refute the spirit that was in Maximilla, but were prevented by others who plainly co-operated with the spirit, and he writes thus: "And let not the spirit which speaks through Maximilla say, in the same work according to Asterius Orbanus, 'I am driven away like a wolf from the sheep. I am not a wolf, I am word and spirit and power.' But let [this spirit] show clearly and prove the power in the spirit, and let [it] through the spirit force those to recognize [it] who were then present for the purpose of testing and conversing with the spirit as it spoke, — eminent men and bishops, Zoticus from the village Cumane, and Julian from Apamea, whose mouths the party of Themiso muzzled, and did not allow the false spirit which deceived the people to be refuted by them."

In the same book, again, after other refutations of the false prophecies of Maximilla, in a single passage he both indicates the time at which he wrote this, and quotes her predictions, in which she foretold future wars and revolutions, and he corrects the falsehood of them as follows: "Has it not been made obvious already that this is another lie? For it is more than thirteen years to-day since the woman died, and there has been in the world neither local nor universal war, but rather by the mercy of God continuing peace even for Christians. . . ."

And after a little he goes on as follows: Wherefore whenever members of the church who have been called to martyrdom for the true faith meet any of the so-called martyrs of the Montanist heresy, they separate from them and die without communicating with them, because they refuse to agree with the spirit in Montanus and the women. And that this is true, and that it happened in our time in Apamea on the Meander, is shown by the case of those who were martyred with Gaius and Alexander of Eumeneia."

> Eusebius (early fourth century) quoting an associate of Apolinarius from the late second century, *Ecclesiastical History* V 14-16[26] (LCL)

75. And in this work he also quotes Miltiades, . . . "But the false prophet speaks in ecstasy, after which follow ease and freedom from fear; he begins with voluntary ignorance, but turns to involuntary madness of soul, as has been said before. But they cannot show that any prophet, either of those in the Old Testament or of those in the New, was inspired in this way; they can boast neither of Agabus, nor of Judas, nor of Silas, nor of the daughters of Philip, nor of Ammia in Philadelphia, nor of Quadratus, nor of any others who do not belong to them.

And again after a little he goes on, "For if the Montanist women succeeded to Quadratus and Ammia in Philadelphia in the prophetic gift, let them show who among them succeeded the followers of Montanus and the women, for the apostle grants that the prophetic gift shall be in all the church until the final coming, but this they could not show, seeing that this is already the fourteenth year from the death of Maximilla."

> Eusebius, quoting Apolinarius who quotes Miltiades of the late second century, *Ecclesiastical History* V 17 (LCL)

76. We have now amongst us a sister whose lot it has been to be favoured with sundry gifts of revelation, which she experiences in the Spirit by ecstatic vision amidst the sacred rites of the Lord's day in the church: she converses with angels and sometimes even with the Lord; she both sees and hears mysterious communications; some [people's] hearts she understands, and to them who are in need she distributes remedies. Whether it be in the reading of Scriptures, or in the chanting of psalms, or in the preaching of sermons, or in the offering up of prayers, in all these religious services matter and opportunity are afforded to her of seeing visions. It may possibly have happened to us, whilst this sister of ours was rapt in the Spirit, that we had discoursed in some ineffable way about the soul.

After the people are dismissed at the conclusion of the sacred services, she is in the regular habit of reporting to us whatever things she may have seen in vision (for all her communications are examined with the most scrupulous care, in order that their truth may be probed). "Amongst other things," says she, "there has been shown to me a soul in bodily shape, and a spirit has been in the habit of appearing to me; not, however, a void and empty illusion, but such as would offer itself to be even grasped by the hand, soft and transparent and of an ethereal colour, and in form resembling that of a human being in every respect." This was her vision, and for her witness there was God and the apostle most assuredly foretold that there were to be "spiritual gifts" in the church.

Tertullian, *A Treatise on the Soul* 9[27] (ANF)

77. Now was absolutely fulfilled that promise of the Spirit which was given by the word of Joel: "On the last days will I pour out of my Spirit upon all flesh, and their sons and their daughters shall prophesy; and upon my servants and upon my handmaids will I pour out of my Spirit." . . . [Paul], when enjoining on women silence in the church, that they speak not for the mere sake of learning (although that even they have the right of prophesying, he has already shown when he covers the woman that prophesies with a veil), . . . goes to the law for his sanction that woman should be under obedience. Now this law, let me say once for all, he ought to have made no other acquaintance with, than to destroy it.

But that we may now leave the subject of spiritual gifts, facts themselves will be enough to prove which of us acts rashly in claiming them for his God. . . . Let Marcion then exhibit, as gifts of his god, some prophets, such as have not spoken by human sense, but with the Spirit of God, such as have both predicted things to come, and have made manifest the secrets of the heart; let him produce a psalm, a vision, a prayer—only let it be by the Spirit, in an ecstasy, that is, in a rapture, whenever an interpretation of tongues has occurred to him; let him show to me also, that any woman of boastful tongue in his community has ever prophesied from amongst those specially holy sisters of his. Now all these signs (of spiritual gifts) are forthcoming from my side without any difficulty.

Tertullian (c 145–c 220 CE), *Against Marcion* V 8 (ANF)

78. After the Bishop of Rome had acknowledged the prophetic gifts of Montanus, Prisca, and Maximilla, and in consequence of the acknowledgment, had bestowed his peace on the churches of Asia and Phrygia, he [Praxeas], by importunately urging false accusations against the prophets themselves and their churches, and

insisting on the authority of the bishop's predecessors in the see, compelled him to recall the pacific letter which he had issued, as well as to desist from his purpose of acknowledging the said gifts. By this Praxeas did a twofold service for the devil at Rome: he drove away prophecy, and he brought in heresy; he put to flight the Paraclete, and he crucified the Father.

Tertullian *Against Praxeas* 1 (ANF)

79. It is on this account that the New Prophecies are rejected: not that Montanus and Priscilla and Maximilla preach another God, nor that they disjoin Jesus Christ (from God), nor that they overturn any particular rule of faith or hope, but that they plainly teach more frequent fasting than marrying. . . . They charge us [Montanists] with keeping fasts of our own; with prolonging our Stations generally into the evening; with observing xerophagies [dry meals] likewise, keeping our food unmoistened by any flesh, and by any juiciness, and by any kind of specially succulent fruit; and with not eating or drinking anything with a winey flavour; also with abstinence from the bath, congruent with our dry diet. They are therefore constantly reproaching us with novelty; concerning the unlawfulness of which they lay down a prescriptive rule, that either it must be adjudged heresy, if (the point in dispute) is a human presumption; or else pronounced pseudo-prophecy, if it is a spiritual declaration.

Tertullian, *On Fasting* 1 (ANF)

80. Apollonius also . . . composed a refutation. . . . "But the deeds and the teachings of this recent teacher show his character. It is he who taught the annulment of marriage, who enacted fasts, who gave the name of Jerusalem to Pepuza and Tymion, which are little towns in Phrygia, and wished to hold assemblies there from everywhere, who appointed collectors of money, who organized the receiving of gifts under the name of offerings, who provided salaries for those who preached his doctrine in order that its teaching might prevail through gluttony."

So he says about Montanus. And a little further on he writes thus about the prophetesses. "Thus we prove that these first prophetesses themselves deserted their husbands from the moment that they were filled with the spirit. What a lie it is then for them to call Priscilla a virgin." Then he goes on saying: "Does not all Scripture seem to you to forbid a prophet from receiving gifts and money? Therefore when I see that the prophetess has received gold and silver and expensive clothes, how should I refrain from blaming her?"

. . . And again he says that Zoticus, whom the former writer mentioned, when Maximilla pretended to prophesy in Pepuza had tried in opposition to confute the spirit which worked in her, but was prevented by those who agreed with her. . . .

Eusebius, quoting Apollonius of the late second or more likely the early third century, *Ecclesiastical History* V 18 (LCL)

V. Women as Teachers of Divine Things in the Early Roman Empire

81. The interval between early morning and evening is spent entirely in spiritual exercise. They read Holy Scriptures and seek wisdom from their ancestral

philosophy by taking it as an allegory. . . . They do not confine themselves to con-
templation but also compose hymns and psalms to God in all sorts of metres and
melodies which they write down with the rhythms necessarily made more solemn.
For six days they seek wisdom by themselves in solitude in the closets mentioned
above, . . . but every seventh day they meet together as a general assembly.

These people assemble after seven sets of seven days have passed, for they
revere not only the simple seven but its square. . . . The feast is shared by women
also, most of them aged virgins, who have kept their chastity not under compulsion,
like some of the Greek priestesses, but of their own free will in their ardent yearn-
ing for wisdom. Eager to have her for their life mate they have spurned the
pleasures of the body and desire no mortal offspring but those immortal children
which only the soul that is dear to God can bring to the birth unaided because the
Father has sown in her spiritual rays enabling her to behold the verities of wisdom.

The order of reclining is so apportioned that the men set by themselves on the
right and the women by themselves on the left. . . . No wine is brought during those
days but only water of the brightest and clearest. . . . When the guests have laid
themselves down . . . the President of the company . . . discusses some question
arising in the Holy Scriptures or solves one that has been propounded by someone
else. . . . The exposition of the sacred scriptures treats the inner meaning conveyed
in allegory. For to these people the whole law book seems to resemble a living
creature with the literal ordinances for its body and for its soul the invisible mind
laid up in its wording. It is in this mind especially that the rational soul begins to
contemplate the things akin to itself and looking through the words as through a
mirror beholds the marvellous beauties of the concepts, unfolds and removes the
symbolic coverings and brings forth the thoughts and sets them bare to the light
of day for those who need but a little reminding to enable them to discern the
inward and hidden through the outward and visible. . . .

Then the President rises and sings a hymn composed as an address to God,
either a new one of his own composition or an old one by poets of an earlier day. . . .
After him all the others take their turn as they are arranged and in the proper order
while all the rest listen in complete silence except when they have to chant the
closing lines or refrains, for then they all lift up their voices, men and women
alike. . . .

After the supper they hold the sacred vigil which is conducted in the following
way. They rise up all together and standing in the middle of the refectory form
themselves first into two choirs, one of men and one of women. . . . Then when each
choir has separately done its own part in the feast, having drunk as in the Bacchic
rites of the strong wine of God's love they mix and both together become a single
choir, a copy of the choir set up of old beside the Red Sea in honour of the wonders
there wrought. . . . Thus they continue till dawn, drunk with this drunkenness in
which there is no shame, then not with heavy heads or drowsy eyes but more alert
and wakeful than when they came to the banquet, they stand with their faces and
whole body turned to the east and when they see the sun rising they stretch their
hands up to heaven and pray for bright days and knowledge of the truth and the
power of keen sighted thinking. And after the prayers they depart each to his

private sanctuary once more to ply the trade and till the field of their wonted philosophy.

Philo (first century CE), *The Contemplative Life*, selections from 28-30, 65, 68-69, 73, 75, 78, 80-81, 83, 85, 89 (LCL)

82. A certain Jew named Apollos, an Alexandrian by birth and an educated man, arrived in Ephesus and interpreted the scriptures powerfully. Having been taught the way of the Lord and seething with the spirit, he spoke and taught accurately the things about Jesus while knowing only the baptism of John. He began to speak publicly in the synagogue. When Priscilla and Aquila heard him they took him aside and explained the way of God more accurately to him. When he wanted to come over to Achaia, the brethren encouraged him and wrote to the disciples to receive him.

Acts 18:24-27 (late first century CE)

83. There were once some highwaymen in the neighbourhood of R. Meir who caused him a great deal of trouble. R. Meir accordingly prayed that they should die. His wife Beruria said to him: How do you make out [that such a prayer should be permitted]? Because it is written Let hatta'im (sins) cease? Is it written hot'im (sinners)? It is written hatta'im (sins)! Further, look at the end of the verse: and let the wicked men be no more. Since the sins will cease, there will be no more wicked men! Rather pray for them that they should repent, and there will be no more wicked. He did pray for them, and they repented.

b Berakoth 10a (not recorded until after 400, though Beruria lived in the early second century) (BT).

84. And while Paul was thus speaking in the midst of the assembly in the house of Onesiphorus, a virgin (named) Thecla—her mother was Theocleia,—who was betrothed to a man (named) Thamyris, sat at a near-by window and listened night and day to the word of the virgin life as it was spoken by Paul; and she did not turn away from the window, but pressed on in the faith rejoicing exceedingly. Moreover, when she saw many women and virgins going in to Paul she desired to be counted worthy herself to stand in Paul's presence and hear the word of Christ; for she had not yet seen Paul in person, but only heard his word. . . . [Accused by her mother of deserting her betrothed, she is condemned, miraculously saved from burning, flees to Paul, and is then arrested for rejecting another man.]

And the governor sent soldiers to fetch Thecla. . . . They sent in many beasts, while she stood and stretched out her hands and prayed. And when she had finished her prayer, she turned and saw a great pit full of water, and said: "Now is the time for me to wash." And she threw herself in, saying: "In the name of Jesus Christ I baptize myself on the last day!" And when they saw it, the women and all the people wept, saying: "Cast not thyself into the water!"; so that even the governor wept that such beauty should be devoured by seals. So, then, she threw herself into the water in the name of Jesus Christ; but the seals, seeing the light of a lightning-flash, floated dead on the surface. And there was about her a cloud of fire, so that neither could the beasts touch her nor could she be seen naked. . . .

And the governor summoned Thecla from among the beasts, and said to her: "Who art thou? And what hast thou about thee, that not one of the beasts touched thee?" She answered: "I am a handmaid of the living God. As to what I have about me, I have believed in him in whom God is well pleased, His Son. For this sake not one of the beasts touched me. For he alone is the goal of salvation and the foundation of immortal life. To the storm-tossed he is a refuge, to the oppressed relief, to the despairing shelter; in a word, whoever does not believe in him shall not live, but die for ever. . . .

And straightway the governor issued a decree, saying: "I release to you Thecla, the pious handmaid of God." But all the women cried out with a loud voice, and as with one mouth gave praise to God, saying: "One is God, who has delivered Thecla!", so that all the city was shaken by the sound. And Tryphaena when she was told the good news came. . . . So Thecla went in with her and rested in her house for eight days, instructing her in the word of God, so that the majority of the maidservants also believed; and there was great joy in the house.

But Thecla yearned for Paul and sought after him, sending in every direction. And it was reported to her that he was in Myra. So she took young men and maidservants and girded herself, and sewed her mantle into a cloak after the fashion of men, and went off to Myra, and found Paul speaking the word of God. . . . And Thecla arose and said to Paul: "I am going to Iconium." But Paul said: "Go and teach the word of God!" . . . And when she had borne this witness she went away to Seleucia; and after enlightening many with the word of God she slept with a noble sleep.

> *Acts of Paul and Thecla* (second century CE) 7, 31, 33-34, 37-38, 40-41, 43 (NTA)

85. A viper of the Cainite heresy [Quintilla?], lately conversant in this quarter, has carried away a great number with her most venomous doctrine, making it her first aim to destroy baptism. . . .

The woman of pertness, who has usurped the power to teach, will of course not give birth for herself likewise to a right of baptizing. . . . But if the writings which wrongly go under Paul's name, claim Thecla's example as a license for women's teaching and baptizing, let them know that, in Asia, the presbyter who composed that writing, as if he were augmenting Paul's fame from his own store, after being convicted, and confessing that he had done it from love of Paul, was removed from his office. For how credible would it seem, that he who has not permitted a woman even to learn with overboldness, should give a female the power of teaching and of baptizing! "Let them be silent," he says, "and at home consult their own husbands."

> Tertullian (c 145–220 CE), *On Baptism*, 1 and 17 (ANF)

86. The Holy Ghost had even then forseen that there would be a certain virgin (called) Philumene an angel of deceit, "transformed into an angel of light," by whose miracles and illusions Apelles was led (when) he introduced his new heresy. . . .

Apelles . . . is far from being "one of the old school," like his instructor and moulder, Marcion; he rather forsook the continence of Marcion by resorting to the company of a woman, and withdrew to Alexandria, out of sight of his most abstemious master. Returning therefrom, after some years, unimproved, except that he was no longer a Marcionite, he clave to another woman, the maiden Philumene (whom we have already mentioned), who herself afterwards became an enormous prostitute. Having been imposed on by her vigorous spirit, he committed to writing the revelations which he had learned of her. Persons are still living who remember them, — their own actual disciples and successors, — who cannot therefore deny the lateness of their date.

Tertullian, *On Prescription Against Heretics* 6 and 30 (ANF)

87. Peter said to Mary, "Sister, we know that the Savior loved you more than the rest of women. Tell us the words of the Savior which you remember — which you know (but) we do not, nor have we heard them." Mary answered and said, "What is hidden from you I will proclaim to you." And she began to speak to them these words: "I," she said, "I saw the Lord in a vision and I said to him, 'Lord, I saw you today in a vision.' He answered and said to me, 'Blessed are you, that you did not waver at the sight of me. For where the mind is, there is the treasure.' I said to him, 'Lord, now does he who sees the vision see it ‹through› the soul ‹or› through the spirit?' The Savior answered and said, 'He does not see through the soul nor through the spirit, but the mind which [is] between the two — that is [what] sees the vision and it is. . . .' [four pages are missing here, and the text begins again in the middle of a vision account, which soon ends:]

"When the soul had overcome the third power, it went upwards and saw the fourth power, (which) took seven forms. The first form is darkness, the second desire, the third ignorance, the fourth is the excitement of death, the fifth is the kingdom of the flesh, the sixth is the foolish wisdom of flesh, the seventh is the wrathful wisdom. These are the seven [powers] of wrath. They ask the soul, 'Whence do you come, slayer of men, or where are you going, conqueror of space?' The soul answered and said, 'What binds me has been slain, and what turns me about has been overcome, and my desire has been ended, and ignorance has died. In a [world] I was released from a world, [and] in a type from a heavenly type, and (from) the fetter of oblivion which is transient. From this time on will I attain to the rest of the time, of the season, of the aeon, in silence.'"

When Mary had said this, she fell silent, since it was to this point that the Savior had spoken with her. But Andrew answered and said to the brethren, "Say what you (wish to) say about what she has said. I at least do not believe that the Savior said this." [A debate follows in which Levi defends to Peter her authority to teach them.]

The Gospel of Mary (A Greek fragment of this text survives from the early third century), Berlin Gnostic Codex 10,1-23; 16,1-14[28]

| Notes

Chapter 1

1. Sarah B. Pomeroy, *Goddesses, Whores, Wives and Slaves: Women in Classical Antiquity* (New York: Schocken Books, 1975); idem, *Women in Hellenistic Egypt from Alexander to Cleopatra* (New York: Schocken Books, 1984); idem, "Selected Bibliography on Women in Classical Antiquity," *Women in the Ancient World: The Arethusa Papers,* ed. by J. Peradotto and J. P. Sullivan (Albany: State University of New York Press, 1984), 343–72; Ross S. Kraemer, "Women in the Religions of the Greco-Roman World," *Religious Studies Review* 9 (1983), 127–39. Collections of sources are also available: Mary Lefkowitz and Maureen B. Fant, eds., *Women's Life in Greece and Rome* (Baltimore: Johns Hopkins University Press, 1982); Ross S. Kraemer, *Maenads, Martyrs, Matrons, Monastics: A Sourcebook on Women's Religions in the Greco-Roman World* (Philadelphia: Fortress Press, 1988).

2. Adolf Harnack, "On the Inward Spread of Christianity: Among the Women," *Mission and Expansion of Christianity in the First Three Centuries,* Vol. 2, from 2nd rev. German ed. of 1906, tr. by James Moffatt (New York: G. P. Putnam's Sons, 1908, 74–84; for his full treatment see the 3rd and 4th expanded eds. of 1915 and 1924 available only in German); Leopold Zscharnack, *Der Dienst der Frau in den ersten Yahrhunderten der christlichen Kirche* (Göttingen: Vandenhoeck & Ruprecht, 1902); Klaus Thräde, "Ärger mit der Freiheit, Die Bedeutung von Frauen in Theorie und Praxis der alten Kirche," *"Freunde in Christus werden . . .": Die Beziehung von Mann und Frau als Frage an Theologie und Kirche* by Gerta Scharffenorth and Klaus Thräde (Gelnhausen/Berlin: Burckhardthaus-Verlag, 1977), 35–128; Elisabeth Schüssler Fiorenza, *In Memory of Her: A Feminist Theological Reconstruction of Christian Origins* (New York: Crossroad, 1983).

3. Else Kähler, *Die Frau in den paulinischen Briefen unter besonderer Berück-sichtigung des Begriffes der Unterordnung* (Zürich: Gotthelf-Verlag, 1960); Elisabeth Schüssler Fiorenza, "Women in the Pre-pauline and Pauline Churches," *USQR* 33 (1978), 153–66; idem, *In Memory of Her,* 160–241; Margaret Y. MacDonald, *The Pauline Churches: A Socio-Historical Study of Institutionalization in the Pauline and Deutero-Pauline Writings* (Cambridge: Cambridge University Press, 1988).

4. This process has now begun in a study on the women's reception of Paul's letter to the Philippians in the context of women's cultural experience in that city: Lilian Portefaix, *Sisters Rejoice: Paul's Letter to the Philippians and Luke-Acts as Seen by First-century Philippian Women* (Stockholm: Almqvist & Wiksell International, 1988).

5. Gerd Theissen, "The Sociological Interpretation of Religious Traditions: Its Methodological Problems as Exemplified in Early Christianity," *The Social Setting*

of Pauline Christianity: Essays on Corinth, ed. by John H. Schütz (Philadelphia: Fortress Press, 1982), 175–200 (from German: *Kairos* 17 [1975], 284–99).

6. See Appendix 1 on Rhetorical Criticism. The classics in Pauline studies are Johannes Weiss, "Beiträge zur paulinischen Rhetorik," *Theologische Studien* (Festschrift B. Weiss, [Göttingen: Vandenhoeck & Ruprecht, 1897], 165–247) and Rudolf Bultmann, *Der Stil der paulinischen Predigt und die kynisch-stoische Diatribe* (Göttingen: Vandenhoeck & Ruprecht, 1910).

7. Strabo, *Geography,* 14.5. 13–15; Dio Chrysostom, *Orations* 34. 22–23.

8. Chaim Perelman and L. Olbrechts-Tyteca, *The New Rhetoric: A Treatise on Argumentation* (Notre Dame: University of Notre Dame Press, 1969; French, 1958) and the more recent summary volume, Chaim Perelman, *The Realm of Rhetoric* (Notre Dame: University of Notre Dame Press, 1982).

9. William Brandt, *The Rhetoric of Argumentation* (Indianapolis: Bobbs-Merrill, 1970), 49–69.

10. Perelman and Olbrechts-Tyteca, *The New Rhetoric,* 4.

11. Perelman and Olbrechts-Tyteca, *The New Rhetoric,* 491. See also Lloyd F. Bitzer's "The Rhetorical Situation," *Philosophy and Rhetoric* 1 (1968), 1–14.

12. However this method does press the interpreter to determine what is the dominant form of persuasion being exercised. See reference to the debate on the rhetorical genre of 1 Corinthians in Appendix 1.

13. For a general introduction to reader-response criticism through essays by some of its key practitioners see two collections. Jane P. Tompkins, ed., *Reader-Response Criticism: From Formalism to Post-Structuralism* (Baltimore: Johns Hopkins University Press, 1980), and Susan Suleiman and Inge Crosman, eds., *The Reader in the Text: Essays on Audience and Interpretation* (Princeton: Princeton University Press, 1980).

14. Jerome Murphy-O'Connor, *St. Paul's Corinth: Texts and Archeology* (Wilmington, Del.: Michael Glazier, 1983).

15. Theissen, "The Sociological Interpretation of Religious Traditions."

16. Victor W. Turner, *The Ritual Process: Structure and Anti-Structure* (Chicago: Aldine Publishing, 1969); Bruce Lincoln, *Emerging from the Chrysalis: Studies in Rituals of Women's Initiation* (Cambridge: Harvard University Press, 1981).

17. Mary Douglas, *Natural Symbols: Explorations in Cosmology,* 2d rev. ed. (Harmondsworth, Eng. and New York: Penguin Books, 1973), 119–31.

18. *Natural Symbols,* and *Cultural Bias* (Occasional Paper No. 35 of the Royal Anthropological Institute of Great Britain and Ireland, 1978).

19. Bruce J. Malina, *The New Testament World: Insights from Cultural Anthropology* (Atlanta: John Knox Press, 1981), 25–50.

20. Wayne A. Meeks, *The First Urban Christians: The Social World of the Apostle Paul* (New Haven and London: Yale University Press, 1983), 75–94; Schüssler Fiorenza, *In Memory of Her,* 160–84.

21. This distinction between textual and structural rhetoric is adapted with changes from Brandt, *The Rhetoric of Argumentation,* 19–23, 99–116.

22. See Appendix 1 and the following summary statements in Perelman and Olbrechts-Tyteca, *The New Rhetoric,* 190–92, and Perelman, *The Realm of Rhetoric,* 48–53.

23. Michael Polanyi, *The Tacit Dimension* (Garden City, N.Y.: Doubleday, 1966).

24. Ferdinand Christian Baur, "Die Christuspartei in der korinthischen Gemeinde, der Gegensatz des petrinischen und paulinischen Christentums in der alten Kirche," *Tübingen Zeitschrift für Theologie* (1831), 61–136; reprinted in *Ausgewählte Werke in Einzelausgaben,* ed. by Klaus Scholder (Stuttgart, Bad Cannstadt: Friedrich Frommann Verlag [Günther Holzboog], 1963, Vol. 1, 1–76); Johannes Weiss, *Der erste Korintherbrief* (Göttingen: Vandenhoeck & Ruprecht, 1910); Hans Conzelmann, *I Corinthians: A Commentary on the First Epistle to the Corinthians* (Philadelphia: Fortress Press, 1975; from 1st German ed., 1969).

25. For example, Graham Shaw, *The Cost of Authority: Manipulation and Freedom in the New Testament* (Philadelphia: Fortress Press, 1982), 62–100 focuses on Paul's argument as manipulation. Isabel Carter Heyward in *The Redemption of God: A Theology of Mutual Relation* (Lanham, Md.: University Press of America, 1982, 25–71), chooses to ignore Paul in her re-imaging of Jesus.

Chapter 2

1. Paul wrote these sentences in the singular, challenging any individual to respond. His address is generic, the particle "any" being both masculine and feminine and appearing as usual with masculine modifiers. To avoid "he or she thinks himself or herself to be . . . ," I reluctantly substitute the plural.

2. "These things" apparently refers back to Paul's silencing of uninterpreted tongues, simultaneous prophecy, and women in the church. See the excursus on 14:34-35 in chapter 7 defending Paul's authorship of this passage.

3. To gauge Paul's general rhetorical style and point of view I limit myself to the letters almost universally attributed to him at the present time: Romans, 1 and 2 Corinthians, Galatians, Philippians, 1 Thessalonians, and Philemon.

4. Chaim Perelman and L. Olbrechts-Tyteca, *The New Rhetoric: A Treatise on Argumentation* (Notre Dame: University of Notre Dame Press, 1969; French, 1958) 8, discuss the line where language crosses over from persuasion to magical action.

5. See below, Argument from Universal Church Practice.

6. When Paul says, "Bear each others' burdens and so fulfill Christ's law" (Gal. 6:2), he is probably referring back to his preceding statement, "The whole law is fulfilled in one word, love your neighbor as yourself" (Gal. 5:14), rather than speaking of a command of Jesus or a revelation from the risen Christ.

7. On divorce: Mark 10:9, 11-12; Matt. 5:32; 19:9; Luke 16:18; on financial support: Matt. 10:10c; Luke 10:7.

8. There are indications elsewhere that Christ's exaltation is to the glory of God (Phil. 2:11), but there is no statement that Christ is subordinated to God.

Chapter 3

1. See chapter 4 under "Judicious Rhetoric" concerning how Paul responds to their letters and the implications of this for understanding their letter topics that he takes up.

2. See Appendix 6 on Wisdom, especially B. Fjärstedt, *Synoptic Tradition in First Corinthians: Themes and Clusters of Theme Words in 1 Cor. 1–4 and 9* (Uppsala: Teologiska Institutionen, 1974), 104–5, 133–35.

3. Norman Young provides a review of the primary evidence. He notes that girls are attested sharing their brothers' paidagogos, but seldom in Greek culture, and in Roman society the arrangement is overwhelmingly for the care of minor males ("Paidagogos: The Social Setting of a Pauline Metaphor," *Novum Testamentum* 29 [1987], 150–76).

4. This departs from contrary views of Käsemann and Schweizer as described in Appendix 5 on Apollos.

5. See chapter 6.

6. This is the position presented in Helmut Köster's review of Hans Windisch, *Weisheit und Torheit* in *Gnomon* 33 (1969), 590–95. See Appendix 6 on Wisdom.

7. For a reading of the 1 Corinthians opponents in the light of Philo's exegesis of Gen. 2:7 in *The Allegorical Interpretation* I 38, III 161, see Birger Pearson's *The Pneumatikos-Psychikos Terminology in 1 Corinthians* (Missoula, Mont.: Society of Biblical Literature, 1973).

8. This effort is supported by a new study of Paul's theology in Romans by E. Elizabeth Johnson called *The Function of Apocalyptic and Wisdom Traditions in Romans 9–11* (Atlanta: Scholars Press, 1989).

9. Modern sociologists widely agree that multiple factors must be considered in any determination of social status, and that status is always a socially perceived phenomenon. One model proposes twenty factors under the five broad headings of demography, associations, influence, culture, and social-psychology (Thomas Lasswell, *Class and Stratum: An Introduction to Concepts and Research* [Boston: Houghton Mifflin, 1965], 3–97, 482). Although there is continuing interest in trying to develop a cumulative or general index of social status as first seen in W. Lloyd Warner and associates' Index of Status Characteristics, there is more concern to deal with factors separately to observe inconsistencies between status factors or to specify the different consequences of change for the same variable (W. Lloyd Warner, Marcia Meeker, and Kenneth Eells, *Social Class in America: Manual of Procedure for the Measurement of Social Status* [New York: Harper & Row, 1969]; Gerald E. Lenski, "Status Crystallization: A Non-Vertical Dimension of Social Status," *American Sociological Review* 19 [1954], 405–13); Robert Hodge, "Social Integration, Psychological Well-Being and Their Socio-Economic Correlates," *Social Stratification: Research and Theory for the 1970's* [ed., E. O. Laumann, Indianapolis: Bobbs-Merrill, 1970], 182–206). The greatest difficulty in adapting methods from sociology for work with texts is that sociology assumes it is possible to test and retest hypotheses in social settings, whereas historians must fashion other tests (Peter Burke, *Sociology and History* [London: George Allen & Unwin, 1980]; G. Theissen, "The Sociological Interpretation of Religious Traditions: Methodological Problems Exemplified in Early Christianity," *The Social Setting of Pauline Christianity: Essays on Corinth* [Philadelphia: Fortress Press, 1982], 175–200). My hypothesis is that rhetorical analysis can sufficiently reconstitute the rhetorical situation in which certain texts were produced so that status determinations can be made, using as control what other texts have taught us about the society in question. I see this excursus falling in the category of small scale investigations recently called for by E. A. Judge and R. Rohrbaugh, although in contrast

to Rohrbaugh I use relational categories to observe social-status mobility broadly conceived rather than to observe economic-political class (E. A. Judge, "The Social Identity of the First Christians: A Question of Method in Religious History," *JRH* 11 [1980], 201–17; R. Rohrbaugh, "Methodological Considerations in the Debate over the Social Class Status of Early Christians," *JAAR* 50 [1984], 519–46). See also note 18.

10. Josephus, *Antiquities of the Jews* XX 34–38, 195; Luke 8:3; Acts 3:50; 17:4.

11. *Antiquities of the Jews* XII 119–28; XIV 213–67; XVI 16–26, 167–73. On the alliance with Rome see Geza Vermes, "Ancient Rome in Post-Biblical Jewish Literature," *Post-Biblical Jewish Studies* (Leiden: E. J. Brill, 1975), 215–24.

12. Pausanius, *Description of Greece*, II 3, 6–7.

13. This is indicated, for example, in Claudius's Edict to the Alexandrians in H. I. Bell, *Jews and Christians in Egypt: The Jewish Troubles in Alexandria and the Athanasian Controversy* (Oxford: Oxford University Press, 1924), 23–29. See also Philo's historical works, *Flaccus* and *Embassy to Gaius*, and Luke's Acts 18:12–17.

14. This is evident in the person of Josephus himself (*Life* 414–30; *Against Apion* I 50–51) as well as in what he says about the restoration of Jewish rights in some Hellenistic cities after the Jewish War and the resistance of some Jews to remnant revolutionary movements (*Jewish War* VII 111, 411–16, 45–50).

15. Thomas Wiedemann, *Greek and Roman Slavery* (Baltimore: Johns Hopkins University Press, 1981), 5–6; W. L. Westermann, "Sklaverei," *Real-Encyclopädie für Altertumswissenschaft* (eds., Pauly-Wissowa, Supplement Vol. VI, Stuttgart, 1935), 894–95, 931–32, 934, cf. 1002; M. I. Finley, *Ancient Slavery and Modern Ideology* (New York: Viking Press, 1980), 80. Beloch, known for conservative estimates of slave population, proposes 280,000 slaves to 520,000 free for Rome in 5 CE (J. Beloch, *Die Bevölkerung der griechisch-römischen Welt* [Leipzig, 1886], 95ff, as quoted in a useful summary of research by Ulf-Rainer Kugler, "Die Paränese an die Sklaven als Modell Urchristlicher Sozialethik," Diss. Erlangen, 1977, 40–441, 290). Galen notes two free adults per slave for Pergamum in the second century CE (Westermann, *RE* Supp. Vol. VI, 999).

16. See chapter 4 and its notes 2 and 3.

17. See Sarah B. Pomeroy, *Goddesses,* 140; idem, "Infanticide in Hellenistic Greece," *Images of Women in Antiquity* (A. Cameron and A. Kuhrt, eds., London, 1983), 207–22.

18. The classical theorists of twentieth-century social mobility study—Pareto, Sorokin, and Keller—reacted against Marx by focusing primarily on the rise and fall of elites seen as the superior leaders in large societies (Vilfredo Pareto, *The Rise and Fall of Elites: An Application of Theoretical Sociology* [1901, reprinted by Bedminster, 1968]; Pitirim Sorokin, *Social Mobility* [1927, revised and reprinted as *Social and Cultural Mobility,* New York: Free Press, 1959]; Suzanne Keller, *Beyond the Ruling Class: Strategic Elites in Modern Society* [New York: Random House, 1963]). Some American studies have contested the functionalist assumption that superior talent rises or that occupation is its best gauge. They call for study of social mobility that separately controls visible mobility and class interest, that deals with varying sets of interrelated mobile factors, and that is observant of the way social institutions are used by those in power to control upward mobility (M. Tumin, "On Inequality," *American Sociological Review* 28 [1962], 25; S. M. Miller, "The Concept and

Measurement of Mobility," and K. U. Mayer and W. Mueller, "Progress in Social Mobility Research?" *Social Mobility*, ed. by A. P. M. Coxon and C. L. Jones (Penguin Books, 1975); Carson McGuire, "Social Stratification and Mobility Patterns," *American Sociological Review* 15 [1950], 195–204). I have yet found only scattered studies on cross-mobility in small groups that have any relevance for the study of Corinth's church (H. Kelley, "Communication in Experimentally Created Hierarchies," *Human Relations* 4 [1951], 39–56; Arthur R. Cohen, "Upward Communication in Experimentally Created Hierarchies," *Human Relations* 11 [1958], 41–53).

19. See Gerd Theissen's careful study of this group, unfortunately taken by him to be more representative of the church leaders at large than the letter supports, in "Social Stratification in the Corinthian Community" (*The Social Setting of Pauline Christianity: Essays on Corinth* ed. by J. H. Schütz, Philadelphia: Fortress Press, 1982], 69–119).

20. The poignancy of this is reflected in the Jewish prayer said to be quoted by a mid-second-century CE rabbi, "Blessed art thou, who did not make me a Gentile. Blessed art thou, who did not make me a woman. Blessed art thou, who did not make me a slave" (*Tosefta Ber.* 7.18; *j. Ber.* 9.1.13; *b. Menach.* 43b).

21. For a statement of some general implications of my study of the Corinthian women prophets, see chapter 9.

22. Other Jews escaped these restrictions by renouncing their Judaism, for example, Antiochus of Antioch (Josephus, *Jewish War* VII 46–53) and Tiberius Alexander of Alexandria, nephew of Philo (*Jewish War* II 220, 309, and VI 237; *Antiquities* XX 100 3).

23. Philo, *Life of Moses* I 148–59, trans. by F. H. Colson for the Loeb Classical Library edition of Philo Vol. 6 (Cambridge, Mass.: Harvard University Press and London: William Heinemann, 1966, 353–59). Compare Philo's allegorical interpretation of Rebecca going down to the spring to fill her pitcher and coming up again as giving up self-conceit and being carried by virtue to the heights of fame, *The Posterity and Exile of Cain* 136.

24. The social and economic changes in the first two hundred years of the empire have been studied from many different vantage points. Rostovtzeff and Oertel emphasize particularly the expansion of trade and commerce in the Roman East, which Rome made no effort to regulate beyond collecting border taxes. Soldiers are cultivated by Augustus as a key class and freedmen multiply in numbers and economic significance. H. H. Scullard traces how the rising new families of wealth are gradually granted senatorial status while Rome draws its skilled doctors and teachers from the East. Edith Hamilton describes the increasing insecurity of the old ruling families as wealth and imperial connections come to be the primary basis of power (M. I. Rostovtzeff, *Social and Economic History of the Roman Empire*, Vol 1 [Oxford: Clarendon Press, 1926], 48–105; F. Oertel, "The Economic Unification of the Mediterranean Region: Industry, Trade and Commerce," *CAH*, Vol. 10. ed. by S. A. Cook, F. E. Adcock, and M. P. Charlesworth [Cambridge: Cambridge University Press, 1928–64], 382–403, 412–24; H. H. Scullard, *From the Gracci to Nero* [London: Methuen & Co., 1959], 333–356; Edith Hamilton, *The Roman Way to Western Civilization* [New York: Mentor Books, 1957], 99–109).

25. Seneca, *Moral Epistles to Lucilium* XLVII 9, LXXXVI 7; Juvenal, *Satires* III and VI; Jas. 4:13; *Gospel of Thomas*, logia 64 and 95.

Chapter 4

1. Sarah B. Pomeroy, *Goddesses, Whores, Wives and Slaves: Women in Classical Antiquity* (New York: Schocken Books, 1975), 126–127, 151; Mary R. Lefkowitz and Maureen B. Fant, *Women's Life in Greece and Rome* (Baltimore: Johns Hopkins, 1982), sections 76, 78, 80, 82, 83, 200, 202; cf. 205.

2. Plato, *Laws* 785B, 833C–D; cf., *Republic* 460E; Xenophon, *Oeconomicus* 7.5; Pomeroy, *Goddesses,* 64; Gerhard Delling, *Paulus' Stellung zu Frau und Ehe* (Stuttgart: W. Kohlhammer, 1931), 37 and n. 349.

3. J. Laurence Angel, "Ecology and Population in the Eastern Mediterranean," *World Archaeology* 4 (1972), 88–105, Table 28, as cited in Pomeroy, *Goddesses,* 169.

4. Ibid., 127–30.

5. Not only does Paul's opening line in chapter 7 indicate that he has received these topics in written form, but the same may be reflected in 1 Thessalonians 4 where Paul addresses the topic of "those who have fallen asleep" and notes that they do not need for him to write on the topics of brotherly love and of periods and times (1 Thess. 4:9, 13; 5:1). This reading of Paul's phrase, "concerning . . . ," to refer to letter topics is not excluded by two studies just available in this area, but it will need review: Ernst Baasland, "Die περί-Formel und die Argumentation(situation) des Paulus," *ST* 42 (1988), 69–87; Margaret M. Mitchell, "Concerning ΠΕΡΙ ΔΕ in 1 Corinthians," *NovT* 31 (1989), 229–56.

6. Hurd makes this useful observation about Paul's change in tone between sections of the letter responding to oral reports and those responding to the Corinthians' letter (John C. Hurd, Jr., *The Origin of 1 Corinthians,* 2d ed. [Macon, Ga.: Mercer Univ. Press, 1983], 74, 82). But it does not follow that Paul is turning from one group to speak to another. In fact the same confident group is addressed throughout. Perhaps in the oral news he got alarmist tales about them and in the letter he got strong assertions from them.

7. H. Strathmann, *Geschichte der frühchristlichen Askese, bis zur Entstehung des Mönchtums im religionsgeschichtlichen Zusammenhange,* I. *Die Askese in der Umgebung des werdenden Christentums* (Leipzig: A. Deichter'sche Verlagsbuchhandlung Werner Scholl, 1914), 206–208.

8. F. Blass and A. Debrunner, *A Greek Grammar of the New Testament and Other Early Christian Literature,* trans. and rev. by R. W. Funk (Chicago: University of Chicago Press, 1961), § 373[3], allows that ἐάν with the aorist subjunctive in the NT can occasionally refer to a condition impending in the past, but this occurs in sentences using past tenses in the main clause.

9. Josephus, *Jewish War* II 560; *Antiquities of the Jews* XX 34–35, 38, 195; Luke 8:3; Acts 16:14; 17:4, 12, 34; 24:24.

10. Only this reading takes with full seriousness both the adversative and intensive particles in the parenthetical 7:21b, and the explanatory particle in 7:22, which refers back to what precedes the parenthesis.

11. F. Blass and A. Debrunner, *A Grammar of the Greek New Testament,* § 399.1.

12. The Greek does not distinguish whether the third-person singular verb is masculine or feminine. The adjective means literally "ripe." Concerning a feminine reading see *Mishna,* Niddah 5, 7. A third alternative translation should be considered, "if she is pregnant, and so it needs to happen . . . let them marry."

13. This noun can mean either "will" in the broad sense or "sexual desire" (see John 1:13). The latter fits this context better.

14. The feminine article before the noun does not appear in 7:28 in all manuscripts, but it is uncontested in 7:36, 37, and 38. The only male "virgins" that appear in the surviving first-century Christian literature are the 144,000 of Revelation 14:4 who follow the Lamb in John of Patmos's apocalyptic vision, hardly a description of daily sexual behavior.

15. Pomeroy, *Goddesses,* 140 and note. See also Sarah B. Pomeroy, "Infanticide in Hellenistic Greece," *Images of Women in Antiquity,* A. Cameron and A. Kuhrt, eds. (London, 1983), 207–22, where statistics drawn from The Delphinion inscriptions in Miletus are evaluated.

16. The variety of readings in the manuscript tradition of the words here signifying the women caution us against putting any great interpretive weight on these terms.

17. Philo, *On The Contemplative Life,* 11–12, 25–29, 32–33, 68, 78, 83–89 (see Selected Texts, no. 81).

18. H. Strathmann, *Geschichte der frühchristlichen Askese,* I, 199–205.

19. Ibid., 188, 212–215.

20. The "both . . . and" form does not appear in all manuscripts, but is more likely to have been dropped than added in transmission. The meaning would not be significantly different without the word signifying "both."

Chapter 5

1. See chapter 4 above on 7:1 for the evidence that "concerning . . ." marks a topic in a letter Paul is answering, also for a proposal on the nature of that letter. A good introduction to the phenomenon of sacrifice to gods and goddesses is provided in C. K. Barrett's, "Things Sacrificed to Idols," *NTS* 11 (1964–65), 138–53. Paul's argument on this issue in 1 Corinthians is analyzed by John C. Hurd, Jr., in *The Origin of I Corinthians,* 2nd ed. (Macon, Ga.: Mercer University Press, 1983), 115–49, and more recently by Wendell Lee Willis in *Idol Meat in Corinth: The Pauline Argument in I Corinthians 8 and 10* (Chico, Ca.: Scholars Press, 1985).

2. Discussions of this passage often set these two reasons for exclusive commitment at odds, usually in order to favor Paul's argument from the common good and to defend him against charges of a magical view of violating God. But Paul uses both arguments, and the issue that interests him is not this dichotomy but the defense in whatever way of full and exclusive participation in Christ. A different analysis of these issues is found in Hans Freiherr von Soden's "Sacrament and Ethics in Paul," available in the full German text most readily in K. H. Rengstorf, ed., *Das Paulusbild in der neueren deutschen Forschung* (Darmstadt: Wissenschaftliche Buchgesellschaft, 1964), 338–79, translated into English in abridged form in *The Writings of St. Paul,* ed. by Wayne A. Meeks (New York: W. W. Norton, 1972), 257–68.

3. Philo, *Flaccus* 89; *On the Special Laws* III 169.

4. On flute girls: Plato, *Symposium* 176e, 212d; Xenophon, *Symposium* II 1–23 (the wives mentioned in II 3 are apparently not present: IV 8, IX 7); on actresses:

ibid. IX 1–7; on courtesans: Athanaeus, *The Deipnosophists* XIII 588d. For other references and analysis see Kathleen E. Corley, "Were the Women around Jesus Really Prostitutes? Women in the Context of Greco-Roman Meals," *Society of Biblical Literature 1989 Seminar Papers,* ed. by David J. Lull (Atlanta, Ga.: Scholars Press, 1989), 487–521.

5. Juvenal, *Satire* VI 1–20, 242–45, 346–54, 398–412; Columella, *On Agriculture* XII Preface 9.

6. Pauly-Wissowa, "Kochkunst," *Real-Encyclopädie der classischen Altertumswissenschaft* 11 (Stuttgart: Metzler, 1921), 957. For some proposals on the significance of meat for the poor and the rich, see Gerd Theissen, "The Strong and the Weak in Corinth: A Sociological Analysis of a Theological Quarrel," *The Social Setting of Pauline Christianity* (Philadelphia: Fortress Press, 1982), 121–43. A caution may be in order on Theissen's thesis that the rich are used to meat and hence will be more likely to demand it. Sacrifice of privileges is also the prerogative of those who have them (8:18). Those who for social, economic, sexual, or other reasons have lacked privileges may have particular interest in demonstrating the prerogative that is no longer the exclusive domain of others.

7. An example: W. Dittenberger, *Sylloge Inscriptionum Graecarum* 1044 (Leipzig: S. Hirzel, 1920; 4th unchanged ed., Hildesheim: G. Olms, 1960).

8. Apuleius, *Metamorphoses* XI 9–10; Pausanius, *Description of Greece*, II 2.7; Lewis Richard Farnell, *The Cults of the Greek States* Vols. II and III (Oxford: Clarendon Press, 1896 and 1907); idem, "Sociological hypotheses concerning the position of women in ancient religion," *Archiv für Religionswissenschaft,* Vol. 7, 1904, ed. by T. Achelis and A. Dieterich, (Tübingen and Leipzig: J. C. B. Mohr), 70–94; Françoise Dunand, *Le culte d'Isis dans le bassin oriental de la Méditerranée* (Leiden: E. J. Brill, 1973), Vol. 2, 168–70, Vol. 3, 163–67, 314–17.

9. Wis. 14:22–28; Philo, *The Contemplative Life,* 50–52, 59–62; Athanaeus, *The Deipnosophists* XIII 588d.

10. John C. Hurd, Jr., in *The Origin of I Corinthians,* 235–37, gives a concise argument for 2 Corinthians 6:14 — 7:1 as a fragment of Paul's pre-1 Corinthians letter. Hans Dieter Betz proposes non-Pauline authorship: "2 Cor 6:14 — 7:1: An Anti-Pauline Fragment?" *JBL* 92 (1973), 88–108. Each reviews the history of research.

11. Idem, 97–98; Elisabeth Schüssler Fiorenza, *In Memory of Her: A Feminist Theological Reconstruction of Christian Origins* (New York: Crossroad, 1983), 194–96.

12. For examples see Athanaeus, *The Deipnosophists* XIV 658–62d; Menander, *Dyskolos,* 393–963, *Aspis,* 216–33, W. G. Arnott, ed., (Loeb Classical Library; Cambridge. Mass.: Harvard University Press and London: William Heinemann, 1979). On this phenomenon see also Pauly-Wissowa, "Kochkunst," *REA* 11, 953–55, 966, and E. M. Rankin, *The Role of the Mageiroi in the Life of the Ancient Greeks* (Chicago: University of Chicago Press, 1907), 55–68, 71.

13. Pauly-Wissowa, "Kochkunst," *REA* 11, 948–49, 955–56.

14. Athanaeus, *The Deipnosophists* VI 275.

15. Philo, *On the Contemplative Life,* 48–56.

16. Pauly-Wissowa, "Kochkunst," *REA* 11, 978.

17. Strabo, *Geography* 8, 6, 23.

18. Pliny, *Natural History* XVIII xxviii 107–108; Pauly-Wissowa, "Kochkunst," *REA* 11, 948–49, 955–56.

19. Columella, *On Agriculture* XII i–iii.

20. Jerome Murphy-O'Connor, *St. Paul's Corinth*, 156; cf. Pauly-Wissowa, "Kochkunst," *REA* 11, 980.

21. Although little attention has been paid to the issue of who prepares the food, several recent studies propose a differential treatment of guests according to wealth or status: Gerd Theissen, "Social Integration and Sacramental Activity," *Social Setting*, 145–63; Jerome Murphy-O'Connor, *St. Paul's Corinth*, 153–64.

22. Xenophon, *Memorabilia of Socrates* III 14, 1; Athanaeus, *The Deipnosophists* VIII 365; Pauly-Wissowa, "Kochkunst," *REA* 11, 957.

23. Philo, *The Contemplative Life*, 40–47; Plutarch, *Table Talk* IV 6.

24. *The Community Rule* VI.

25. Philo, *The Contemplative Life*, 67–81.

Chapter 6

1. Strabo argues from the common knowledge that the women are more religious than men (*Geography*, 7.3.4). For Plutarch it is the lack of experience and information about life that qualifies the peasant girl to be a channel of the Delphic Apollo (*Oracles at Delphi*, 405CD). Simplicity and purity ensure that the songs of Sappho and the prophecies of the Sibyl are valid (397A). In general Plutarch considers a less rational nature more receptive to divine impressions and presentiments about the future, "like a tablet without writing" (*Obsolescence of Oracles*, 432CD).

2. This metaphorical meaning of *kephalē*, "head," has recently been demonstrated by Fitzmyer and Grudem to have been known usage in Paul's time. An earlier study by Scroggs argued that "head" here must mean "source" rather than "one having authority over" because the Greek did not use the word in the latter sense. However, Grudem's exhaustive study has shown that the majority of citations with this meaning are in the Septuagint and New Testament, suggesting Paul's possible dependence on the Jewish tradition (Joseph A. Fitzmyer, S.J., "Another Look at ΚΕΦΑΛΗ in 1 Corinthians 11:3," *NTS* 35 [1989], 503–11; W. Grudem, "Does κεφαλή ['Head'] Mean 'Source' or 'Authority' in Greek Literature? A Survey of 2,336 Examples," *Trinity Journal* 6 [1985], 38–59; Robin Scroggs, "Paul and the Eschatological Woman," *JAAR* 40 [1972], 283–303, and an update in the same journal, 42 [1974], 532–37).

3. See Appendix 8. On hairstyles and coverings in the Roman East, see note 13 below.

4. Jacob Jervell, *Imago Dei. Gen 1,26f im Spätjudentum, in der Gnosis und in den paulinischen Briefen* (Göttingen: Vandenhoeck & Ruprecht, 1960), 26–46, 84–112.

5. On further historical developments in this kind of exegesis see Elaine Pagels, *Adam, Eve and the Serpent* (New York: Random House, 1987).

6. Num. 12:8; Ps. 17:15 (LXX 16:15). תְּמוּנָה, more often translated ὁμοίωμα (likeness, form), is translated δόξα (glory) in reference to God.

7. Wis. 7:26; 9:9-11; *b Baba B* 58a; *Gen R* 8, 1 and 10; 12, 6; *Pirke R El* 4.4; *Eccles R* 8, 1–5; *Pesiqta* 4, 36a–38; J. Jervell, *Imago Dei*, 21; 38–40; 96–107; Johannes Weiss, *Der erste Korintherbrief* (Göttingen: Vandenhoeck & Ruprecht, 1910), 272, n. 3.

8. *j Ket* 11.3: "The wife of R. Jose, the Galilean, caused him much annoyance. R. La'azar went up to see him. He said to him: 'Rabbi, divorce her for she is not thy glory.' He replied: 'A great dowry is upon her.' R. La'azar said to him: 'I will give thee the dowry and do thou divorce her.' He gave him the dowry and he divorced her. She went and married the guardsman of the town. He was brought down from his wealth and became blind. And she was walking him about all the town, leading him. One time she took him all round the town and nothing was given to him. He said to her: 'Is there not here another neighbourhood?' She said to him: 'There is the neighbourhood of him who divorced me, but I cannot enter there.' He began to beat her. Just then R. Jose, the Galilean, passed by and heard them quarrelling in the street. He took them and put them into a house which was one of his own, and he also kept them in food as long as they lived." Translation by J. T. Marshall, *Manual of the Aramaic Language of the Palestinian Talmud* (Leiden: E. J. Brill, 1929), 184–85.

9. It is highly unlikely that Paul is requiring only married women to cover their heads. The lack of a definite article before "woman" in the phrase, "the head of a woman is the man," and before "man" in the phrase, "the woman is the glory of a man," can reflect Paul's drawing his sanctions from the marriage relationship. But when he says, "Each woman who prays and prophesies uncovered shames her head," he has generalized the instruction to all women. If she claims to have no husband, hence no "head," a father or even a son will suffice. To substitute the terms "husband" and "wife" for "man" and "woman" is a possible alternative translation of the Greek, but would not make sense in this text. For example, "Yet the wife is not apart from the husband nor the husband apart from the wife in the Lord; for just as the wife is [created] from the husband, so also the husband is [born] through the wife."

10. Rom. 1:21-23; 3:23-26; 5:1-5; 8:15-18; 1 Cor. 1:26-31; 2 Cor. 1:20-22; 3:18; 4:15.

11. This proposal is made by M. D. Hooker as the basis for a somewhat different interpretation of the chapter in "Authority on her Head: An Examination of I Cor XI," *NTS* 10 (1963–64), 414–15.

12. *Life of Adam and Eve* 13–17; *Gen R* 8, 10; *Eccles R* 6, 9, 1; J. Jervell, *Imago Dei*, 38–39, and 100; M. D. Hooker, "Authority," 415.

13. See Selected Texts, nos. 17, 84. For the full texts, *The Prayer and Confession of Aseneth* 15.1, *The Apocryphal Old Testament*, ed. by H. F. D. Sparks (Oxford: Clarendon Press, 1984), 488 (see chapter 7, n. 26, concerning title); *The Acts of Paul and Thecla* 40, *New Testament Apocrypha*, Vol 2, ed. by E. Hennecke and W. Schneemelcher (Philadelphia: Westminster Press, 1964), 363–64; see also *Acts of Thomas* 14, *New Testament Apocrypha*, Vol 2, 449–50.

14. Rom. 8:29; 1 Cor. 15:49; 2 Cor. 3:18; 4:4. The distinctiveness of 1 Corinthians 11:7 in Paul's thought is recognized by J. Jervell who reads it as a response to a Corinthian interpretation of Genesis 1:26-27 (*Imago Dei*, 231–32, 292–98).

15. Hans Dieter Betz, *Galatians: A Commentary on Paul's Letter to the*

Churches in Galatia (Philadelphia: Fortress Press, 1979), 181–85 and other literature mentioned there on pre-Pauline traditions, 185–201 on Paul's interpretation; Elisabeth Schüssler Fiorenza, *In Memory of Her: A Feminist Theological Reconstruction of Christian Origins,* (New York: Crossroad, 1983) 208 and n. 12, 237 on pre-Pauline tradition, 205–41 on Paul's use of it.

16. Jervell, *Imago Dei,* 107–9, 161–65; Wayne Meeks, "The Image of the Androgene: Some Uses of a Symbol in Earliest Christianity," *HR* 13 (1974), 165–208; Betz, *Galatians,* 197–200; Schüssler Fiorenza, *In Memory of Her,* 211–13; and most recently Dennis Ronald MacDonald, *There is No Male and Female: The Fate of a Dominical Saying in Paul and Gnosticism* (Philadelphia: Fortress Press, 1987), 14–63. I part with MacDonald's study only at the admittedly crucial point where he tries to prove the priority in the Christian baptismal tradition of a gnostic dominical saying affirming original androgyny over the social understanding of "not male and female" (113–26). Paul's subordination of sexual to ethnic social equality itself presupposes an earlier social function of the claim to be *not* male and female in Christ. His unquestionably social struggle with the women prophets in Corinth is good evidence of this.

17. Jervell, *Imago Dei,* 84–92.

18. On distinctive functions of shame and honor for male and female in Mediterranean culture, see Bruce Malina, *The New Testament World: Insights from Cultural Anthropology* (Atlanta: John Knox Press, 1981), 25–50, especially 42–47.

19. The positive use of the same word is found in 1 Clement 45, 1, again applied to the Corinthians. Due to the author's respect for 1 Corinthians, this usage cannot have been taken from Paul's letter where the irony cannot be missed — though perhaps the author of 1 Clement could miss it if anyone could.

20. Compare 1 Corinthians 2:21-25, which opens by describing an act of will — God in wisdom chose to save those who believe through the announcement's foolishness — and ends with a maxim directly stating the paradox of God's foolishness.

Chapter 7

1. Mary Douglas, *Natural Symbols: Explorations in Cosmology,* 2nd rev. ed. (Harmondsworth, England and New York: Penguin Books, 1973), 88–90, 102–10, 130–35, 153–59; idem, *Cultural Bias* (Royal Anthropological Institute of Great Britain and Ireland, Occasional Paper No. 35, 1978), 21, 46–54.

2. Hans Dieter Betz proposes that in 1 Corinthians Paul retracts his position stated in Galatians 3:28, using similar words in 1 Corinthians 11:11-12 but arguing in the opposite direction due to difficulties with the emancipation of women (*Galatians: A Commentary on Paul's Letter to the Churches in Galatia* [Philadelphia: Fortress Press, 1979], 200).

3. Cf. Luke 2:34-35; Matt. 13:13. This view is also held by Johannes Weiss in *Der erste Korintherbrief* (Göttingen: Vandenhoeck & Ruprecht, 1910, 331–34), and Hans Lietzmann in *An die Korinther* (I/II, Handbuch zum Neues Testament, 5th ed. revised by W. G. Kümmel, Tübingen: J. C. B. Mohr [Paul Siebeck], 73). Karl Maly, after rejecting Weiss, tries to incorporate the testing function of "sign" with what he takes to be its major function as a standard to attract people, prophecy

attracting to belief and tongues to unbelief (*Mündige Gemeinde: Untersuchungen zur pastoralen Führung des Apostels Paulus im 1 Korintherbrief* [Stuttgart: Katholisches Bibelwerk, 1967], 206–11).

4. See Nils Ivar Johan Engelson, "Glossolalia and Other Forms of Inspired Speech according to 1 Corinthians 12-14," Yale Dissertation, 1970. Thomas Gillespie argues that ecstatic speech in Corinth was integral to prophecy as its authenticating sign and that Paul worked to dissociate it from prophecy by limiting it to prayer ("A Pattern of Prophetic Speech in First Corinthians," *JBL* 97 [1978], 81–84).

5. David E. Aune identifies these two passages as eschatological theophany oracles. See *Prophecy in Early Christianity and the Ancient Mediterranean World* (Grand Rapids: Wm. B. Eerdmans, 1983), 250–53, 325.

6. The role of ecstatic speech in prayer in the Nag Hammadi corpus can be observed in *Allogenes* 53,36 and *Zostrianos* 52,17; 118,18-21; 127,1-5; see also the more extensive prayers in *The Three Steles of Seth*. These texts can be found in English in *The Nag Hammadi Library in English*, 2d rev. ed. by James M. Robinson (San Francisco: Harper & Row, 1988).

7. Another view of gifts is reflected in the RSV translation where the verb "speak" is read "bring" — "how shall I benefit you unless I bring you some revelation or knowledge or prophecy or teaching" (14:6). This implies the person has the gift before the group comes together. Second-century texts include rules against prophecy in private, in response to questions, and in return for money (*Shepherd of Hermas, Mandate* 11; *Didache* 11). The lack of any such warnings in 1 Corinthians suggests that prophecy as private consultation is not yet occurring in Corinth when Paul writes.

8. David Aune, *Prophecy*, 320–27.

9. Eusebius, *Ecclesiastical History* V 16, 17. See Selected Texts: Women Who Speak for the Divine, nos. 44, 74.

10. Epiphanius, *Panarion* 49,1. See Selected Texts: Women Who Speak for the Divine, no. 40.

11. Though the text has no disjunctive particle ("or") in this series, the particle *hekastos* (each) stands for an individual in opposition to the whole group even when the verbs are given in the plural (H. G. Liddell and R. Scott, *A Greek-English Lexicon* [Oxford: Clarendon Press, 1968], 499b). Paul's usage of "each" without "or" (1:12) also means that one does one thing and another does another.

12. Gerhard Dautzenberg traces Christian prophecy back to a two-stage process of vision and interpretation found in Jewish apocalyptic sources (*Urchristliche Prophetie: Ihre Erforschung, ihre Voraussetzung im Judentum und ihre Struktur im ersten Korintherbrief* [Stuttgart: W. Kohlhammer, 1975], 118–21, 290–91, 298–304). Plato and Plutarch each speak of the words of Greek mantics being interpreted by other prophets (*Timaeus* 71e–72b; *Oracles at Delphi* 407BC; *Obsolescence of Oracles* 438B). Aune, *Prophecy*, 31, 33–34, 39, argues that there is no evidence that the Pythia at Delphi ever spoke incomprehensibly; interpreters probably only made her speech more elegant.

13. Paul's arguments on prophecy, speaking in tongues, and women's speech have elements in common that can be visualized as follows:

PAUL'S EVALUATION OF EACH LEVEL ↓	SOCIAL DESCRIPTION ↓		
	Communal speaking	*Orderly sequence of individuals speaking*	*Reflection on previous speaking*
Most constructive			Others discerning the prophecy (14:29)
Constructive		Two or three prophesying one after another (14:29-33)	One person interpreting the prayers (14:27)
Provisionally acceptable	Prophesying together (14:24-25)	Two or three praying in tongues one after another (14:27-28)	Woman alone asking questions at home (14:35)
Destructive	Praying in tongues together (14:23)	Two or three women praying or prophesying one after another (14:34-35)	
Most destructive	Praying in tongues and prophesying together, women and men (14:34-35)		
WOMEN PROPHETS' APPARENT → EVALUATION	*Productive*	*Less productive*	*Least productive*

14. On the Latin and bilingual Greek-Latin traditions see particularly Hermann Josef Frede, *Altlateinische Paulus-Handschriften* (Vetus Latina 4, Freiburg: Herder, 1964) and Bonifatius Fischer, "Das Neue Testament in lateinischer

Sprache: der gegenwärtige Stand seiner Erforschung und seine Bedeutung für die griechische Textgeschichte" (*Die alten Übersetzungen des Neuen Testaments, die Kirchenväterzitate und Lektionare*, ed. by K. Aland [Berlin and New York: de Gruyter, 1972]), 1–92. Two earlier studies set research directions on the bilinguals: P. Corssen, *Epistularum Paulinarum codices Graece et Latine scriptos Augiensem Boerneranum Claromontanum examinavit . . .* (Kiel: Program des Gymnasiums Jever, I 1887, II 1889); Karl Th. Schäfer, "Der griechisch-lateinische Text der Galaterbriefes in der Handschriftengruppe DEFG," *Scientia Sacra: Theologische Festgabe zugeeignet . . . K. J. K. Schulte . . .* (Köln: J. P. Bachem and Düsseldorf: L. Schwann, 1935), 41–70. Although the Old Latin 1 Corinthians texts have not yet been collated by the Beuron Vetus Latina Institute in their project to edit the full Pauline corpus, work has been completed on several shorter Pauline-type letters. This work has provided the basis for a determination of text types and their patterns of development: H. J. Frede, *Vetus Latina 24/1: Epistula ad Ephesios* (Freiburg: Herder, 1962–64); idem, *Vetus Latina 24/2: Epistulae ad Philippenses et ad Colossenses* (Freiburg: Herder, 1962–64); idem, *Vetus Latina 25/1 and 2: Epistulae ad Thessalonicenses, Timotheum, Titum, Philemonem, Hebraeos* (Freiburg: Herder, 1975–incomplete).

15. F. H. Scrivener counts only 200 "real" variant readings between F and G in the entire New Testament and Frede argues that even these are errors of one copyist or the other (F. H. Scrivener, *Codex Augiensis* [Cambridge: Deighton, Bell, and Co.; London: Bell and Daldy, 1859], xxv–xxviii; Frede, *Altlateinische Paulus-Handschriften*, 84–85). The parallel omissions of major units of material in the Greek and Latin of F and G confirm their common source (see Nestle-Aland, *Novum Testamentum Graece* [Stuttgart: Deutsche Bibelstiftung, 1979], 690, 714). For an effort to reconstruct a narrative of the origins of F and G from X, see Frede, *Altlateinische Paulus-Handschriften*, 73–77, 83–85.

16. In 14:34a "women" is supplied with the adjective "your" and the verb "be subordinate" appears in infinitive rather than third-person imperative. In 14:35c "woman" appears in the plural, "church" in the plural, and the words "speak in church" are reversed in order. Also, of course, the entire two verses are displaced to the end of the chapter.

17. See a summary of the research in Fischer, "Das Neue Testament in lateinischer Sprache," 24–26, 67–73, 80–83; Frede, *Altlateinische Paulus-Handschriften*, 88–101; Bernhard Weiss, *Textkritik der paulinischen Briefe* (Leipzig: J. C. Heinrichs, 1896), 1–2.

18. The Book of Armagh (a 61), the Budapest Lat. med. aevi I (b 89), Ambrosiaster and Sidulius-Scotus are all classified by Frede as Old Latin texts of the "I" (first European) type. I have not been able to locate any texts of this type or any other Old Latin type that read 14:34-35 at the numerical position. The UBS Greek New Testament cites it/dem, it/x, it/z for the numerically correct placement of 14:34-35 (*Greek New Testament*, ed. by K. Aland, M. Black, C. M. Martini, B. Metzger, and A. Wikgren [London, New York, Edinburgh, Amsterdam, and Stuttgart: United Bible Societies, 1966], 611–12). But elsewhere Bruce Metzger indicates that it/dem (Codex Demidovianus, Beuron 59) and it/x (Codex Bodleianus Laudianus) are no longer generally regarded as Old Latin but as Vulgate with some Old Latin readings, and the manuscript it/z (Codex Harleianus, Beuron 65) is Old

Latin only in Hebrews 10–13 (Bruce M. Metzger, *The Early Versions of the New Testament: Their Origins, Transmission and Limitations* [Oxford: Clarendon Press, 1977], 285–362, especially 295, 302, and 306).

19. Although the Vulgate puts 14:34-35 back into its numerical order, at least one Vulgate manuscript, Codex Vaticanus Reginensis lat. 9, retains the Old Latin sequence. But this cannot be taken as an independent attestation of late placement of these verses since even our earliest Vulgate in the Pelagian commentaries already shows signs of conservative reversion to the Old Latin. A second Vulgate manuscript, Codex Fuldensis, was corrected in 578 by Victor of Capua using a text very close to Reginensis (B. Fischer, *Lateinische Bibelhandschriften im frühen Mittelalter*, [Freiburg: Herder, 1985], 57–59, 63). When he found in Fuldensis the early placement of 14:34-35, Victor inserted 14:36-40 in the margin *before* 14:34-35 to match the sequence of the Reginensis, without, however, eliminating the 14:36-40, which already followed 14:34-35 in Fuldensis according to the usual Vulgate order (E. Ranke, *Codex Fuldensis* [Marburg and Leipzig: N. G. Elwert, 1865], 226 and 485; checked in microfilm of manuscript). The resulting deutero-graph is thus indirect evidence of the continued influence in Vulgate texts of the Old Latin placement of 14:34-35. Metzger and Ellis apparently misread the Fuldensis gloss after 14:33 to be 14:34-35 rather than 36-40 and Ellis takes this as early evidence that Paul glossed his own letter in this way (Bruce M. Metzger, *A Textual Commentary on the Greek New Testament*, [London and New York: United Bible Societies, 1971], 565; E. Earle Ellis, "The Silenced Wives of Corinth (I Cor. 14:34-5)," *New Testament Textual Criticism: Its Significance for Exegesis*. Essays in Honor of Bruce M. Metzger, ed. by E. J. Epp and G. D. Fee [Oxford: Clarendon Press, 1981], 213, 218–220).

20. K. T. Schäfer, "Der griechische-lateinische Text der Galaterbriefes," 54–55; Fischer, "Das Neue Testament in lateinischer Sprache," 24–25; Frede, *Altlateinische Paulus-Handschriften*, 88–101. G. Zuntz recognizes the common origin of all Old Latin texts, now extant only in the d text and the nonvulgate quota-tions of the Latin fathers. He takes Tertullian and the Greek archetype of DFG as the other two witnesses to the Western text proper (*The Text of the Epistles: A Disquisition upon the Corpus Paulinum* [London: Oxford University Press, 1953], 84–86).

21. Franz Hermann Tinnefeld, *Untersuchungen zur altlateinischen Überlie-ferung des I Timotheusbriefes: Der lateinische Paulustext in den Handschriften DEFG und in den Kommentaren des Ambrosiaster und des Pelagius* (Wiesbaden: Otto Harrassowitz, 1963), 62.

22. See note 20.

23. Kurt Aland and Barbara Aland, *The Text of the New Testament: An Intro-duction to the Critical Editions and to the Theory and Practice of Modern Textual Criticism*. Grand Rapids: Wm. B. Eerdmans; Leiden: E. J. Brill, 1987, 129 on ms 88 and 116 on ms Ψ, with keys to abbreviations, 105–6, 127–28.

24. Only in the placement of 14:34-35 does 88 read with all Old Latin and bilingual texts against all other Greek texts. Its relation to the "Western" tradition is not strong. The UBS Greek New Testament 1 Corinthians shows 88 reading with D and/or G among other witnesses 23 times and against both of them 33 times. Due to UBS Greek New Testament's narrow selection of strictly "Western" variants, the

88 microfilm was checked for such variants found in Nestle-Aland[26] (which does not cite 88 readings). Eighty-eight consistently did not share such variants, except where they were also attested by Ψ and by the majority of manuscripts, such as: 3:3 "with dissentions"; 5:3 "as" before "when present"; 7:34 "the wives and the unmarried virgins"; 7:39 "by law" after "given"; 11:2 "brethren"; 12:31 "stronger/better" in place of "greater/better." These, with the late placement of 14:34-35 (in 88 only) are probably survivals of "Western" readings in the broader tradition. Zuntz's argument that, because P[46] agrees with both the Western and majority texts at certain points, the conjunction of the latter two even without P[46] could be evidence of the "second-century reservoir" of all these traditions, would not apply in any case to the placement of 14:34-35 where the reading appears only once outside the "Western" tradition (*The Text of the Epistles*, 55–57, 212–15).

25. Dautzenberg, *Urchristliche Prophetie*, 254–55.

26. The Greek language can use the masculine to refer to personhood in general or abstract concepts signifying many people even when women alone are in view (R. Kühner and B. Gerth, *Ausführliche Grammatik der griechischer Sprache* II, Part 1, 3d ed. [München: Max Hüber, 1963], 82–83). But Paul's contrast of their local work to worldwide mission better explains the inclusive language here.

27. Dautzenberg, *Urchristliche Prophetie*, 257–73, 397–98.

28. See chart, note 13.

29. Luke 2:36-38; Acts 21:9; Philo, *On the Contemplative Life* 68, 87–89; *Testament of Job* 46–52; *The Confession and Prayer of Aseneth* 11,19–15,8. See Selected Texts, nos. 59, 70, 81, 19, and 17 respectively, where full texts are cited. (On the title of the Aseneth text see C. Burchard, *Untersuchungen zu Joseph und Aseneth* [Tübingen: Überlieferung-Ortsbestimmung, 1965], 50–54; Marc Philonenko, *Joseph et Aséneth: Introduction, texte critique, traduction et notes* [Leiden: E. J. Brill, 1968], 128; J. H. Charlesworth, *The Old Testament Pseudepigrapha* II [Garden City, N.Y.: Doubleday, 1985], 181–82, 202; Ross S. Kraemer, *Maenads, Martyrs, Matrons, Monastics: A Sourcebook on Women's Religions in the Greco-Roman World* [Philadelphia: Fortress Press, 1988], 408–9).

30. Rev. 2:20-24; *j. Hagigah* II.2:77d, 78a; Irenaeus, *Against Heresies* 1, 13, 1–4; Eusebius, *Ecclesiastical Histories* V, 18–19. For the first, third, and fourth of these texts see Selected Texts, nos. 71, 72, and 80.

Chapter 8

1. See Karl Barth, *The Resurrection of the Dead. University Lectures on I Cor. 15*, trans. by H. J. Stenning (New York: Fleming H. Revell, 1933; German 1924), 95–107.

2. Michael Bünker takes 15:1-11 as a new *exordium* and *narratio*, respectively preparing the audience and laying the foundation for the coming argument by telling the story as the speaker sees it (*Briefformular und Disposition im 1 Korintherbrief*, Göttinger Theologische Arbeiten 28 [Göttingen: Vandenhoeck & Ruprecht, 1984], 62–67).

3. The Greek term for hard labor here, κοπιάω, associates Paul with slaves in a society where a people of status did not work. See Richard L. Rohrbaugh,

"Methodological Considerations in the Debate over the Social Class Status of Early Christians," *JAAR* 52 (1984), 536–37.

4. Within this interpretation the proposal that "miscarriage" was first an epithet used against Paul could make more sense. From the Corinthians' viewpoint he is born too *soon* in the spirit before reaching the full breadth and depth of wisdom, perhaps misshapen by struggles to survive against impossible odds.

5. H. Grass, *Ostergeschehen und Osterberichte* (Göttingen: Vandenhoeck & Ruprecht, 1962), 109, 111, 183–85. Hans Conzelmann does not mention the issue (*I Corinthians*, Hermeneia Series [Philadelphia: Fortress Press, 1975], 256–59).

6. Hans Dieter Betz, *Galatians*, Hermeneia Series (Philadelphia: Fortress Press, 1979), 199–200.

7. Michael Bünker, *Briefformular*, 62, can see this because he is analyzing the chapter as argument, but most commentators take Paul's claim at face value.

8. Wedderburn suggests that Paul misrepresents rather than misunderstands them. But he does not clearly develop the nature and function of this misrepresentation (A. J. M. Wedderburn, *Baptism and Resurrection: Studies in Pauline Theology against its Greco-Roman Background* [Tübingen: J. C. B. Mohr (Paul Siebeck), 1987], 36).

9. So begins the argument that has drawn such debates concerning its precise logical form: T. G. Bucher, "Die logische Argumentation in 1 Kor. 15:12-20," *Biblica* 55 (1974), 465–486; M. Bachmann, "Zur Gedankenführung in 1 Kor. 15:12ff," *TZ* 34 (1978), 265–76; W. Stenger, "Beobachtungen zur Argumentationsstruktur von 1 Kor. 15," *LB* 43–46 (1978–79), 71–128; M. Bachmann, "Rezeption von 1 Kor. 15," *LB* 51 (1982), 79–103; T. G. Bucher, "Allegemeine Überlegungen zur Logik im Zusammenhang mit 1 Kor. 15,12-20," *LB* 53 (1983), 70–98.

10. See Bünker, *Briefformular*, 68–72, and Simone Frutiger in a structuralist analysis, "La mort, et puis . . . avant? I Corinthiens 15," *ETR* 55 (1980), 199–229.

11. The saying is from Menander's *Thais*, the only quotation of a text not considered scripture in Paul's extant letters. The authority he claims here is proverbial rather than literary. It does suggest someone has misled them and for this they are scolded, as happens earlier in the struggle over Apollos in 3:10-17 and 4:14-21.

12. A quick explanation from the different presuppositions concerning life and death in Greek philosophy and Jewish apocalyptic would seem to obviate this guesswork. But Paul and other Hellenistic Jews use apocalyptic thought only in certain contexts, and many Greeks who were synagogue-worshipers or converts of Paul would share elements of it. Therefore the views of the Corinthian believers cannot be specified from their Greek heritage, but only ferreted out by the ways Paul argues to persuade them.

13. For an interesting parallel link of initiation and holy food in Hellenistic-Jewish wisdom see *The Confession and Prayer of Aseneth, Daughter of Pentephry* 14–17, Greek text in Marc Philonenko, *Joseph et Aséneth: Introduction, texte critique, traduction et notes* (Leiden: E. J. Brill, 1968) 176–90; English translation in H. F. D. Sparks, ed., *The Apocryphal Old Testament* (Oxford: Clarendon Press, 1984), 486–91. See selections from Selected Texts, no. 17.

14. See for example Plato, *Timaeus* 36D, 40A–41B; Philo, *On the Creation of the World* 27; 73; 144; *On Dreams* I, 135; Plotinus, *Ennead* IV 4, 8, 22, and 42. Gerhard Sellin suggests that this commonplace of Hellenistic thought has its origin

in Stoic physics, citing *Stoicorum Veterum Fragmenta*, John of Arnim, ed., 1964, 127, 142, 200ff (*Die Streit um die Auferstehung der Toten: Eine religions-geschichtliche und exegetische Untersuchung von 1 Korinther 15* [Göttingen: Vandenhoeck & Ruprecht, 1986], 218-220).

15. This could represent a critique of Middle Platonic body/soul dualism on Paul's part. He may be functioning within the Hellenistic-Jewish wisdom tradition, which occasionally, in asserting the transcendent power of the divine spirit, disparages the human soul as of lesser power (Philo, *On Dreams* I 118-19). However, the particular distinction Paul makes between people or bodies who are spiritual and those who are ensouled (2:14-15; 15:44-46) is not found in Philo and may represent a development of wisdom exegesis of Genesis parallel to the development later found in Gnosticism (Birger Pearson, *The Pneumatikos-Psychikos Terminology in 1 Corinthians: A Study in the Theology of the Corinthian Opponents of Paul and its Relation to Gnosticism*, Missoula, Mont.: Society of Biblical Literature, 1973, 82–85).

16. An alternative reading of Paul's argument here sees it concluding *a minore ad maius*, i.e., if the soul has a God-created body, how much more the spirit (cf. Rom. 5:8-10, 15, 17). But the "how much more" has to be supplied, and that concept is not developed anywhere in the context.

17. In a recent helpful collation and analysis of Paul's uses of Scripture this passage is explained as an example of Paul's expansion of a text to include his own interpretation: Dietrich-Alex Koch, *Die Schrift als Zeuge des Evangeliums: Untersuchung zur Verwund und zum Verständnis der Schrift bei Paulus* (Tübingen: J. C. B. Mohr [Paul Siebeck], 1986), 134–37.

18. Philo Judaeus and the Wisdom of Solomon are the most often cited examples of this tradition. For the literature see Appendix 12 on Resurrection. My discussion is dependent on Tobin's analysis of the second and third of the stages in the pre-history of Philo's Genesis 2:7 interpretation, which he identifies as: first, anti-allegorical exegesis; second, separate and conflated accounts of one creation of humanity (Tobin uses the word "man" for both generic and male meanings); third, accounts of two separate creations of humanity; fourth, Philo's own allegory of two minds (Th. H. Tobin, S. J., *The Creation of Man: Philo and the History of Interpretation* [Washington, D.C.: Catholic Biblical Association of America, 1983]). See also Gerhard Sellin's critique of Tobin in *Die Streit*, 171–72, n. 226.

19. This is the conclusion of Birger Pearson in *The Pneumatikos-Psychikos Terminology*, 24–26. See more recently Gerhard Sellin, *Die Streit*, 78–79, 188–89; Dennis Ronald MacDonald, *There is No Male and Female: The Fate of a Dominical Saying in Paul and Gnosticism* (Philadelphia: Fortress Press, 1987), 92–98.

20. Theodotion's translation of Isaiah does read the past tense with some variations in manuscript traditions (Hans Conzelmann, *I Corinthians* [Philadelphia: Fortress Press, 1975], 292). But this only confirms that this past tense proclamation of victory over death originates in Christian use of the Isaiah text and then appears in both Paul and Theodotian.

21. Note that "the will" means God's will in Romans 2:18. The same meaning is attested without the article in Ignatius's *Ephesians* 20.1.

22. Apollos' possible absence as Paul writes does not explain adequately why there is no greeting from him. If he was often asked to accompany the letter and

did not, he could well have softened his demur by sending a greeting through Paul.

23. It has been proposed that their Latin names, especially the geographical reference in Achaicus's name, could signify they are of freed families relocated from Rome to Corinth and therefore of some social standing (Wayne A. Meeks, *The First Urban Christians: The Social World of the Apostle Paul* [New Haven and London: Yale University Press, 1983], 56-58). It is also possible they could be slaves born in a Roman house or free Greeks given Latin names at birth in a Roman colony such as Corinth.

Chapter 9

1. This can be seen throughout the Apocryphal Acts, as in Acts of John 63; 113; Acts of Paul 9–10; Acts of Thomas 11–14; 82–98.

2. See for example Luke 2:36-37; Acts 21:9; Rev. 2:20; Philo, *On the Contemplative Life* 29, 68, 78, 83–89; Plutarch, *The Oracles of Delphi* 405CD; *Testament of Job* 45–52; *j Hagiga* 2.2 and *b Sanhedrin* 23c (the euphemism is that when men raise them off the ground they lose their powers); Eusebius, *Ecclesiastical History* V 18.2-3. See Selected Texts, nos. 59, 70, 71, 81, 49, 19, and 80, respectively. Due to dating questions, the Talmudic texts above were not included in this collection.

3. An analysis of the variety of this type of work with bibliography is found in John H. Elliott's "Social Scientific Criticism of the New Testament: More on Method and Models" (*Semeia: Social-Scientific Criticism of the New Testament and its Social World* 35 [1986], edited by John H. Elliott, 1–33). Malina's *Christian Origins and Cultural Anthropology: Practical Models for Biblical Interpretation* (Atlanta: John Knox Press, 1986) adapts a number of contemporary anthropological and social paradigms for biblical study. He uses his own form of Mary Douglas's "group/grid" model as an integrating paradigm, working from her 1973 revised edition of *Natural Symbols: Explorations in Cosmology* (London: Barrie & Jenkins and New York: Pelican Books; reprinted by Penguin Books, 1978; reprinted with new preface, New York: Pantheon Books, 1982; first edition, 1970). In *Christian Origins* he distinguishes "group" as social control from "grid" as assent to social symbol systems, assigning marginal "catchment areas" to those not assenting although they may well be the majority. This interpretation of "grid" tends to reverse the meaning of high and low "grid" as Douglas uses the model. See the charts throughout Malina's study beginning with his "group/grid" model on pages 14–15.

4. The "group/grid" model was first developed in *Natural Symbols: Explorations in Cosmology*, 1970 and 1973, and further developed in *Cultural Bias*, Occasional Paper No. 35 of the Royal Anthropological Institute of Great Britain and Ireland (London: Royal Anthropological Institute, 1978), reprinted with other relevant studies in *In the Active Voice* (London: Routledge & Kegan Paul, 1982). For a critical review of the early development of her thought and its application in religious studies see Sheldon K. Isenberg and Dennis E. Owen, "Bodies Natural and Contrived: The Work of Mary Douglas," *Religious Studies Review* 3 (1977), 1–16, and more recently James Vernon Spickard, "Relativism and Cultural Comparison in the Anthropology of Mary Douglas: An Evaluation of the Meta-theoretical

Strategy of her Grid-group Theory," Ph.D. Dissertation, Graduate Theological Union, 1984.

5. Here the work of E. A. Judge has been particularly important: *The Social Pattern of the Christian Groups in the First Century: Some Prolegomena to the Study of New Testament Ideas of Social Obligation* (London: Tyndale, 1960); "The Early Christians as a Scholastic Community," *JRH* (1960), 4–15, 125–37; "Paul as a Radical Critic of Society," *Interchange* 16 (1974), 191–203; "The Social Identity of the First Christians: A Question of Method in Religious History," *JRH* 11 (1980), 201–17; *Rank and Status in the World of the Caesars and St. Paul*, University of Canterbury Publications 29, University of Canterbury, 1982; "Cultural Conformity and Innovation in Paul: Some Clues from Contemporary Documents," *Tyn Bul* 35 (1984), 3–24. Among major recent works in the social history of the Pauline churches are the following: Gerd Theissen's articles collected in *The Social Setting of Pauline Christianity* (Philadelphia: Fortress Press, 1982); Ronald F. Hock, *The Social Context of Paul's Ministry: Tentmaking and Apostleship* (Philadelphia: Fortress Press, 1980); Wayne A. Meeks, *The First Urban Christians: The Social World of the Apostle Paul* (New Haven and London: Yale University Press, 1983); Peter Marshall, *Enmity in Corinth: Social Conventions in Paul's Relations with the Corinthians* (Tübingen: J. C. B. Mohr [Paul Siebeck], 1987).

6. Jerome H. Neyrey, "Body Language in 1 Corinthians: The Use of Anthropological Models for Understanding Paul and his Opponents," *Semeia: Social-Scientific Criticism of the New Testament and Its Social World* 35 (1986), edited by John H. Elliott, 127–70.

7. Jerome H. Neyrey, "Body Language," 162.

8. See Excursus on the Social Status of the Corinthian Women Prophets and of Paul, chapter 3, and chapter 3 notes 20–22.

9. Peter Marshall, *Enmity in Corinth: Social Conventions in Paul's Relations with the Corinthians* (Tübingen: J. C. B. Mohr [Paul Siebeck], 1987).

10. For reference to some of the important studies being done on Greek and Roman women and their religion see Ross S. Krämer, "Women in the Religions of the Greco-Roman World," *Religious Studies Review* 9 (1983), 127–39, and Sarah B. Pomeroy, "Selected Bibliography on Women in Classical Antiquity," *Women in the Ancient World*, ed. by J. Peradotto and J. Sullivan (Albany: State University of New York Press, 1984), 315–77. Two excellent collections of primary sources are now available: Mary R. Lefkowitz and Maureen B. Fant's *Women's Life in Greece and Rome* (Baltimore: Johns Hopkins University Press, 1982) and Ross S. Krämer's *Maenads, Martyrs, Matrons, Monastics: A Sourcebook on Women's Religions in the Greco-Roman World* (Philadelphia: Fortress Press, 1988). Especially relevant to this point, though focused on the city of Rome in the previous century, is Suzanne Dixon's "A Family Business: Women's Role in Patronage and Politics at Rome 80–44 BC," *Classica et Mediaevalia* 34 (1983), 91–112.

11. Here Marshall distinguishes between patronage that strictly benefits the receiver and "patronal friendship" where an appearance of reciprocity is maintained by the love and honor with which the receiver responds (*Enmity in Corinth*, 143–44). Because most patronage seems to have significant social benefits for the giver, or at least this is the case in all the relations in the church that might be so classified, I use the word "patronage" here in this patronal friendship sense.

12. Marshall, *Enmity in Corinth*, 233–58, 397–98. I do not consider the status of the "rival apostles" and Paul's relations to them because they do not appear explicitly until 2 Corinthians.

13. Marshall, *Enmity in Corinth*, 178–218, quoting 194.

14. Elisabeth Schüssler Fiorenza, *In Memory of Her, A Feminist Theological Reconstruction of Christian Origins* (New York: Crossroad, 1983), 60–64.

15. Rosemary Radford Ruether, *Sexism and God-Talk: Toward a Feminist Theology* (Boston: Beacon Press, 1983); Dory Previn, "Sheba and Solomon," *USQR: Ad Feminam* 43 (1989), issue edited by Alice Bach, 59–66.

Notes to Selected Texts from the Early Empire

1. Texts cited are those widely dated to the Early Roman Empire, broadly conceived as mid-first century BCE to second century CE, including Tertullian who writes just before and after the turn into the third century. Where the stories are about women prophets before the imperial period, the texts are cited as evidence of early imperial views of women's prophecy. Third- or fourth-century authors are included only where they provide direct quotations of early imperial writers or speakers which are thought by many to be genuine.

2. References to prophecy in this period that do not distinguish gender must also be considered as possible evidence for women's prophecy. See for example Josephus, *Jewish War* I 347, *Didache* 10. 7, *Barnabas* 16. 10, Tertullian, *Against Marcion* 24, 4 (see also note 18 below). Greek use of masculine plural nouns may also incorporate women.

3. The following abbreviations are used for the names of major series and collections:

AOT   *The Apocryphal Old Testament*, H. F. D. Sparks, ed., Oxford: Clarendon Press, 1984.

ANF   *The Ante-Nicene Fathers*, Alexander Roberts and James Donaldson, eds., Grand Rapids: Wm. B. Eerdmans.

BT   *The Babylonian Talmud*, I. Epstein, ed., London: Soncino Press, 35 Vols., 1935–1952.

LCL   Loeb Classical Library, London: William Heinemann and Cambridge: Harvard University Press.

NTA   *New Testament Apocrypha*, Wm. Schneemelcher, ed., Philadelphia: Westminster Press. Vol. 1, 1963, Vol. 2, 1965.

OTP   *Old Testament Pseudepigrapha*, James H. Charlesworth, ed., Garden City, N.Y.: Doubleday & Company, Vol. 1, 1983, Vol. 2, 1985.

4. Where translators render with "man" or "men" Greek terms which unmistakably include all people, I make appropriate substitutions in square brackets. Otherwise the recent changes in English usage toward the use of "man" in the strictly masculine sense lead to a misunderstanding of the original text. This is especially problematic in the light of the gender-specific questions of this study.

5. The poet proclaims the fulfillment of an oracle of the Cumean Sibyl whose name is most often the one associated with the mysterious arrival of the oracle

books in Rome as told above. References to the various Sibyls appear in literature throughout this period, as, for example, in Strabo, *Geography* 14. 1. 37.

6. The text continues in indirect discourse to recount Varro's description of the ten Sibyls, citing his sources in each case. This translation of Lactantius by Sister Mary Francis McDonald is from the series: *Fathers of the Church: A New Translation*, ed. Roy Joseph Deferrari (Washington D.C.: Catholic University of America Press, 1964), 32–33.

7. Compare Hannah's song in Pseudo-Philo's *Biblical Antiquities* 51:3-6, which in part is spoken as a prophecy.

8. Compare with this a probably somewhat later version of the story (with the stories of other women prophets) in the Babylonian Talmud Megilla 14ab.

9. The story of Deborah is extended and many prophecies attributed to her in Pseudo-Philo 30–33. Compare also the probably mid-second century BCE depiction of Rebecca's dreams and prophecies in Jubilees 25:11-22; 27:1-3; 35:6-7, 27.

10. *Sifre to Numbers: An American Translation and Explanation*, Jacob Neusner, Brown Judaic Studies 119, (Atlanta: Scholars Press, 1986), Vol II, 57.

11. *Midrash Rabbah: Genesis*, Vol. I, trans. by H. Freedman and Maurice Simon (London: Soncino Press, 1939), 385. See also *Genesis Rabbah. The Judaic Commentary to the Book of Genesis: A New American Translation*, Vol. II Jacob Neusner, Brown Judaic Studies 105 (Atlanta: Scholars Press, 1985), 152–153.

12. Compare with a similar "oracle" to Alexander told by Plutarch in *Alexander* 14.4 and to a riddle oracle in Plutarch's *Obsolescence of the Oracles* 412CD.

13. Some other sayings attributed to women prophets are found within the stories in the following sections.

14. This appears to be an oracle against Rome and is attributed to the Sibyl, perhaps dating from 32 BCE. I append to it here the conclusion of the collection of oracles in which it is preserved. Since no Sibyl is attested in this period, this and the following oracle may be pseudonymous and the attribution to a woman could be part of the fiction.

15. Most of the Delphic oracles surviving from this period are indirect discourse, partially preserved, or of questionable provenance or authenticity. For these translations of three oracles and for other Delphic responses from literature and inscriptions of this period see J. Fontenrose, *The Delphic Oracle: Its Responses and Operations, with a Catalogue of Responses* (Berkeley, Los Angeles and London: University of California Press, 1978), 262–64, 349–51. For the Greek texts see H. W. Parke, *The Delphic Oracle, Vol 2, The Oracular Responses* (Oxford: Basil Blackwell, 1956), to which Fontenrose is cross-referenced.

16. The translations of this ode and the following are taken from James H. Charlesworth's *The Odes of Solomon: The Syriac Texts*, Society of Biblical Literature Text and Translations Series 13 and Pseudepigrapha Series 7 (Chico: Calif., Scholars Press, 1977), 82–83, 120–21. The virgin here has been variously interpreted as Wisdom, the Church, the Spirit, or Christ speaking. This assumes a literary fiction and possible male authorship. But see note 17.

17. It is the feminine point of view reflected in the imagery of many of the odes that supports the thesis of an origin in women's songs or prophetic oracles. For example, here the concern is with breasts which are full and must be released, but without waste. The obvious correction of the feminine imagery of God in this

ode, so that the one giving milk from "her bosom" receives the name of Father, indicates a process of adaption in the reuse, collection, or writing of these odes.

18. Translation from Herbert Musurillo, *The Acts of the Christian Martyrs* (Oxford: Clarendon Press, 1972), 109–113, 117–119. The translator puts certain words from the text into parentheses to indicate that they are to be read as comments by the narrator.

19. My translation of these eight oracles and their introductions was made from texts collected in Kurt Aland's "Bemerkungen zur Montanismus," *Kirchengeschichtliche Entwuerfe* (Gütersloh: Gerd Mohn, 1960), 145–46. Other oracles cited by Tertullian in his various writings are attributed to the spirit, the paraclete, or the new prophecy, without stating which Montanist prophet spoke them. These may well also come from Prisca or Maximilla: see Aland, #8. 9, 20, 21, 22, 23, 25, pp. 144, 147–48. To study the literary contexts of the oracles translated above, see Tertullian (ANF) and Eusebius (LCL), the latter as #74 of this collection. The relevant parts of Epiphanius's *Panarion* are not yet (to my knowledge) translated into a modern language. An English translation by Frank Williams, *The Panarion of Epiphanius of Salamis,* Book II, is anticipated from E. J. Brill in Leiden and New York. These texts may be included in the selections from the *Panarion* forthcoming as Epiphanius, *The Panarion of St. Epiphanius, Bishop of Salamis,* trans. by Philip R. Amidon (New York: Oxford University Press, 1990).

20. H. W. Parke suggests that the prophetess at Delphi may be chosen from among a "guild of consecrated women" who keep the eternal fire burning: *Delphic Oracle,* Vol. 1, 35–36.

21. Translation from Lucan, *Pharasalia: Dramatic Episodes of the Civil Wars* (Baltimore: Penguin Books, 1957), 110–12.

22. English translation by Douglas Garman of Robert Flaceliere's French rendition in *Greek Oracles* (London: Paul Elek, 1976). The Greek text is available in L. Robert's *Etudes anatolienne* (Paris: Boccard, 1937), 130.

23. The New Testament translations are mine.

24. A further reference to Veleda and her successor Ganna appears in Cassius Dio's *Roman History* 47. 5. 3 (LCL).

25. The translator in ANF identifies the Montanists as those under attack in this passage although the Latin text does not. There is no extant Greek text. The context makes clear that Irenaeus is affirming a paraclete-identified prophecy here, not opposing it.

26. See also the third-century attack on the Montanists by Hippolytus in the *Refutation of All Heresies* 8.12, where again the focus is not on heresy in theology but on "novelty" in practice.

27. Compare this with Firmilian's description of another woman prophet in a third-century letter to Cyprian. She is accused by the writer of being possessed by a demon and of seducing a presbyter and a deacon: Cyprian, *Epistles* 74, 10 (ANF).

28. Translation by Douglas Parrott, "Gospel of Mary (BG 8502, 1)," *The Nag Hammadi Gospel in English,* 3d. revised edition, James M. Robinson, ed., (San Francisco: Harper & Row, 1988), 525–26.

Index of Biblical and Other Ancient Literature

NEW TESTAMENT

GREEK AND LATIN AUTHORS

EARLY CHRISTIAN LITERATURE

NAG HAMMADI

Index of Modern Authors

Index of Subjects

Abstinence, sexual. *See* Sexual
  asceticism.
Adam, 121, 168, 186
  and Eve, 100, 119, 174, 244
  typology, 119, 123, 165, 171,
    172–173, 174, 176, 234
Analogy
  argument by, 37–38
  building, 43
Androgyne, 125, 221, 281 n.16
Angels, 121 22, 127, 132, 133, 143,
  221
Antithesis, 54–56
Apocalyptic
  and Corinthians, 60
  and dualism, 214
  for Paul and other Hellenistic Jews,
    287 n.12
  and prophecy, 226, 227
  and resurrection, 233
  and wisdom, 212, 214–15
Apollos, 25, 27, 37, 51, 66, 69, 129,
    145, 209–11, 287 n.11, 288–89
    n.22
  in Acts, 50, 129–30, 179, 210
  ally of women prophets, 177–78,
    183
  as Christ's mediator, 44
  as God's wisdom, 43
  and John the Baptist, 210
  as leader of opposition, 41–43, 48
  modern research on, 209–11
  Paul's discrediting of, 44, 46
  and resurrection, 160–61
  and spiritual leaders, 153
Arguments
  and authority, 9–11
  based on structure of reality, 7, 12,
    28, 47, 49–54
  by dissociation of concepts, 7, 12,
    13–23, 47, 54–58
  establishing structure of reality, 12,
    35–38, 47, 58–62

function of persuasion, 2–4
quasi-logical, 7, 12, 23–27
typology of, 7, 198–99
Aseneth, 122, 235, 242–44
Audience, 3–4
Authority, 98–115
  of the bible, 9–11
  claimed by Corinthian women, 14,
    102–12, 121, 133, 161, 183–84,
    186
  claimed by Paul, 45–46, 99–100,
    152–58, 159–60
  exemplified by Israel, 99
  and freedom, 13, 45, 111–12
  on the head, 21, 121, 127–28,
    132–33
  limitations of, 99
  patriarchal, in Paul's appeal, 207
  of the spirit, 96, 113, 183
  as unexercised right, 132

Baptism
  Corinthian view of, 37, 167, 173
  for the dead, 166, 167
  and new humanity, 127, 167–68
  and resurrection, 166, 168
  and spiritual identity, 111
  tradition in the New Testament,
    167
Baptismal confession, 123–26, 126,
    131, 137–38, 186
Blessings, 141, 180
Boasting, 14–15, 44, 59, 194
Body, 77, 90, 100
  authority over one's own, 82–83,
    93, 94, 182
  consecrated, for women, 95
  as metaphor, 136, 138.
  See also Spiritual body
Brothers, 41–42, 74

Cephas, 37, 41, 42, 51, 66, 102, 162
Chloe, 41, 42, 50, 66

Women (*cont.*)
  See also Restriction of women, by
    Paul; Marriage; Virgins; Widows;
    Women prophets; Women
    teachers; Women's head cover-
    ing; Women's leadership;
    Women's power; Women's sexual
    behavior; Social history, research
    in women's
Women prophets, 237–69
  in early Christianity, 260–65
  Greco-Roman, 245–48
  Jewish, 240–45
  in New Testament, 83, 93.
  See also Women prophets,
    Corinthian
Women prophets, Corinthian,
    156–58
  and baptism, 69
  common life of, 181–83
  and common meals, 108–9, 182
  communal homes, 181–82
  conduct and functions, 181–84
  confidence of, 129, 157–58
  ethnic status of, 63–64
  gifts of, 40, 103, 183, 186, 187
  and honor, 122, 127, 128–29, 158
  and household subordination,
    227
  and idol meat, 102–13
  inclusive identity of, 156
  and integration into Christ, 131
  as mediators, 134
  in New Testament, 83, 93
  in opposition to Paul, 15, 38, 130,
    184, 185, 188, 189
  Paul's silencing of, 30, 34–35
  rank in community, 65
  in Roman context, 70–71
  and resurrection, 174, 175–76
  self-understanding of, 93–97,
    110–12, 184–88
  and servitude, 64
  social power of, 130, 158

  social status of, 63–66, 188–89,
    192
  among the strong, 105, 110
  theology of, 93–97, 112–13, 134,
    184–88
  and Timothy, 177–78
  and tongues, 144
  with uncovered heads, 117–18,
    122–23, 129, 130–31.
  See also Consecration; Prayer and
    prophecy; Prophecy; Sexual
    asceticism; Virgins; Widows;
    Women's leadership
Women teachers, 50–51, 265–69
Women's head covering, 18, 19, 27,
    116–34, 220–23
  and Corinthian practice, 29–30, 38,
    183
  and church practice, 32–33,
    129–30
  and God's image, 132
  and idolatry, 131
  and new creation theology, 137–38
  and prayer in tongues, 140
  as problem for modern reader, 220
  reinterpretations of, 220–21
  and scriptural allusions, 29–30
  and shame, 20–21, 25, 128–30
  for unmarried women, 280 n.9
Women's leadership, 38, 50–51, 102,
    153, 155, 183–84, 202, 207
Women's power, through historical
    reconstruction, 6
Women's sexual behavior, in Roman
    context, 90–93. *See also* Sexual
    asceticism.
Women's social history. *See* Social
    history, research in women's
Word of the cross, 23, 49, 55, 59,
    67–68
Worship, order in, 153–54

Yeast image, 17, 29, 76–77, 90

Zipporah, 240